THE GLASS OF
FREDERICK CARDER

FREDERICK CARDER, in 1953 at age ninety. *Rockwell Gallery*

THE GLASS OF
FREDERICK CARDER

by PAUL V. GARDNER
Curator, Division of Ceramics and Glass,
National Museum of History and Technology,
Smithsonian Institution

Introduction by PAUL N. PERROT, Director,
The Corning Museum of Glass

CROWN PUBLISHERS, INC.   NEW YORK

Contents

Acknowledgments

THE MAJOR CONTRIBUTOR TO THIS VOLUME WAS FREDERICK CARDER UNDER WHOSE guidance, first at the Steuben Division and later at the Corning Glass Works, my interest and knowledge in the art of glassmaking was initiated and fostered. He gave freely of his time and expertise throughout our entire association and was especially helpful in the preparation of this book, by granting many interviews and providing photographs and other memorabilia from his personal files, scrapbooks, and reference library. Much of this material was not available before, as he had always been reluctant to divulge his secrets. It is hoped this work will give an indication of the accomplishments of this outstandingly talented and versatile Englishman.

In addition, I wish to express sincere appreciation to my many friends and colleagues who have contributed to this book. Among those who have given so generously of their time and talents and aided me immeasurably in the preparation of the manuscript are: Dr. Philip W. Bishop, Donald T. Bonnell, Dr. Robert H. Brill, Mrs. Harry A. Erwin, John J. Graham, Henry Hanley, Otto Hilbert, Dr. Harrison P. Hood, Mr. and Mrs. Daniel Philip Hoover, Arthur A. Houghton, Jr., Mr. and Mrs. William P. Hudson, Mrs. Joseph Kelly, Frederick H. Knight, Mr. and Mrs. Karl H. Koepke, Robert J. Leavy, J. Jefferson Miller II, Jennifer M. Oka, Paul N. Perrot, Kathryn Pinney, Robert H. Rockwell, Frederick Schroeder, Jane S. Shadel, Joseph Sporer, Dr. and Mrs. Laverne G. Wagner, Mr. and Mrs. Gillett Welles, Hubert Williams-Thomas, Kenneth M. Wilson, and H. W. Woodward.

I also wish to thank Raymond F. Errett, Corning Museum of Glass; Stanley Weisenfeld, Corning Glass Works; and Henry A. Alexander, Richard K. Hofmeister, and Robert G. Myers, Smithsonian Institution, for their exceptionally fine photographs, without which this book would not have been possible.

Introduction

DURING THE LAST FEW YEARS THE PUBLICATION OF BOOKS, MONOGRAPHS, CATALOGUES, and articles on various aspects of glass history has reached almost tidal proportions. As one peruses many of these works a strange paradox emerges: the more recent the subject matter is, often the more superficial the contributions appear, as if their authors were hesitant to ferret out the comments of contemporaries or to seek out those anecdotes that might provide precious insights unavailable from any other sources.

In the literature on Gallé, Daum, Lalique, Tiffany, or Marinot, rarely do we find that the authors were able to establish that personal link with subjects and surroundings that contributes so much for a deeper understanding of the psychological or other factors, and which could provide the base upon which future historical perspectives could develop.

It is perhaps for these reasons that the publication of this volume, on one of the great figures of English and American glass, is so welcome. For not only did its author work in close association for over a decade with Frederick Carder, but during later years he remained his keen observer and close friend.

The active career of Frederick Carder extended over three-quarters of a century. During this entire period he was involved with glass, first as a student, then as a designer, next becoming the manager of a large industrial enterprise, and—finally—continuing to work creatively in the material for over twenty-five years after retirement. Over this period he saw his works rise from obscurity to commercial success and international reputation, then fall to neglect and rejection until the start of a triumphant return as they were sought after by discriminating collectors and glass students.

Few men have lived long enough to find themselves, and their works, entering the pages of history after surviving the ebb and flow of changing popular tastes. Even fewer have done so without losing their zest and their desire to remain active, participating members of society. Frederick Carder was one of these.

A short, lean, wiry, brusque man, Carder had a strong temper, a sharp tongue, and a quick mind. Under these externals were concealed great kindness, an understanding of human foibles, and an infinite generosity for those who wanted to learn. He was strong in his convictions, perfectly willing to admit that others could have different points of view even though often skeptical that they were any "damn good." But he was always willing to give the fellow a

1

chance and give him a helping hand if needed. For falseness and pretense he had but contempt and had no hesitation to show it.

When I met Frederick Carder in 1952 I had never heard of him and knew virtually nothing about glass. He was then eighty-nine years old: still active in school affairs, still going to his office everyday, still operating one or two furnaces in which he constantly strove to develop new glasses or new forms that he could execute himself without assistance. Eagerly soaking up any scrap of information that I could find on glass history or glass manufacture, I visited his studio regularly. At first I was received with courtesy, but this later developed into a close personal friendship of that rare kind that overcomes discrepancies in years and degrees of experience.

The personal aspects of Frederick Carder's life perhaps do not come through these pages as strongly as they might, no doubt because of the understandable reticence of an author who was, in so many ways, close to his subject. What does emerge with sparkling clarity is the tremendous variety of his approaches toward glass, his superb understanding of its physical, chemical, and manipulative properties, and his close participation in all the phases of production, from original concept to final marketing.

His technological standards were exacting—he was as demanding of his suppliers, whose raw materials he had no hesitation to assay and reject if they did not reach his specifications, as he was of his workers, whose mistakes were mercilessly smashed. He was keenly aware that research was essential, not only for growth but for mere survival. This research was not of the theoretical type, involved with concepts and abstractions. It was the research of an activist who achieved results through ceaseless personal experimentation with raw materials, crucibles, and furnaces.

For Carder, glass was synonymous to color, and even in the last year of his life, ninety-nine years after his birth and seventy-three years after he climbed the three hundred meters of the Eiffel Tower (the year it was completed), his passion for its infinite varieties remained unchanged. In this lies his kinship with that great contemporary Louis C. Tiffany. Both understood glass: one with a complete practical familiarity with all of its potential, the other as a genial creator of forms and as an impresario who was able to orchestrate a multitude of talents to express his ideas.

Those who knew Frederick Carder, and were privileged to attend his memorable birthday parties in the late 1950s and until 1963, will find in these pages some of his biting humor and the twinkle in his eye as he was saying something "shocking." They will also find a panorama of his production, a discussion of his techniques, and an inventory of his contributions, which make this the definitive volume on his life and his glass.

Frederick Carder demonstrated the keenness of his judgment when, in 1929, he selected Paul Gardner as his assistant. Their relationship has done well for glass history.

PAUL N. PERROT
Director
The Corning Museum of Glass

1

Carder in England— From Stourbridge to Steuben

FREDERICK CARDER, WHO IN 1903 FOUNDED THE STEUBEN GLASS WORKS AT CORNING, New York, spent over eighty years of his century-long life making fine glass. From the time he started work as a teen-ager at the English glass factory of Stevens & Williams until his retirement at age ninety-six, he worked in this medium. During his long career he produced such an amazing variety of glass objects in so many techniques, styles, and colors that he emerges as one of the giants of glassmaking.

Carder was born on September 18, 1863, in Brockmoor, Kingswinford, Staffordshire, England, one of six children of Annie and Caleb Carder. The first forty years of his life were spent studying and working within about five miles of his birthplace. This is a highly industrialized area known as the Black Country because of its characteristic smoky atmosphere. Prior to the seventeenth century, coal mining, iron making, and pottery manufacturing were its principal industries. In the early 1600s, itinerant glassmakers from Lorraine, France, settled here.[1] Their glasshouses and those built later by English workmen, which dotted

Ill. 1. ORIGINAL MOOR LANE, Brierley Hill, glasshouse built c. 1740 by the Honeybourne family and worked 1824–1870 by the forebears of the present Williams-Thomas family. *Stevens & Williams Limited*

the area from Kingswinford to Stourbridge, established glassmaking as an important industry in the district. These industrial surroundings were to have a marked bearing on Frederick Carder's career.

At age seventy-four, Carder wrote of his early schooling: "My earliest recollections are being expelled from a Dame School for throwing a slate at the principal. I had at that time a violent temper."[2] This incident took place when, as a punishment for some infraction of the rules, he was required to stand in a corner with a slate on his head. Not surprisingly, the result was immediate expulsion.

He was next enrolled in the Clark School in nearby Brierley Hill. On his first day there he punched the nose of the boy seated next to him because he "hated his velvet suit." The headmaster, David Clark, a Scotsman whom Carder remembered as a very strict disciplinarian, took immediate action and there is no record of further classroom disturbances by Carder during his years at that school.

In addition to controlling young Frederick's conduct, Headmaster Clark was also able to stimulate in the boy an interest in his studies. These included geography, physics, chemistry, Latin, and Greek, along with the basics. Years later Carder recalled, "I liked them all—except mathematics. This I hated, and often I was sketching fellow pupils' heads instead of doing math."

Carder's father and paternal grandfather owned the Leys Pottery, also in Brierley Hill, which produced salt-glazed stoneware articles. The factory fascinated young Carder. The boy's grandfather encouraged his interest by allowing him access to the rooms where the wares were made. Moreover, he gave his grandson a copy of Muspratts's *Chemistry* and advised him to "learn as much as he could about everything." The boy took the advice literally and began an avid search for knowledge that continued throughout his lifetime. He promptly supplemented his hobby of sketching and modeling with experiments in chemistry and physics, in addition to his assigned schoolwork. By the time he was fourteen he had applied himself so diligently to his studies that he was "top boy" in his class at the Clark School.

Carder's eagerness to excel in schoolwork was exceeded only by his interest in working with clay, which had become an obsession. He began spending all his spare time after classes and on Saturdays at the pottery, making objects in clay and modeling portraits of the factory workers. As he wrote later, "This got such a hold of me that I begged to go to work at the pottery." His father, however, failing to realize how vital this creative urge was to his son, refused to take the boy's repeated requests seriously. Finally young Frederick could bear it no longer, and in a sudden willful outburst he announced that he was quitting school to go to work in the pottery. Later, he recalled that his father "did his damnedest" to dissuade him, suggesting other schools and reminding the fourteen-year-old that his excellent scholastic record would virtually assure his entrance into Oxford or Cambridge. Carder doggedly insisted that nothing would satisfy him but work at the pottery, which he envisioned as "great fun." Sensing the futility of further arguments, his father reluctantly gave in to the boy with the trite but ominous admonition, "All right, young man—you have made your bed. Now you will lie on it." And he put the boy to work in the pottery—shoveling coal!

This was not the job Carder had anticipated. He had to report for work at six in the morning and put in twelve sweaty hours shoveling, sieving, and transferring wheelbarrow after wheelbarrow of coal from the storage bins to the fireboxes of the giant kilns. Before a week had passed he regretted his choice, and told his father he would go back to school. But now his father was adamant. He reminded young Carder that the situation was of his own doing. So the boy resignedly continued to shovel coal, realizing how foolish he had been.

Soon his self-pity was dissolved by his determination to extricate himself from his plight and seek training in art. For this he enrolled in night classes at the School of Art in Stourbridge, three miles from the Leys Pottery. Three evenings a week after his long, hard day at the pottery, he would clean up, eat a hurried meal brought from home in the morning, and walk the three miles to school. By the time he had finished his classes and walked home again, it would be about eleven o'clock. Later he reminisced, "All ideas of play were abandoned" in those days, but he insisted that they were always "challenging days of work and accomplishment."

Carder had stoked the pottery kilns for nine months when his father, secretly pleased by the young man's change in attitude and pursuit of more education, promoted him to a job in the "fettling room." In this part of the factory, handles were applied to the bottles and jugs and other finishing work was done to the greenware. Carder soon enlarged his activities to include throwing on the potter's wheel and assisting with glazing and firing.

Becoming intensely interested in the possibility of improving the factory's products, Carder also now experimented with various clays and other ceramic materials. He soon realized that he needed more than Muspratts's *Chemistry* to achieve his goal and gave over two more evenings a week for schooling. The additional evening classes in chemistry, electricity, and metallurgy were taken at the Dudley Mechanics Institute, also three miles from the pottery, but he continued his art classes in Stourbridge for three evenings a week. In his nineties, Carder loved to recall his enthusiasm during this period. "To be at work at six in the morning and work to six in the evening, and walk three miles each way for study five nights per week seems now tough, but I enjoyed it. Through the long days when I had a monotonous job, I would be going over in my mind the previous lessons. All this hard work served me in good stead in the years to come."

For the next year Carder was completely happy. Each day at the factory offered opportunities to apply his growing knowledge and express his artistic ability. Each evening brought new knowledge from his art and science courses. He looked forward to a career in clay-working and hoped to carry on the family pottery. Then suddenly, in 1878, the prospect changed. His grandfather died and the factory became the property of Carder's father and two uncles. "From then on . . . there was trouble." One of his uncles "resented his constant experimentations, rebuffed his suggestions for technical improvements, and ridiculed his sketches for new designs." For months Carder endured the uncle's hostility and tried to win his approval. But when all such efforts failed, he decided that eventually he would have to leave the pottery.

Just at this time Carder learned that John Northwood, the father of a fellow student, had made a copy in glass of the celebrated Portland Vase.[3] Young

Ill. 2. MARBLE PLAQUE, carved by Frederick Carder. Note signature and date at bottom. Dimensions are 12 by 7⅞ inches, by 1 inch in thickness. *Welles Collection. Raymond Errett Photograph*

Ill. 3. STEVENS & WILLIAMS as it appeared in 1900. *Stevens & Williams Limited*

Northwood's description of the work involved in this achievement so intrigued Carder that he coaxed his father to take him to see the cameo glass masterpiece. The visit to John Northwood's studio changed Frederick Carder's life. As he wrote later, "When I saw this vase, I was struck by the possibilities of glass and determined, if possible, to get into the business."

John Northwood, in turn, was impressed by a small marble head that Carder had just finished carving and had brought along. He promptly invited the boy to spend Saturday afternoons at his studio learning the art of cameo glassmaking. Carder accepted with enthusiasm.

After a few months of carving in glass and marble under Northwood's tutelage (Ill. 2), the fledgling artist showed such promise that Northwood recommended him to the Brierley Hill firm of Stevens & Williams (Ill. 3), which was looking for a glass designer. Overjoyed at the prospect of leaving the pottery, Carder accepted instantly when Stevens & Williams offered to hire him. Thus in 1880 he began his career in glassmaking.

Carder at Stevens & Williams

As draftsman and designer for Stevens & Williams, Carder's official working hours were nine in the morning to five in the evening. However, he was still so interested in clay modeling and sculpture that, whenever possible, he continued working at the pottery both before and after his normal factory day, modeling sculptural objects and relief panels in terra-cotta for architectural decorations. He now owned a bicycle, which greatly eased his travel between the factories in Brierley Hill (Ill. 4), his schools in Stourbridge and Dudley, and his home in Wordsley. But after about a year, this regimen became too exhausting even for

Carder, and he stopped his early morning stint at the pottery though he still executed special orders in ceramic sculpture in the evenings and on weekends (Ills. 5, 6, 7). Moreover, he continued spending Saturday afternoons at Northwood's studio and often took along his work done during the week for the master's criticism. He spent hours in the studio painstakingly reproducing, in wax relief, figures from one of the Wedgwood copies of the Portland Vase.[4] And while Northwood was working on the famed Pegasus Vase (Ill. 14), now in the Smithsonian Institution, Carder carved a cameo glass plaque, "The Immortality of the Arts" (Color Plate IC; Ills. 15, 16), in The Corning Museum of Glass.

Ill. 4. BRIERLEY HILL in 1952. The Royal Brierley Crystal Glass Works (Stevens & Williams) appears in middle ground. *Stevens & Williams Limited*

Ill. 6. TERRA-COTTA RELIEF PANEL, modeled by Frederick Carder, 1889. Approximately 30 by 18 inches. *Corning Glass Works Photograph*

Ill. 5. FREDERICK CARDER modeling a terra-cotta griffin, Brierley Hill, England, 1885.

Ill. 7. PLAQUE "CERES," plaster of Paris. Designed and modeled by Frederick Carder in 1900. Diameter 3½ feet.

For this first year at Stevens & Williams, Carder was treated as an apprentice. His work included copying new designs to scale in a special cost book and making full-size drawings of the cut and engraved patterns currently in production. Next he began designing original glass forms and cut decorations. The first of his designs for cut glass to be accepted and produced, about 1881, was a handsome crystal glass decanter (Ill. 8).

Colored glass had been made in the Stourbridge area at least as early as the seventeenth century. Records show that Stevens & Williams were using it for cased wares in the 1830s.[5] As the century progressed, the popularity of colored glass decreased, and in the decades after the Great Exhibition of 1851 the demand for colorless glass predominated.[6] By the time Carder began working in glass, the bulk of the Stourbridge district productions were of "cut crystal" glass. Carder considered many of these designs "the quintessence of vulgarity" and felt that there were far greater artistic possibilities in reviving colored glass—a trend already noted in some of the other English glasshouses.[7]

After much persuasion, the "principal" of the factory, J. F. Williams-Thomas, consented to have some colored glass designs produced on a trial basis. Carder

Ill. 8. CUT GLASS DECANTER, the first design by Carder accepted for production at Stevens & Williams in 1881. Height, about 10 inches. *Welles Collection. Raymond Errett Photograph*

Ill. 10. COLOGNE BOTTLES, crystal glass with cut decoration. Made at Stevens & Williams in the 1880s. Height, about 6 inches. *Welles Collection. Raymond Errett Photograph*

Ill. 9. COLOGNE BOTTLE, amber glass with ruby accents; cut decoration. Designed by Frederick Carder at Stevens & Williams in the 1880s. *Welles Collection. Raymond Errett Photograph*

recalled that these sample pieces were "jeered at by everyone in the factory." Nevertheless, the "principal" agreed to "give them a trial," and they were sent to London for sale. Carder vividly remembered how he lay awake the next few nights fearful of being called into the "principal's" office and told there was no further need for his services. His fears proved groundless when, a few days later, an elated "principal" summoned him to the office and jubilantly told him his designs were "selling like hot cakes." He congratulated the young artist on his foresight, encouraged him to widen his creative activities, and promised him greater freedom to work out his ideas. Carder was now well started on his career in glassmaking, and for the next two decades many productions of Stevens & Williams reflected the impact of his talents (Ills. 9–13; Color Plates I, II).

The demand for cameo glass articles was increasing so rapidly that the factories of Thomas Webb & Sons and Stevens & Williams began producing it on a commercial scale. As the volume of orders mounted, Stevens & Williams sent many of their finer pieces to Northwood's studio for finishing.[8] Artists in this highly specialized technique were scarce, and one by one Northwood's workmen were offered positions in the nearby factories. Tom and George Woodall, two of his best artists, were hired by Thomas Webb & Sons, and Carder heard that Northwood himself was considering closing his studio and working at Webb's. When Carder repeated the rumors to his "principal," Mr. Williams-Thomas immediately offered Northwood the position of art director and works manager at Stevens & Williams. Northwood accepted the position about 1881 and remained with the factory until his death in 1902.

This teaming of teacher and pupil proved most successful: Northwood and Carder collaborated on many artistic and technical glassmaking projects. One of their first successful ventures was made in competition with Thomas Webb & Sons. This was the polishing of engraved designs on clear crystalline glass to give an effect similar to rock crystal pieces[9] produced in the sixteenth and seventeenth centuries.[10] Such glass pieces have continued in varying degrees of popularity until the present day (Ills. 17–20). Other techniques that Carder and Northwood introduced or improved included thinning overlays on cameo glass articles to speed production (Color Plate IA); the use of an intaglio lathe (Ill. 21) for cutting art nouveau designs;[11] perfecting silver threading;[12] and producing double, triple, and quadruple glass casings. They also designed patterns for the factory engravers and cutters to apply to the more traditional shapes of tablewares.

During these years Carder consistently kept up with his evening classes, amassing an ever increasing number of awards and certificates[13] from the Science and Art Department of the Committee of the Council on Education in South Kensington. How he found time for romance in his crowded schedule is not recorded; but that he did is evidenced by his marriage to Annie Walker in the Parish Church of St. James, Dudley, Worcestershire, on May 21, 1887. In later years, Annie Carder reminisced that during much of their courting the only communication she had with her admirer all week long was the rhythmic sound of a stick being dragged along the pickets of the iron fence before her house by her "Freddie" as he bicycled past on his way to work or evening classes. "It was," she confided, "one of the sweetest, most exciting sounds I ever heard."

Marriage and family life seemed to give an added impetus to Carder's work and study programs.[14] In 1888, he won a silver medal in the National Competi-

Ill. 11. AMBER GLASS VASE with sulfide medallion of Queen Victoria commemorating her Jubilee year, 1887. Height, about 4 inches. Designed by Frederick Carder at Stevens & Williams. *Corning Museum. Raymond Errett Photograph*

Ill. 12. RUBY GLASS VASE with applied elephant-head handles and mat-su-no-ke decoration in crystal glass. Designed by Frederick Carder at Stevens & Williams in the 1880s. Height, approx. 7 inches. *Corning Museum. Raymond Errett Photograph*

Ill. 15. PEGASUS VASE. Cameo glass carved by John Northwood, Wordsley, Staffordshire, England. Completed 1882. *John Gellatly Collection, Smithsonian Institution*

Ill. 13. CAMEO GLASS VASE designed by Carder, executed by Will Northwood at Stevens & Williams (c. 1887), and now in their collection. *Stevens & Williams Limited*

Ill. 14. TERRA-COTTA VASE, designed and made by Frederick Carder in the 1880s. Height, about 12 inches. *Corning Museum. Raymond Errett Photograph*

Ill. 16. FREDERICK CARDER'S HANDS, demonstrating how he carved the cameo glass plaque "The Immortality of the Arts." Photographed about 1959. *Raymond Errett Photograph*

Ill. 17. "ROCK CRYSTAL" engraving in art nouveau style on a goblet. Designed by Frederick Carder at Stevens & Williams in the 1890s and now in their collection. Height, approx. 5 inches. *Stevens & Williams Limited*

Ill. 18. "ROCK CRYSTAL" engraving in art nouveau style on a goblet. Designed by Frederick Carder at Stevens & Williams in the 1890s and now in their collection. Height, approx. 6½ inches. *Stevens & Williams Limited*

Ill. 19. "ROCK CRYSTAL" wineglasses with engraved decoration, designed by Frederick Carder at Stevens & Williams in the 1890s. Height, approx. 5 inches. *Welles Collection. Raymond Errett Photograph*

Ill. 20. "ROCK CRYSTAL" engraved decanter. Stevens & Williams, about 1895. Height, 9 inches. *Welles Collection. Raymond Errett Photograph*

Ill. 21. ("JOSH") HODGETTS, intaglio decorator, 1900. Photograph taken by George Carder, Frederick's brother. *Stevens & Williams Limited*

tion of Schools of Science and Art for a vase design, "Cupid and Psyche" (Ill. 28), modeled in white wax relief on dark amethyst glass. The next year brought an even greater honor, the gold medal in the National Competition, for "The Muses," a dark blue glass vase decorated in white wax relief (Ill. 29), which simulated the cameo glass technique he admired so passionately. These honors and his achievements as an art instructor (he was now teaching) were acknowledged at the annual meeting of the Stourbridge School of Art on October 4, 1889. They were noted again at the Wordsley Art Class prize-giving in April, 1890, when the local member of Parliament made the formal presentation of the gold medal he had won a few months earlier.

In 1891, Carder qualified as an entrant in the national art competitions in London, and won his Art Master's Certificate and the Gold Medal of the Year for his thirty-inch copy of the heroic bronze, "The Archer," by Hamo Thornycroft (Ill. 30). This achievement also entitled him to a national scholarship, which would have enabled him to study for three years in Paris, Rome, or London. It was a bitter disappointment to Carder when Stevens & Williams refused to release him from his contract, thus forcing him to forego this opportunity for further full-time study. The scholastic committee was powerless to intervene, but was able to arrange for his use of some of the funds during several of his short annual vacations. He utilized these trips to study glass collections in the leading museums in England and on the Continent. Drawings made during these years show the impact of these important collections on his art (Ill. 33).

Ill. 22. ART NOUVEAU INTAGLIO GLASS made at Stevens & Williams. Reproduced from a magazine page of the 1890s, which had been kept by Frederick Carder in his files. *Smithsonian Institution Photograph*

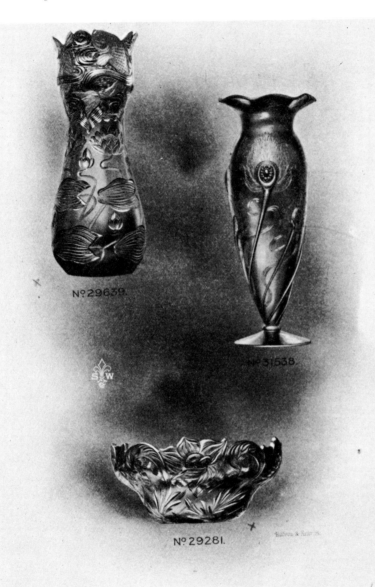

Nº 29639.

Nº 31538.

Nº 29281.

INTAGLIO GLASS.

From
STEVENS & WILLIAMS
Brierley Hill Glass Works
Stourbridge, England.

*Designed by
Fredk Carder*

" The bold sweeping cuts and delicate modelling lend themselves to producing the happiest results, and are particularly adapted to floral decoration " (See Text.)

Ill. 23. GLASS CUTTER, England, 1900.

Bottom left:
Ill. 24. CASED GLASS BISCUIT BOX with silver cover; dark amber over pale yellow. Cut decoration is in cameo style. Made at Stevens & Williams in the 1890s. Height, 6 inches. *Welles Collection. Raymond Errett Photograph*

Ill. 25. CASED GLASS BRANDY BOTTLE, amethyst over crystal; engraved design. Made at Stevens & Williams in the 1890s and used from then until 1943 by Mrs. Carder. Height, 7 inches. *Welles Collection. Raymond Errett Photograph*

Ill. 26. CRYSTAL GLASS BISCUIT BOX with engraved decoration.
Stevens & Williams, about 1890. Height, 7 inches. *Welles
Collection. Raymond Errett Photograph*

Ill. 27. GLASS CUTTING SHOP at Stevens & Williams in 1928, almost
the same as it was at the turn of the century. *Stevens & Williams
Limited*

Ill. 28. "CUPID and PSYCHE" VASE, modeled by Frederick
Carder. Height, 19⅞ inches. Dark amethyst glass;
white wax relief decoration. Awarded silver medal in
National Competition of Schools of Science and Art,
1888. *Corning Museum. Raymond Errett Photograph*

Later in 1891, the local authorities invited Carder to establish an art school in Wordsley where talented workmen could attend night classes. He eagerly seized this opportunity to impart his artistic ideas and technical knowledge to those interested in improving their skills. He had learned through his association with the glassworkers that many could not visualize from line drawings the objects to be made; they needed to have a model or actual piece of glass to copy. He felt that much time and expense could be saved by teaching these men at least the rudiments of line drawing. Accordingly, he set up classes in drawing, painting, and sculpture on Monday, Wednesday, and Friday nights. On Tuesdays and Thursdays he instituted classes in glassmaking to supplement the art training. This program consisted of actually making melts of glass to test basic formulas, the effects of coloring oxides, variations in melting temperatures, and other production problems.

Classes were scheduled from 7:00 to 9:00 P.M., but interest was so great that they usually ran until 10:30 or 11:00 P.M. Though only 8 students enrolled the first year, their reaction was so enthusiastic and the results so beneficial to them and their employers that within five years the enrollment had increased to 150.

In the midst of this activity, Carder experienced his "greatest thrill" when his bronze "Study of a Child's Head" was accepted for the 1893 Exhibition of the

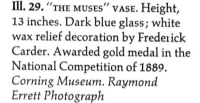

Ill. 29. "THE MUSES" VASE. Height, 13 inches. Dark blue glass; white wax relief decoration by Frederick Carder. Awarded gold medal in the National Competition of 1889. *Corning Museum. Raymond Errett Photograph*

Ill. 30. "THE ARCHER" BRONZE. Height, 30 inches. Modeled by Frederick Carder in 1891 from the heroic figure by Hamo Thornycroft. For this bronze, Carder was awarded the national gold medal by the Science and Art Department of the Committee of the Council on Education. *Welles Collection. Corning Glass Works Photograph*

Royal Academy of Arts.[15] This appealing sculpture was stolen from the exhibition and no trace of the culprit or the object was ever found. Carder always felt the thief might have been someone who had lost a child resembling the little bronze head so strongly that the urge to steal it was irresistible. Fortunately the plaster-of-Paris model was preserved, and another bronze casting, now in the Welles collection, was made to replace the stolen statuette. The model Carder used for this charming study was his own baby daughter, Gladys.

When Carder started the Wordsley School of Art in 1891, classes were held in the Wordsley Institute. Plans for a new building were immediately formulated, but it was eight years before the building was completed and formally opened with appropriate ceremonies in February, 1899. The brick facade of the building was ornamented by terra-cotta relief panels (Ills. 39–40) and other embellishments designed and modeled by Frederick Carder and his brother George. The staff was headed by Carder as art master.

As a result of the practical classes at the Wordsley School of Art, the numbers and skills of the glassworkers available in the Stourbridge area increased greatly, a development so much appreciated by the local glass industry that in 1902 the South Staffordshire County Council sent Carder on a tour of the glassmaking

Ill. 31. Annie Carder's monogram appears in the corners of the lace handkerchief design done by her husband. Carder's design for an overmantel decoration followed a musical theme. Both 1880s. *Raymond Errett Photographs*

Design for Lace Handkerchief.

Ill. 32. DESIGNS Carder made in 1886.

centers of Germany and Austria. When the report of his trip was published, Carder's already favorable impression on "the trade" was greatly enhanced,[16] and the council recommended him for another fact-finding mission, this time to glass centers in the United States.

Accordingly, in the winter of 1903, Carder sailed for the United States, arriving in New York about March first. He found New York City "dirty and cold," commenting later that the only place where he had ever seen more filth was Prague. Pittsburgh was his next stop. There Andrew Mellon, to whom he had letters of introduction, welcomed him most cordially. Carder was always very grateful to Mellon for helping him make many of the contacts and arrangements he needed to ensure the success of his trip.

Ill. 35. STUDY OF A CHILD'S HEAD, bronze; height with base, 6 inches. Modeled by Frederick Carder and exhibited at the Royal Academy of Arts, London, in 1893. Actually, it is a portrait bust of his daughter Gladys at eleven months. Signed "F. Carder, 1890." *Welles Collection. Raymond Errett Photograph*

Ill. 33. SKETCHES FROM LIFE made by Carder in the 1890s. *Raymond Errett Photographs*

Ill. 36. CYRIL, bronze portrait bust of Carder's son Cyril at the age of five. Height with base, 8 inches. Modeled by Carder in 1898 and signed with his FC monogram and '98. *Welles Collection. Raymond Errett Photograph*
◄

Ill. 34. CARDER removing a waste mold from a plaster-of-Paris casting. England, about 1885.

Ill. 37. STANLEY, 1898; bronze ► plaque made by Carder, portraying his son who died in 1899 at the age of seven. *Welles Collection. Raymond Errett Photograph*

STANLEY

Ill. 38. THE FREDERICK CARDER FAMILY about 1895. Stanley and Cyril are at their mother's right. Gladys is seated in the foreground. *Courtesy Gladys Carder Welles*

After surveying the glass factories in the Pittsburgh area, Carder spent a day or two sight-seeing in Washington before proceeding to Corning, New York. His trip by rail to Corning was an experience he later said he would "a damn sight rather tell about than do again!" The worst part was a three-hour, predawn layover in Elmira, New York. It was bitterly cold, and the only possible diversion in the Erie Railroad Station was watching a man clean cuspidors. Carder kept warm by "cussing his stupidity in ever coming to this cockeyed country and vowing he would lose no time getting out of Yankeeland." By the time he boarded the train again, he was so furious that he gave vent to his feelings to an old chap with white hair who happened to sit next to him. The man seemed highly amused at Carder's comments. He willingly traded quips with the English visitor and made spicy comments on the strange names of the towns they passed en route, such as Horseheads and Big Flats. Not until Carder was about to get off the train did he learn that his companion was Mark Twain, traveling to lecture in Rochester!

Carder's first view of Corning was from the platform of the Erie Railroad Station at the corner of Pine Street and West Erie Avenue. It was bleak and uninviting. The wooden sidewalk, partially obscured with soot-blackened snow,

Ill. 40.

A. TERRA-COTTA RELIEF FIGURE (life size). Modeled by Frederick Carder in 1899 as a decoration for the Wordsley School of Art (see Ill. 39). Note Portland Vase form in the left hand.

B. TERRA-COTTA RELIEF FIGURE (life size). Modeled by Frederick Carder in 1899 as a decoration for the facade of the Wordsley School of Art (see Ill. 39).

Ill. 39. WORDSLEY SCHOOL OF ART, about 1900. Terra-cotta panels and entrance arch were designed and modeled by Frederick Carder.

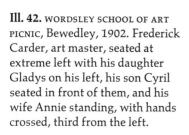

Ill. 41. ANNOUNCEMENT of Wordsley School of Art courses, 1902-1903 — front and back of the brochure. Courses of instruction and schedules were listed inside.

GLASS MANUFACTURE.

A Special Class in this subject is held on Mondays. The Course includes—Composition of Glass generally—Modes of Manufacture—Special properties of Glass—Construction of Furnaces, &c.—Chemical Changes during Manufacture—Composition of Materials used, including colours—Moulds and Tools—Various Methods of Decoration, &c., &c.

The above Syllabus is both *theoretical* and *practical*, and is divided into three grades—Preliminary, Ordinary, and Honours. It is designed to cover the ground of the City and Guilds of London Institute. In the Honours Grade students are expected to possess some knowledge of design, and to attend a class on that subject.

Special attention will be given to Continental methods of work, as studied by the Instructor during the past vacation in Germany and Austria.

Mondays, Preliminary and Ordinary, 7-30 to 9-30.

Honours, 7-30 to 10 p.m.

FEES .. .. .. 2s. 6d.; and Honours, 5s.

Money Prizes, value £4, and Medals are offered by the City and Guilds; and Free Studentships (Money Prizes, value £3, £2, £1), by the Staffs. County Council.

Instructor ... F. CARDER.

E. R.

. WORDSLEY .
School ✦ of ✦ Art,
(SESSION 1902-3)
Commencing Monday, September 29th.

SUBJECTS :—

Art :

Elementary—Tuesdays and Fridays .. } 7·15
Advanced—Tuesdays, . Wednesdays, } to
and Fridays .. } 9·15.
Morning Classes—Wednesdays . and } 10-30 to
Fridays .. .. } 12-30.

Science :

Geometry and Mechanical Drawing— } 7·15
Mondays .. .. } to
TECHNICAL SUBJECTS : } 9·15.
Glass Manufacture—Mondays.. .. }

STAFF—

Art Master :—F. CARDER, Gold Medallist
Assistants :—Misses E. & M. A. RICHARDSON, and N. WILKES.
Science Master :—B. F. MASON.
Glass Manufacture :—F. CARDER.

Hon. Secs.: } W. NORTHWOOD,
} C. DUDLEY.

looked nearly as hazardous as the unpaved street with its frozen ruts. As he walked the short block north to Market Street and continued on past Corning's leading hostelry, the Dickinson House,[17] facing Pine Street Square, he caught his first view of the Corning Glass Works. He promptly dubbed this sprawling plant with its ten smoking chimneys "The Smokestack University," a name he used consistently from then on (Ill. 46).

Later that morning, after meeting Alanson B. Houghton and other Corning Glass Works officials, he was taken on a tour of the plant and was impressed by its size and by the quantity of glass produced. But the electric light bulbs, glass tubing, and other items mass-produced here were of only mild interest to a man whose career was devoted to making handcrafted glass. He was anxious to get on to his next objective, a meeting with Thomas G. Hawkes. Hawkes was the

Ill. 42. WORDSLEY SCHOOL OF ART PICNIC, Bewedley, 1902. Frederick Carder, art master, seated at extreme left with his daughter Gladys on his left, his son Cyril seated in front of them, and his wife Annie standing, with hands crossed, third from the left.

president of T. G. Hawkes & Company, a firm that had carried on an extensive glass decorating business in Corning since 1880.

It is intriguing to surmise how much planning Carder and Hawkes may have done for this meeting in Corning, which proved to be so vital to Carder's career. There would have been ample opportunity for them to get acquainted in England, for Hawkes had been buying glass blanks from Stevens & Williams for many years. The speed with which the results of their meeting were announced in the press suggests not only that it was prearranged, but also that the documents that were to associate these two men had been prepared earlier and were ready for signature. The *Corning Leader* of March 11, 1903, bore the headlines AN-OTHER GLASS INDUSTRY IN CORNING, and continued, "Articles of incorporation of the Steuben Glass Works[18] were filed with the Secretary of State at Albany on Mon-

Ill. 43. THE CARDER FAMILY in Frederick Carder's home, Kingswinford, England, 1902. *Left to right, standing,* Mrs. George Carder (sister-in-law of Frederick), Mrs. Frederick Carder (Annie). *Seated,* Cyril Carder, George Carder's daughter, Gladys Carder (Frederick's daughter, later, Mrs. Gillett Welles), Caleb Carder (Frederick's father), and Frederick Carder.

Ill. 44. ERIE RAILROAD STATION, Corning, New York, about 1900. *Corning Glass Works*

Ill. 45. CORNING GLASS WORKS, Main Plant, Corning, New York, about 1905. *Corning Glass Works*

day, March 9." Since Carder had probably arrived in Corning no earlier than March 6 or 7, he very possibly signed the papers on his first day there. All he would ever say of this momentous meeting in Corning was that Hawkes was "so damn persuasive" that he could not refuse.

Carder's alacrity in accepting Hawkes's offer, though characteristic of his decisiveness, also reflected his long-pent-up desire to leave Stevens & Williams. His resentment over losing the full benefits of the scholarship won in 1891 had continued to rankle despite efforts to suppress it. More pertinent, perhaps, was the deterioration of his friendship with John Northwood. The congenial comradeship of their early years was gone, and Northwood had gradually become first "lukewarm," then "openly hostile" toward everything that Carder did.

Several things contributed to the rift between these two men: For one, Carder believed that Northwood had become somewhat jealous of his success at the Wordsley School of Art. He also thought that Northwood wanted to be sure that his own son, John Northwood II, would fall heir to his position at Stevens & Williams, a position Carder felt should rightfully come to him. Whatever the reason, the break between them never healed. And after Northwood's death in 1902, this son was, in fact, appointed to the position his father had held at the Stevens & Williams plant. Thereby Carder's chances for further advancement at the Brierley Hill factory were effectively blocked.

Ill. 46. DICKINSON HOUSE on the corner of West Market and Pine streets (now Centerway), about 1900. *Corning Glass Works*

Ill. 47. BRIDGE STREET, Corning, New York, looking north, about 1903. *Corning Glass Works*

Ill. 48. DENISON PARK, Corning, New York, about 1909. *Corning Glass Works*

Ill. 49. ORIGINAL STEUBEN GLASS WORKS, Corning, New York, as it appeared about 1907. The four buildings shown here, formerly the Payne Foundry and Machine Shop, were converted to house the Steuben Glass Works in 1903. The only change from the 1903 appearance was the addition, in 1907, of the third story and cupola to the building at extreme right bearing the name STEUBEN GLASS WORKS. *Corning Glass Works*

Even if this situation had not existed, it is doubtful that Carder could have resisted the temptation to establish and run a factory of his own. He later admitted that when he heard Hawkes's offer, he "felt like jumping up and down." And the more he learned of the possibilities, the more attractive the project seemed. Hawkes already owned a building (formerly the Payne Foundry, on what is now Denison Parkway), which, he assured Carder, could be converted into a glass factory within a few months. Moreover, for his decorating shops, which then employed over four hundred people, Hawkes agreed to take all the glass blanks that Carder could make. With such assurances, the success of the venture seemed certain.

Carder's return to England and the announcement of his decision to go to America startled and shocked the district. Sir Graham Balfour, director of the education committee of the South Staffordshire County Council, was highly incensed that Carder would think of leaving the country after having just returned from a trip financed by the council. He gave Carder "a goddamn fine dressing down" and prevented publication of Carder's report on his American trip. Stevens & Williams offered to triple Carder's wages and were understandably irritated by his determination to resign.[19] Even sixty years later, Hubert Williams-Thomas confessed that they were still angry at Fred Carder for "walking out" on them.

The Wordsley School of Art felt Carder's loss keenly and presented him with a beautifully engrossed "illuminated address" in appreciation of his years of service. Still, in but little more than three months, he had settled his business and personal affairs in England. And on July 15, 1903, Carder and his family left Liverpool on the R.M.S. *Oceanic*, bound for New York.

Before leaving England Carder granted an interview, which was published in the *Brierley Hill Advertiser* on June 20, 1903. It contains some highly interesting notes relating to his new venture:

> He referred to Corning, in the State of New York, as the Wordsley of America, having about 13,000 inhabitants (a few more than Brierley Hill) and comparable to Malvern with a little bit of Brierley Hill thrown amongst it! With reference to the glass industry in America compared with that on the Continent, he states, "I found the Americans were taking all the best mechanical devices which the Continent produces. . . ." The number of glass cutters employed in the city of Corning alone impressed him, "In one factory 400 men are employed, in another 200, and another 80 and there are several smaller factories with 60 to 30 men; so that in this city alone are engaged many more cutters than in the whole of the Stourbridge district." He also commented on the natural advantages such as an abundance of natural gas for manufacturing, the vast extent of the country and the wealth of the population.
>
> Three weeks hence Mr. Carder will leave England to take up his new work. Other conditions being equal, he would rather stay in England, which, in contrast with the "wild rugged character" of the scenery to which he goes is "like a well laid-out garden." In his adopted city, the railways run along the streets and there are many other strange features to one who has been reared on English soil; but he says the liking of America grows upon one. He has this satisfaction, that in the sphere he is leaving he has done his work with modest faithfulness as with marked ability; and the good wishes of all who know him will accompany him into his exile, where we hope he may find, in every sense of the word, a new home.

2

Carder in America
The Start-Up

THERE WAS NO TIME FOR CARDER TO REGRET HIS "EXILE" ONCE HE ARRIVED IN CORNING. He was eager to start glass production and fulfill the optimistic statement of the *Corning Leader* that the Steuben plant would be in operation very soon.[20] That the factory would be making glass before the year ended must have seemed unbelievable to those unfamiliar with Carder's resourcefulness, but Corningites were soon to learn that this newcomer was at his best under pressure.

As soon as he accepted Hawkes's offer, Carder began planning the staff and equipment of the Steuben Glass Works. While still in England, he quietly arranged for some fifteen glassworkers to come to work for him in America. He decided on a ten-pot, deep-eye, natural draft furnace, fired with soft coal, as the most desirable type for his new factory, and obtained plans for it from the Dixon Company of Pittsburgh. Construction of the furnace started soon after Carder's arrival in Corning (Ills. 50, 51). Having seen similar furnaces operating in Austrian and German factories, Carder actively supervised the building of his furnace, which continued in use for the next fifteen years.

All was going well when suddenly, in early October, word came that his English glassblowers had been denied admission to the United States and were being held in Montreal, Canada.[21] Investigation disclosed that British and American unions claimed the Alien Contract Labor Law was being violated. The action of the unions probably resulted from previous disagreements between Carder and union officials in the Stourbridge area. When they learned of Carder's plan to move English workmen to Corning, they had notified their American counterparts, who took prompt and effective steps. In spite of all Carder could do, the unions won—a few days later the English glassworkers were deported.

This left Carder with a glass factory fully equipped and nearly ready to start production—but no glassmakers. He stubbornly continued his preparations, but a search for workmen was now his major problem. The solution came unexpectedly when a Swedish glassblower named Henning Overstrom applied to Carder for a job. He was hired at once. It developed that Overstrom had worked at the Mosaic Glass Company in Addison, New York,[22] which had failed a few months before. Although he had subsequently found work at the Dorflinger Glass Factory in White Mills, Pennsylvania, he was dissatisfied there and anxious to leave. Overstrom soon got in touch with other Swedish glassblowers, and

Ill. 51. VIEW OF GLASS FURNACE EXCAVATION. Carder is on the upper level at the extreme right, next to the man holding onto the top of the ladder. *Rockwell Gallery*

Ill. 50. EXCAVATION FOR TEN-POT GLASS FURNACE of Steuben Glass Works, July, 1903. Carder is at center with pick on right shoulder. *Rockwell Gallery*

Ill. 52. HENNING OVERSTROM, the first glassmaker to be hired by Carder for the Steuben Glass Works in 1903. *Corning Glass Works*

around them as a nucleus Carder formed a blowing-room force that enabled him to start making glass by late October, 1903.

Productions during the first months consisted of crystal glass blanks for T. G. Hawkes & Company to decorate with cutting and engraving, as Hawkes and Carder had agreed earlier. Such an assured market for the output of his factory would have satisfied the usual factory manager, but Carder "damn well soon got tired of that." By early in 1904 he was running experimental melts of colored glasses and spending every available moment on the perfection of gold-colored iridescent glass, which he was able to register September 6, 1904, under the now-famous name of Aurene (Color Plate III).

Financial as well as artistic success was almost instantaneous. Carder loved to recall, with justifiable pride, that he "bought the materials, built the furnace and retired 40 percent of the $50,000 indebtedness in the first year of operation."

The Steuben Glass Works was a one-man operation, with Carder devising the glass formulas, designing the ware, supervising production, and dictating sales policies. New colors, classic and exotic forms, and drawings for engraved and cut decorations poured out of Carder like salt from the legendary little red mill. At least half of the more than one hundred recorded colors and the over eight thousand design forms (which made up the Carder record from 1903 to 1932) were initiated before World War I. In addition, hundreds of specially designed glass shapes were made in quantity as blanks for T. G. Hawkes & Company.

Early Merchandising

Although Carder had registered the name Aurene in the United States Patent Office in the fall of 1904, several months passed before he was able to develop the rich, full-bodied, velvety iridescence that is now the accepted quality of Aurene. A market survey indicated that, in addition to making ornamental wares of this glass, the production of Gold Aurene shades for gas and electric lighting fixtures would be lucrative (Ill. 59). Later results proved the survey to have been a sound appraisal—large quantities of these shades were sold during the next years.

Upon the advice of T. G. Hawkes, the Aurene shades were sold at first through manufacturers' agents who had showrooms in New York, Boston, Philadelphia, Chicago, and other large cities. The agents operated on a commission, which Carder recalled as being 14 percent. From the start, he was dissatisfied with the volume of business done by this method, and there were constant arguments about the commissions. Finally, he decided to send his sample shades directly to the fixture manufacturers, with the result that he "sold more shades in a day than those damn fools did in a week!" But as soon as the agents learned of Carder's new arrangement, they demanded a commission on all sales of Steuben glass made in their territories. Carder refused, and so this method of merchandising came to a sudden end.

Soon afterward Carder decided to employ his own salesmen, and they were so successful that from then on the major portion of the Steuben output was sold by a selected group of personable traveling representatives. Steuben adver-

Ill. 53. GOLD AURENE VASE with applied trefoil handles and hooked threadings forming elongated feather motifs. Carder made the notation in wax pencil (partially illegible), which refers to the date made—"1905"—and "G. Hole," probably the experimental atmosphere of the glory hole at the time the vase was given the stannous chloride spray. Height, about 8 inches. *Corning Museum. Raymond Errett Photograph*

Ill. 54. GOLD AURENE VASE, probably made about 1904 or 1905, has the reddish purple tone found in very early pieces. Given to the author by Frederick Carder in 1930. Marked "Aurene" (no number). Height, 6⅞ inches. *Smithsonian Institution Photograph*

Ill. 55. GOLD AURENE VASE, No. 135; height, 8½ inches. About 1905. *Collection Mr. and Mrs. George Jamison. Raymond Errett Photograph*

Ill. 56. AURENE GROUP. *Left to right,* Bowl, Blue Aurene with hooked decoration; height, 3 inches. Vase, Calcite with Gold Aurene lining and hooked decoration; height, 4¼ inches. Vase, Calcite with Gold Aurene and green glass hooked decoration; height, 5¼ inches. All made about 1905. *Corning Library. Raymond Errett Photograph*

Ill. 57. CRYSTAL GLASS BOWL with machine threading in green and engraved floral decoration. Carder said this was the first engraved piece made at Steuben, about 1904. Diameter, 8½ inches. *Corning Museum. Raymond Errett Photograph*

tising was aided by small brochures (Ill. 60) issued from time to time, which were distributed at factory and department store showrooms, as well as by these men.

The most glamorous and successful of the salesmen was Charles Potter, who came to the Steuben Glass Works in about 1906 or 1907 and continued to be Carder's ace representative until about 1932. A tall, lithe man, Potter had a handsome, aquiline nose, enhanced in his later years by an elegant pince-nez. With his expensively tailored clothes, courtly manners, and charming personality, he became known as the "man who kept Steuben running." So large were his sales of Calcite glass lamps and shades when these were introduced about 1915 that customers and competitors alike affectionately dubbed him "Calcite Charlie."

Potter was not salaried but worked strictly on commission, even owning the trunkloads of samples he carried from city to city on his cross-country sales trips. He planned his itinerary to include regional glass shows, and on the completion of a tour would sell his samples to the last buyer on the circuit and ship the empty trunks back to the Steuben plant to be refilled for the next trip.

Although Potter's commission was only 10 percent, his volume of sales was so great that his income averaged about $20,000 a year for most of his time with Steuben. His elegant Pierce Arrow limousine, his residence (only one block below that of his "boss"), and his farm and stables all attested to his affluence. Soon Hawkes and others tried to persuade Carder that Charlie was making too much money on a commission basis, and urged transferring him to a salary plus an expense account. This Carder refused to do, arguing that it would dampen Potter's enthusiasm and result in a smaller sales volume, which would be detrimental to all concerned. Later, the Corning Glass Works urged the same change. But Carder again stood firm and Potter continued on the straight commission basis for his entire career with Steuben.

Ill. 58. AVENTURINE CRACKLE VASE, green with gold flecks and random bubbles, made about 1910 to 1917. Probably a limited production item. Height, 8 inches. A Steuben paper sticker on the base gives the price as $25. *Corning Museum. Raymond Errett Photograph*

Ill. 59. ELECTRIC and GAS LIGHTING SHADES, made from about 1905 to 1920. *Corning Museum. Raymond Errett Photograph*

Ill. 60. AURENE and HAWKES brochure covers designed by Frederick Carder about 1905. *Smithsonian Institution Photograph*

Ill. 61. CALCITE GLASS LAMP, No. 2383, with engraved floral design. Made about 1916. Height, about 14 inches.

Ill. 62. CALCITE LIGHTING BOWL, No. 963. Engraved design is Rosette. Made about 1916 in the following sizes: *Width   Depth*

Width	Depth
10"	x 5"
12"	x 5½"
14"	x 6"
16"	x 8¾"

Charlie often brought back samples of competitors' wares to the factory and insisted that Steuben produce similar items. This always touched off an argument with Carder, who preferred to design his own forms and often refused to copy an object. Though Carder usually had his way, Charlie would sometimes sweep aside all arguments by showing a large initial order from a quantity buyer. Even Carder could not hold out against such odds, and his capitulations account for many of the Steuben forms that closely resemble shapes known to have been produced in European and contemporary American factories. There was considerable criticism then and later, and the term "copyist" has often been applied to Carder for allowing the manufacture of these items.

Although most critics would not condone the practice, it must be borne in mind that in the glass and ceramic industries the purloining of competitors' shapes and patterns of decoration has gone on from the earliest periods. Some eighteenth-century German porcelain pieces are almost exact duplicates of oriental prototypes. And styles of decoration on glassware can be traced from Egyptian and Roman pieces through Venetian and other European productions to the present day. Moreover, eighteenth-century American glassmakers produced shapes and decorations in imitation of and in competition with European designs; and late nineteenth-century American factories copied popular colors and shapes from each other, often renaming a color or changing a form slightly to avoid a lawsuit.

To Carder, every piece of glass was a challenge. He had a compulsion to see whether he could duplicate or excel the work of another glassmaker or factory. It is easy for faultfinders to point out a derivation and easier still to cry "copy," but the more astute will note that Carder's aim was to add his own touch to a form or to carry a technique to a higher degree of perfection.

Tiffany Lawsuit

Steuben glass was not only sold by its representatives but also through a few selected outlets. Among them, from about 1910 to 1914, was Haviland and Co., with offices at 11 East 36th Street, New York City. It was from Arthur Veel Rose, the general manager of this company, that Carder received the first indication that he was going to be sued by Louis Comfort Tiffany. A letter to Carder from Rose, dated October 23, 1913, said in part:

> L.C.T.'s lawyer called on me yesterday and asked me if he was right in supposing that I was closing out Aurene Glass. I said, "Why do you want to know?" and he replied that, "If I was not closing it out he had instructions to proceed against the manufacturer and against me!" I said, "If that's your game go as far as you like—I have no intention of closing it out but on the contrary I will at once proceed to stock up."
>
> P.S. . . . I told that "legal guy" you were making glass in England in 1898 or 1899 and that as far as L.C.T. was concerned he did not know the first thing about making Favrile Glass but that Arthur Nash was the "whole thing" and I could prove it.

Carder had heard the increasingly persistent rumors that Tiffany Furnaces was feeling the competition Steuben Aurene was giving their Favrile. But in spite of Rose's warning, he was shocked at being served a subpoena dated November 3, 1913, to answer a bill of complaint by Tiffany Furnaces.

This bill of complaint was voluminous. It alleged in part that Tiffany Furnaces "at the expenditure of large sum(s) of money . . . has produced a distinctive and original kind of glass, having a peculiar gold iridescence. . . . This glass has been designated for a number of years . . . with the plaintiff's trademark 'Favrile' and by marking each piece with the letters 'LCT' or 'L.C. Tiffany—Favrile' . . . referred to by the public as 'Tiffany Glass.' "

The bill went on to charge "that the defendant, Steuben Glass Works . . . has employed a workman who was trained in the plaintiff's employ and who learned while in the plaintiff's employ the method of producing such ornamentation of glass; and was hired in order that the defendant might learn from such workman how plaintiff produced some of the plaintiff's glass."

The bill stated further that the defendant (Steuben) was manufacturing a glass so closely resembling Tiffany glass "that it is difficult to distinguish the imitation glass and glassware which is manufactured by the defendant from the genuine glass . . . manufactured and sold by the plaintiff unless carefuly examination is made to determine whether the glass . . . offered for sale bears the initials 'LCT' or 'L.C. Tiffany—Favrile.' "

The bill ended with "Sale of the imitation glass . . . has greatly injured the plaintiff's business . . . and has resulted in actual loss of business to the plaintiff

... to the amount of $50,000.00 for which plaintiff demands judgment, together with costs of the suit."

Carder began immediately to prepare his refutation of the allegations, and in this Rose proved to be an invaluable ally. In a letter to Carder dated November 13, 1913, he wrote:

> Arthur J. Nash [Tiffany's manager] took lunch with me at the Club [The Manhattan Club, Madison Square, New York], as arranged. There are one or two points you should know, first he says that Anderson [the attorney for Tiffany] called on me without his [Nash's] or L.C.T.'s instructions probably thinking that he could frighten *me!* Well! You know what Anderson got for his trouble! Then Nash said, "of course we shall win the case against Steuben just in the same way that Macbeth of Pittsburgh won a similar case." I don't know what that case was but it was evidently a famous case, so it's up to your lawyer to find out and look it up! Then he said that you did not know how to make a piece of Aurene until you took away a young man from L.C.T.'s factory who had previously been in your employ at Brierley Hill. Now it's up to you to find that young man. . . .

"That young man" proved to be Edwin Millward, who had a room at the home of Samuel Baggett, 87 West Erie Avenue, Corning, New York. On November 26, 1913, Millward signed a long affidavit, which stated in part that he:

> ... never taught or tried to teach Mr. Carder or anyone connected with the Steuben Glass Works how to imitate the methods or processes used by Tiffany Furnaces. . . . I do not know how to make colored glass . . . do not know the processes or the formula used by Tiffany Furnaces in making, decorating or coloring glass . . . while employed by Tiffany Furnaces, all I did was to gather glass. Neither Mr. Carder or anyone connected with Steuben Glass Works asked me to tell them how Tiffany Furnaces made colored or decorated shapes . . . no one ever offered me any inducement or in any way tried to get me to leave the Tiffany Furnaces and come to Corning to work for Steuben Glass Works.
>
> When I started at Steuben Glass Works that concern was then making the same kind of glass wares [as Tiffany] . . .

On November 25, 1913, Carder executed a demand for a bill of particulars, which asked information as to

> ... what designs were copies . . . what plaintiff's samples were procured. . . . Name of workman . . . customers, times, places and names of persons as to whom it is alleged . . . the purchasing public has been deceived. . . .

After this was submitted, Tiffany Furnaces was silent for over six weeks. Then the Carder forces, sensing that perhaps the Tiffany lawyers were beginning to have misgivings concerning the success of their case, decided to take further action. In January, 1914, Carder requested the court to order Tiffany Furnaces to answer his interrogations. The silence of Tiffany's lawyers was finally broken when Carder received a notice of discontinuance of the action dated March 5, 1914.

Carder never met Tiffany until years after the threatened lawsuit. They encountered each other at a medal-awarding ceremony in New York City.[23] Carder related that they "got on famously," and after shaking hands agreed to "let bygones be bygones."

Ill. 63. SIXTEEN-POT FURNACE used in the Steuben blowing room from 1908 until the 1930s. Actually, each arch of this furnace could hold one large pot or two small pots, as shown by the center arch in the photograph. The iron kettles on wheels in the left foreground were used for draglading. *Corning Glass Works*

Ill. 64. ("ART") FERMER, gaffer at Steuben, finishing the blowing of a Calcite glass lighting bowl. Note the cherrywood molds and forming tools in the foreground. Photograph was taken about 1915. *Corning Glass Works*

Ill. 65. BLOWING ROOM, Steuben Glass Works, about 1910. Note the gaffer's chair and tools in center and foreground. *Corning Glass Works*

Ill. 66. STEUBEN GLASS WORKS, Corning, New York, as it appeared from about 1908 until the buildings were demolished in 1963. The buildings on the left were added about 1908. Photograph was taken in 1962.

Ill. 67. STEUBEN GLASS WORKS. The corner building, formerly the grain warehouse of Heyneger, Pitt and Company, was acquired about 1912 to complete the Steuben factory complex. It housed the Steuben offices, including Carder's, which was located on the second floor corner. The showroom occupied the center portion of the third floor (see Ill. 74). Carder occupied these offices from 1912 until 1932 (except for about six months in 1920), when he was moved to the Corning Glass Works main plant office building. He returned to this building in 1944 and reoccupied his former offices and studio until he retired in 1959.

Ill. 68. STEUBEN GLASS WORKS in the foreground, the Corning Glass Works main plant in the background. About 1915. *Corning Glass Works*

Growth

The Steuben factory grew steadily during the first fifteen years. In 1908, the
sixteen-pot furnace (Ill. 63) was added and the blowing room expanded to its
maximum size. By 1912, additional plant buildings extended eastward along Erie
Avenue from the original Payne Foundry to the corner of Chestnut Street and
around the corner about half a block up the Chestnut Street hill (Ills. 66–68).

The Steuben Glass Works was in the midst of its most vital period by 1916. A
large variety of tablewares, decorative items, and lighting devices were being
produced in a wide range of colors and designs. The demand for "brilliant"
period cut glass, at its height when Steuben was founded, continued during the
first two decades the factory was in operation. The cutting shop produced much
more of this type of cut glass than is generally realized. The designs in general
conformed to the styles that were currently in vogue throughout Europe and
America. Bowls, pitchers, candlesticks, and various decorative and useful pieces
decorated with V-cuts, diamonds, hob-stars, pinwheels, and other popular
motifs were made in considerable quantities. All these pieces were sold as
Steuben productions. Steuben blanks made for T. G. Hawkes & Company and

Ill. 71. DECORATING ROOM, Steuben Glass Works, about 1915. Designs are being applied to Calcite lighting bowls in "wax ink" prior to the acid etching. *Corning Glass Works*

Ill. 72. STOCKROOM, Steuben Glass Works, about 1915. *Corning Glass Works*

Ill. 73. STOCKROOM, Steuben Glass Works, 1917. *Corning Glass Works*

Ill. 74. THE SHOWROOM, Steuben Glass Works, about 1915. Mrs. McElroy, the saleslady, can be seen in the background. *Corning Glass Works*

Ill. 75. OUTER OFFICE, Steuben Glass Works, about 1915. Frederick Carder stands next to post. ("Charlie") Carlson, wearing cap, is seated. *Corning Glass Works*

decorated at the Hawkes factory were sold as Hawkes pieces, with no reference made to Steuben.

The Steuben decorating room, where etched glass was produced, was operating at capacity, and the variety of objects in the stockroom (Ills. 72, 73) and on display in the showroom (Ill. 74) indicates the success Carder's venture had achieved. Calcite glass, which had been introduced about a year earlier, was still an important contributor to the volume of business, and the gaffers were kept busy making large lighting globes and bowls, as well as lamps and tablewares. The office force, like the rest of the factory, was subject to close supervision by Carder, who dictated all policies and kept a sharp eye on every employee.

The Sale to Corning Glass Works

World War I brought an end to the autonomy of the Steuben Glass Works. The factory was classified by the government as a nonessential industry producing luxury items, and was denied the right to purchase raw materials earmarked for the war effort. The Steuben stockholders[24] were faced with the choice of closing the factory—thus throwing about 270 people, mostly long-time employees, out of work—or selling it. They chose the latter course, and on January 8, 1918, the Corning *Daily Journal* announced that the Steuben Glass Works had become the Steuben Division of Corning Glass Works, a firm founded by the Houghton family and located in Corning since 1868.

The sale of Steuben was a blow which, in its impact on Carder, was second only to the loss of his son, Lieutenant Cyril Frederick Carder, D.S.C., who was killed in action in France in July of the same year. Carder had expected Cyril to assist and eventually succeed him at the Steuben plant. Now he had to adjust to radical changes in both his work and his homelife.

Corning officials retained Carder as managing director of the Steuben Division, but soon after their purchase of the plant, the bulk of its ornamental glass production was replaced by the production of bulbs, tubing, and optical glass. Carder chafed under the domination of "The Smokestack University," and as the months passed, his discontent and irritation increased. In August, 1919, Dr. John C. Hostetter was appointed assistant manager of the Steuben Division, and Carder was made art director.[25] Having to relinquish part of his authority over the Steuben Division was so galling to Carder that he felt he must get away from Corning. He needed time to think things through and "see what the 'ell to do next." So in the spring of 1920 he and Annie Carder sailed for Europe.

They first went to France to see the grave of their son Cyril, then proceeded to the Stourbridge area in England to visit family and friends. While there, Carder toyed with the idea of resuming his career in his native land. But despite his love for England, after a six-months holiday and a careful appraisal of his feelings, he grudgingly admitted his roots were now in "Yankeeland," and the couple returned to Corning, where Carder eventually resumed the management of the Steuben plant.[26]

Ill. 76. FREDERICK CARDER'S RESIDENCE, 249 Pine Street, Corning, New York, which he and his family occupied from 1903. He died here December 10, 1963.
Raymond Errett Photograph

Although Carder damned the regulations imposed by the "Smokestack," he was given a fairly free hand with Steuben. The factory's products in the 1920s were much like they had been before World War I. The essential wartime commodities such as sheet glass, bulbs, and tubing were mostly phased out. The blowing room, now using only the sixteen-pot furnace, continued to make the Aurenes, rubies, greens, blues, and dozens of other glowing colors that Carder loved so well (Color Plates V, VI, XXII, XXVIII, XXIX; Ills. 77–85). Steuben was once again almost his—from office to blowing room to shipping platform.

In the late 1920's, Carder's routine day began with a brisk fifteen-minute walk from his home to the factory, where he arrived at his office about nine o'clock. Carder's office resembled a museum storage room, with glass pieces everywhere. Dozens of vases, bowls, candlesticks, plates, and other glass objects—the accumulation of his years at Stevens & Williams and at Steuben, plus a sampling of the wares of European and American competitors—were crammed on shelves behind the glass doors of floor-to-ceiling cases. Other fragile objects occupied the tops of bookcases, crowded the windowsills, and poised precariously on the top of his dark oak rolltop desk. A sizable number of pieces even lined the walls along the floor. No one was allowed to touch this cumulative arrangement because Carder, knowing the accustomed place of each object, had at his fingertips an amazing visual reference file of technical and artistic achievements in glass. He used this collection to illustrate a color or technique to his staff. Or he might humble an overconfident young scientist who had brought a newly discovered color or glassmaking technique to show him, by reaching into the depths of a dust-covered shelf and bringing forth an object of exactly the same color or of similar form, with the comment "Dammit, I did that in 1896!"

Seated at his desk, which was piled high with papers, brochures, glass pieces, and his pipes and cigars, he read the morning mail and attended to any pressing office business. This might involve urgent letters, discussing sales and other administrative problems with his office manager, Robert J. Leavy, and reviewing his schedule for the day.[27]

Ill. 77. PAIR OF COMPOTES, Celeste Blue with mica-flecked ball stems. 1920s. No. 6063; height, 8¼ inches. *Collection of Mrs. Harry A. Erwin. Raymond Errett Photograph*

Ill. 78. COMPOTE, Celeste Blue with amber stem. No. 6058, made in the 1920s. Height, 8¼ inches. *Private Collection. Smithsonian Institution Photograph*

Ill. 79. CANDLESTICKS, 1920s. *Left to right,* Dark Amethyst, No. 379 (variant). *Corning Museum.* Royal Purple, No. 2956. *Mrs. Raymond J. Howar Collection.* Dark Amethyst; height, 10 inches. *Corning Museum. Raymond Errett Photograph*

Ill. 80. WATER-LAMP BASES. *Left,* Pomona Green with crystal glass handles and feet, No. 84202; height, 10½ inches. *Right,* crystal glass with Pomona Green handles, feet, and hooked horizontal ring, No. 8405; height, 10 inches. These were designed to be filled with water, and the bulb socket and shade holder fastened to an insert that fit into the neck like a cork. Made in the late 1920s for Art Lamp Company. *Private Collection. Smithsonian Institution Photograph*

After attending to these matters, which he finished with all possible speed, he was ready to begin his "morning round" of the factory. This was a tense period for all departments—each section boss or production supervisor awaited "the Old Man's" appearance with apprehension, hoping that all would be in order when he arrived. When Carder's temper was aroused at any point en route, everyone else "caught hell all down the line."

Carder's first stop was at the laboratory where the glass formulas were kept. These were written in code with numbers denoting the ingredients, and were relayed to the mixing room as needed. Pull tests, color comparisons, and other determinations of glass quality were all made here. The color samples, either in the form of rods about the size of a lead pencil or Prince Rupert's drops, were laid out for Carder's inspection and approval. The decisions as to which glass pots could be worked that day, what formulas needed correcting, and what batches were to be mixed for future melts were also made here. As a rule the session in this area, with John Graham in control, went smoothly.[28]

His next stop was at the office and design room, next to the laboratory, which the author shared with John Graham for several years. Since Carder had been raised on the apprentice system, he felt every designer should serve time in that status before being allowed to assume a more responsible role. Accordingly, when I arrived at Steuben, fresh from the college campus, to work as Carder's assistant, he outlined my duties and put me to work as an apprentice in the etching room, with the comment, "You'll be no damn good to me for three years!" This two-months assignment in the heat of melting wax combined with acid fumes and augmented by the summer temperature was to test my mettle, Carder admitted later, and see whether I could adapt to factory working conditions.

After this tour in the etching room, I settled into the factory routine, but still was treated as an apprentice. My first duties were to make line drawings to scale for the factory catalogs and full-size outlines of Carder's designs in ink on tracing paper, to be blueprinted for use by the gaffers in the blowing room. In these first months, Carder's visits to my office were usually fairly serene. He would make random checks of the work at hand, spotting at once the wavering of a line with such comments as, "Can't you see that damn' flat spot on the goblet's bowl? They'll make it rotten enough in the blowing room without your help! You're nothing but a damn' Yankee kid, and more trouble to me than a row of 'ouses!"

He would then demonstrate, with a sure swift stroke, how the line should be drawn, humming softly to himself meanwhile and watching to see if the technique was being absorbed by his probationary assistant. When a line was particularly cramped, his favorite criticism was, "You're drawing it pinchey-cot"— a word he never defined, but which made his point.

After a few months, he apparently felt I had gained sufficient facility to make finished drawings of engraved designs. At first he assigned me practice drawings of the simpler floral shapes, stressing the necessity of memorizing each element in a flower and its position in relation to the other parts. After these and other motifs were mastered, I was allowed to copy patterns, first from Carder's sketches and then from actual glass objects, usually new additions to the Steuben line.

The first time I was given a glass object to copy, the results were disastrous.

Ill. 82. COMPOTE, pale green with Celeste Blue applied tooled decorations in Venetian style. Possibly a variation of No. 5123. Made in the 1920s. Height, 6 inches. *Welles Collection. Raymond Errett Photograph*

Ill. 83. COMPOTE, dark amethyst glass with optic foot and bowl, crystal glass mereses. Late 1920s. No. 2847½; height, 5¾ inches. *Private Collection. Smithsonian Institution Photograph*

Ill. 81. WATER-LAMP BASE, French Blue, No. 6585; height, 15½ inches. *Private Collection. Smithsonian Institution Photograph*

Ill. 84. DECANTERS, No. 6400; height, about 16 inches. BOWL, No. 6539 (variant); diameter 15 inches. FLOWER BLOCK with Buddha figure, No. 6721; height overall, 12 inches. 1920s. *Photograph from Carder's files*

The object was a clear glass goblet, ten inches in height; it had a black glass casing over the bowl with an elaborate cut and engraved pattern. This handsome piece was the only sample of a new design scheduled to retail at about $185 a dozen. Carder gave the sample to me late one afternoon, with instructions to keep it in my office and complete the drawing the next day, so I left it on the drawing table when I went home for the night. Next morning, to my horror, I found the goblet shattered on the floor—a victim of the vibration caused by the Erie Railroad trains passing outside, combined with the slight tilt of the table-top. For the next long hour and a half, in the company of a sympathetic John Graham, I awaited Carder's routine arrival. The fragments of the goblet were tenderly piled on the drawing table.

At last Carder came in. For a brief uncomprehending second all was well. Then, spying the wreckage, he shouted, "Sacrébleu!" and strode cursing to the table. After giving me one piercing look, he shouted, "Glue it!" and departed at once in a mood that boded ill for his next contact. I worked all day gluing the pieces together.

Fortunately, the accident was an isolated instance. Carder left the patched-up goblet in the design room where it served as a sorry reminder that may have paid off rather handsomely. I cannot recall smashing another Steuben glass piece of any importance during my twelve-year career as Carder's assistant.

As the months passed, more interesting tasks came my way, such as carving plaster-of-Paris models for architectural glass molds. I was also gradually allowed to include my own ideas and work out original designs, which Carder criticized on his visits.

On his daily rounds, Carder next crossed the passageway to the fascinating domain of Walter Herriman, another Englishman who had come to America and found work at the Steuben plant. Herriman had been hired about 1910. He continued at Steuben through the rest of Carder's regime and later, until his retirement in the 1950s.

Herriman was a super jack-of-all-trades. Whenever Carder had a special problem, such as a complicated mounting for a glass fountain or a metal fitting for a unique vase, a tool or piece of apparatus for a special job in the blowing room, Herriman would contrive the solution. If he failed to work out the answer in his workshop-office at the Steuben plant, he would continue his efforts after hours in his private garage, where he welded, soldered, glued, and fabricated his ingenious ideas into the objects he would later submit in triumph to his "boss." Herriman's considerable contribution to the success of Steuben was deeply appreciated by Carder, who relied on his ingenuity and valued his friendship throughout their long association.

From Herriman's place Carder went to the blowing room, where Frederick Schroeder and Joseph Sporer, the superintendents, were always ready for him with problems ranging from routine operations involving broken glass pots and gas pressures to the difficulties of producing some of his new designs. Carder sometimes took problems dealing with equipment and glassmaking ingredients back to the office for study and research, but the fabrication of new objects he dealt with on the spot. Often, all that was needed was a change in the tempo of manipulation or a simple maneuver that would allow the molten glass to take the desired form. Usually after the "trick was turned," the gaffer would com-

Ill. 85. CENTERPIECE. Canoe-shaped bowl is mold-blown in bubbly-green glass (possibly Antique Green). Probably a modification of No. 6515; about 12 inches long. Cast bronze figures are mounted on the polished glass base. Made about 1929. *Welles Collection. Raymond Errett Photograph*

ment, "Now why didn't I think of that?" Sometimes Carder's insistence that a routine technique *had* to produce the desired result provided the extra pressure that made the difference between success and failure.

If there was time before lunch, Carder visited the cutting shop and etching rooms. In the 1920s and early 1930s, Ray Inscho was in charge of the cutting shop, which was located in the west end of the factory on the top floor of one of the original Payne Foundry buildings. A tall, rangy, handsome man with graying hair, Inscho ran the operation in a relaxed manner that was deceptive. Beneath the jovial exterior of this former glass cutter, now foreman, was a stern character that keenly resented any workman's taking advantage of his kindness. Inscho might look the other way when a workman was polishing a nicked rim on a vase obviously brought from home for repair, or even stay after hours to cut a "special" wedding or anniversary present for a fellow employee. But if production lagged or privileges were abused, the culprit was supervised from then on with such vigor and diligence that he rarely overstepped a second time.

The etching rooms were below the cutting shop. During the last decade of Carder's management, these rooms were in the charge of Bolaslav Manikowski, a former house painter whom Carder had hired about 1917 as a worker in the etching rooms, and promoted to foreman in the early 1920s. Manikowski had learned to etch the master patterns on the steel and glass plates used to make the transfer prints in wax, which were applied to the glass objects being decorated. Carder would sketch the design full scale on white or black paper, depending on his mood, and Manikowski would transfer a tracing of the design to the wax coating of the steel or plate glass, cut the pattern in the wax with a stylus, and etch the plate with acid.

As the years passed, Manikowski became critical of Carder's designs and sometimes undertook to "improve" them when he transferred the pattern from the original to the etching pattern plates. This tampering did not escape Carder's notice, but often he would allow the pattern plate to be etched as Manikowski had restyled it, after having "cussed him out" for his changes. In the next few patterns produced, Carder's drawings would be more strictly adhered to, but in time the cycle would be repeated—Manikowski would again impose his ideas, with the inevitable repercussions from Carder.

When I was assigned to work in the etching rooms, I found Manikowski a most affable supervisor who went far beyond the required courtesies in supplying information and helping a new assistant adapt to the Carder regime. During this time, Carder had several occasions to reprimand Manikowski for changes in the plate designs. He would take the stylus in his hand and correct the design as far as the remaining wax-coating permitted, cussing with every stroke. After such sessions, Manikowski would philosophize that Carder had to make these changes to show he was the boss. However, when Manikowski went too far in his design changes for Carder's tolerance, he was required to redo the plate. Many etched pieces produced in the late 1920s show the results of Manikowski's revisions.

Carder usually completed his rounds before noon. If some emergency delayed him until the noon whistle blew, he had to suspend operations because all departments stopped work for the noon hour. Often he lunched at the Corning City Club, which he had helped organize and had served as president. This group of

Ill. 86. TABLEWARE TO MATCH LENOX CHINA, engraved in Fountain pattern. GOBLET, No. 6565; height, 9½ inches. CANDLESTICK, No. 6594; height, 7 inches. This pattern was made in Marina only, for Marshall Field and Company in the late 1920s. *Photograph from Carder's files*

local business and professional men had a private dining room at the Baron Steuben Hotel. Once a week Carder attended the Rotary Club luncheon, also held at the Baron Steuben, and on other days he either ate at home or with visiting friends or business acquaintances. After lunch he either finished his factory rounds or worked in his office, with excursions to the factory as emergencies or other needs dictated.

Most of Steuben's production was now sold by exclusive shops and leading department stores. Marshall Field and Company in Chicago was among the first to display table settings (Ill. 86) featuring Steuben glass made to match Lenox china. Sales to buyers for these stores were usually made at the glass shows held every year in Pittsburgh, Chicago, and New York (Ill. 87). Carder continued to design all forms and decorations, drawing preliminary sketches on black paper with a white pencil (Ill. 88). Finished designs from these sketches were done full-size, in India ink on tracing paper as noted earlier, and blueprints were made for use in the blowing room, cutting shop, or the engravers' studios.

Carder's policy during the 1903 to 1932 period was to continue to make an object as long as it sold. "Designs discontinued themselves," he often said, and usually added, "Sometimes when a vase or stemware group doesn't move, I double the price and it sells like shot!" This accounts for some seeming dis-

Ill. 87. EXHIBITION BOOTH of the Steuben Division, Corning Glass Works, at Grand Central Palace in New York, April, 1929.

Ill. 88. CARDER, photographed about 1930 while designing an engraved decoration for a goblet. *Corning Glass Works*

crepancies in dating Carder Steuben pieces. Carder cataloged his designs in numerical order, beginning with No. 1 in 1903 and ending with No. 8,578 in 1932. A low number usually indicates one of the earlier pieces. However, many of the popular designs were produced during almost the entire 1903 to 1932 period, and a few of his designs continued long after his regime ended. Line drawings of all surviving factory catalog numbers are reproduced in Chapter 9.

Just before 1920 a change in public taste began to develop. The elegant forms and elaborate decorations derived from traditional styles were losing their appeal. Now "functional" and "modern" designs became the trend. Art nouveau extravagances were particularly singled out as targets for derision—even hatred— by champions of functional forms, and by the mid-twenties demand for them had begun to decline everywhere.

Carder made some grudging concessions to the new trend. A few of his designs in the late 1920s and early 1930s show his ability to produce, however reluctantly, in the accepted mode of these years (Color Plate XVII B). But he detested these designs, and characterized them as being composed of "straight lines and pot hooks."

For Carder-Steuben glass, the final blow fell in the early 1930s when color in glass also went out of favor. Now the clear colorless glass of Orrefors in Sweden, Lobmyer in Austria, and Baccarat in France led the fashion.

The stock market crash of 1929 and the general economic depression that followed further aggravated the problems of the Steuben Division. Sales of their Carder glass were no exception to the decline in sales everywhere, especially of luxury items. Corning Glass Works officials decided something must be done about the Steuben Division. Carder was ordered to discontinue many of his traditional forms and introduce designs by artists whose ideas seemed to express contemporary taste better. But Carder was by now well beyond the average retirement age. This fact, combined with his stubborn inflexibility and his resistance to many of their plans and suggestions, had the inevitable result. In February, 1932, John MacKay was appointed to Carder's position at Steuben, and Carder was named art director of Corning Glass Works. Along with me, he was moved from his office in the Steuben Division to the Corning Glass Works main plant office building at the foot of Walnut Street.

In retrospect, it seems that this change should not have had such an impact on Carder as it did. The average man appears to accept semiretirement to a less demanding position with equanimity. But Carder was not an average man. His exceptional vitality and his love for his work as manager of Steuben made him feel that the transfer meant an end to his career.

Art Director, Corning Glass Works

The fortitude with which Carder met this crisis was superb. Outwardly he showed no sign of the wounds the drastic transfer had inflicted, but his family and those close to him in the factory realized the terrific strain of those first few weeks. At age sixty-nine, with his life's work in glassmaking apparently terminated, many a man would have become irrevocably submerged in self-pity and given way to weak resignation. Not Carder. The very qualities that had contributed to his removal from Steuben carried him through this new situation. His vast experience and technical knowledge in the field of glassmaking assured him of a position of continued importance in the glassmaking community.

A long-time friend, Dr. Eugene C. Sullivan, glass scientist and co-inventor of Pyrex glass, was at that time vice-chairman of Corning Glass Works.[29] Probably closer to Carder than any other Corning Glass Works official, Dr. Sullivan did much with his understanding friendship to reassure Carder that his career was far from ended. He encouraged him to experiment with unexplored glassmaking techniques and do designing for other Corning plants and departments. On the social side, he lifted Carder's spirits by frequently suggesting they take the afternoon off and play golf at the nearby Corning Country Club.

With this moral support and the urging of his own zestful personality, Carder began to plan new activities. In a few weeks it seemed that the transition was over its roughest part. Then suddenly, on a Monday morning a few months after his transfer, word came out that during the weekend all the glass remaining in the stockroom of the "Old Steuben" had been smashed by the new regime. This news was spread with lightning speed and with varying degrees of emotion, both by word of mouth and by the press.

Like many other sensational stories, this one was greatly distorted and the importance of the episode exaggerated at the time. Statements made years later by several of the men who had been involved in the incident cast a different light on it:[30] They point out that space was urgently needed; that since Carder never discontinued a design, the stockroom held nearly a thirty-year accumulation of his glass; that most of this stock was then outmoded and unsalable, and that many pieces were defective, damaged, or incomplete sets. For months the company had been selling these items to employees and others at a small fraction of their retail price. Thus, a considerable quantity had already been sold. But even the space occupied by the remaining pieces was needed. So the Steuben manager and others went carefully through the stock, removed and preserved the pieces they believed to be significant and valuable, then ordered the rest to be smashed. According to Robert J. Leavy, who was present at the time, only "culls" were involved in the smashing. Since the majority of Steuben stock items then retailed for less than ten dollars, the monetary loss incurred by this act has probably been greatly overestimated.

Had there been better communication between Carder and those directly involved in the incident, much of his tribulation could have been avoided. But this lack, coupled with the emotional tension on both sides, conspired to create a situation that only a character as strong as Carder's could have survived. He found this latest indignity to be almost unbearable. Although it had been fourteen years since Steuben had been sold, he still thought of the factory as his own and its glass productions as his treasures. Knowing nothing of the reasons for

Ill. 89. GUTZON BORGLUM, sculptor of the Mt. Rushmore memorial, and Frederick Carder in a candid photograph taken in Carder's office about 1937. Carder made several castings of the model of Lincoln's head (seen in Carder's hand), a prototype for the gigantic portrait at Mt. Rushmore. *Corning Glass Works*

the apparent sacking of his creations, he concluded that the intent had been to eliminate all remaining evidence of his influence in the Steuben factory, and he symbolized his feelings about the affair, which he regarded as a crucifixion, by modeling in clay and later casting in glass a head of Christ crowned with thorns.[31]

Although Carder was angry and hurt, his fighting spirit came to his rescue and tranformed his nadir into the start of the final and most triumphant phase of his career. He plunged into experimentation with glass casting by the cire perdue process (see Chapter 7) and developing architectural glass applications.

To pursue these new projects, Carder immediately started converting his new office into a studio-workshop. The commodious room on the fifth floor of the main office building became at once a sanctuary and a creative center. A plywood screen partially separated the studio from the outer office space assigned to his assistant. Behind the screen, Carder gradually installed enough equipment to enable him to model small sculptures, cast plaster-of-Paris molds, experiment with glass castings in pâte de verre, and, finally, melt glass in a homemade furnace. This furnace was ultimately used for perfecting the cire perdue process of glass casting.

Ill. 90. FREDERICK CARDER and a cabinet containing his glass pieces, mostly made by the lost wax process. Photographed in his office by the National Geographic Society, 1942. *Courtesy National Geographic Society*

As the main plant office building was relatively new at the time and the luxurious offices of the top executives of the Corning Glass Works were on the floor directly below Carder's office, the installation of the furnace and other melting equipment was somewhat surreptitious. In his experiments with casting glass by the cire perdue process, it was necessary to melt the wax models from their ceramic molds by steam. Customarily Carder placed the ceramic mold containing the wax model over a pan of water, which was kept boiling by an electric hot plate. This he had quietly purchased at a local store, to avoid any questions that might be raised if he requested one from the factory's supply division. The hot plate sat on a flat-topped desk, which Carder had taken the precaution of covering with a sheet of fireproof "Transite."

For several months, the melting operations were carried on without incident or the knowledge of the downstairs neighbors. But one afternoon Carder left the office early to play golf on a spur-of-the-moment invitation from his friend, Dr. Sullivan. As he had already started melting a wax model out of the ceramic mold, he instructed me to turn off the hot plate when I left the office at 5:00 P.M. This I forgot to do. Several hours later, Carder was called at home by an excited night watchman, who informed him that smoke from "something burning" was filling the office. Surmising that the water had boiled away and the melted wax had caught fire, Carder made a fast trip to the office, where the efficient watchman had already extinguished the burning wax with inconsequential damage. The watchman, who had known Carder for years, minimized the episode in his report and the incident was closed—except for the monumental "bawling out" I received the next morning!

Although Carder seemingly had been relegated to an inactive status as far as current Steuben productions were concerned, he was consulted regularly by the scientists and management of the Corning organization as well as by collectors, museum officials, and others interested in the many aspects of glassmaking. George S. McKearin and his daughter Helen were writing their incomparable books on American glass, and they, as well as Ruth Webb Lee, Alexander Silverman, Gutzon Borglum, Lee Lawrie, and many others were welcome guests at the fifth floor studio-office and at his Pine Street home.

It was at this time that Carder was commissioned to produce a sculptured glass panel fifty-five feet long by fifteen feet high for the RCA Building in Rockefeller Center. This panel, designed by Lee Lawrie, was cast in Pyrex glass. It can still be viewed in the entrance loggia of the RCA Building (Ills. 190–195).

One distinguished visitor was Carl Milles, the Swedish sculptor, who visualized a thirty-five-foot-high glass sculpture for the courthouse in Saint Paul, Minnesota. Milles had brought along a small scale model of his sculpture, which was based on an American Indian theme and depicted the Great Spirit rising from a ceremonial campfire. He wished to discuss the possibility of having Carder produce the statue in glass, and Carder was thrilled at the challenge the project presented. He assured Milles the casting could be done by the cire perdue process in seven five-foot sections. Milles left in high spirits, with the understanding that he would return in a few weeks, accompanied by the Saint Paul officials involved, to see a sample casting.

For this demonstration, Carder modeled a traditional Indian head forty-six

inches in height by twenty-nine inches in width at the base (Ills. 203, 204), and
cast it in Pyrex glass by the cire perdue process. Through some misunderstand-
ing, the officials from Saint Paul arrived in Corning to inspect the sculpture a
week before the date scheduled. Carder felt he should accommodate them and let
them view the glass casting, and so the ceramic mold casing was broken away
even though the glass was still too hot to be exposed to room temperature. The
sudden cooling created a strain that cracked the large glass casting horizontally
across the middle, just above the end of the nose. Everyone was disturbed that
the premature viewing had caused the damage, but the officials were convinced
that Carder could cast the statue in glass and Milles was highly pleased. They
left with assurances that they would submit a favorable recommendation, giving
Carder high hopes of producing the world's largest glass sculpture.

The deliberations in Saint Paul took many weeks, and when word finally came
it was a great disappointment. The awarding of the contract had become a polit-
ical issue. The Depression was still on, and some politicians felt that the dollars
appropriated should not be paid to a New York State firm but kept in Minnesota.
So it was decided to have the Milles sculpture done in Mexican onyx by artists in
Saint Paul. Carder's experimental glass casting of the Indian head is now in the
Rockwell Collection.[32]

In addition to carrying on his experimentation with the cire perdue castings
and his pioneering work in architectural glass, Carder and I designed and carved
plaster models and drew designs for many other divisions of Corning Glass
Works, including the first Pyrex top-of-stove ware, and the pressed tablewares
and ornamental pieces manufactured at the Macbeth-Evans Division at Charleroi,
Pennsylvania. At the beginning of World War II, when German Christmas tree
ornaments were suddenly unavailable, Carder's office was called on to design a
line of these decorations. The request came at 9:15 A.M., and Carder delegated
the job to me. I finished sketches of around twenty designs for the salesman to
take to New York with him on the 4:00 P.M. train. About a dozen of these designs
were chosen by the New York buyers and were successfully sold in quantity for
the next several years.

Earlier his experimentation with ceramic molds for cire perdue casting led to con-
sultation with Dr. George V. McCauley and Dr. John C. Hostetter, the Corning
Glass Works scientists in charge of producing the two hundred-inch glass tele-

Ill. 92. FREDERICK CARDER at age
eighty-nine, in a candid photograph
taken at the opening of a special
exhibition, "The Life and Work of
Frederick Carder," at the Corning
Museum of Glass in 1952. *Corning
Glass Works*

Ill. 93. CARDER in his library at 249 Pine Street, Corning, about 1954.

Ill. 94. FREDERICK CARDER in his library about 1954. *Rockwell Gallery*

scope disk for Mount Palomar Observatory. Carder's ideas and experiments with mold materials were a considerable contribution to the success of this notable achievement.

In January, 1943, I left for active duty with the United States Navy, and from then on Carder carried out his experiments without an assistant. In 1944, his studio-office was moved back to the old Steuben plant, where he occupied the same suite of rooms he had used as offices up to 1932 (Ill. 91). During the next fifteen years, until he was ninety-six, he continued to put in a full working week at his factory-studio. In addition, he performed his duties as president of the Corning Free Academy School Board and participated in other civic activities, as well as regularly attending Rotary Club luncheons, Masonic Lodge meetings, and golfing at the Corning Country Club.

The World War II years were saddened by Mrs. Carder's illness and her death in 1943. But Carder continued his work with cire perdue castings, culminating in the production of the Diatreta pieces (Plate XXXII A & B), which were inspired by the fourth-century cage cups produced in the Rhineland. These unique cast and carved glass pieces, produced while Carder was in his eighties and nineties, were executed completely by him except for some grinding and polishing, which was done at the Steuben finishing rooms.

In 1959, Carder decided to "retire." He moved many of his treasured pieces from his factory studio-office to his Pine Street residence (Ill. 76), and donated the remaining contents of the office to The Corning Museum of Glass.

For the next four years, until he scored his century, Carder held court at 249 Pine Street. As the dean of American glassmakers, his position as a leading authority and artist-technician in glass was unchallenged. He was lionized by admirers and sought after by writers and connoisseurs of glass from all over the world. And recognition came in many other forms as well. His long and fruitful service on the Corning Free Academy School Board was acknowledged by the naming of a new elementary school in his honor.[33] On April 9, 1962, Alfred University conferred on him the honorary degree of Doctor of Fine Arts at a special ceremony in Corning, the only occasion in the history of that university when a degree was conferred outside its campus. His art glass was now avidly sought by collectors, and they flocked to his home to meet him, have him authenticate and sign his Steuben pieces, and autograph photographs.

Carder remained in remarkably good health during these last years, making periodic visits to his daughter, Gladys, and her husband, Gillett Welles, in Hudson, Ohio, until he was ninety-eight. He continued to attend the weekly luncheons of the Corning Rotary Club, which he had founded in 1921 and of which he was a past president. His presence there was traditional—he could be counted on to fill any conversational gaps with anecdotes and current comments always embellished with a fluent supply of "cuss words." In March, 1963, seven months before his one-hundredth birthday, he made tapes of autobiographical data and descriptions of important Steuben glass processes and pieces, which were edited into a longplaying record.[34]

One of Carder's retirement projects was reactivating a third-floor studio in his house. When unearthing some long-idled artist's gear, he commented, "I hadn't used that easel and palette for over forty years." For the next four years, however, he turned out landscapes in oils and watercolors by the dozens, often amazing a casual visitor by telling him to choose a gift painting from the twenty or thirty unframed ones leaning against the wall (Color Plate XXXII C).

Between visits from his friends and family (which now included a great-great-grandson), Carder worked in his flower garden or went for drives in the country. He stopped driving his own car after a cataract operation in 1957 made him feel his vision was not good enough for this activity. But his physical accomplishments and alert mentality constantly made news. He had been in the local headlines for years with his golf scores—CARDER SHOOTS A 78 AT 87—or civic duties —CARDER WORKS HARD, MISSES LITTLE, AT 96.

In the 1950s he began giving his own birthday parties, explaining that he was reversing the usual custom so that he could invite whom he "damn well pleased." These events consisted of a black tie dinner in the penthouse dining room of the Baron Steuben Hotel in Corning, followed by an evening of toasts and reminiscences. The first few such dinners were depressing because of the unavoidable thought that each gathering might be Carder's last. But as he continued his steady climb toward the century mark with scarcely any visible changes in his amazing health and vitality, they became birthday celebrations in the true sense of the word, and his informally issued invitations were eagerly accepted by those fortunate enough to be included.

On September 18, 1963, the guests Carder had invited to his ninety-ninth birthday celebration were enjoying the traditional toasting, which had come to be the main after-dinner feature, when the accolades were suddenly varied by a toast proposed by Robert Rockwell. It characterized Carder as a "fine artist but a poor mathematician." In explanation, Rockwell stated that he had recently received official word from England that Carder's birth date was September 18, 1863, thus confirming that on that very day, September 18, 1963, Carder was a centenarian.

Before the guests fully comprehended the significance of the announcement, Carder quipped, "I've been a goddamn liar for ninety-nine years!" and added, "As everyone knows, the good die young." This characteristic retort put Carder in immediate command of the situation, and the rest of the evening was a jubilant celebration of his newly announced centennial.[35]

About three months later, on December 10, 1963, Frederick Carder spent the evening at home with Robert Rockwell in pleasant conversation about their favorite subject, glass. Soon after Rockwell left, Carder told his housekeeper he had decided to "go up to bed." She asked if he would like assistance in ascending the steep, winding stairs. "Not on your life," he answered. "I've climbed these stairs for sixty years, and I'll climb them tonight!"

That night, Frederick Carder died peacefully in his sleep.

3

Special Color Techniques
"At the Fire"

CARDER OFTEN SAID IT WAS POSSIBLE TO USE ALL HIS COLORS TOGETHER WITH NO more fear of their clashing than the multicolored flowers in a garden. The list of colors given here was compiled from factory records, advertising brochures, and discussions with Carder, Robert Leavy, John Graham, Otto Hilbert, and others, all of whom were most helpful. However, the list contains a good many colors that, up to the present time, have not been identified. Carder frankly admitted that he himself could not remember the shade of some colors, such as the No. 5 Green, although he was sure such a color had been made and his certainty was substantiated by catalog references.

It has been possible to identity many of the colors that were made in quantity, and most of the special types Carder originated or perfected are discussed in the pages that follow. The others listed and not described are colors that are produced by the addition of standard coloring oxides or by formulas too well known to need description.

Carder Steuben Glass Colors

Alabaster (Color Plates XXV C & XXVI C)
Alabaster, Henna
Amber (Color Plate XXIX B)
Amber, Special
Amethyst (Color Plate XXVIII A)
Amethyst, Dark
Amethyst, Light (Color Plate XV A)
Aqua Marine (Color Plate XI B)
Aurene, Blue (Color Plates IV & V)
Aurene, Brown (Color Plate IX A)
Aurene, Gold (Color Plates III & VI)
Aurene, Green (Color Plate VIII A)
Aurene, Light Green
Aurene, Opaline
Aurene, Red (Color Plate VII)
Black (Color Plate XXVI B)
Blue, Antique Rita
Blue, Calcite

Blue, Celeste (Color Plates XV A & XXVIII B)
Blue, Cobalt
Blue, Dark Jade (Color Plate XXIV B)
Blue, Dark Turquoise
Blue, Extra Dark
Blue, Extra Dark Flemish
Blue, Flemish (Color Plate XXII A)
Blue, Hard Flemish
Blue, French (Color Plate XXII A)
Blue, Light Jade (Color Plates XXIV B & C)
Blue, Light Turquoise (Color Plates IX B & XI A)
Blue, Peacock
Blue, Persian
Blue, Rita
Blue, Rose
Blue, Tiffany
Blue, Vigilite
Blue Black

Burmese

Cairn Gorm (nearly a dark amber)
Calcite
Canterbury (perhaps a pale purple)
Cardinal Red
Carrara Marble
Celadon
Cintra* (Color Plates XVI & XVII)
Cluthra* (Color Plate XVIII A)
Coral
Crystal
Crystal, Smoke
Cyprian (Color Plate XI B)

Diatreta* (Color Plates XXXII A & B)

Flint, Brown
Flint, Crystal
Flint, Soda
Florentia* (Color Plate XXX B)

Green, Antique
Green, Cairo
Green, Dark Olive
Green, Jade
Green, Light Flint
Green, Medium
Green, Nile
Green, No. 5
Green, Olive
Green, Opaque
Green, Pale
Green, Pomona (Color Plates XV A & XXII B)
Green, Spanish (Color Plate XXII B)
Green, Tiffany
Green, Wheeler
Green, Window Glass
Grenadine

Heliotrope

Intarsia* (Color Plates XX & XXI)
Ivory (Color Plate XXV B)
Ivrene (Color Plate XXV A)

Jade, Plum (Color Plate XXVII B)
Jade, Rose

Lavender

Marbelite (used for shades)
Marble Glass
Marina (Color Plate XXVIII B)

Millefiori* (Color Plate XIV)
Moonlight
Moss Agate* (Color Plate XXXI)
Mother of Pearl

Old Rose
Opal (Color Plate XVIII C)
Opal, Straw (Color Plate XV B)
Opalescent, Amber
Opalescent, Blue
Opalescent, Pink
Opalescent, Yellow
Orchid
Orchid Rosaline
Oriental Jade (Color Plate XXX A)
Oriental Poppy (Color Plate XXX A)
Or[r] Verre

Peach
Peach Blow
Plum (probably Plum Jade)
Purple, Light
Purple, Pale
Purple, Royal

Quartz, Alabaster
Quartz, Amethyst (Color Plate XVIII B)
Quartz, Blue
Quartz, Green
Quartz, Peach
Quartz, Rose (Color Plate XVIII B)
Quartz, Yellow

Rosa (Color Plate XIX B)
Rosa, Dark
Rosa, Soda
Rosaline
Rose (Color Plate XXV C)
Rose Blue
Rose DuBarry
Rouge Flambé (Color Plates XXIII A & XXIV A)
Ruby, Amethyst Gold
Ruby, Brownish-yellow Gold R
Ruby, Cerise (Color Plate XIII B)
Ruby, Cinnamon Gold (also called Cinnamon)
Ruby, Pink Gold (usually called Gold Ruby)
   (Color Plates XIII A & C)
Ruby, Selenium (same as Cerise Ruby)

Silverine

Topaz (Color Plate XXIX B)
Topaz, Amber (Color Plate XXIX B)
Topaz, Dark

* Actually a technique; made in several colors.

Topaz, Light (Color Plate XV A)

Tyrian (Color Plate XII)

Verre de Soie (Color Plate XI A)

White

Wisteria (Color Plate XXVIII C)

Yellow, Bristol (Color Plate XXIX A)

Yellow, Canary

Yellow, Carbon

Yellow, Citron

Yellow, Jade (Color Plates XXVI A & XXIX A)

Yellow, Mandarin (Color Plates XXIII B & XXIX A)

Yellow, Topaz

Iridescent Colors

Aurenes

Gold Aurene was the first decorative iridescent colored glass produced at the Steuben Glass Works. In the 1890s, while he was still at Stevens & Williams, Carder had become intrigued by the golden and rainbow-colored iridescence on Roman glass of the First to Fourth centuries A.D. On ancient glass, such iridescence is caused by a partial disintegration of the glass surface through the action of chemicals in the soil in which it was buried. In England, Carder experimented for years with methods of producing a similar effect, and was about ready to produce his iridescent glass when he came to America. How near he was to success is shown by the historic vase dated 1904 (Color Plate III A), which he made within a year after he started the Steuben Glass Works.

Louis Comfort Tiffany, who also had been inspired by the Roman glass, produced his iridescent Favrile glass in the early 1890s.[36] Whenever it was suggested that Tiffany's glass motivated Carder's production of Aurene, Carder stoutly maintained that he had started his experiments in England long before he saw Tiffany's Favrile pieces in the Paris Exposition of 1900. Probably the only influence Tiffany's iridescent glass had on him was to assure him it could be done and challenge him to equal Tiffany's achievement. Recent laboratory tests showing Carder's and Tiffany's glass to be from different formulas[37] have confirmed Carder's contention that these two creative glassmakers arrived at their very similar results independently.

The name Aurene was coined from the first three letters of *aurum*, the Latin word for gold,[38] combined with the last three letters of *schene*, the Middle English form of sheen, which describes the gold sheen of the glass. The velvety-soft iridescence of this glass was a remarkable technical achievement. While it was being produced at Steuben, Carder always resisted explaining how it was made—generally ending any interview with, "Why the 'ell should I tell you everything in five minutes that it took me years to find out?"

In 1920 he described this glass and its properties in a book he planned to dedicate to his son Cyril,[39] which was never published. The handwritten manuscript was given to the author by Carder to assist him in writing this book. The excerpt that follows is from the section entitled "Aurene Glass or Metallic Lustre Glass":

This glass depends entirely upon the property of certain glasses being able to keep in solution in an oxidized state salts of the rare metals. This glass when

Ill. 96. GLUE CHIP and ENAMEL PIECES. *Top,* Jade Green bowl with "glue chip" decoration. The surface of the bowl was covered with glue, which shrank as it dried, and pulled away flakes of the glass surface. An acid bath then removed the sharp edges and produced the satin-finish texture. No. 2687; height, 3¾ inches. Probably made in limited quantity in the 1920s. *Below,* Crystal bowl with enameled decoration in yellow, blue, and green. Carder said this was a unique trial piece. Steuben did not use enameled decoration on production items. Probably a variant of No. 2687; height, 3¼ inches. *Corning Museum. Raymond Errett Photographs*

Ill. 95. GOLD AURENE VASES. *Top, left to right,* No. 230; height, 11 inches. No. 257; height, 11½ inches. *Below:* No. 256; height, 11 inches. All made about 1905. *Contemporary Steuben Catalog Photograph*

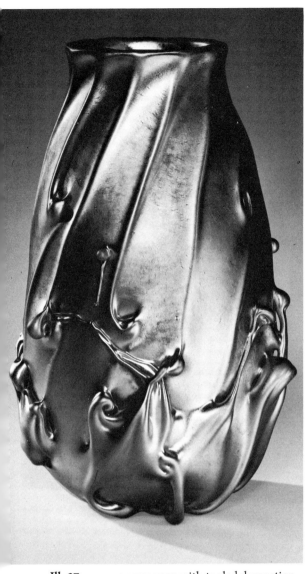

Ill. 97. GOLD AURENE VASE with tooled decoration and swirled ribbing was probably made about 1910. Possibly unique. Height, 7 inches. *Corning Museum. Raymond Errett Photograph*

Ill. 98. GOLD AURENE CANDLESTICKS in art nouveau style, No. 7613; height, 10 inches. Made in the 1920s. *Collection of Mrs. Harry A. Erwin. Raymond Errett Photograph*

made into articles and subjected to the reducing flame of either gas or oil becomes coated by reduction with a film of the metal, varying in intensity with the proper adjustment of flame. This development requires care on the part of the artist and when the reduced metallic film is sufficiently dense, it is sprayed with a solution of tin salt and then heated in an oxidizing flame. Iridescent colors will be produced, these varying in intensity and color values according to the heat treatment it undergoes. . . . Under a microscope Aurene has many thousand lines to the inch . . . which reflect and refract the light rays, giving the iridescent or lustrous sheen. If iron chloride be sprayed on instead of tin salt, or after spraying with the iron chloride it is followed with the tin salt, a golden color is produced. The beauty of the article produced depends entirely upon the artistic manipulation of the workman. He must know how far to heat the piece on hand and know just when to stop.

The description continues with the information on Blue Aurene and the types of decorations put on Aurene glasses that has been incorporated in later pages here.

Carder's statement that the Aurene glass formula contained salts of the rare metals, coupled with the golden hue of Gold Aurene, has led many to think its surface is actually metallic gold. To my knowledge—and I have had the advantage of seeing formulas in possession of the Corning Glass Works—the only "rare" metal ever used in the Aurene formula was silver.

If the tin and iron chloride sprays were not used, the surface would retain a high mirrorlike gloss. Indeed, some pieces of Aurene have bright areas caused by careless application of the chloride spray. Such bright spots are more likely to occur near the base of an object or where a projection of the form cut off the spray. Pieces with these bright spots were considered less desirable by Carder, who preferred the complete surface to have a mat texture.

Some pieces of Aurene have bright cracks in the mat coating. These occur when the object is manipulated and shaped after the spray has been applied. They are more pronounced on flaring rims (Ill. 96) or radially on the Aurene disks, such as that shown in Color Plate III A. The effect is intentional; it is caused by the stretching of the molten glass under the metallic coating, which splits into iridized "islands" between which the bright glass surface beneath can be seen. Like snowflakes, probably no two pieces of Aurene are exactly alike because of the manipulation during the spraying and the slight variations in atmospheric conditions at the fire.

As noted, Gold Aurene was first made in 1904, and the name was registered that same year in the United States Patent Office.[40] Steuben Aurene glass was in continuous production from 1904 until about 1933 (Color Plates VI A & B; Ills. 95–98).

Blue Aurene, introduced about 1905, was essentially the same formula as Gold Aurene with cobalt added to the batch.[41] The iridescence was produced at the fire with a spray of tin chloride, as in the Gold Aurene process. Blue Aurene was produced through the entire time Carder was in charge of the factory and continued to be made until about 1933. It was also often called Cobalt Blue and Cobalt Blue Aurene by the Steuben factory workmen (Color Plates IV & V).

A number of other iridescent glasses made by Carder at Steuben have been called Aurenes. Although he considered the Gold and Blue the only true Aurenes, he often referred to objects with Aurene decorations and combinations of Aurene with other iridized glasses as Aurenes. Brown Aurene, Red Aurene, and Green Aurene are so listed in factory records, and are described in the pages that follow.

The names Platinum Aurene and White Aurene are not found in the factory records. Blue Aurene sometimes developed a silvery tone, and pieces having this coloring seem to be the ones erroneously called Platinum Aurene. The pieces referred to as White Aurene generally prove to be Ivrene or Verre de Soie (Color Plate XI).

The so-called Brown Aurene is similar to the Gold and Blue Aurenes in that it has an iridescent surface that was produced by tin chloride sprayed at the fire in the same manner. The glass itself is a brown glass colored with iron or nickel oxide and cased (or flashed) over Calcite glass (Color Plate IX A).

The name Red Aurene is rather broadly applied to the group of glass objects usually made from Calcite or Alabaster glass either partially or entirely cased with Gold Ruby, and having applied Aurene decorations, usually in feather motifs or trailed threadings, often combined with floral and leaf forms. There are also a few solid ruby glass pieces with Aurene trailed decorations and the entire surface slightly iridized that are in the Red Aurene classification. Most Red Aurene pieces were made during the first few years the Steuben factory was in operation (Color Plates VII & IX C).

Rouge Flambé is sometimes erroneously called Red Aurene (Color Plate XXIII A). This glass, which is colored with cadmium sulfide and selenide, has a bright surface and was not sprayed with the oxides mentioned above. It is not iridescent.

Green Aurene designates a group of Calcite or Alabaster glass pieces either entirely or partially cased with green glass and having Aurene decorations in the same styles as the Red Aurenes. The designs for these, and most of the other Aurene pieces having the trailed, feather, and millefiori decorations, were first done in 1904 and 1905 (Color Plate VIII).

Calcite

Calcite glass, perfected about 1915,[42] was named for the mineral it resembles. It has a creamy white tone with a warm ivory translucency. Carder was very proud of this glass. Bowl-shaped ceiling fixtures made from it gave a pleasing and efficient interior illumination, the inside surface reflecting more light (according to Carder) than any other lighting glass in existence. The transmitted light was so soft that it was, as he often said, "very easy on the eyesight."

This unique effect was not accidental. The glass batch contained calcium phosphate (bone ash) in a carefully regulated formula—"just enough to give translucency and not opacity." The high degree of reflectivity was produced by what Carder called a "damn good trick." The glass used in each bowl was gathered in three separate layers. This was accomplished by gathering about a third of the total amount needed and cooling it in a wooden block. The first gather was then covered with a second, which was also cooled by rotating in the block. A third and final layer was added the same way. The result was a bowl made of three fused layers of glass, each having reflecting and refracting surfaces (Ills. 61, 62).

The outside surface was often sprayed, while still ductile, with a tin chloride in the same manner as Aurene and Verre de Soie, which gave it a slightly iridescent surface. These bowls were made in various sizes from about ten to twenty-six inches, and were often decorated with acid-etched or engraved designs. A brown oxide, such as burnt umber or ocher mixed with linseed oil and turpentine, was frequently rubbed into the etched surfaces to accent the design. This color was not fired on, but was a fairly permanent air-dried pigment. Calcite bowls were soon in great demand for both office and residential lighting. One of the early installations was in the Commonwealth Edison Company, of Pittsburgh, Pennsylvania, about 1915.

Calcite glass was also used extensively in smaller shades for electric- and gas-lighting fixtures, table lamps, ornamental objects, and tablewares. It is often found as the inner or outer casing for the Gold and Blue Aurenes. As noted earlier, it was also the matrix glass for the Red, Green, and Brown Aurenes, which were usually embellished with the familiar spider, leaf, feather, and other applied decorations.

Ivrene

Ivrene, a translucent whitish glass with an iridescent surface, was a standard production item at Steuben. It was the nearest Carder ever came to making a milk-white glass. "Glass should be transparent or translucent—not opaque!" was his answer whenever lovers of milk-white glass asked why he did not make items of this popular color. The Ivrene batch contained feldspar and cryolite, and the iridescence was produced by the use of stannous chloride spray applied at the fire in much the same manner as for Aurene and Verre de Soie.

The bulk of the production of this glass was in the 1920s. It has sometimes erroneously been called White Aurene (Color Plate XXV A; Ill. 99).

Ill. 99. IVRENE URNS, No. 7468; height, 12 inches. Made in 1930. *Private Collection. Smithsonian Institution Photograph*

Tyrian

The name of this very rare type of Carder Steuben was suggested by its subtle overtones of purple, which reminded Carder of the color of the imperial purple fabrics that were the fame of ancient Tyre.

Tyrian is an opaque glass, which is exceptional for Steuben. The quality of shading from green to bluish purple was governed by the heat treatment at the fire. When the glass was first gathered from the pot it was green, and it would remain green in color if worked directly from the glass pot without reheating. The purple color was developed by reheating the partially formed object in the glory hole under oxidizing conditions. The longer the glass was reheated, the deeper the purple coloring became. Carder preferred the pieces in which the greenish-turquoise top shaded to a purple base. His two favorite pieces are shown in Color Plate XII A.

Tyrian pieces were usually decorated with applied Gold Aurene leaves and trailed threads, which were smoothed to the level of the glass. These Aurene decorations were, as usual, sprayed with stannous chloride to give them their iridescence and to give the Tyrian glass its characteristic sheen, especially in the areas of the applied decorations. A few vases have a hooked decoration of Aurene around the neck, superimposed on white and rubbed smooth with the glass surface. A few pieces have part of the trailed threading in relief. A relatively small number of Tyrian pieces were produced, all made about 1916.

Verre de Soie, Aqua Marine, and Cyprian

Verre de Soie was another iridescent glass that was a standard production from the early years of the Steuben Glass Works until the end of the Carder era. As the descriptive French name indicates, this glass has a smooth silky surface, which was produced by spraying crystal glass, while it was still nearly molten, with stannous chloride. The spraying resulted in a rainbow-hued iridescence very delicate in tone, almost like a soap bubble with a frosty radiance. V.D.S., as this glass was commonly called in the factory, was used in a multitude of forms ranging from elegant vases to stemware services and cologne bottles. Its satinlike sheen varies from a slightly tinted, frosty surface to the full chromatic spectrum (Color Plate XI A).

When first made, this color was called Flint Iridescent, but Carder soon changed it to the more romantic Verre de Soie.[43]

Aqua Marine, perhaps most easily described as Verre de Soie with a greenish tint, is often mistaken for that glass. It was produced in much smaller quantity. Here again, the iridescence was the result of a stannous chloride spray at the fire. The greenish tint is clearly seen when pieces of Aqua Marine and Verre de Soie are compared. (See Color Plate XI B.)

Cyprian[44] is a pale greenish iridescent glass with a Celeste Blue ring applied at the rim. The blue rim is the only apparent difference between this glass and Aqua Marine, and it, like Aqua Marine, is frequently mistaken for Verre de Soie. Verre de Soie was often made with a turquoise ring, which also contributes to the confusion in identification. Cyprian was made at least as early as 1915 and continued to be made into the 1920s (Color Plate XI B).

Ill. 101. SATIN GLASS VASE with air-trap decoration, made about 1905. No. 596 variant; height, about 5 inches. *Corning Library. Raymond Errett Photograph*

Other Colors and Effects

Air Trap

Decoration in which a pattern was produced by enclosing air between two layers of glass in a controlled design was very popular while Carder was working in England in the late nineteenth century. He continued this decorative technique at Steuben (Ills. 100–103). The process is similar to that for producing controlled bubbles. The parison is placed in a dip or two-part hinged mold that has a protruding pattern of diamonds, circles, or some other design for the air-trap shapes. After these patterns are impressed on the semicooled parison, a second gather locks the air in the indentations and forms the air-trap pattern.

Ill. 100. GOLD RUBY SATIN GLASS BOWL with air-trap decoration, made about 1905. Probably unique. Height, 5 inches. *Corning Library. Raymond Errett Photograph*

Ill. 102. CRYSTAL SILVERINA AIR-TRAP GOBLET, probably unique. Height, 9 inches. Made in the 1920s. *Corning Library. Raymond Errett Photograph*

Bubbles

Bubbles in glass have long annoyed glassmakers striving for clear, flawless glass. Carder loved bubbles—he said they "gave life to the metal," and he often used them decoratively either in controlled designs (Ill. 104) or random arrangements (Ills. 105, 106).

Controlled bubbles were made by two methods: flat spike molds and two-piece hinged iron molds. The former were wooden slabs about an inch in thickness, varying in size from about four to eight inches in width by about twelve to eighteen inches in length. Iron spikes were driven through the slabs to protrude about one-half inch above the surface, arranged in the desired bubble pattern. The slab was placed on the marver, where the molten gather was rolled

Ill. 103. AMETHYST SILVERINA AIR-TRAP VASE, No. 6545 variant; height, 7 inches. Made in the 1920s. Rare in this color. *Collection of Dr. and Mrs. L. G. Wagner. Raymond Errett Photograph*

Ill. 104. LUMINORS, solid crystal glass with controlled bubbles; mounted on square black glass bases containing light fixtures. About 1928. PINEAPPLE, No. 6971; height with base, 10 inches. BALL, No. 6821; height with base, 7 inches. These were often sold with blue and red glass disks about 1/16 inch in thickness, which fitted into a metal ring inserted into the black base below the luminor ball or pineapple, to give a colored light. *Steuben Catalog Photograph*

Ill. 105. SMOKE CRYSTAL BOWL with random bubbles, No. 6118; diameter, 10 inches. Made in the late 1920s. *Private Collection. Smithsonian Institution Photograph*

Ill. 106. FAN VASES, No. 6287; heights 8¼, 6¼, and 4¼ inches. Made in a variety of colors with random bubbles, engraved decorations, and plain. Popular items of the 1920s. *Photographs from Carder's files*

Ill. 107. COLOGNE BOTTLE, probably unique; height, about 6 inches. Black and white Cintra center is surrounded by a heavy clear colorless glass casing with random bubbles. Facet cut. *Collection Dr. and Mrs. L. G. Wagner. Raymond Errett Photograph*

over it. The spikes impressed a pattern in the surface of the hot glass, and another gather of glass was then applied to lock in the air and form the controlled design.

The same effect was also obtained by an iron mold, either in the form of a dip mold or an open-and-shut hinged mold, with spikelike projections in the desired patterns on the inside. These produced impressions in the hot glass that formed the controlled bubble design when covered with another gather of glass.

Random bubbles were produced in Carder Steuben glass by an unbelievably simple process known as "sticking the pot." Just before bubbled wares were to be made, a freshly cut willow pole about two inches in diameter and four to five feet long was pushed into the pot opening and through the molten glass to the bottom of the pot, then was withdrawn almost at once. This sudden introduction of green wood caused the glass to bubble as a result of the gases released, and gathers of glass taken for the next half hour or so would contain bubbles of various sizes. The process was repeated as often as necessary to keep the glass bubbly.

Carder also used this process to change the color of the glass in the pots. A greenish tint resulting from iron impurities in the sand used in mixing the batch was eliminated by adding manganese to the molten glass. The right amount of manganese would eliminate the greenish tint and produce a clear, colorless glass. If too much manganese was added, the glass acquired a pinkish tint. When Carder saw pinkish samples he would order, "Stick the pot with a withy pole," and the same procedure as that used for producing random bubbles was used, thus lessening or eliminating the pink tinge. Sometimes it was necessary to "stick the pot" more than once to eliminate the pinkish color entirely and produce colorless glass. The supply of fresh willow poles was replenished by sending a factory workman out to cut new ones from the willows growing on the banks of the nearby Chemung River.

Cintra

Cintra glass was produced by rolling a molten gather of crystal glass over powdered glass (or frost) of various colors, which had been spread on a marver.

Usually, a second gather of crystal was added to enclose the colored particles, which remained suspended in the clear glass casing. Carder evolved the name Cintra from the verb *to sinter,* and the objects made by this technique exemplify the definition: "to cause to become a coherent solid mass without completely melting."

Cintra pieces have very small bubbles or none at all, as compared with the myriad of many-sized bubbles found in Cluthra. (A description of Cluthra glass follows.) The colored glass used in Cintra pieces was much more finely powdered than that in Cluthra, as the coarser particles were removed by sifting.

Cintra pieces were made in monochromes, two colors with shaded effects, and variegated colors (Color Plates XVI & XVII; Ills. 107–109). One of the most distinctive Cintra techniques is found in pieces designed with vertical stripings of alternating colors, usually of blue and pink, or blue and yellow. Blue and pink stripes were created by placing finely powdered blue glass on the marver and rolling a gather of molten crystal glass over it. After the blue glass was "rolled in" until it was fairly smooth, the gather was reheated and blown into a rib mold, which caused the blue glass to form vertical stripes separated by bulges of clear glass. The molded piece was rolled again on a marver, covered this time with powdered pink glass. The protrusions of clear glass picked up the pink powder. Then the pink and blue striped object was reheated, smoothed out, and enclosed in a final gather of crystal glass.

Additional decorations applied at the fire usually included black or blue edge rings, or applied threads, which were pulled by a hook to form feather or leaf borders. Cintra pieces might be formed either with or without an outer crystal

Ill. 108. VASE, perhaps a variant of No. 8430 or a unique trial piece combining Cintra and Florentia techniques, has yellow ground and pale orange leaves. Height, 7 inches. 1920s. *Raymond Errett Photograph*

Ill. 109. PUFF BOX, No. 6688; height, 4¾ inches. Blue and pink Cintra with heavy casing of clear colorless glass containing controlled bubbles. Facet cut. Late 1920s. Carder used this as an ashtray on his desk at the factory and later in his library at home. *Corning Museum. Raymond Errett Photograph*

Ill. 110. CLUTHRA VASE, No. 7083; height, 8¼ inches. White Cluthra shades to black. Heavy casing is clear colorless glass with random bubbles. Cut decoration. Made in the 1920s. *Corning Museum. Corning Glass Works Photograph*

glass casing. Striped Cintra pieces were produced about 1917; with other variations in patterns, the technique continued in use into the 1920s.

A variation of the striped technique called Lace glass was made about 1930. These pieces were usually somewhat thinner than Cintra pieces made in cased crystal glass, and contained more bubbles. Specimens of the short-lived Lace glass are extremely rare. About sixteen shapes were made, usually with blue and white, pink and white, or black and white stripings. (See catalog numbers 7159–60, 7164–70, 7193–94, 7196–98.)

Cluthra

Cluthra was one of several Carder Steuben glasses that utilized a powdered glass technique similar to that used for Cintra. In making Cluthra, the glass "frost" was not sifted and consequently the particles varied considerably in size. Carder said he mixed "a chemical"[45] with the glass frost on the marver to produce the myriad of variously sized bubbles that are a distinguishing feature of Cluthra. In most Cluthra pieces, after the desired amount of frost was picked up on the molten gather, another layer of crystal glass was gathered to cover the colored frost and lock it, together with the bubbles, in a transparent casing giving an optical illusion of depth. Carder emphasized that the best effects were obtained when the last crystal glass gather was put on at "just the moment" when the bubbles were forming so that they would be locked in at varied levels and sizes.

Cluthra pieces were also cased in white and other translucent colors, as well as in crystal. They were usually used as blanks for acid-etched designs, primarily lamp bases (Color Plate XVIII A; Ills. 110, 111).

Ill. 111. CLUTHRA VASES, No. 6882; height, 8 inches. Black and white. Late 1920s. *Corning Museum. Raymond Errett Photograph*

The question of the pronunciation of the word Cluthra constantly arises. Carder preferred to pronounce the first syllable with an "oo" sound; as he said: "Clooth to rhyme with tooth." At the time it was being produced, many of the factory workers pronounced it to rhyme with "doth," and others called it "cloother." In later years Carder himself used either vowel sound. The origin of the name is obscure; the only clue Carder would offer was that it meant "cloudy."[46]

Cluthra was made in monochromes as well as in shaded and variegated colors.

Florentia

In this decorative technique, the leaf-shaped elements were prepared from powdered glass in the shape and color desired, usually green or pink. These elements were then picked up on the hot crystal glass gather and fused and worked into a vase or other desired form. After annealing, the entire surface was given a mat finish by acid etching or sandblasting. Color Plate XXX B shows two vases made in this manner, and a goblet with mica flecks, which was left with a bright finish. These pieces date from the late 1920s or early 1930s.

Intarsia

The Intarsia glass made at Steuben in the late 1920s and early 1930s was considered by Carder to be his greatest achievement in artistic glassmaking. The name was probably adapted from *intarsiatura*, a type of fifteenth-century Italian marquetry or inlaying. In 1960, Carder recalled that he had experimented with a type of Intarsia about 1916 or 1917, but did no commercial productions until 1920 or 1921. He said this type of Intarsia was done by laying out the colored

Ill. 112. INTARSIA VASE; unique. Height, 7½ inches. Dark blue design in crystal glass. Engraved facsimile signature "Fred'k Carder" appears at base of bowl. Made about 1929. *David Williams Collection. Smithsonian Institution Photograph*

Ill. 113. INTARSIA VASES made about 1929. *Left to right,* No. 7050, black and crystal, Vermicelli design; height, 6½ inches. No. 7060, black and crystal, Ivy design; height, approx. 5¾ inches. No. 7050, black and crystal, Chinese Floral design; height, 6½ inches. Present whereabouts unknown. *Steuben Glass Works Catalog Photograph*

Ill. 114. INTARSIA BOWLS made about 1929. *Left to right,* No. 7051, amethyst and crystal, Vermicelli design; height, 3¼ inches. No. 7059, black and crystal, Geometric design; height, 4 inches. No. 7051, black and crystal, Modern design; height, 3¼ inches. Present whereabouts unknown. *Steuben Glass Works Catalog Photograph*

Ill. 115. INTARSIA GLASS. *Left to right*, VASE, possibly a variant of No. 7041; height, 7 inches. Dark blue design with applied foliate forms in clear colorless glass with cut decoration. *Rockwell Collection.* GOBLET, unique form; height, about 9 inches. Amethyst design in clear colorless glass. GOBLET, unique form; height, about 6 inches. Black design in clear colorless glass. Both goblets, *Corning Museum. Raymond Errett Photograph*

Ill. 116. INTARSIA VASE, made about 1929. Height, about 8 inches. Dark blue design in crystal. *Lucy Maltby Collection. Raymond Errett Photograph*

design in fragments on the marver. These were picked up on the parison and covered with a layer of clear colorless glass before being formed into the finished object. Up to the present time, no documented pieces made by this technique have come to light.

The Intarsia pieces made about 1930 usually range from about one-sixteenth to one-eighth inch in thickness and are in reality three layers of glass: two colorless crystal glass layers encasing a layer of colored glass that forms the ornamental design.

To achieve this effect, an elongated parison of crystal glass varying with the size of the piece desired, but averaging about 3 inches long by 1½ inches in diameter for a 6- to 8-inch vase, was cased while molten with a thin layer of colored glass. The two-layered gather was cooled, and a design etched through the outer colored casing. This bubble shape with the etched design was then reheated and covered with another layer of clear glass. Next the triple-layered bubble was expanded and worked, usually into a vase or bowl, by offhand blowing. The result was a fusion of the three thin layers of glass into a homogeneous layer, usually from one-eighth to one-sixteenth inch in total thickness. The more the piece was blown out, or worked, the thinner the layers became and the lighter the color of the design.

NEW INTARSEA WARE

791   792   789

Ill. 117. BROWN AURENE VASES with
Intarsia pattern on Aurene border.
Left, No. 2748; height, 9¼ inches.
Right, No. 2411 variant; height,
4¼ inches. Both made about 1910.
*Corning Museum. Raymond Errett
Photograph*

Ill. 118. NEW INTARSEA WARE. Note
the spelling error that appeared on
the early Steuben catalog page.

All Intarsia pieces sold were signed with a facsimile signature, "Fred'k Carder," engraved on the lower side of the bowl above the foot or stem, not on the underside of the foot as in the case of Aurene and other pieces. There are a few unsigned pieces, which were either trials or not made for sale. Production was limited. Probably only about one hundred pieces were made, all around 1930, most of them being vases or bowls. A few goblets and wineglasses are known. Black, blue, and amethyst are the most common colors for the floral and arabesque designs always encased in crystal glass. Three bowls in the Corning Museum with Pomona Green foliate designs and one French Blue vase with amethyst floral pattern have no signatures and may be experimental pieces. They are the only known Intarsia pieces in these colors. In the Rockwell collection there is a heavy Intarsia vase about one-half inch in thickness with applied crystal leaves, probably a variant of No. 7041. (See Color Plates XX & XXI; Ills. 112–119.)

In the early years of the factory, Carder called two other types of decoration Intarsia, though these are entirely different in appearance from the 1930 pieces just described.[47] One form included a crisscross design usually applied to the Aurene glass necks of vases or the borders of lampshades; it consisted of overlapping threads of glass pulled with a hook to give a zigzag pattern. These applied decorations were "rubbed down" while the glass was hot, and so were pushed into the matrix glass and actually formed an inlaid decoration, which justified the name Intarsia. This type of Intarsia decoration was also used on Tyrian and Brown Aurene, and is occasionally found on other colors (Color Plate IX A; Ill. 117).

Ill. 119. NEW INTARSEA WARE
Photograph from an early Steuben catalog

Ill. 120. VASES AND COMPOTE. *Left to right,* No. 2785 variant; height, 6 inches. No. 6577 variant; height, 9 inches. No. 6561; height, 10 inches. No. 3174 variant; height, 7 inches. No. 2776; height, 6 inches. All are rare pieces with mica-flecked decoration, made in the 1920s. *Corning Museum. Raymond Errett Photograph*

Another form of Intarsia, called New Intarsia Ware by Carder, consisted of Gold Aurene vases with trailed decorations of leaves and stems in green, marvered into the Aurene matrix. The employee who lettered the catalog photographs (Ills. 118, 119) probably was responsible for the spelling Intarsea. Carder's handwritten notation by No. 786 in the pattern books is "New Intarsia Ware." Since there are only nine numbers allotted to this group (786–794), these pieces were probably made about 1905 or 1906.

Mandarin Yellow

Ming yellow Chinese porcelain inspired this translucent color. Less than a dozen pieces are known, and nearly all are cracked because of internal strains or have actually broken and been repaired. The shapes indicate a dating of about 1916, and the small number surviving are attributed to a limited production coupled with the "fugitive" quality of this glass. The color of all known pieces is fairly consistent and varies only slightly from those in the Corning Museum (Color Plate XXIII B).

Mica-Flecked Decoration

This technique was known long before Carder used it at Steuben. It consists of picking up pulverized mica flakes from the marver on the hot gather of glass and covering them with another layer of glass before the whole mass is worked into the desired form. The flakes varied in size and density of application, as can be seen from Ills. 120 and 121. It will be noted that the silvery color of the mica flecks changes and assumes tints of the color of the covering glass. Mica flecks were also combined with air-trap decoration and called Silverina (Ills. 102, 103), not to be confused with the Silveria made by Stevens & Williams.

Millefiori or Mosaic Glass

Objects formed by fusing together fragments of variously colored glasses have been highly esteemed since ancient times.[48] Some authorities have contended that the Murrhine bowls[49] mentioned by classical authors and described by Pliny might have been made of this type of glass. Others feel these Murrhine pieces were made from semiprecious stones such as agate, sardonyx, or madrepore, and that the millefiori glass objects now known were glassmakers' imitations of them. Glass vessels of Mediterranean origin dating from the first century B.C. that are made from mosaic and millefiori elements exist today in museums and private collections. They were made from pieces of colored glass and millefiori cane segments fused together by mosaic techniques in much the same manner as Carder used (which is described on the following pages).

The name millefiori (thousand flowers) was not used to describe the technique until it was revived by the Venetians in Renaissance times.[50] Since then, it has often been applied to all glass pieces made by this process whether they are ancient or modern. Collectors of paperweights, especially, are familiar with the

Ill. 121. CELESTE BLUE CANDLESTICK with amethyst and mica flecks in the stem was made in the 1920s. Height, 9¾ inches. This form was also made in amber and other colors. *Private Collection. Smithsonian Institution Photograph*

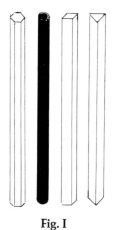

Fig. I

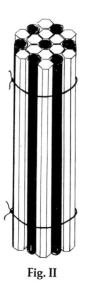

Fig. II

millefiori technique, as it reached a high degree of perfection in the mid-nineteenth century productions of Baccarat, Clichy, St. Louis, and Whitefriars, and in later productions elsewhere in Europe, the Orient, and America.

In company with the artist-craftsmen of the past, Carder produced a limited number of millefiori glass pieces. Most of these were bowls or plates, made a few at a time, from about 1909 until the mid-1920s.[51] A few small pieces, mostly flat panels, were made about 1936 at Steuben by the author, in order to learn the technique. One of these panels appeared on the market in recent years and was purchased by a collector who brought it to the Smithsonian for identification, along with other glass he was giving the museum. He was greatly surprised to learn the facts about its production, since it had been identified by some authorities as Venetian.

To produce millefiori glass, it is necessary to make melts of glass in the various colors chosen for the final design of the object. These glasses must have the same coefficient of expansion in order to "work together"; otherwise, the millefiori object would shatter in cooling. The millefiori technique depends upon the basic physical property of ductility in a mass of molten glass: that is, a gather of molten glass can be pulled or "drawn out" into a rod or cane of the size and form desired. At the Steuben factory in Carder's day, the glass rods were drawn by hand. For this purpose, a section of the blowing room was equipped with smooth boards laid end to end on the floor, forming a series of catwalks. To these were fastened wooden crosspieces about an inch thick, at intervals of about a foot. A space of about three feet between these low racks allowed the workmen to pass alongside.

At the start of the rod-drawing process, the glassworker took a gather of glass of the desired color from the glass pot. The size of the gather varied with the size of the rod to be formed, but it averaged about six to eight inches in length by two to three inches in diameter for rods of one-half inch or less. This gather was made into the selected rod shape either by being rolled on a marver into a round rod or molded to form a square, hexagon, or another shaped rod. The gather was then reheated, if necessary, and a pontil iron attached to one end. The first glassworker held this iron, with its glass gather, horizontally; the second, usually a boy, attached a pontil iron to the free end of the gather and walked or ran with it along the wooden racks, thus drawing out the glass rod, which came to rest in a hardened state on the wooden crosspieces, where it could cool evenly. Considerable skill was required of the runner, whose speed, in effect, controlled the size of the emergent rod. Moreover, an even pull was necessary or a rod of varying thickness would result (see Figs. 1–7).

Mechanical processes have long since been introduced at Corning Glass Works and elsewhere to ensure greater control of the size and quality of drawn rods and tubing. The tendency of molten glass to "thread" is utilized in producing commercial glass tubing, clinical thermometers, and threads for glass fabrics, and mechanization has resulted in much lower production costs and the greater precision necessary for scientific needs. The production drama of the handmade glass rod and tubing is, nonetheless, well worth seeing in the small European shops where it is still practiced.

After glass rods in the colors and shapes needed were hand drawn as described above, they were cut in about six-inch lengths, arranged in a fasces or bundle to form the design, and held together with iron wire (Fig. II). The bundle of rods was next heated until fused together; then the wire was removed and the molten bundle "stuck up" on a pontil iron and marvered smooth (Fig. III). After smoothing, the bundle was dipped in molten glass to enclose the fused rods in a layer of clear or colored glass (Fig. IV). More layers of various colors of glass could be added at this point, if desired. Now the mass of molten glass was drawn into a new rod by repeating the same process. It retained the same shape and design in miniature as in the original fasces (Fig. V). Moreover, the elements of color remained in the same relative positions regardless of how far the molten piece was drawn out.

After the rod had cooled, it was cut or chopped into sections (Fig. VI) by a mosaic cutter. (Carder used a "guillotine" type.) The cold sections of glass rod were then arranged in a shallow iron or pottery mold in a mosaic-type design, along with sections cut from other millefiori or single-color rods (Fig. VII). (The iron mold was coated with a solution of clay and plaster of Paris, to prevent the glass from sticking during reheating.) The filled mold was heated either in the glory hole or in a special furnace until the sections of rod fused together. After this, while the mass was still molten, it was rubbed with a wood polisher to remove unevenness and make the glass more uniform in thickness. Now a pontil iron was affixed to the center so that the molten mass of glass could be lifted from the mold to be heated again in the glory hole, then shaped with a wooden paddle. Finally, surplus portions were sheared off and it was fashioned into its permanent form. Usually a ring of colored glass was applied to the edge, which strengthened the object and added an attractive decoration.

A variation of the technique in which the millefiori object had a crystal glass inside casing was produced by placing a previously blown ball of transparent glass, which was still molten, upon the mosaic pattern after it had been smoothed with the wood polisher but before it was removed from the mold. This ball was pushed down by the blowing iron until it enveloped the entire mosaic pattern. The mass was then taken from the mold upon the ball, marvered down, blown out, and formed into whatever shape was wanted.

Most Steuben millefiori pieces were made by "Johnny" Jansen, whom Carder considered the best glassmaker ever to work at Steuben. Jansen came to the factory as a gatherer about 1905 or 1906, and showed such marked ability that he

Fig. III

Fig. IV

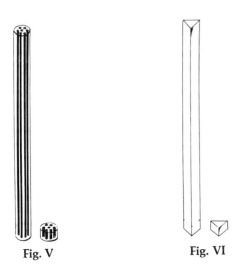

Fig. V   Fig. VI

Fig. VII

was promoted to gaffer within a year. He was still working at Steuben in the 1930s. Carder said that he made "all the best pieces," including the Intarsias (Color Plate XIV).

Moss Agate

Moss Agate pieces were made in emulation of the ancient Roman and later Venetian marbleized glasses, but by different techniques. Powdered glass was spread on the marver in the colors desired, picked up on the parison, and formed into the object. Effects in imitations of semiprecious stones such as moss agate and chalcedony were varied with other marbleized effects. Carder used this technique at Stevens & Williams (Color Plate II A) and at Steuben from about 1910 to the 1920s (Color Plate XXXI).

Opalescent Glasses

The Steuben opalescent colors were inspired by the opal gemstone and usually imitated the cloudy phosphorescence of the fire opal. The opalescence was developed at the fire and was dependent on the bone ash (calcium phosphate) in the glass batch. Steuben made four basic opalescent colors by adding metallic oxides to the batch: chromium for green, gold for pink, uranium for yellow, and copper for blue. A popular variation of the Yellow Opal was a glass that shaded from opal to a pale yellow tint and was called Straw Opal (Color Plates XV B & XVIII C).

The opalescence was developed by suddenly cooling the partially formed object while it was still on the blowing iron, with a jet of compressed air, and then reheating it in the glory hole. If the entire piece was suddenly cooled and reheated, the whole object became opalescent. If only a portion, such as the top of a vase, was cooled, a shaded effect resulted. An opalescent pattern could be obtained by pushing the molten gather into an iron mold and then directing cool air onto the surface as it was revolved by the workman. This caused the higher portions of the design (such as ribs) to be cooled, while the lower areas stayed hot, and, after reheating, gave an opalescent design on a clear background.

Rose Quartz

This glass resembles the mineral for which it was named, but in basic production technique it is similar to Cintra. Usually it was made in heavy glass forms about one-quarter to three-eighths of an inch in thickness. In addition to the powdered glass that gave the object its color, a crackled effect was added. To obtain the crackle, a gather of crystal glass was formed into a teardrop or bubble shape, and while it was still molten, it was plunged into cold water. The sudden change in temperature caused the surface of the glass to shatter; however, since the subsurface was still molten, the gather remained intact on the iron. The shattered surface re-fused when reheated in the glory hole, but a pattern of crackle scars

Ill. 122. ROSE QUARTZ BOWL; No. 6856; height, 7 inches. Crackled inside. Applied and etched decorations. Satin finish has polished highlights. Made about 1930. *Private Collection. Smithsonian Institution Photograph*

remained. The gather was again reheated, then rolled in finely crushed ruby "frost" and "threads," reheated once more, and the threads and frost pulled into a textured effect with a "hook" and marvered smooth.

The mass was now enclosed in another gather of crystal glass and formed into the final shape. Tooled leaf and stem decorations of crystal glass were then applied at the fire.[52] After the vessel was annealed, the acid-etched decoration was added and the entire exterior surface given a dull or satin finish with "mat acid." Highlights were produced by polishing the raised surfaces with pumice and rottenstone on a rotating buffer (Ill. 122). These pieces were usually marked with the fleur-de-lis and Steuben scroll, acid-etched in relief in the base or lower side of the object.

Other colors made by this technique were Alabaster Quartz, Amethyst Quartz, Blue Quartz, Green Quartz, Peach Quartz, and Yellow Quartz. As mentioned above, the color of the frost determined the color of the finished piece (Color Plate XVIII B).

Rouge Flambé

Like Mandarin Yellow, Rouge Flambé was also inspired by Chinese porcelains; both these glasses were made in shapes suggestive of oriental ceramics, and both were difficult to produce and particularly vulnerable to breakage caused by strains within the glass.

Rouge Flambé pieces range in color from a rich red, as in Color Plate XXIII A, which was the color Carder was seeking, to an orange or coral tone. The color was produced by the addition of selenium and cadmium sulfide to the glass batch. As a result of the production difficulties, Rouge Flambé was made for only about two years, probably in 1916 and 1917. (See also Color Plate XXIV A.)

Ruby Glasses

Carder produced two basic types of ruby glass at Steuben: Gold Ruby and Selenium Ruby (Color Plate XIII). The Steuben Gold Ruby is a delicate pinkish color made by adding 22-karat gold in solution to the batch. Selenium Ruby is a rich blood red, sometimes shading to almost a garnet color in heavier pieces. When Carder was asked why he did not make a copper ruby, he dismissed the subject with the remark that copper ruby was all right for signal lights and machine-made pieces, but not beautiful enough for handmade art glass.

Carder's Gold Ruby was nearly always used as a casing over crystal or Alabaster glass, the thin casing resulting in a very beautiful pink color. The gold was dissolved in aqua regia and added to the sand of the batch. The Gold Ruby glass melt is the result of a colloidal system, and great care had to be taken not to overbalance the formula with carbonate, and to maintain an oxidizing condition to keep the gold in suspension. If the oxidizing conditions were not met, the colloidal gold would separate and collect at the bottom of the pot, forming metallic beads and spoiling the color.

The transparent Gold Ruby was not worked directly from the pot; instead, it was gathered and formed into solid lumps about an inch in diameter and two or three inches long—called "sausages" by the workmen. When first gathered they were yellowish in color, but when reheated or placed in the lehr under a reducing flame, the ruby color gradually developed and turned darker and darker until the sausages finally appeared almost black.

These glass sausages were very valuable because of their high gold content, and as Carder said were "always kept under lock and key" until needed for use. When a Gold Ruby piece was to be made, a sausage was reheated, worked into a "cup," and used to case the object.

The often quoted story that the Gold Ruby glass was colored by tossing gold coins into the molten glass in the pot was blasted by Carder as "damned tommy-rot," with the additional practical comment that "Coins would go to the bottom of the pot and stop there." Another delightful tale that credits the discovery of Gold Ruby glass to the accidental dropping of a glassmaker's gold ring into the molten glass batch was discredited for the same reason.

Other Gold Ruby colors made at Steuben by adding coloring oxides to the basic ruby batch were Purple Gold Ruby (gold and cobalt), Amethyst Ruby (gold and manganese), Brownish-Yellow Ruby (gold and iron), and Cinnamon Ruby (gold and uranium).

Steuben's other standard ruby was made by the addition of cadmium selenide plus zinc sulfide to the glass batch. Selenium Ruby is also a colloidal glass system. This formula produced the rich red color found in most of the uncased items. Occasionally this glass developed an orange tint in areas such as the ends of handles or places where variations in temperature occurred during manufacture.

Steuben is said to have made a Cadmium Ruby. This is probably the same as the Selenium Ruby and may have been so-called because the coloring agent was actually the cadmium selenide mentioned above. It can be considered as an alternative name for the Selenium Ruby (Color Plate XIII).

4

Standard Techniques "At the Fire"

DECORATIONS DONE AT THE FIRE ARE A TRUE TEST OF THE GLASSWORKER'S SKILL AND his ability to control the molten metal. The applied decorations done at Steuben included threading, reeding, rings, rigaree, pinchings, prunts, dabs, flowers, fruit, and a wide variety of handles and knobs. Among the variations of threading that were done chiefly with Aurene glass and listed in the catalog as types *A* through *T* were zigzag or herringbone, leaf, feather, spot, whorl, and a random allover trailed threading called spider. Millefiori flowers were also used.

Most of the applied decorations used at Steuben are shown in the Color Plates, illustrations, and catalog sketches, or described in the glossary.

Casing or Flashing

Some authorities differentiate between the terms casing and flashing. Carder used them interchangeably, and when questioned about the difference and pressed for an answer, he indicated that he generally thought of a flashing as being a thinner layer of glass than a casing. In no sense did he use the word flashing to indicate a stained coating. Stained wares were not Steuben production items.

Casing is the term used by glassmakers to describe placing one layer of glass upon another. There are two ways this can be done—casing inside and casing outside.

Inside casing consists of taking a small gather of the color of glass desired for lining an object, and shaping it until it is concentric with the blowpipe. It is then dipped into a pot of glass of the color chosen for the outside, and either rotated in the wood block or shaped on the marver until this coating is spread evenly over the first gather. The double-layered gather is thereafter worked into the desired form.

Outside casing, sometimes called cupping, consists of blowing a small cup or bowl of the glass selected for the outside color. This is removed from the blowpipe and placed either in a mold or on a thin iron table specially made with a hole cut in it to receive the glass cup. A mass of glass of the desired inside

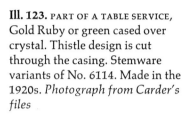

Ill. 123. PART OF A TABLE SERVICE, Gold Ruby or green cased over crystal. Thistle design is cut through the casing. Stemware variants of No. 6114. Made in the 1920s. *Photograph from Carder's files*

Ill. 124. CASED VASE, Gold Ruby or green over crystal. Cut in Spanish Ship pattern. No. 3400; height, 16 inches. Made in the 1920s. *Photograph from Carder's files*

color is then gathered on the blowpipe and shaped to a concentric form slightly smaller than the cup of the outside color, which has been kept at fusing temperature in the iron mold or table. This second gather is placed carefully inside the cup, allowing it to touch the bottom of the cup first and then gradually to fill the cup. During the process the worker keeps pressing down on the blowpipe to prevent air bubbles from becoming locked between the two layers. After this operation is completed, the mass is rolled on the marver or wood block to make it concentric and true before it is blown out and fashioned into the article (Color Plate VII B & C; Ills. 123, 124).

Two layers of glass were the usual number used in Carder Steuben pieces. Crystal glass cased outside with Gold Ruby, blue, or green was the most common type for table services. These were decorated with a design cut, engraved, or etched through the outer layer. Another popular type was Calcite with either Blue or Gold Aurene lining.

Three layers of glass were sometimes used, as in the Plum Jade color, which has a Dark Amethyst layer cased with Alabaster and then the two encased with an outer layer of amethyst.

To produce cased objects, the two or more glasses used must have the same coefficient of expansion in order to "work together." Carder worked out the glass formulas scientifically to make them compatible. Even though the batch formulas were theoretically correct, it was always necessary to make practical tests in the laboratory before the actual pieces were fabricated in the blowing room. This was done by "pull tests," which are described later.

Ring Casing

Carder claimed that he originated the method of providing a border ring casing of Gold Ruby, or of the other clear transparent colors such as No. 5 Green or Flemish Blue, for engraved or etched decoration. The process consisted of blowing a cylinder of colored glass about two inches in diameter and twelve to eighteen inches long. After annealing, the cylinder was sent to the cutting shop and cut into rings of the width desired for the border color—usually 1 to 1¼ inches wide. The rings were brought back to the blowing room, reheated, and

applied to the parison that had been gathered to make the object, such as a bowl or goblet, and completed by offhand blowing. The cased ring was usually cut or engraved (Ill. 125).

Shading

Shaded effects were obtained by a variation of the inside casing technique. To describe this process, let us assume the object is to be shaded from crystal glass to green. A gather of green glass would be shaped or marvered to be concentric with the blowing iron. It was then slightly inflated in such a manner that the bottom part of the bubble was very thin, gradually increasing in thickness as it came to the place where the gather was attached to the blowing iron. This bubble was dipped into the pot of crystal glass and the lower (thinner) part of the green covered with a layer of crystal glass, which was thickest at that point and became thinner as it approached the thicker green portion near the blowing iron. The two colors were then blown out together and worked to the desired form. The "grotesque" vases and bowls in Color Plate XIX A are examples of shaded glass done by this method.

Another technique of shading colors in glass involved chilling or reheating glasses having special ingredients in their formulas. This effect is called "striking"; it was used in many English and American factories. Tyrian and opalescent glasses were produced in this way. Carder also made a few pieces in Burmese, a revival of a popular art glass color of the 1880s (Ill. 126).

Another shading technique, called at Steuben a "die away" cup, was begun by attaching a hot pellet (disk) of colored glass to the end of the blowing iron. The disk varied in size according to the size of the object to be made. For a small bowl, it would be about the size of a quarter and about one-eighth to three-eighths of an inch thick. After being attached to the iron, the disk was reheated and a hole pierced in the center of it, making it into a ring that was concentric with the blowing iron. The ring was then covered with a gather of crystal and blown out to a bubble. As the bubble was formed, the colored glass of the ring would flow into the crystal and "die away" an inch or so from the iron, shading from full color at the iron to clear crystal at the end of the bubble, which could then be worked into whatever object was planned.

Threading and Other Applied Decorations

The technique of decorating glass pieces with applied threads dates from Egyptian times. Carder used applied threads manipulated in many variations and techniques during his entire career. At Steuben, when the threads were put on close together in a regular spiral by a machine, the piece was designated as having a "threaded" decoration (Ill. 57). When they were applied irregularly by the gaffer, the piece was said to have "reeded" decoration (Ills. 127, 128). Hooked and marvered threadings are shown in many illustrations.

In hand threading (reeding), the gaffer touches a molten gather of glass to the hot glass object, which is still attached to the pontil (or in rare instances the blowing iron), and revolves the object on the arms of the gaffer's chair, allowing

Ill. 127. CELESTE BLUE SUGAR BOWL AND CREAMER, made in an "o.g." mold and reeded. No. 6771. Creamer height, 5⅜ inches. Made in the late 1920s in several transparent colors. *Corning Museum. Raymond Errett Photograph*

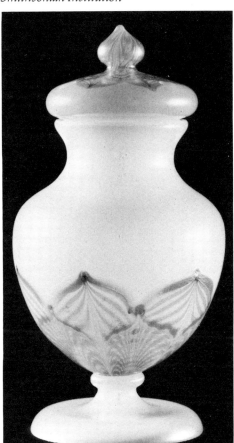

Ill. 128. COCKTAIL SET in crystal with black reeding. No. 7056. Jug height, 9½ inches. Also made with green and rose reeding. 1920s. *Photograph from Carder's files*

Ill. 129. COVERED JAR, No. 2822; height, 6 inches. Alabaster with hooked decorations in Gold Aurene and green. Made about 1919. *Smithsonian Institution*

the hot glass to thread around the object until the threading extends over the desired area.

Other decorations applied at the fire are tooled and pincered leaves and nodes (Ills. 130, 131), prunts and edge rings (Ill. 132), fruit and flower handles and finials (Ills. 133, 134), fins on fish, and random marvered threading (Ill. 136).

Ill. 130. CRYSTAL FLOWER-BLOCK CANDLEHOLDERS, No. 7516. Height varies from about 2½ to 3½ inches. Each leaf is applied separately and shaped at the fire, which accounts for the variation in size. *Private Collection. Smithsonian Institution Photograph*

Ill. 131. GOLD AURENE VASES. *Left,* No. 2741; height, 6 inches. *Right,* No. 2744; height, 7 inches. *Corning Museum. Raymond Errett Photograph*

Top right:
Ill. 132. CRYSTAL BOWL WITH AMETHYST PRUNTS AND HANDLE RINGS, No. 2801 variant; diameter, 12 inches. Matching goblet, No. 3120; height, 6½ inches. About 1918. *Smithsonian Institution*

Center right:
Ill. 133. CENTERPIECES made in Flemish Blue and other transparent colors about 1918. *Left to right,* No. 2942; height, 8 inches. No. 2962; height, 15 inches. No. 2965; height, 8 inches. *Photograph from Carder's files*

Ill. 134. DARK AMETHYST CENTERPIECE with pear decoration in realistic color. No. 5034; diameter, about 14 inches. Made in the 1920s. *Collection of Mrs. Raymond Inscho. Raymond Errett Photograph*

Ill. 135. DECORATIVE PIECES. FISH VASE, No. 6421; height, 12 inches. Also made without swirl as shown in 10-inch fish vase on right. CENTER BOWL, No. 6380; height, 5 inches. VASES, No. 6339; height, 5½ inches. Made in the late 1920s in crystal and transparent colors. *Photograph from Carder's files*

The Use of Molds at Steuben

Although most pieces of Carder Steuben are free blown, some objects were molded, or a type of molding operation was employed in one or more steps in their production. Most of the fully molded or pressed pieces are easy to detect—such as the architectural glass panels, which were obviously produced by means of iron molds. Most of Carder's molded pieces were given a great deal of hand-work after they were annealed, such as polishing, mat and satin finishing, the removal of rough edges, and other refinements.

Some circular shapes such as cruets and decanters were formed by blowing the basic form into a paste mold (which see). After the pieces were removed from the molds, spouts, pouring lips, handles, or other applied portions were added. This method speeded production, tended to result in more uniform capacity in container-type objects, and enabled Carder to use less experienced glassmakers for this phase of production.

Rib molds were employed to give optic and swirl effects (Ill. 137). Air-trap diamonds were produced by putting an unexpanded gather into the diamond mold and then encasing it in the second gather, thus trapping the diamond-

Ill. 136. RED AURENE VASE has light iridescence with random Aurene threading. Possibly an experimental piece made between 1905 and 1910. Height, 2½ inches. Signed in the 1960s "F. Carder Aurene." *Private Collection. Smithsonian Institution Photograph*

Ill. 137. TABLEWARE GROUP with swirl decoration, usually made in ruby, green, or blue with crystal stems and feet. FAN VASES, No. 6287; 8¼ inches high. Made in the 1920s. *Photograph from Carder's files*

Ill. 138. LOTUS BLOSSOMS, pale amethyst and other colors, No. 6927; height, 9½ inches. Used as luminors and bookends. Made by stamping (a variation of pressing) about 1930. *Raymond Errett Photograph*

Ill. 139. AMETHYST VASE, No. 6876; height, 6 inches. Blown in a mold and cracked off. Top edge is ground and polished. No pontil mark. Made about 1929, this is one of the few Steuben designs produced by this method. *Private Collection. Smithsonian Institution Photograph*

shaped air bubbles between the two layers of glass. The vessel was completed by the usual forming process.

Oblong, square, hexagonal, and other angular shapes made for such objects as cigarette boxes, window vases, and a few shallow bowls were shaped in iron molds and the excess glass cut off and the top edge finished after annealing.

Square feet for stemware and urn-shaped vases were also molded and then applied to the free-blown bowls. The ornamental lotus flowers and Buddhas (see Catalog Nos. 6927 and 7133) were done by a process Carder called "stamping." This was actually a variation of the pressing technique using hand-operated molds (Ill. 138).

So few Carder Steuben pieces were molded that some of these items are rarer than the free-blown pieces (Ill. 139).

Steuben paste molds were iron molds coated on the inside with a mixture of boiled linseed oil, burgundy pitch, and beeswax. This viscid coating was sprinkled with a layer of finely ground sawdust. (Applewood was best for this purpose.) After the sawdust coating was applied, the mold was dried in an oven at a temperature of 150 degrees centigrade for twenty-four hours. It was then put in the lehr to bake the coating further until it assumed a nut-brown color. When ready, it was removed to the blowing room, where a workman blew a light ball of glass into the mold, rotating the hot glass constantly to make the mold surface completely smooth. This action burned the surface and formed a carbon coating. It was necessary to dip the mold in water at just the right point in the operation in order to stop the burning at the proper carbonization of the wood. As the mold was used, it was dipped in water after each object was molded, so that the carbon coating would retain enough moisture to create a steam film between the hot glass and the mold, thus eliminating mold marks and producing a brilliant surface on the blown object.

PLATE I

A

A. CAMEO GLASS GROUP designed by Carder in the 1880s for Stevens & Williams. Height of vases, from 4 to 6 inches. Plate diameter, 8⅛ inches. *Corning Museum. Raymond Errett Photograph*

B. CAMEO GLASS VASE, rose DuBarry ground with white casing. Designed by Carder for Stevens & Williams about 1886. Height, 5 inches. *Corning Museum. Stanley Weisenfeld Photograph*

C. CAMEO GLASS PLAQUE, "Immortality of the Arts," carved by Frederick Carder about 1887. Diameter, 10 inches. *Corning Museum. Raymond Errett Photograph*

B

C

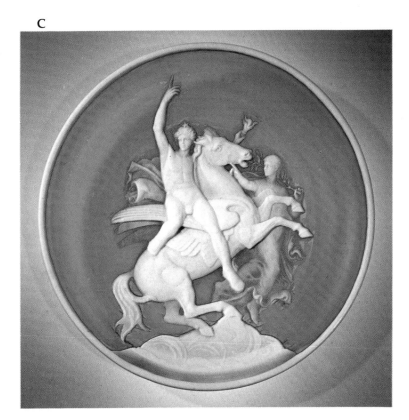

PLATE II

A

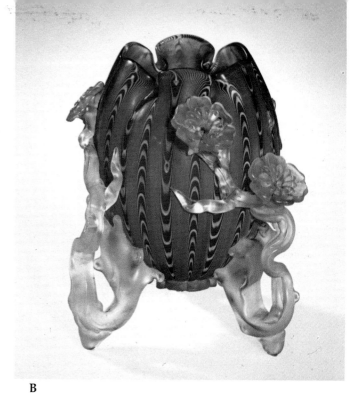

B

C   D

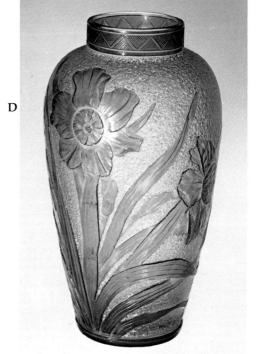

A. MOSS AGATE VASE with cut decoration, designed by Carder for Stevens & Williams about 1884. *Corning Museum. Raymond Errett Photograph*

B. THREADED-DECORATION VASE. Done by the "pull-up" machine; applied tooling in mat-su-no-ke style. Height, 5 inches. Designed by Carder for Stevens & Williams in the 1880s. *Welles Collection. Raymond Errett Photograph*

C. LACE GLASS made at Stevens & Williams about 1887 to 1889. This adaptation of the Venetian filigree technique proved to be very expensive to produce. *Left to right*, BOWL; diameter, 7⅝ inches. *Rockwell Collection.* COMPOTE; height, about 7 inches. *Florence Bushee Collection.* PLATE; diameter, 6 inches. FINGER BOWL; height, 3 inches. *Corning Museum. Stanley Weisenfeld Photograph*

D. CAMEO GLASS VASE with "pecked" ground, designed by Carder and made at Stevens & Williams in the 1890s. In this special technique, which Carder said he originated, the crystal glass background was roughened by pecking with a steel stylus powered by a sewing machine mechanism that had been adapted for the purpose. Only a few vases were made, as the machine "pecking" tended to break the glass, and the cost of perfecting the technique was not warranted by the sales of these objects. Height, about 7 inches. *Corning Museum. Stanley Weisenfeld Photograph*

PLATE III

A. FIRST GOLD AURENE PIECES. Vase at the left dated 1904 was the first successful trial piece. *Corning Museum.* The vase on the right, also dated 1904, was the first production piece. *Rockwell Collection.* The disk dated in the 1920s shows the full development of the color. Diameter, 10½ inches. *Otto Hilbert Collection.* *Stanley Weisenfeld Photograph*

B. GOLD AURENE PIECES. The three decorated vases on the right (height, *left to right*, 6, 5½, and 10⅞ inches) and the vase on the extreme left (No. 170; height, 6 inches) were made about 1905. The other pieces date from about 1910 to 1920. *Corning Museum. Raymond Errett Photograph*

PLATE IV

A. BLUE AURENE DECORATED PIECES, made about 1905. *Far left,* No. 571; height, 4⅝ inches. *Second from left,* No. 296 (variant); height, 6 inches. Marked with date 1905 by Carder. *Corning Museum. Raymond Errett Photograph*

B. ETCHED VASE, Blue Aurene cased over Jade Yellow, No. 8392; height, 8¼ inches. Made in the 1920s. *Corning Museum. Raymond Errett Photograph*

PLATE V

A.

A. BLUE AURENE GROUP. Cologne bottles with light Jade Blue and black stoppers, made about 1930. No. 3426; height, 6¾ inches. *Private Collection.* Vase with applied white glass decoration, possibly 1920s, is No. 2683 or 6299. Height, 6½ inches. *Rockwell Collection. Raymond Errett Photograph*

B. BLUE AURENE VASES. *Left to right,* No. 7100; height, 12 inches. No. 3285; height, 16½ inches. *Corning Library. Raymond Errett Photograph*

C. BLUE AURENE GROUP. Jack-in-the-pulpit vase, on left, No. 130a, is 6½ inches high. Vase in center, No. 5054 variant, measures 10¼ inches. *Rockwell Collection. Raymond Errett Photograph*

B

C

PLATE VI

A   B

A. GOLD AURENE GROUP. Tall vase, second from right, is Jade Yellow cased with Blue Aurene. Probably intended to have an acid-etched decoration. Height, 12 inches. All made in 1920s. *Rockwell Collection. Raymond Errett Photograph*

B. GOLD AURENE VASES made in the late 1920s. *Left to right,* No. 8479; height, 11 inches. (A lamp base made for Art Lamp Co.) No. 7104; height, 14½ inches. No. 7097; height, 12 inches. *Corning Library. Raymond Errett Photograph*

C. CALCITE GLASS, with Gold and Blue Aurene linings. *Left to right,* No. 1980; height, 4⅞ inches. No. 1952; height, 6⅛ inches. Bonbon dish; diameter, 6 inches. No. 346; height, 10 inches. No. 5069; height, 9½ inches. No. 1454 (variant); height, 5½ inches. Made in the 1920s. *Rockwell Collection. Raymond Errett Photograph*

C

PLATE VII

A. RED AURENE GROUP, made about 1910. Vase at left and two at far right, *Rockwell Collection*; second from left, *Mrs. L. H. Wagner Collection*; third from left, *Corning Library*; tall vase in rear, *Otto Hilbert Collection*; third from right, *Corning Museum. Raymond Errett Photograph*

B

C

B. RED AURENE VASE, made about 1910. Gold Ruby over Alabaster, with Gold Aurene applied decorations and lining. No. 279 variant; height, 12 inches. *Rockwell Collection. Stanley Weisenfeld Photograph*

C. RED AURENE VASE, made about 1910. Gold Ruby casing with applied Gold Aurene decoration and lining. No. 298; height, 10½ inches. *Rockwell Collection. Raymond Errett Photograph*

PLATE VIII

A. GREEN AURENE GROUP, made about 1910; Alabaster glass with applied green glass and Gold Aurene decorations. *Corning Library. Raymond Errett Photograph*

B. GREEN AURENE VASE, No. 504, style K; height, 10½ inches. Made about 1905. BOWL, No. 2696; diameter, 9 inches. Made about 1910 to 1915. *Rockwell Collection. Stanley Weisenfeld Photograph*

C. ALABASTER GLASS VASE with Gold Aurene and green glass decoration. Made about 1908 to 1915. No. 534; height, 7½ inches. *Rockwell Collection. Stanley Weisenfeld Photograph*

B

C

PLATE IX

A

B

C

A. BROWN AURENE VASES, made about 1915. The hooked decoration on the necks was called Intarsia at that time. *Left to right*, No. 2466 (variant); height, 13 inches. No. 2426 (variant); height, 11 inches. No. 2461 (variant); height, 10 inches. Vase on left, *Smithsonian Institution*. Others, *David Williams Collection. Smithsonian Institution Photograph*

B. AURENE DECORATED VASE AND BOWL, made 1908–1910. Vase, Jade Yellow cased over Gold Aurene with applied Gold Aurene decoration in style D. No. 600; height, 7 inches. Bowl, turquoise with Gold Aurene decoration. No. 647; height, 3 inches. *Corning Museum. Stanley Weisenfeld Photograph*

C. ALABASTER GLASS VASE (*left*) with Blue and Gold Aurene applied decoration. The pinkish iridescence was produced by a tin chloride spray "at the fire" in the same manner as Gold Aurene. This is an experimental piece made about 1917. Height, 5¼ inches. GOLD RUBY VASE (*right*) cased over Calcite with Gold Aurene lining, foot, and applied decoration. Made about 1917. No. 541; height, 12 inches. *Corning Museum. Stanley Weisenfeld Photograph*

PLATE X

A. WHIMSIES, made in the 1920s. The Blue Aurene objects on the extreme left and right are probably weights, although they are hollow. Stocking darners seem to be among the most popular of these after-hours items. The paper knife is 8⅛ inches long. The paperweight was signed by Carder as being made at Steuben; it is now in the *Corning Museum*. All others, *Rockwell Collection. Raymond Errett Photograph*

B. PAPERWEIGHTS. Not Steuben productions. All were made in the 1920s and 1930s by Steuben workmen after hours. *Otto Hilbert Collection. Raymond Errett Photograph*

PLATE XI

A. VERRE DE SOIE BOWL with turquoise glass prunts and threading, made about 1916. No. 2612 (variant); diameter, 10¼ inches. *Smithsonian Institution*

B. AQUA MARINE, CYPRIAN, and VERRE DE SOIE PIECES dating from 1915 to 1920. *Left to right,* Aqua Marine sherbet and plate. *Otto Hilbert Collection.* Cyprian handled vase (height, 10½ inches) and bowl (with blue ring at edge), and Verre de Soie compote and handled vase. *Rockwell Collection. Raymond Errett Photograph*

A

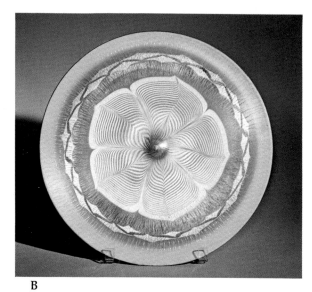

B

A. TYRIAN GLASS, made about 1916. Carder felt these two pieces were the finest in color of all the Tyrian produced, and kept them for his private collection. *Corning Museum.* Bowl, perhaps a variation of No. 2409, is 10½ inches in diameter. Vase, No. 2422; height, 10½ inches. *Raymond Errett Photograph*

B. TYRIAN GLASS DISK, made about 1916; diameter, 15⅞. *Otto Hilbert Collection. Raymond Errett Photograph*

C. TYRIAN GLASS, made about 1916. Vase on left is unusual because of the raised threading. Probably a variation of No. 2434. Height, 14 inches. *David Williams Collection.* Vase on right is a variation of No. 2445. *Private Collection. Smithsonian Institution Photograph*

D. TYRIAN GLASS, made about 1916. Carder said about 100 pieces like the vase form (No. 2433) on the left were made for lamp bases for a Chicago firm. Height, 16 inches. *Otto Hilbert Collection.* Vase on right was an experimental piece with raised threading and a bright surface. No. 2447; height, 9 inches. *Corning Museum. Stanley Weisenfeld Photograph*

C

D

PLATE XIII

A

A. TABLE SERVICE, Gold Ruby cased over crystal, made in mid-1920s. A special engraved design on No. 8351 stemware for L. P. Fisher using the Fisher Body shield and LPF monogram on all pieces. Large plate: diameter, 14 inches; goblet: height, 10 inches. *Rockwell Collection. Raymond Errett Photograph*

B. SELENIUM RUBY GLASS DUCKS, made in the late 1920s. No. 6332; height, 4 and 7 inches. *Welles Collection. Raymond Errett Photograph*

C. PLATE, Gold Ruby cased over crystal, is cut and engraved in Spanish Ship pattern. Diameter, 17⅜ inches. Made in the 1920s. *Otto Hilbert Collection. Raymond Errett Photograph*

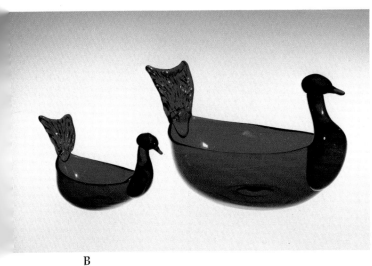

B

C

PLATE XIV

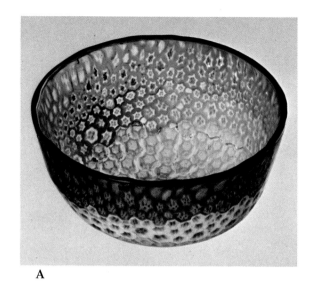

A

B

A. MILLEFIORI BOWL, made at Steuben between 1915 and 1920. Diameter, 6¼ inches. *Corning Library. Stanley Weisenfeld Photograph*

B. MILLEFIORI BOWL, 1915–1920. *Corning Library. Stanley Weisenfeld Photograph*

C. MILLEFIORI PLATE; diameter, 10 inches. 1915-1920. *Corning Museum. Stanley Weisenfeld Photograph*

D. MILLEFIORI PLATE; diameter, 12½ inches. *Corning Museum. Stanley Weisenfeld Photograph*

C

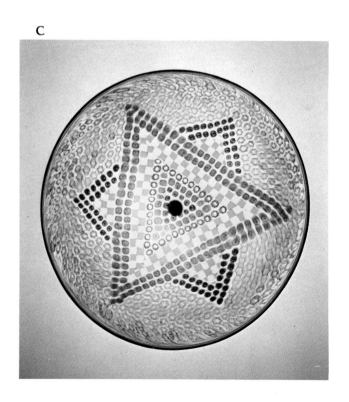

D

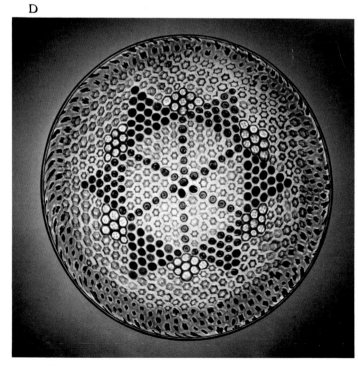

PLATE XV

A. COLORED GLASS, made at Steuben in the 1920s. *Left to right*, Vase, No. 6017; height, 15 inches. Celeste Blue with Royal Purple handles. Center Bowl, No. 2926; height, 8 inches. Topaz with Celeste Blue accents. Covered Jar, No. 3114 variant; height, 13½ inches. Topaz with flower finial. Covered Jar, No. 6847; height, 18 inches. Light Amethyst; engraved Marina. Cologne, No. 6048 variant. Pomona Green with cinnamon foot and finial and mica-flecked stem and stopper top. *Smithsonian Institution*

B. STRAW OPAL VASES, made about 1907. All about 10 inches in height. No. 313 (*left*) and No. 182 (*right*), *Corning Museum.* No. 311 (*center*), *Private Collection. Raymond Errett Photograph*

PLATE XVI

A. CINTRA VASES, made about 1917. Vase on left, height, about 4½ inches; vase on right, height, 9½ inches. Both pieces unique. *Corning Museum. Raymond Errett Photograph*

B. CINTRA BOWL AND CANDLESTICKS, orange with turquoise rims and handle rings. Bowl, No. 2942; height, 8⅝ inches; diameter, 9⅞ inches. Candlesticks, No. 3236; height, 10 inches. Made about 1917. *Rockwell Collection. Raymond Errett Photograph*

PLATE XVII

A

B

A. CINTRA COLOGNE BOTTLE, made about 1928. The heavy crystal casing encloses controlled bubbles. Cut decoration. Probably unique. Height, 11¼ inches. *Smithsonian Institution*

B. CINTRA VASE with heavy crystal casing and cut decoration, made in the 1920s. No. 6713; height, 7½ inches. *Otto Hilbert Collection. Raymond Errett Photograph*

C. CINTRA VASE. The unique decoration was produced by "picking up" the bird form (in powdered glass glued to a paper backing) from the marver. The paper burned away in the reheating, leaving the design fused to the matrix. The outline of the paper is faintly visible. Height, 9¾ inches. *Corning Museum. Stanley Weisenfeld Photograph*

D. CASED VASE, Cintra over crystal, probably unique. The design is etched through a layer of Cintra. The black accents were painted and probably fired on at a low temperature as the final decorating step. Height, 9 inches. *Dr. Edwin G. Sensel Collection. Raymond Errett Photograph*

C

D

PLATE XVIII

A.

A. CLUTHRA GLASS GROUP, 1920s. *Left to right,* Vase, No. 2683; height, 6 inches; Dark Amethyst. Vase, No. 2939; height, 10 inches; blue with Opal handles. Puff, No. 6881; height, 4 inches. White with Pomona Green cover and crystal knob. Vase, No. 6898; height, 10 inches. Shaded green to white with crystal handles. Vase, No. 6870; height, 10 inches. Shaded blue to white. Bowl, No. 6415; height, 4½ inches; Light Amethyst. *Rockwell Collection. Raymond Errett Photograph*

B. AMETHYST QUARTZ BOWL (No. 6856; height, 7 inches) and ROSE QUARTZ VASE (No. 6766 variant; height, 11 inches). Both made in the 1920s. *Dr. and Mrs. L. G. Wagner Collection. Raymond Errett Photograph*

C. OPAL TABLEWARE, made in the 1920s. The goblets are 7⅛ inches in height; they and the champagne glass have Cintra stems. Signature "Steuben" and "F. Carder" on the 8-inch plate were added by Carder in the 1950s. *Raymond Errett Photograph*

B

C

PLATE XIX

A. GROTESQUE VASES AND BOWLS. Flemish Blue, ruby, amethyst, Pomona Green, and amber, all shaded to crystal. *Left to right*, No. 7090; height, 9 inches. No. 7090; height, 11 inches. No. 7090; height, 11½ inches. No. 7091; height, 4¾ inches. No. 7521; height, 12 inches. No. 7277; height, 5⅛ inches. No. 7090; height, 9¼ inches. Made in the 1920s. *Rockwell Collection. Raymond Errett Photograph*

B. ROSA BOWL AND CANDLESTICKS, with Pomona Green feet and prunts. No. 6154; diameter of bowl, 12 inches; height, 5¾ inches. Candlesticks; height, 12 inches. Made in the 1920s. *Rockwell Collection. Raymond Errett Photograph*

PLATE XX

A. INTARSIA GROUP, made about 1929, all signed with the facsimile signature "Fred'k Carder" at the base of the bowl, above the foot and stem. *Corning Museum and Private Collections. Raymond Errett Photograph*

B. INTARSIA VASES, made about 1929. *Left,* blue-black and crystal glass; height, 9⅝ inches. *Smithsonian Institution. Right,* amethyst and crystal glass; height, 7⅛ inches. *Corning Museum.* Both have the facsimile signature "Fred'k Carder" engraved on the base of the bowl.

PLATE XXI

A. INTARSIA GROUP, made about 1929. The French Blue vase with amethyst foliate design *(second from left)* is the only one of this color combination known. The green and crystal glass bowl *(extreme right)* is one of three of this color known. This bowl, the wineglass, and the bowl on the extreme left are unsigned. All the other pieces have the facsimile signature "Fred'k Carder" engraved at the base of the bowl above the foot and stem. *Welles Collection and Corning Museum. Raymond Errett Photograph*

B. ENLARGEMENT of vase second from left in **A,** showing Carder's engraved signature. *Raymond Errett Photograph*

C. INTARSIA VASE, said by Carder to be the first successful piece made in this technique (about 1929) Note the bubbles, which do not appear in most later pieces. Height, 5½ inches. *Private Collection. Raymond Errett Photograph*

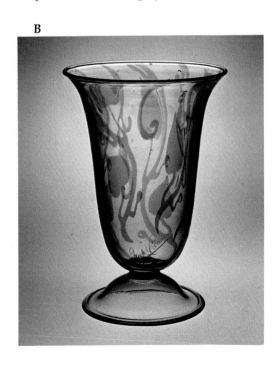

PLATE XXII

A. BLUE GLASS GROUP. *Left to right,* Tumble-up, No. 3064; height, 6¼ inches. Vase, No. 6287; height, 11 inches. Goblet, No. 6220; height, 6½ inches—all Celeste Blue. Goblet, No. 6358; height, 7¾ inches; French Blue. Goblet, No. 6869; height, 6½ inches; Flemish Blue. *Rockwell Collection.* No. 6869, *Private Collection.* *Raymond Errett Photograph*

B. GREEN GLASS GROUP. *Left to right,* Cream and sugar, No. 6139; height, 5¾ and 5¼ inches; Pomona Green with topaz handles. Bowl, No. 6444; diameter, 13¼ inches; Pomona Green. Sugar bowl (not shown in catalog sketches, but cutting matches No. 6183 goblet), unidentified green (possibly No. 5 Green) casing over crystal; height, 4½ inches. Low candlesticks, No. 6384; height, 3⅞ inches; Pomona Green. Goblet, unidentified color and shape (possibly No. 476 variant in Nile Green); height, 9 inches. Goblet, unidentified shape and color; height, 7 inches. Goblet, No. 6114; unidentified color (perhaps Antique Green). Candlesticks, No. 6356; Spanish Green—reeded and bubbly; height, 14¼ inches. *Rockwell Collection.* No. 6114, *Corning Museum. Raymond Errett Photograph*

PLATE XXV

A

A. ALABASTER COVERED JAR with Aurene decoration. No. 2812; height, 9¼ inches. Made about 1910. This is also often called Aurene because of the Aurene decoration. The iridescence is produced by the same spray as that used for Gold Aurene. *Otto Hilbert Collection.* IVRENE CANDLESTICKS, No. 7563; height, 8⅜ inches. 1920s. *Rockwell Collection. Raymond Errett Photograph*

B. IVORY VASE. Acid-etched Stamford pattern. No. 2683; height, 10½ inches. *Rockwell Collection. Raymond Errett Photograph*

C. ETCHED GROUP, 1920s. Rose cased over Alabaster. *Left to right,* No. 7441; height, 8⅛ inches; Gordon pattern. No. 6034; height, 12 inches; Matzu pattern. No. 6468; height, 9¾ inches; Sculptured pattern. Puff Box, No. 5074; height, 4¾ inches. *Rockwell Collection. Raymond Errett Photograph*

B

C

PLATE XXVI

A. ETCHED VASES, Blue Aurene cased over Jade Yellow. Made in the 1920s. *Left to right*, No. 8491; height, 10 inches. Probably a variant of No. 6095; height, about 14 inches. No. 8392; height, 8 inches. *Private Collection. Stanley Weisenfeld Photograph*

B. ETCHED VASE, Gold Aurene cased over black. Made in the 1920s. No. 6211 (in a larger size); height, 6¼ inches. *Otto Hilbert Collection. Stanley Weisenfeld Photograph*

C. ETCHED BOWL, No. 2687; Blue Aurene cased over Alabaster. Compton pattern. Made in the 1920s. Diameter, 8 inches. *Rockwell Collection. Stanley Weisenfeld Photograph*

PLATE XXVII

A. ETCHED VASES. *Left*, Rose Quartz, No. 6650 variant; height, 12½ inches. *Center*, white over Celeste Blue, No. 8413 variant; height, 12½ inches. *Right*, No. 8494; height, about 14 inches. *Corning Museum. Stanley Weisenfeld Photograph*

B. ETCHED BOWLS, Plum Jade, made in the 1920s. No. 2928; diameters, 6 and 8 inches. *Rockwell Collection. Stanley Weisenfeld Photograph*

C. DOUBLE-ETCHED VASE, Blue Aurene cased over Pomona Green. Height, 12½ inches. Made in the 1920s. *Private Collection. Raymond Errett Photograph*

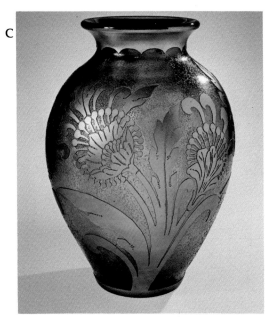

PLATE XXVIII

A.

A. DARK AMETHYST GROUP. Covered compotes, No. 3384; height, about 7 inches. Clear colorless knobs and mereses. Candlesticks, No. 2596; height, 10 inches. Stems are topaz. Decanter, No. 2910½; height, 10 inches. The knob is clear colorless glass. Wineglasses, which match goblet No. 1692, have clear colorless stems. *Welles Collection and Corning Museum. Raymond Errett Photograph*

B. MARINA AND CELESTE BLUE GROUP. *Left to right*, Marina bowl, No. 6983, with etched Ducks pattern; height, 6¾ inches. *Otto Hilbert Collection*. Marina vase, No. 6561; height, 12 inches. *Corning Museum*. Goblet with Celeste Blue bowl and amethyst foot and stem, No. 5160; height, 9 inches. *Corning Museum. Raymond Errett Photograph*

C. WISTERIA GLASS, made about 1920. Goblet, No. 6395; height, 10 inches. Vase, No. 7607; height, 9 inches. Finger bowl with cut decoration, No. 7305; height, 3 inches. *Dr. and Mrs. L. H. Wagner Collection*. Goblet with cut decoration, No. 7384; height, 6⅛ inches. *Corning Museum. Raymond Errett Photograph*

B

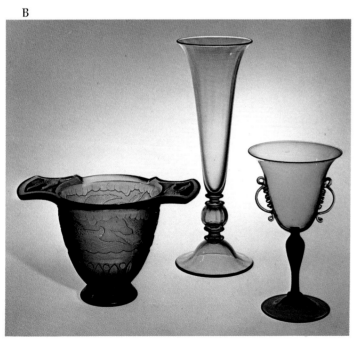

C

PLATE XXIX

A. YELLOW GROUP. *Left to right,* Mandarin Yellow vase; height, approximately 5 inches. *David Williams Collection.* Jade Yellow etched jar; height, 6⅛ inches; Bristol Yellow vase; height, 12 inches. *Private Collection.* Engraved cologne bottle on the extreme right, a Steuben yellow as yet unidentified. *Corning Museum, Smithsonian Institution Photograph*

B. AMBER AND TOPAZ GROUP, made in the 1920s. Two candlesticks; height, 10 inches. *Private Collection.* All others, *Corning Museum. Raymond Errett Photograph*

PLATE XXX

A

A. ORIENTAL JADE AND POPPY GROUP. *Left to right,* Vase, No. 6500; height, 5 inches; Oriental Jade. Vase, No. 6031; height, 7 inches; Oriental Poppy. Vase, No. 6030; height, 7 inches; Oriental Jade. Pair of Colognes, No. 6237; height, 9¼ inches; Oriental Poppy and Oriental Jade. Candlestick, No. 6597; height, 6 inches; Oriental Jade. Candlestick, No. 6614; height, 6 inches; Oriental Poppy. *Rockwell Collection. Raymond Errett Photograph*

B. FLORENTIA GLASS, made about 1930. Vase, No. 6780; height, 7 inches. Vase No. 8436; height, 12 inches. *Dr. and Mrs. L. H. Wagner Collection.* Goblet, No. 6615; height, 10 inches. *Corning Museum. Raymond Errett Photograph*

C. Probably experimental Steuben pieces, although they are not positively documented. Vase on left; height, 10⅞ inches. *Rockwell Collection. Raymond Errett Photograph*

B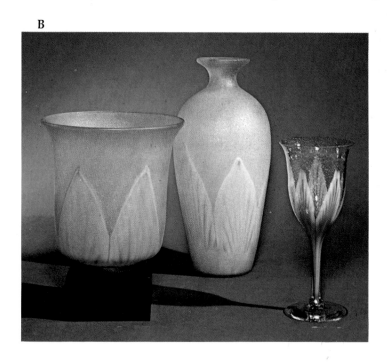

C

PLATE XXXI

B

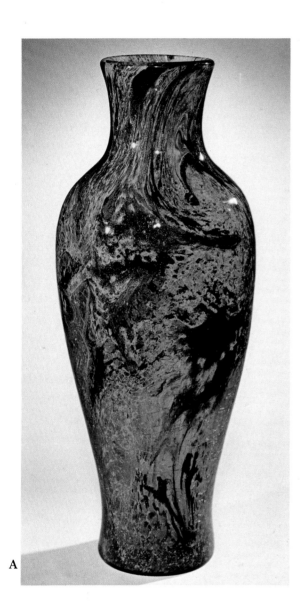

A

C

A. MOSS AGATE VASE, No. 6152; height, about 15 inches. Very rare color; probably unique in this size. *David Williams Collection. Raymond Errett Photograph*

B. MOSS AGATE VASE; height, about 10 inches. *Corning Museum. Stanley Weisenfeld Photograph*

C. MOSS AGATE VASE. Unique shape, or a variant of No. 3280. Height, 14 inches. About 1923. *Smithsonian Institution*

PLATE XXXII

A. DIATRETA VASES, variegated amethyst. Vase *(left)* has inscription "Life Is Short, Art Is Long" in gold. Height, 9 inches. Signed on bottom "F. Carder 1955." Vase on right (height, 6⅜ inches) is signed "F. Carder 1953." Both unique. *Corning Museum. Raymond Errett Photograph*

B. DIATRETA VASE, variegated blue-green; height, 7¼ inches. Unique. Signed on bottom "F. Carder 1952." *Corning Museum. Raymond Errett Photograph*

C. *Ohio Winter Scene*, oil painting done by Carder in 1955. *Private Collection. Raymond Errett Photograph*

The repoussé goblets of German silversmiths were the inspiration for a few unusual pieces made at Steuben in skeleton molds. The operation of the skeleton mold utilized a principle similar to that of opening and closing the ribs of an umbrella. The mold was first placed on the floor of the blowing room with the ribs open in a pattern radiating from the mold base. The bulb-shaped gather of molten glass was placed at the center of the mold, and a sliding ring encircling the ribs was pulled slightly upward, causing the hinged ribs to close like a partially folded umbrella. This ring held the ribs in place until the glass gather had been expanded into and through the cagelike form of the ribs. The ring was then lowered, allowing the ribs to fall away from the glass object, which was then finished offhand by adding the applied foot and other elements and fire-polishing the top. The completed form had a pillared effect, surmounted by a row of convex shapes with a lenslike appearance. An engraved decoration was usually added to accent and enhance the molded forms (Ill. 140).

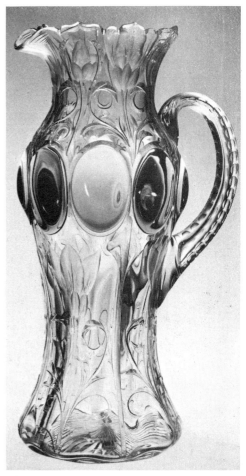

Ill. 140. SKELETON-MOLDED PITCHER, with engraved decoration. This may possibly be a Stevens & Williams prototype for Steuben's No. 1284. Height, 11 inches. Made about 1910. *Photograph from Carder's files*

Ill. 141. CRYSTAL GLASS SLIPPERS, No. 6486; length, 8 inches. Made in the late 1920s. Carder said the original pair was used in *A Kiss for Cinderella*, but this has been impossible to verify. *Corning Museum. Raymond Errett Photograph*

Pressed Glass

Relatively few pressed glass statuettes and ornamental pieces were made at Steuben. Nearly all produced from about 1928 to 1932, these consisted mainly of inserts for flower blocks (Ills. 142, 143), relief-decorated panels and grilles, and decorative intaglio panels usually sold with supporting bases of glass or metal (Ills. 144, 145; see also Catalog Nos. 7223, 7224, 8460, 8461). The last-

Ill. 142. CRYSTAL FLOWER BLOCKS with molded figure inserts. The satin-finish figures are on pegs ground to fit the holes in the hand-blown bases. The flower block in the center is cut from a solid piece of glass to imitate ice. The others are decorated with applied looped rings with pincered accents. Blocks and bases were also made in Pomona Green, Celeste Blue, Bristol Yellow, and other colors. FISH, No. 7064; height, 7½ inches. FEMALE FIGURE, No. 7039. DIVING GIRL, No. 6483; height, 15 inches. BUDDHA, No. 7133. ELEPHANT, No. 7231. *Photograph from Carder's files*

Ill. 143. DETAIL OF FLOWER BLOCK AND FIGURE, No. 7039. *Photograph from Carder's files*

named also included a portrait head of Washington (Catalog No. 7452) and one of Lincoln (Catalog No. 7491).

An intaglio panel portrait of Thomas A. Edison about the same size as the Washington portrait, seven by ten inches, was produced in 1929. This was never offered for sale, as it was a special order for about 350 pieces, all of which were used as favors at the Golden Jubilee Banquet given by Henry Ford for Edison at the Henry Ford Museum in Dearborn, Michigan, October 21, 1929 (Ill. 146).

The architectural pieces (Catalog Nos. A-2000–A-2156) were made in iron molds, as was the glass sculptured panel for the RCA Building in Rockefeller Center.

Pull Tests

Cased glass objects are subject to strain and breakage if the two or more layers of glass do not have a compatible coefficient of expansion. Tests show that cased glass pieces in which the two or more layers of glass have exceeded the limits of compatibility will sometimes crack or shatter completely when a sudden change in temperature occurs—even many years later. Perhaps the most noted instance of this kind of breakage occurred when the Northwood copy of the Portland Vase cracked about three years after the blank was made, while John Northwood was washing it in warm water when he had nearly finished carving the cameo design.

Carder used a relatively simple method to determine the compatibility of his cased glasses—a method called a pull test. When two glasses were to be "worked together" (one cased over the other), a rod about one-quarter inch in diameter and six to eight inches long was made from the glass pot of each of the glasses to be used. The two rods were taken to the laboratory, melted together, and pulled into a thread, which was detached and placed flat on the table. If it remained fairly straight, the two glasses were compatible and could be worked together. If the thread bent to a curve, one glass was contracting more on cooling than the other. When the curvature exceeded certain known limits, the formula for one glass batch had to be altered to make that glass contract like the other. The pull test was repeated when the corrected glass was again ready. If the thread made from the two glasses was now straight, or within the curvature limits, the word was passed to the blowing room to go ahead with the production of cased objects using these glasses.

Ill. 144. MOLDED CRYSTAL LUMINOR with intaglio figure, No. 7223; height with base, 12 inches. Black glass base contains electric light. Late 1920s. *Photograph from Carder's files*

Ill. 145. MOLDED CRYSTAL LUMINOR with intaglio seahorses, No. 7224; height with base, 13½ inches. Black glass base contains electric light. *Photograph from Carder's files*

Ill. 146. THOMAS A. EDISON, relief portrait modeled in Plastelina on plate glass by Carder in 1929. An iron mold made from this model was used to produce crystal glass plaques with the portrait intaglio, which were used as favors at the banquet given by Henry Ford in Dearborn, Michigan, October 21, 1929, to celebrate the fiftieth anniversary of Edison's invention of the electric light and the opening of the Henry Ford Museum. *Photograph from Carder's files*

Ill. 147. COVERED BOWL, No. 6566 variant; height, 14¾ inches. Color is Moonlight. Cut decoration. Made about 1928. *Smithsonian Institution*

5

Decoration after Annealing

Cut Decorations

CARDER NEVER WOULD SAY THAT HE LIKED CUT GLASS. HE WAS FORCED TO DESIGN CUT glass patterns at Stevens & Williams, and because cut glass was still in demand when he came to America, he felt it was good business to establish a cutting shop at Steuben soon after he began selling his glass to other outlets than Hawkes. He grudgingly admitted that "when well designed, cut glass has a brilliancy like no other material except the diamond." And although he shivered, literally, when he handled some designs, he found use for the cutting shop the entire time he managed the factory. Occasionally he bowed to popular demand and made some pieces that were "cut all over" and cut so deep they were "painful to pick up." But these were in the minority, and most of the Steuben cut glass pieces rank with the best productions of the period (Ills. 147–154).

Carder often combined cutting and engraving in his designs, and some of his most beautiful stemware relies for its artistic appeal on the strong cut motifs contrasting with the more delicately engraved details (Ills. 155, 167). Cruets and decanters with facet-cut stoppers, goblets with fluted stems, and massive cologne bottles with cut paneled sides framing Cintra and bubbly centers were also very successful. Table decorations in the form of pouter pigeons, pheasants, and eagles in heavy cut crystal glass sparkled with deep V-cuts and faceted diamonds, which accented the brilliance of the fine lead glass (Ill. 152).

The Steuben cutting shop used equipment and techniques typical of most cutting shops of the period in Europe[53] and America. The cutters worked seated at lathes, which held the iron, stone, and wooden wheels that were used in that order to rough-cut, smooth, and polish the cut designs. These wheels varied in diameter from a few inches to about two feet, and had narrow or wide edges shaped to form the types of cut desired—usually flat, rounded, or V-shaped. The flat edge was used for panels, plain-surface cutting, or wide flutes. A rounded edge on the wheel gave a hollow circular shape, which was sometimes called a "printie" or "thumb cut," and was also used for deep flutes. It was used to remove pontil marks as well.

A V-shaped edge, of course, gave the much-used miter or V-cut. In order to save time, the edge of a single flat wheel was often shaped to contain two or more V-cuts, thus making two or more parallel V or line cuts in a single manipu-

Ill. 148. COLORED GLASS GROUP. Left to right, CANDLESTICK, No. 3571 — bobeche and base are Flemish Blue cased over crystal. Acid-etched design. CANDLESTICK, No. 3571, and COMPOTE, No. 3569, have decoration cut through blue casing to crystal. All three have air-twist crystal stems. WHISKEY BOTTLE, No. 6255; height, 11½ inches. Bristol Yellow with cut design. DECANTER, No. 5170 variant; height, 15½ inches. Gold Ruby cased over crystal. Cut design. WINEGLASSES, No. 6959 variant. Gold Ruby cased over crystal. Acid-etched design. All made in the 1920s. *Corning Museum. Raymond Errett Photograph*

Ill. 149. CONSOLE SET. CANDLESTICKS, No. 3454; height, 16 inches. BOWL, No. 3399; height, 9 inches. Probably amber or topaz; cut decoration. *Photograph from Carder's files*

Ill. 150. CRYSTAL COLOGNE BOTTLE, No. 6432; height, 6¼ inches. Crown shape cut from a globular exterior wall. Made in the 1920s. *Corning Museum. Raymond Errett Photograph*

Ill. 151. CRYSTAL CANDLESTICK with cut decoration. Unique experimental form. Height, 10½ inches. *Private Collection. Smithsonian Institution Photograph*

lation. These were called "gang cuts." Obviously, as many sizes and shapes of wheels were made as there were forms of cuts to be executed.

In the cutting process the design, usually geometric in form, was laid out on the glass in lines, usually with a mixture of red lead and turpentine. Then the "rougher" used the iron wheel to make the first rough cuts of the design. He held the glass on top of the wheel, as did the other cutters, in order to see how deep a cut he was making. As the wheel turned, a fine abrasive (usually carbo-

Ill. 152. ONE OF A PAIR OF EAGLES in cut crystal glass, No. 6502; height, 8 inches. Made in the late 1920s. *Corning Museum. Raymond Errett Photograph*

Top right:
Ill. 153. CRYSTAL VASE, with cut decoration in art nouveau style, *Stevens & Williams prototype;* diameter, 10 inches. *Corning Museum. Raymond Errett Photograph*

Ill. 154. CUT CRYSTAL PLATE; diameter, 17½ inches. *Hilbert Collection. Raymond Errett Photograph*

Ill. 155. PLACE SETTING; No. 7181. GOBLET, height, 9½ inches. Crystal cased with black; cut and engraved Poussin pattern. Made in the late 1920s. It was a goblet of this design that fell from the author's drawing table. *Photograph from Carder's files*

rundum) mixed with water was fed onto its rim from a hopper directly above it.

The "smoother" in his turn went over the same cuts with the stone wheel, kept moist with a trickle of water. The stone wheel had the same shape as the iron one used by the rougher. Then the "polisher" went over the smoothed cuts with wooden or cork wheels of identical shape, fed with putty powder, pumice powder, or rouge, which polished the surface to the brillance of the original glass. Polishing was also done by dipping the smoothed cut ware into a mixture of hydrofluoric and sulfuric acids, which restored the brilliance of the cuts and was much less laborious than polishing each cut on the wooden or cork wheels as mentioned above. It is easy to see why cut glass was expensive to produce, and why pressed glass imitations of cut patterns eventually ruined this phase of the glass business.

In addition to executing artistic cut decorations, the Steuben cutting shop functioned in many less glamorous capacities, such as grinding out and polishing pontil marks and flattening bases of bowls, vases, and other objects. These practical applications of the cutting techniques, combined with Carder's ingenious combinations of cut and engraved patterns, probably accounted for the continuation of this department long after the vogue for cut glass had passed.

Cut Glass Patterns

In this list, the catalog number or numbers at the right of each pattern name indicate one or more of the glass forms decorated with that specific pattern.*

---

* It is hoped that a more complete coverage of the cut, engraved, and etched patterns can be published at a later date.

Popular forms were not limited to one pattern, but were decorated with whatever design the buyer specified. There are probably additional pattern names not included in this list, which was compiled from factory records, sales brochures, and other reliable sources presently available. Many patterns in this list and in the engraved and etched lists that follow have not been identified, as up to the present time no catalog has been found with drawings of all the patterns.

Numbers in parentheses preceded by 32 are illustrated in the appendix to the 1932 Steuben Catalog reproduced following the catalog line drawings. In this appendix, designs designated with a T prefix were done by Walter Darwin Teague.

Pattern Name	Catalog Number	Pattern Name	Catalog Number
ABURN	1105	CHASE	1297
ADAMS*	1492	CHATEAU†	7309
ALASKA	1298	CHATHAM†	(32–7236)
ALBERT	1007	CHELWIND	1435
ALBION	1271	CLIFTON	1486
ALDEN	1255	CLIMAX	1299
ANTIQUE	1169	CLINTON	1099
ARCTIC	1077	CLUSTER	1422
ARLINGTON	1422	COLUMBIA	1118, 1300
ARVID	7406	COMO	1525
ASTOR	1159	CONCAVE	1225
ASTORIA	1171	CONCORD	1081
AZTEC	1032	CORNELL	1225
		CREOLE	1171
BALDWIN	1262	CRESCENT*	1099
BALTIC*	1433, 1451	CRYSTAL	1080
BARYMORE	1487	CUSTOR	1047
BEARING	1168	CUT	(32–6828)
BELLFORT	1449	CUT No. 1§	
BERNICE	1647	CUT No. 2§	
BERTON	1022		
BOAT		DAISY*	1003
BOLTON	1339	DALTON	1304
BRADLEY	1489	DANBURY†	(32–7237)
BRILLIANT	1173	DENVER	1103
BRYWOOD	1273	DIAMOND	1537
		DOLPHIN	1272
CAMPANIA	1459	DOMESTIC	1119
CARIO	1173	DORCAS	1482
CARMEN	1598	DUDLEY	1040
CEDRIC	1422, 1525	DURO	1261
CELTIC	1274		
CENTRAL	1305	ELDRED	(32–7233)
CEYLON	104	ELDRIDGE	1172
CHARLESTOWN	1280	ELECTRIC	1307

---

* Also the name of an engraved pattern.
† This pattern is composed of cut and engraved motifs.
‡ Also the name of an etched pattern.
§ Several designs are noted in catalogs as "Cut No. 1" and "Cut No. 2."

Pattern Name	Catalog Number	Pattern Name	Catalog Number
ELITE	1008	MADRID	1527
ELMER	1447, 1525	MAJESTIC	1168
EMPIRE*	1225	MANTON*	1119, 1531
ERIE	1146	MARION	1255
ETHEL	1526	MARS	1165
EUREKA*	1253	MELBOURNE	1483, 1539
		MELBA†	6596
FAVORITE	1450	MODERNE	
FELTON	1289	MOSELLA†	(32–7234)
FESTIVE*	1533	MUNROE	1490
FISH	6371		
FLORENCE	1277	NEVADA	1180
FLUTED	1433	NEWPORT	1024
FRISCO	1108	NIAGARA	1083
		NORMAN*	1024
GEORGIA	1215	NORWOOD	1099
GEORGIAN	7270	NUMBER 1§	(32–6515),
GIBSON	1143		(32–6559),
GLADYS	1109		(32–6763),
			(32–7407)
HANOVER*	1107	NUMBER 75	1141
HEAVY CUT	(32–6636),	NUMBER 76	1140
	(32–6687),	NUMBER 77	1144
	(32–6688),	NUMBER 79	1142
	(32–7035)	NUMBER 80	1138
HECTOR	1510	NUMBER 81	1139
HEXAGON	1514	NUMBER 84	1125
HINDOO	1072	NUMBER 85	1126
HOLLAND	1289	NUMBER 86	1127
HORNDALE	1597	NUMBER 89	1128
		NUMBER 91	1121
		NUMBER 92	1129
IMPERIAL	1269		
		ODESSA	1422
JAPAN	1403, 1404	OREGON	1072
KENLWOOD† (sic)	7292	PARISIAN	1024
		PEERLESS	1599
LA FRANCE	7023	PEMBROKE	1337
LABURNUM	1226	PLUTO	1072
LAMBERT	7405	PRINCESS	1464
LAWRENCE	1340	PRISM	1159
LEADER	1171	PUNTY	(32–7289)
LEAVES	(32–6936)		
LEICESTER	1434	QUEEN	1589
LENOX	1214	QUEEN ANNE	(32–6268)
LEYLAND	1172	QUEEN ANNE,	
LILY	1104	MODIFIED	6268
LINCOLN	1224		
LONDON	1254	RAISED DIAMOND	1526
LORRAINE*	1534	RAYMOND	1542
LOTUS*	1082, 2039	RELIANCE	1099
LUNA	1164	RENO	1009

Pattern Name	Catalog Number	Pattern Name	Catalog Number
RIDGEWAY	1590	THOMAS	1599
RODNEY	1422	TOLDIC	1168
ROSEWOOD	1529	TRAYMORE	7401
ROXBURY†	6960	TREMONT	1522
ST. LOUIS*	1227, 1296	UNION	1006
SATURN	1167		
SEAWEED	1373	VERONA	1444
SHELBY	1484	VESTA	1166
SHELL*	1422	VICTOR	1055
SHIELDS	1422	VIOLA	1171
SPANISH SHIP	6371	VIOLET	1341
STAR	1417, 1570		
STARLIGHT	1225	WAKEFIELD	1506, 1526, 1530
STERLING*	1457	WALDORF*	1172
STEUBEN	1099	WARSAW	1040
STRAWBERRY		WARWICK‡	1099, (32–6268),
DIAMOND	1526		(32–6936)
STRAWBERRY		WASHINGTON	1244
MANSION†	(32–7238)	WELLINGTON†	6861
SYLVIA*	1433	WESLEY	1485
		WESTERN	1297
TARTAN	1422, 1430, 1432	WESTON	1535
TEUTONIC	1276	WHIRLWIND	1005
THISTLE	3396, (32–6183),	WILBERT	1300
	6192	WOOSTER	1288

Engraved Decorations

During Carder's administration, the engraved decorations were done in the homes of the engravers in Corning and not in the factory. It was common to see Joseph Libisch, Henry Keller, and the other engravers walking from the Steuben plant carrying home one or two baskets filled with Steuben blanks. A day or so later they would return, bringing back the engraved pieces for Carder's inspection. If approved, these were shipped to the waiting customers, most orders being for special patterns or monograms. Only a few standard engraved patterns were carried in stock.

Carder designed all the hundreds of engraved patterns listed in the factory records, beginning about 1904 with floral motifs (Ill. 57). He usually sketched the design of a goblet, for example, on an actual-size outline drawing with a white chalk pencil or with crayon on black paper (Ill. 88). Sometimes the engraver would work directly from Carder's original sketch. More often, Carder would make a finished drawing in India ink on tracing paper. This would be blueprinted, thus allowing the original to be kept on file, and the blueprints would be given to the engravers as needed.

All Steuben engravings were done in intaglio[54]—that is, the design was sunk into the glass, the reverse of relief decoration. Indeed, the Steuben engravers could not do the latter, and his inability to get relief done was one of Carder's

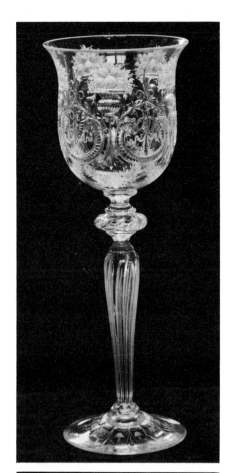

Ill. 156. ORNAMENTAL PIECES. *Left to right,* VASE, No. 6417; height, 14 inches. COVERED VASE, No. 6429; height, 20 inches. Both engraved Grape pattern. VASE, No. 6441; height, 10 inches. Swirl decoration. All made in the late 1920s. *Photograph from Carder's files*

Ill. 157. STEMWARE GROUP. The first four glasses *(left to right)* have cut and engraved patterns. The champagne *(second from right)* has green and opaque white twist in the stem. The goblet on the far right has light optic pattern in bowl and stem. All made in the 1920s. *Corning Museum. Raymond Errett Photograph*

Ill. 158. CRYSTAL GOBLETS, No. 6727 *(top)* and No. 8351; height of both, 10 inches. Both have engraved designs. *Photograph from Carder's files*

few failures. At one point, an important order was received for a set of goblets to be decorated with cameo heads in relief, and Carder decided to "give it a try." He designed a tall, elegant goblet, and the blowing room placed a two-layer glass medallion in the spot designated on the side of the goblet bowl. Carder then designed a cameo-type female head, and gave the drawing along with the trial goblet to the best engraver, who said immediately that he could not do a relief cameo. Carder insisted. The engraver tried and failed. Carder cussed, but still insisted. The engraver made several more attempts, all miserable failures. Carder tried other engravers, with even worse results. Finally he "called it quits" and reluctantly informed the customer he could not fill the order. Two souvenirs of this unsuccessful project were kept, from then on, in Carder's office collection, and after his retirement one became the property of The Corning Museum of Glass (Ill. 164) and the other of the Rockwell collection.

The engraving process used at Steuben is so well known that a short description will suffice.[55] The engraver copied the design on the glass with either India ink, a solution of whiting and gum, or some other method of marking. He then engraved the pattern by using copper wheels of various sizes and profiles, which were inserted into the chuck of a small lathe. The engraver held the glass under the copper wheel (not on top, as the glass cutter does) and sank the design into the glass by means of an abrasive consisting of emery powder and oil, applied by the various copper wheels selected to achieve the required design.

A dozen or two copper wheels mounted on tapered spindles were kept in a rack within easy reach of the engraver. These disks varied from about the size of a common pinhead to wheels three or four inches in diameter. Some Steuben engraved patterns were done with small stone wheels, but these were in the minority.

Ill. 159. CRYSTAL CHALICE, made in the 1920s. Unique. Height, about 15 inches. Engraved decoration. *Corning Museum. Raymond Errett Photograph*

Ill. 160. CRYSTAL PLATES; diameter, 10 inches. One at left is engraved Holbein; at right, Melba. Made in the 1920s. Notation on back of photograph in Carder's handwriting: "$138.00 dn." *Photograph from Carder's files*

Ill. 161. CRYSTAL COLOGNE BOTTLES. *Above,* No. 6604, height, 8¼ inches. *Below,* No. 6604 variant; height, 8 inches. Engraved decoration. Made in the 1920s. *Photograph from Carder's files*

Ill. 162. CASED GOBLETS, Gold Ruby over crystal. *Left,* No. 8351; height, 10 inches. *Right,* No. 6765; height, 9¼ inches. Gold engraved decoration. *Photograph from Carder's files*

Ill. 163. MARINA COVERED VASE, No. 6611; height, 12 inches. Engraved in Rugby pattern. Made in the 1920s. *Photograph from Carder's files*

Ill. 164. CRYSTAL GOBLET with applied cameo-type medallion of white glass over turquoise. No. 6861; height, 10 inches. The relief engraving of the cameo medallion is of poor quality, as the Steuben engravers at that time were unable to do engraving in relief. *Corning Library. Raymond Errett Photograph*

Ill. 165. CRYSTAL COVERED VASE. No. 7078; height, 13¼ inches. Engraved in La France pattern. Made about 1929. *Photograph from Carder's files*

Ill. 166. GOBLETS. *Left to right*, No. 7079; height, 7⅛ inches. Crystal glass engraved in La France pattern. No. 7080; height, 8 inches. Pale amethyst engraved in Crest pattern. No. 7081. Crystal glass engraved in Coat of Arms pattern. All made in the late 1920s. *Photograph from Carder's files*

Ill. 167. CRYSTAL GOBLETS. *Left to right,* No. 6947; height, 7 inches. Cut and engraved in Lambeau pattern. No. 6959; height, 6 inches. Cut and engraved in Freyberg pattern. No. 6960; height, 6¼ inches. Cut and engraved in Mariette pattern. *Photograph from Carder's files*

Ill. 169. CRYSTAL CONSOLE SET, probably a special order. CANDLESTICKS, 24 inches tall. BOWL, 21 inches long. Engraving is "Rock crystal" type. *Photograph from Carder's files, with notation in his handwriting*

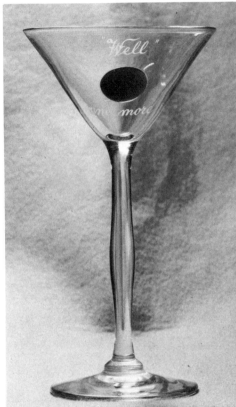

Ill. 168. CRYSTAL COCKTAIL GLASS, No. 7284; height, 6¾ inches. Olive is applied in green. Engraved, "Well" one more. Private Collection. Smithsonian Institution Photograph

Ill. 170. CRYSTAL COLOGNE BOTTLES with engraved decoration, No. 6675; height, 8½ inches. Made in the 1920s. *Photograph from Carder's files*

Ill. 171. CASED CONSOLE SET, Jade Green over Alabaster, is engraved in Grapes pattern. Height, 8 inches. BOWL, No. 6081; 15 inches long. Also made in crystal and colors in the 1920s. *Photograph from Carder's files*

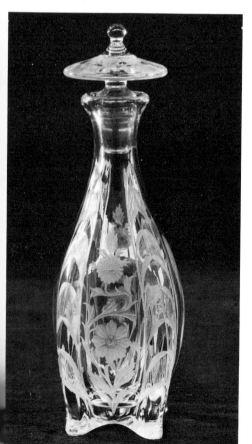

Engravings were left with a mat texture (called gray in the factory) as they came from the copper wheels, or they were polished in the style of rock crystal pieces. Sometimes a combination of mat and polished motifs was used. Polishing was done with a revolving fiber brush, fed first with pumice and water, and then with putty powder and water. Acid polishing was also done—by dipping the glass in a solution of sulfuric and hydrofluoric acids. In acid polishing, the portions of the object that were not engraved were protected from the acid during the dipping process by a wax coating. A pebbled effect was obtained by acid polishing an engraving that had been done with a coarse abrasive. Polished engravings gave the effect of rock crystal, and were done at Steuben in the same manner Carder had used at Stevens & Williams in the 1880s and 1890s.[56]

Engraved Glass Patterns

In this list, the catalog number or numbers at the right of each pattern name indicate one or more of the glass forms decorated with that specific pattern. Popular forms were not limited to one pattern, but were decorated with whatever design the buyer specified. There are probably additional pattern names not included in this list, which was compiled from factory records, sales brochures, and other reliable sources presently available.

Numbers in parentheses preceded by 32 are illustrated in the appendix to the 1932 Steuben Catalog reproduced at the end of the catalog line drawings. In this appendix, designs designated with a *T* prefix were done by Walter Darwin Teague.

Pattern Name	Catalog Number	Pattern Name	Catalog Number
ACACIA	6022, 6043	ADELPHIA	6017
ACME		AJAX	
ADAMS*	6510, 6931	ALBA	6567

* Also the name of a cut pattern.
† This pattern is composed of cut and engraved motifs.
‡ Also the name of an etched pattern.

Pattern Name	Catalog Number	Pattern Name	Catalog Number
ALBANY	6034	CHATHAM†	(32–7236)
ALBERTA	7234	CHELSEA	6074
ALDINE		CHESTER	6949
ALLBRIGHT	6709	CHRISTY	
ALPINE	7344	CLAREMONT	7237
ALVIN	1412, 1640	CLARKIA	6605
ANGELA VERONA	6233	COAT OF ARMS	6087, 7081
ANTIQUE		COLONIAL	
ANTONIO	6977, 7058	COLUMBIA	6976
ARCADIAN	2028	CORDON	
ARDSLEY		CORDOVA	6728
ARGONNE	6051	CORNFLOWER	1433
ARIZONA	6955	CRESCENT*	6505, 6820, 7032
ATLANTIC		CRESOTA	
ATLAS	7032, 7054	CREST	7348
AUBURN	6429	CREST,	
AURORA‡	7080	HORSES HEAD	7028
AUTUMN	6401, 6668, 7392	CREST,	
		MOUNTAIN GOAT	6963
BALTIC*	1406, 1422, 1424,	CREST, SHIELD	7336
	1444	CREST, SWAN	7336
BARLEYCORN	6220	CRESWELL	1415
BARTON		CROSLEY (CROSSLEY)	7171, 7241
BASEBALL BAT AND			
MONOGRAM	7336	DAFFODIL	1955
BAT	2039	DAISY*	2160, 7203
BAYARD	(32–6928)	DANBURY†	(32–7237)
BEAUMONT	6073	DANUBE	7234
BELMAR†	3585, 6539, 6868	DAULTON	6947
BEVERLY	6220	DEARBORN	6505
BIZARRE	6966	DEITCH	1621
BLUE TREE	6863	DELPHIC	6621, 6669
BLUE TREEN	6705	DERBY	1415
BORDEN		DEVON	6959
BORGIA	7234	DIAPER	7040, 7296
BOUCHER	6972	DU FRENE	6897
BOUQUET	6257	DUCK	(32–2989)
BRADFORD	3598	DUPONT	6505, 7032
BRENTON	6735	DUVEEN	6901
BROMLEY	6505, 7031		
BRUNSWICK	6704, 6734	ELAINE	6900
BUDWORTH	6947	ELCHO	6277
BURGUNDE	6017	ELKAY	(32–7250)
BURLINGTON	(32–6599),	ELM	
	(32–6626)	EMPIRE	1554
BUTTERCUP	1923	EMPRESS	8351
		ETRUSCAN†‡	6397, 6398
CAIRO		EUREKA	6220, 6226
CAMILLO	1984, 3370		
CAROLINA		FAN	1411
CASTLE	6433	FERN	2028
CECELIA	6955, 7341	FESTIVE*	1533
CEDAR		FESTOON	7156, 7176
CHATEAU†	6595, 7309	FIGURE(S)	6706

Pattern Name	Catalog Number	Pattern Name	Catalog Number
FIRCONE‡	6081	KENNELWORTH	
FISH	6754	(KENNILWORTH)	2028
FITCHBERG	7290	KENLWOOD† (sic)	7292
FLAGS	1044	KENNETH	
FLORIAN	7345	KENSINGTON	6269
FONTAINE	6929	KENTON	
FORGETMENOT	2156	KING	1410
FOUNTAIN	6594, 6672		
FRANKFORT	7094	LA FRANCE	
FRENCH HOUSE	6287	(Ills. 165, 166)	(32–7078)
FRENCHA	6277	LAMBEAU (Ill. 167)	6947
FREYBERG (Ill. 167)	6959	LAUREL SPRAY	1917
		LAURERITE	
		LEANDER	
GABRIEL	6820	LINDEN	3586
GALVESTON	6977	LOCKWOOD	6044, 6062
GARFIELD	7046, 7174	LONSDALE	6715
GARLAND	3386	LORRAINE*	8351
GENOA	6693	LOTUS*	3600
GEORGIAN	6280	LOUIS SEIZE‡	6671
GLENDALE	6505, 7032	LUXOR	3600
GLENMORE	6505	LYON'S HEAD	8351
GLOBE		LYONS	6567, 7235
GLORIA	6898		
GOBELIN	7343	MAGNOLIA	
GOTHIC TAPESTRY	3579	MAINE	
GRAPES (GRAPE)‡		MALAY (MALAYA)	6604
(Ill. 156)	6023, (32–6034),	MANON	6574
	6419, (32–6893)	MANSON	
GROTTO	7081	MANTON*	1445
GUNS	(32–2989)	MAPLE	
		MARCHAIL	3179
		MARCO	7092
HANGING FLOWER	2382	MARGURITE	2138, 7372–7381,
HANOVER*	6692		(32–7402, 7403),
HARVARD	6505, 8380		(32–7472)
HEYDEN	7174	MARIETTE (Ill. 167)	6960
HILDA		MARINA (MARINE)	6706, 6847, 6869
HOLBEIN (Ill. 160)	2028, 6395	MARINE	(32–6869)
HUDSON*	7032, 7117, 7254	MARZINI	6717
HUNT FRIEZE	6183	MAUSER	
HUNTER	7056	MAXIM	
HUNTING DOG	(32–2989)	MAY	
HUNTINGTON	6505, 7118	MEDIEVAL TAPESTRY	3578
		MELBA† (Ill. 160)	6747
IVY	6401, 6869	MELROSE	1431
		MERCER	3387
		MIDANA	6596
JACOBIAN (sic)	6268	MIGNON	6577
JASMINE	6167	MILLET	6844
JEFFERSON		MONTREX	6037
JETTE D'EAU	6394, 6395	MOOSE	2989
JONQUIL	2158	MORA (MORO)	6902, 6919
		MOREAU	6729
KABU		MOSELLE	
KAHN	6716	(MOSELLA)†	(32–7234)

Pattern Name	Catalog Number	Pattern Name	Catalog Number
Mystic	6583, 6664, 6665	Rideau (Riddau)	8351
		Riverside	
Narcissus	1585, 1645	Rocaille	2159
Nemo†	6869	Rock Crystal	1509
Nora		Rococo (Rococo	
Norma	6245	Festoon)	1916
Norman*	7031, 7032	Rome	
Noyon	(32–6126), 6261,	Rooster	6333
	6262	Rosaline	
Number 10001	2682	Rosemary	6277
Number 10007	2028	Rosette	
Number 10008	6106, 6119, 6225	Rosslyn	6861
Number 10011	6225	Rowen	6575
Number 10018	(32–938)	Roxbury†	6860
Number 10035	6912	Rubens	6955
Number 2	(32–7349)	Rugby (Ill. 163)	6611, 6612
		Russian	
Oakhurst	6987	"Rye"	1475, 6516
Olympic			
Orient			
Orsin	3325	St. Louis†	1497, 6062
		Saratoga	6947
		Sedgwick	7248
Paragon	6841	Shell	1422, 1472, 1614
Paris		Sherate	2956
Parisean	3327	Ship	6433
Partridge	2989	Shirley	(32–6505)
Pekin		Sidney	6949
Percival	6844	Siegbert	6505, 7031
Persian‡	1481, 3598, 6759	Spiraea	6505, 6510
Persian Tapestry	3579	Spray (see Laurel Spray)	
Pheasant	(32–2989)	Standish	6998
Phlox	6606	Sterling*	(32–7245)
Phoenix	6278	Strawberry	
Phyllis		Mansion†	(32–7238, 7239)
Piedmont	6982	Sunflower	1955
Pilsen	7174	Sydney	6949
Plymouth		Sylvia†	1433
Polo	(32–2989)	Syringia	6021
Polo Sticks and			
Monogram	7336		
Poussin	(32–6844), 7094	Taragon	6841
Primrose	2012	Tennis	(32–2989)
Prince Charles	2013	Texas	6977
Princess	6596	Thistle†	1727
Princeton		Tiffany	2908
Priscilla	6714	Torino	(32–6596), 6765,
			(32–6768)
Rajah	6675	Torio	
Raleigh		Traymore	(32–7401)
Ralston	1426		
Ramsey	7253		
Regal	(32–7046)	Uno	6919
Renwick	7304, (32–7372 to		
	7381), (32–7387,		
	7388), (32–7472)	Van Dyke	6081, 6257, 6737
Rheo	2909	Venus	

Pattern Name	Catalog Number	Pattern Name	Catalog Number
VERDUN	6109, 6257	WAVERLY	6354
VERMONT	3579	WEDGWOOD	3601
VERNON	6026, 6062	WELLINGTON†	(32–6861)
VERONA (see ANGELA VERONA)		WHITCOMBE	6955
VERRA	6567	WHITNEY	6030, 7033
VERSAILLES‡	6977	WIELD	6899
VICTORIA	8351	WILD DUCK	2989
VIENNA	6576	WINDSOR	6768
VIENNESE	7249	WOLF DOG	2989
VIRGINIA		WOODSTOCK	6394, 6418, 6429,
(VIRGINIAN)	(32–62727)		6430
WALDORF*	6844		
WALES	6596	YALE	
WATER LILY	6754	YORK	6034, 6106

Acid-etched Decorations

Carder established the etching room at Steuben about 1906. He had become familiar with the process of etching designs on glass early in his career at Stevens & Williams, where he used it as the first step in the production of cameo glass. The acid-etched pieces produced at Steuben were made by transferring the design to the glass by means of a print made on paper in a "wax ink"[57] (Color Plates XXVI & XXVII).

This print was taken from a plate etched with the reverse, or negative, of the pattern desired. The plate could be of glass or metal. Carder usually used a sheet of plate glass about one-quarter inch thick because it was cheaper than steel or copper. The pattern plate was warmed slightly, and the etched portion filled with "ink," which was a compound of asphaltum, beeswax, gum mastic, and turpentine. These elements were proportioned to form a paste that, when warm,

Ill. 173. ALABASTER "SCULPTURED" VASE, No. 6443; height, 10½ inches. Acid-etched design accented with raw umber. Made in the 1920s. *Photograph from Carder's files*

Ill. 172. "SCULPTURED" ALABASTER GLASS URN, No. 8007; height, 16 inches. BOWLS, No. 6368; diameter, 10 inches. The acid-etched designs are accented with raw umber. Made in 1920s as a special order for Crest Co. *Photograph from Carder's files*

was about the consistency of peanut butter—it spread easily into every detail of the etched pattern. After the excess ink was scraped off, a special transfer paper was placed on the warm ink and rubbed down just enough to make the ink adhere to the paper when the paper was peeled back from the plate. The paper with the design in ink was then applied to the glass object and rubbed down with a felt "rubber" to ensure a perfect union between the glass and the ink. Next, the paper was moistened with water and peeled away, leaving the ink pattern on the glass object to be etched. The portions of the glass not covered with the pattern were painted with wax to protect them from the etching acid.[58] Then the object was immersed in the etching acid for the time required to etch the designs to the desired depth. Afterward, the wax coating was removed, revealing the completed etched design. Etched patterns were discontinued about 1934 (Ills. 172–189).

Etched wares were also advertised as "carved" and "sculptured." Carder usually used these terms to describe the more expensive designs (No. 6702),

Ill. 174. "SCULPTURED" VASE, No. 6391; height, 16 inches. Produced in several sizes and colors, including Alabaster. Made in the 1920s. *Photograph from Carder's files*

Ill. 175. CASED VASE, black over Jade Green, No. 6147 (small size); height, 5½ inches. Deep-etched design. Probably a unique trial piece made about 1917. *Corning Museum. Raymond Errett Photograph*

Ill. 176. CASED COVERED VASE, Jade Green over Alabaster. No. 5020 variant; height, about 12 inches. Acid-etched Dragon pattern. Teakwood base and cover. Made in the 1920s. *Photograph from Carder's files*

Ill. 177. CASED VASE, rose over Alabaster, with acid-etched Butterfly design. Height, about 10 inches. Made in the 1920s. *Photograph from Carder's files* ▶

Ill. 178. DOUBLE-ETCHED VASE, amethyst cased over crystal. No. 7000; height, 14 inches. Called double-etched because the background design was produced by a second acid bath. *Collection of Dr. and Mrs. L.G. Wagner. Raymond Errett Photograph*

Ill. 179. DOUBLE-ETCHED VASE. "Green flashed on Alabaster" appears on the photograph in Carder's handwriting. No. 6148; height, about 8 inches. *Photograph from Carder's files*

Ill. 180. MAT CRYSTAL BOWL etched in Ducks pattern, No. 6681; height, 4 inches. Made in the 1920s. *Photograph from Carder's files*

Ill. 181. DOUBLE-ETCHED VASE, black cased over crystal, No. 668 variant; height, about 15 inches. *Photograph from Carder's files*

Ill. 182. CASED CANDLESTICK, Jade Green over Alabaster, wth acid-etched design. No. 6063 variant; height, 10 or 12 inches. *Photograph from Carder's files*

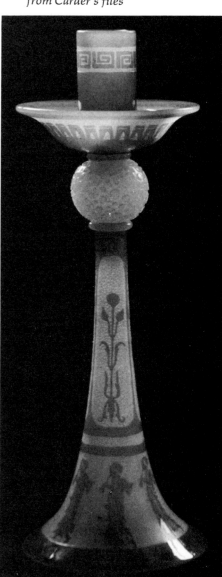

Ill. 183. DOUBLE-ETCHED VASE, black cased over Celeste Blue, No. 6094; height, 15 inches. *Corning Museum. Raymond Errett Photograph*

Ill. 184. CASED DISK, Gold Aurene over Alabaster; diameter, 15 inches. Acid-etched with a unique design by Bolas Manikowski for Frederick Schroeder, who worked at Steuben as superintendent of the blowing room during Carder's entire tenure. *Raymond Errett Photograph*

Ill. 185. ALABASTER "SCULPTURED" LIGHTING BOWL (actually acid-etched), No. 7393; diameter, 18 inches. The raised design is accented with a brown background produced by applying raw umber mixed with turpentine. Made about 1925. *Photograph from Carder's files*

Ill. 186. DOORSTOPS & ACID-ETCHED VASES. DOORSTOPS, No. 7257 variants; height, about 3½ inches. This size doorstop with various bubble and thread arrangements is the only one listed in available records as a production item. Other doorstops and paperweights made at the Steuben Glass Works were usually made by workmen after hours for personal use, with or without permission. VASES are black cased over Alabaster. *Left to right*, No. 6272 variant; height, 10 inches. Stamford pattern. No. 2683; height, 12 inches. Hunting pattern. No. 6078; height, 8 inches. Nedra pattern. *Photograph from Carder's files*

Ill. 187. DOUBLE-ETCHED BOWL in Chinese pattern is green cased over Alabaster. No. 5002; diameter, 10 inches. Made in the 1920s. *Photograph from Carder's files*

particularly the Calcite and Alabaster pieces that had the raised designs accented with brown air-dried pigment, and Rosaline lamp bases like No. 5190. The word "sculptured" was also used to describe the pieces with applied leaves and vines, like vase No. 6766.

Etched Glass Patterns

In this list, the catalog number or numbers at the right of each pattern name indicate one or more of the glass forms decorated with that specific pattern. Popular forms were not limited to one pattern, but were decorated with whatever design the buyer specified. There are probably additional pattern names not included in this list, which was compiled from factory records, sales brochures, and other reliable sources presently available.

Numbers in parentheses preceded by 32 are illustrated in the appendix to the 1932 Steuben Catalog reproduced at the end of the catalog line drawings. In this appendix, designs designated with a *T* prefix were done by Walter Darwin Teague.

Ill. 188. DOUBLE-ETCHED COVERED JAR in Chinese pattern is Rosaline (also called rose) cased over Alabaster. No. 5000; height, 6 inches. Made in the 1920s. *Photograph from Carder's files*

Ill. 189. DOUBLE-ETCHED VASE in Hare Bell pattern; black cased over Celeste Blue. No. 2148; height, 10 inches. *Corning Museum. Raymond Errett Photograph*

Pattern Name	Catalog Number	Pattern Name	Catalog Number
Acanthus	2938, 5000, (32–6406), (32–6415)	Bouquet	2217, 2541
		Brandon	6777
		Bristol	6389, 6744, 7294, (32–8413)
Acorn	2774, 2938		
Adams	6094	Bryony	2487, 2854
Adams Rosette	2346	Butterfly	6678
Adams with heads	995	Calais	2593
Adams with shield	995	Calla Lily (Calles Lily)	6382
Alhambra	6078, 6199, 6703	Cameo	6457
Alicia	(32–7443)	Canterbury	2682
Anchusa	6272	Canton	(32–2687)
Anethea	6272	Cat Tails	6914
Assyrian	6578, 6613	Celanese	7002
Astrid	6702, 6706, 6855	Chambord	7001
Atlas	7394	Chang	6094, (32–6112)
Aubusson	6467	Chester	2485
Aurora*	8485	Chinese	(32–5000), 6109, 8506
Aytic	8511		
Azalia	5000	Chippendale	6368
		Cliffwood	
Bacchus	8436	Clodian	6777
Bat	5000	Colleone	2774
Bedford	6078	Cologne	6953
Belgrade	6272, 7001	Colombo	7000
Bellani	6468	Columbine	6183
Bird (Number 1)	(32–938)	Como	6756
(Number 2)	5000, 6373, 6679	Compton	(32–2687)
Boothbay	(32–7007)	Corinthian (Corinthia)	6272
Bosque	6468		

* Also the name of an engraved pattern.
† Also the name of a cut pattern.

Pattern Name	Catalog Number	Pattern Name	Catalog Number
CORNUCOPIA	995	GREEK HEADS	6088
CRYSANTHEMUM	6199, 6382	GREEK KEY	2774
CUPID	2328	GRETA	(32–7444)
DAGMAR	6019	HARE BELL (Ill. 189)	2184, 6019
DAMASCUS	6914	HARTWICK	(32–7391)
DAPHNE	8522	HEATON	7001
DAYTON	6273	HEPPLE	2654
DEBUT	6881, 6885	HOFFMAN	6272
DELWOOD	(32–7442)	HOLLYWOOD	(32–7036)
DENVER	6128	HONESTY	6535, 6608
DERBY	6112, 6227	HONEYSUCKLE	6227
DONATELLO	2938	HUNTING (Ill. 186)	(32–2683), 7007
DOVER	6094		
DRAGON (Ill. 176)	6094, 7106	INDIAN	(32–6272)
DRESDEN	6276	INVICTA	7107
DUCKS	6681	IONIC	6272
		IRIS	5000
EGG AND DART	2938	IVY LEAF	2328
ELIZABETHAN	995, 2774		
ELIZABETHAN,		JAPANESE	2217, 2485
RAISED	2487		
EMPIRE	2485	KELSO	7260
ETRUSCAN*	7389	KENILWORTH	2346
EVELYN	(32–7440)	KEY BORDER	
FANTAN	6276	LANDSCAPE	995, 6272, 6370
FESTOON	2512	LEAF	2241, 8414
FIGURE	6400	LION	6578, 6650,
FIGURE AND HORSES	5190		(32–6680)
FIGURE, DANCING	2228	LOTUS	2144, 5000, 6229
FIGURE FESTOON	2774	LOUIS XV	2682
FIGURE ROSETTE	2346	LOUIS PHILIPPE	2682
FIRCONE	5000, (32–6078),	LOUIS SEIZE*	6227
	6512	LUMENE	2346, 2730
FISH (Ill. 174)	7083		
FLEUR DE LIS	6229	MADISON	6406, 6482, 6805
FLORAL	(32–6078), 6224,	MAJESTIC	6227, 6229
	6369, 6375	MANCHU	2683
FLORENTIA	7288, 8553	MANSARD	(32–6501), 6760,
FLORIDA	(32–6468)		6804
FULLERTON	7103	MANTELLA (sic)	2683, 6078
		MAPLEWOOD	(32–7442)
GALLEON	5000, 6370	MARIGOLD	(32–7426)
GEORGIAN	2346	MARLENE	(32–938),
GOBELIN	6467		(32–6034),
GODFREY	7002		(32–6078),
GORDON	(32–7441)		(32–6389),
GOTHIC	2346, 2592, 7083		8389
GRAPE(S)*	6222	MATSER	6078
GREYSTONE	6680	MATZU	(32–938),
GREEK FIGURE	995, 2328		(32–5000),
GREEK FRET	2590		6034, (32–6078)

Pattern Name	Catalog Number	Pattern Name	Catalog Number
MAYA	8511	RORSTRAND	
MAYFAIR	(32–7442)	(ROSTRAND)	6457, 6702
MEDALLION	2541	ROSARIO	(32–7445)
MILLEFIORI	(32–7494) etched with applied millefiori buttons as flower centers	ROSE	6183, 7032
		ROSETTA	
		ROSETTE	6571
MING	6222	ST. CLOUD	6034
MOCKING BIRD	6078, 7034, 8494	SALUBRIA	6415, 6508
MODERNE	6706, 6837	SAMARKAND	5000
MONARCH	2217, 2487	SCROLL	2744
MONROE	6680	SCULPTURED	5000, (32–6199), (32–6391), (32–7425)
MURILLO	2687		
MUSIC	2346		
		SCULPTURED LEAVES	(32–7439)
NANETTE	6272	SEA HOLLY	(32–6078), 6389, 7036
NEAVEAU	6230		
NEDRA (Ill. 186)	5000, (32–6078)	SEMPER	6787, 6857
NEPTUNE	6857	SEVRES	2682
NEWPORT	6149	SHELTON	(32–2683)
NIMROD	7034	SHERATON	2512, 2771
NORFOLK	2683	SHERWOOD	6078, 8483
		SHIELD AND	
OAK LEAF AND		FESTOON	2567, 2938
ACORN	2346	SPEZA	6111
OPHELIA	6094	SPIDER	
ORIENTAL	6288	SPRINGTIME	5000
ORTEGA	7000	STAMFORD (Ill. 186)	(32–2683)
OSIRIS	2730	STRATFORD	2938
OXFORD	6468	SUPINO	7100
		SWIRL	2687
PAGODA	2683, 6097	SWISS	2593
PARIS	6872		
PEACOCK	6679	TAPESTRY	2989
PEKING	6223	TEAZLE	(32–2683), 6272
PEONY	(32–7391)	THISTLE*†	5000, (32–6415), 6559, 7289
PERSIAN†	6125		
PIEDMONT	8408	TOLEDO	2487
POMPEIAN	2346, 2566	TRENTHAM	6806
POPPY	6291, 6390	TRENTON	2774
PRIMROSE	6389	TRIANON	6467
PUSSYWILLOW	(32–2683)	TROPIC	
		TUDOR	6223
RACIENT	6034, 6078		
RAINY DAY	6534, 8388	VALENCIA	6986
RALEIGH	6595	VALERIA	(32–7391)
RECTOR	6391	VALLOIS	5000
RENAISSANCE	2247	VARIEGATED	6221
RENOR	2683	VENDEE	6572, 6578
RHODEIAN	6283	VENTURE	
RODIN	6098	VENTURIE	
ROMA	6854	(VENTURIS)	6222, 6482

Pattern Name	Catalog Number	Pattern Name	Catalog Number
VERMICELLO	8023	WILD GOOSE	6370
VERSAILLES*	995, 2774, 2938	WINTON	(32–7424)
VINE	6304, 6390	WYCOMBE	6703
WALLCREST	2683	ZENITH	2683, 6078
WARWICK†	2487, 6078		

Finishing Pontils and Bases

Practically all Steuben glass was hand blown, and the pontil (or punty) mark was usually ground off and the surface polished. There were some exceptions. The pontil was sometimes left rough (just as it broke from the iron) on pieces where a high foot-ring kept the rough spot from coming into contact with table-tops or other surfaces that might be marred. The rough pontil is more often found on less expensive items or experimental pieces, although it sometimes appears on Aurenes, Quartz, and Cluthra pieces.

The concave depression left by grinding out the pontil was polished on transparent pieces where a rough grinding would show. It is found "rough ground" or partially polished on pieces made from translucent colors such as ivory and the jade glasses.

A waffle or crisscross pattern pontil is also found on many Steuben pieces. This type of pontil was formed after a small gather of hot glass had been put on the pontil rod and pressed into a crisscross mold before being attached to the bottom of the hot glass object. The waffle pattern remains on the object after the pontil is broken away. These waffle indentations reduce the area of the pontil surface adhering to the object, allowing the pontil to be separated from it more easily.

Pad pontils are the result of an extra gather of glass being applied to the base of the object before it was "stuck up" on the pontil rod. This was rarely done at Steuben, but a few pieces are known with pad pontils. These were usually put on to reinforce the base when the piece seemed too thin at that point.

Sometimes, particularly on plates and heavy flat-bottomed pieces, the entire base of the pieces was flattened and polished, leaving no evidence at all of the pontil; or perhaps only a slight scar or two may mark the spot where the pontil was. Robert Leavy says the pontils on Steuben plates were small (about one-half inch in diameter), or the bottom was ground flat and polished, eliminating the pontil entirely, as noted above. In contrast, plates made by the Sinclair Glass Company had large, concave pontil marks an inch to 1½ inches in diameter. Since many Sinclair and Steuben plates are almost identical in form and color, the large pontil will help to identify products of the Sinclair factory.

6

Architectural Glass

I<small>N THE LATE</small> 1920<small>S, STEUBEN FURNACES BEGAN PRODUCING</small> "<small>DECORATIVE CAST GLASS,</small> in full or partial relief and in intaglio, in panels or grilles, and in the round," as stated in a contemporary brochure.

The possibilities of glass as an architectural element had been apparent to Carder for many years, and he was finally successful in having architects include Steuben glass as both an exterior and an interior architectural feature. One of the earliest interior installations was the lighting frieze in the elevator lobbies of the Empire State Building in New York City. The intaglio panels were designed by the architects Shreve, Lamb & Harmon. The models were carved by the author about 1930 and the glass made at Steuben.

During the last few years Carder was manager of the Steuben Division, the architectural glass business gradually increased, and he continued his interest after he became art director of Corning Glass Works. The largest installation was the already-mentioned panel over the entrance doors of the RCA Building facing Rockefeller Plaza. Carder, with my assistance and that of four laborers from Corning Glass Works, made a full-sized model in clay enlarged from sculptor Lee Lawrie's plaster-of-Paris small-scale model. Several tons of clay were used, the work being done in an area lent to Carder by the Pot and Clay Division of Corning Glass Works. After the clay model was completed, it was divided into sections that were cast in plaster of Paris, which in turn formed the models for the iron molds in which the Pyrex glass sculpture was finally cast. When completed, the panel was assembled at Corning, and after approval by the architects and others concerned, was shipped to New York City and installed in the RCA Building, where it can be seen today (Ills. 190–195).

Ill. 190. <small>PLASTER-OF-PARIS SCALE MODEL</small> by Lee Lawrie, showing location of glass panel in the facade of the RCA Building, Rockefeller Center, New York. Note that the glass panel is continuous behind the pillars. *Photograph from Carder's files*

Ill. 191. DETAIL SCALE MODEL in plaster of Paris showing complete glass panel design (55 by 15 feet) extending over six doorways. *Photograph from Carder's files*

Ill. 192. CORNING WORKMEN (Antonio Mayo on left) finishing the full-scale plaster-of-Paris model from which iron molds were made for the production of the glass panel. Note model for a panel section in the foreground. *Photograph from Carder's files*

Ill. 193. COMPLETED GLASS PANEL. It was cast in sections in Pyrex glass and assembled at Corning Glass Works for approval prior to shipment to New York for installation. *Photograph from Carder's files*

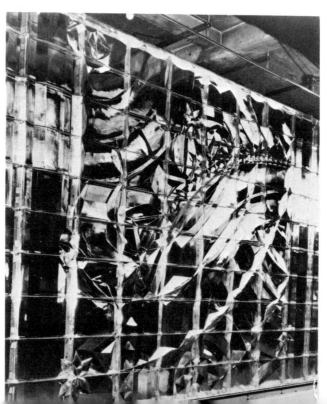

Ill. 194. DETAIL VIEW OF CENTER SECTION OF PANEL, photographed at Corning Glass Works before shipment. *Photograph from Carder's files*

Ill. 195. CENTER SECTION OF PANEL, installed above the entrance to the RCA Building, Rockefeller Center, New York. When this photograph was taken, the glass still had a bright finish. The present frosted effect on the interior surface was applied later to cut down the glare. *Photograph from Carder's files*

Ill. 196. ARCHITECTURAL LIGHTING DOMES, No. A-2068; 17 inches square and 9 inches high. Photograph was taken during installation in the ceiling of a New York theatre marquee. *Photograph from Carder's files*

The architectural pieces shown in the catalog sketches Nos. A-2000 to A-2156 were designed by Carder or various architects for special projects. These range from No. A-2000, designed by architect Raymond Hood for the elevators of the Daily News Building in New York, to the grilles used in the dining salons of the S.S. *Oriente* and the ill-fated S.S. *Morro Castle*. "Standard shapes" such as Nos. A-2011 and A-2034 were incorporated in shops, restaurants, and private residences. These pieces were produced from about 1929 to 1934.

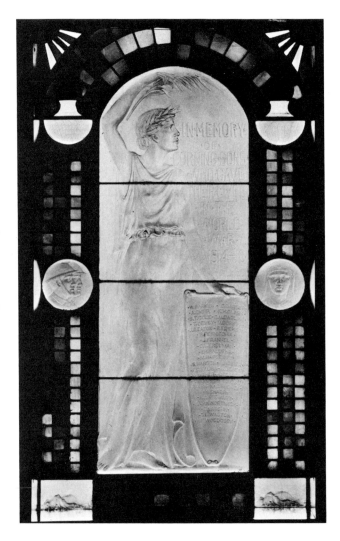

Ill. 197. WORLD WAR I MEMORIAL WINDOW in Corning Public Library, designed by Frederick Carder and made at Steuben Glass Works about 1930. The center panel and medallions are in Bristol Yellow glass made in iron molds cast from Carder's wax model. Border is made of variegated squares set in lead. About 4 by 7 feet in size. *Raymond Errett Photograph*

7

The Cire Perdue (Lost Wax) Process

WEBSTER'S NEW INTERNATIONAL DICTIONARY, SECOND EDITION, 1934, DEFINES CIRE perdue as follows: "[F., lit., lost or waste wax.] adj. Designating, or pertaining to, a process for casting bronze statues, etc., which consists in constructing a model with a wax surface of suitable thickness, forming the outside mold about this, heating so that the wax melts and runs out, and filling the vacant space with metal."

The very wording of this definition, which was published about the time Carder started his cire perdue experiments, implies that the use of this process for casting glass had not yet become well enough known to be included, though glass is referred to in the trade as "metal." Although he had seen the lost wax glass pieces that Decorchemont, Rousseau, and other French glassmakers had produced many years earlier, this knowledge and some practical experience with lost wax bronze castings were about all the tangibles Carder had when he started his experimentation on casting glass by the cire perdue process in the early 1930s. But he had one other essential ingredient—dogged perseverance—which carried him through to success.

His basic idea of the process was a relatively simple concept. If bronze and other metals could be cast by this process, why not glass?

The perfecting of the process was one of the rewards of his being relieved of the command of the Steuben factory. After months of experimentation in 1933 and 1934 in his fifth-floor studio-office at the Corning Glass Works, he worked out the process in the following steps. (To simplify the explanation, we will assume the object to be made in glass by this process is a statuette about eight inches high.)

1. The original statuette was modeled in clay. (A modeling wax like Plastelina was also often used for the original model.)
2. A plaster-of-Paris replica of the original clay statuette was made by the usual process employed by sculptors and ceramists.
3. A "gelatin"[59] mold was made from the plaster-of-Paris statuette. This mold, a reverse of the statuette, was in two or more sections, which fitted into an external plaster shell. The plaster shell was necessary to give the gelatin the support needed to keep it from collapsing.

4. A wax replica of the statuette was made from the gelatin mold.[60] Usually only two or three wax castings could be taken from the gelatin mold. After that, the mold surface became worn and details of the modeling were lost.

5. The wax statuette (which was a replica of the original clay model) was covered, or "invested," with the ceramic mold. This covering was a formula containing plaster of Paris and powdered calcined clay, the ingredients being mixed with water to form a liquid about the consistency of thick cream, and poured over the wax model while still liquid. They were allowed to "set," which occurred in about fifteen minutes as a result of the plaster content.

6. This mold was allowed to dry about twenty-four hours, and then was placed over boiling water. The steam melted the wax, which ran out of the mold leaving, in the ceramic shell, the molded impression in reverse of the original model. The ceramic mold was allowed to air-dry and then fired to a temperature high enough to drive off the volatiles in the plaster content.

7. Cold glass in the form of rods or lumps was now placed in the mold, and mold and glass were fired in a kiln to a temperature high enough to melt the glass and cause it to run into every portion of the mold.

8. Mold and glass were next cooled at a rate slow enough to anneal the solid mass of glass now filling the mold. Carder usually annealed his castings in the studio kiln he had constructed, which contained electric heating elements and allowed him to control the rate of cooling. Usually, this took from one to two days or longer depending on the size of the glass casting. After cooling, the mold was broken away and the glass casting of the original model was revealed.

Although this was a long and tedious process, it was comparatively easy once the formula for the ceramic mold was perfected. This formula had to fulfill two requirements: 1) It must be a mixture that could be poured over the wax model, but would "set" sufficiently hard to allow the wax to be melted out; 2) It must be sufficiently friable to break away from the glass readily after casting, but of sufficient strength to hold the weight of the glass during the melting process.

The problem of strength was one of the most stubborn obstacles Carder had to overcome. Trial after trial would reveal that small chunks of the mold had broken off as the glass flowed by and had become enmeshed in the glass, ruining the cast. "Never say die—say damn!" was Carder's comment as he tossed a ruined glass casting into the trash barrel, and went doggedly back to work making another trial mold.

He saved some of these damaged castings and ground the mold fragments out of others. Some trial pieces that found their way to the market have given rise to harsh criticism of Carder's ability as a sculptor. It should be noted that very few of his sculptured glass pieces were considered "finished objects" by their creator. During experimentation, when it was almost a certainty that the glass casting would be ruined, it is understandable that Carder would use a wax model that might have been made when the gelatin mold was old and had partially destroyed the modeling. Or he would bend a wax model to a more difficult angle as his castings became more successful. This would spoil the model, but advance the process.

Ill. 198. CARDER modeling a high relief portrait of Rubinoff in Plastelina, which was later cast in glass by the lost wax process about 1950. *Corning Glass Works*

Ill. 201. CRYSTAL VASE with black flakings, an early cire perdue trial piece made about 1933. The black flakes were a deposit from the ceramic mold that were "locked in" as the glass fused. This condition was corrected in later castings. Height, 7 inches. *Corning Museum. Raymond Errett Photograph*

Ill. 199. CARDER in his studio at the Corning Glass Works about 1944, carving a wax model. One of the steps of the lost wax process. *Rockwell Gallery*

Ill. 200. CARDER carving the finishing details on a glass sculpture, using an abrasive wheel on a flexible shaft. Photograph was taken April 5, 1954, about five months before his ninety-first birthday.

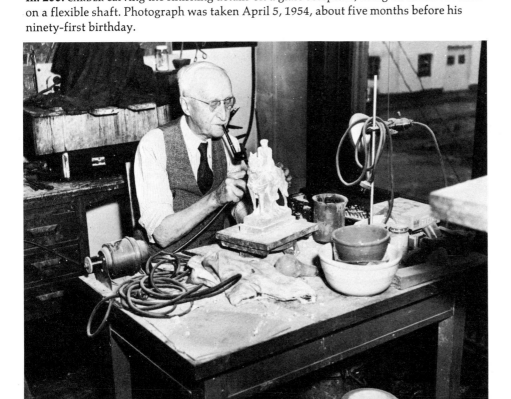

Ill. 202. SCULPTURED GLASS produced by Frederick Carder by the cire perdue process in his studio at the Corning Glass Works in the 1930s. Pieces are all between approximately 4½ and 7½ inches in height. Some are in private collections, some in the Corning Museum. *Photographs from Carder's files and Corning Glass Works*

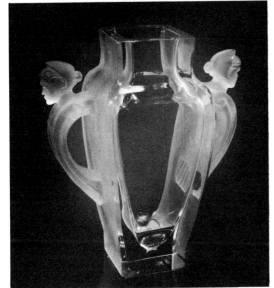

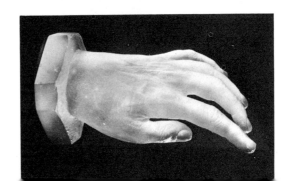

Ill. 203. FREDERICK CARDER completing the clay model of the Indian head he used to demonstrate that a piece of glass this large (46 inches high) could be cast by the lost wax process. The clay is still moist, as indicated by the dampness on the wooden stand. *Photograph from Carder's files*

Ill. 204. PYREX GLASS INDIAN HEAD, the largest piece of glass Carder ever cast by the lost wax process. The cracks across the center of the face and through the headdress resulted from removing the glass from the ceramic mold while it was still too hot to stand the strain of exposure to room temperature. Thickness at nose, about 12 inches. *Rockwell Gallery*

When such a deformed model resulted in a successful glass casting, Carder would dismiss the artistic deficiency with "It's only a trial piece," and proceed to a more difficult phase in his experiments. He reasoned that if he could prove a casting could be made, then he would make a first-rate wax model and reproduce it in glass. His "finished" pieces are relatively few, as he could not resist the temptation to go a step further with each new sculpture. Many of his "trials" are new bringing high prices as collector's items, but are often adversely criticized by people who assume, with good reason, that these pieces were the best he could produce. One has only to see the bronze sculptures and plaster-of-Paris models he made throughout his long career to know that he was capable of producing sculptures of anatomical accuracy and relief carvings of delightful sensitivity (Ills. 198–204).

Pâte de Verre

One of the more notable techniques that Carder revived and perfected in his later years was Pâte de Verre (glass paste).[61] This process of melting powdered glass in molds to form objects resembling those made from semiprecious stones or other minerals was known to the Egyptians as early as 1500 B.C. Small sculptured heads of Pâte de Verre having an Eighteenth Dynasty dating are in the collections of the Victoria and Albert Museum and the Smithsonian Institution.

Carder had studied these ancient pieces, and also objects produced in France by Henri Cros, François Decorchemont, and others in the late nineteenth and early twentieth centuries.[62] Some Steuben Pâte de Verre figures were offered for sale in the 1920s.[63] Carder produced a few more in the 1930s, as one of the steps in his experimentation with the cire perdue process. Perfecting the ceramic mold for the lost wax process enabled him to use his procedure for Pâte de Verre, as well as for his sculptured and Diatreta pieces.

After the ceramic mold (prepared by the method described for cire perdue) was fired and cooled, it was filled with powdered glass. As a source for his powdered glass, Carder used any cullet available that had the colors he needed. He was very casual about the glass he pulverized, often tossing in fragments of broken Steuben pieces he brought from home—an unwitting contribution by careless help in the Carder kitchen. Since the powdered content tended to result in a homogenous mixture, and since the individual particles were so small, the need for glasses with compatible coefficients of expansion was greatly minimized. No breakage is known to have resulted from this carefree mixing of the ingredients.

The process continued with heating the ceramic mold and its powdered glass contents in his studio furnace to the fusing temperature of the glass. Usually more powdered glass was added during the melting period, as the glass shrank into a denser and consequently smaller mass when fused than when it was a loose powder. This additional glass was put in by opening the furnace at peak temperature and sliding a few tablespoonfuls of it down a hastily constructed V-shaped piece of metal, which Carder held precariously in his asbestos-gloved hands. The sudden introduction of cooler air and powdered glass sometimes

Ill. 205. PÂTE DE VERRE PANEL — white figures in low relief on a light green ground. About 9 inches wide. Thickness varies from about ¼ to ½ inch. *Corning Museum. Raymond Errett Photograph*

caused the mold to crack. When this occurred, the melted glass would flow into the cracks and form fins, which protruded from the surface of the finished piece. Carder ground off the fins with abrasive wheels, and as the surface of most Pâte de Verre pieces was given a mat texture, these imperfections were for the most part invisible. On occasion, when he ran out of the basic color, Carder added whatever powdered glass came easily to hand—perhaps white or another shade of the basic mix. If the mold cracks were deep, this second color sometimes ran into them, and when the fins were ground away the evidence still showed on the surface as veinings. Quite often these enhanced the finished pieces, giving the effect of marble. Marbleized pieces were also done intentionally, as were variegated and cameo effects.

Nearly all the Pâte de Verre pieces were simply trials—as soon as one was completed Carder lost interest in making it in any quantity. He felt these pieces were a stepping-stone to the more complicated sculptured and Diatreta objects—objects that required far greater patience and skill to produce (Ill. 205).

Diatreta

Carder's Diatreta glass was inspired by the rare ancient cage glass pieces made about the fourth century A.D., which were produced by massive cutting of a

Ill. 206. DIATRETA VASE IN SATIN FINISH CRYSTAL; height, 5⅝ inches. Signed "F. Carder 1958." *Corning Museum. Raymond Errett Photograph*

Ill. 207. DIATRETA VASE IN VARIEGATED ROSE AND CRYSTAL; satin finish. Height, 7 inches. Signed "F. Carder 1952." *Lent to the Smithsonian Institution by the Corning Museum of Glass*

heavy-walled vessel, as stated earlier. Carder's Diatreta pieces were made by the cire perdue process, demonstrating how fully he had perfected this method of glass casting.

All Diatreta pieces were made between about 1945 and 1959, and like the other cire perdue objects, were done entirely by Carder in his factory-studio with the exception of some finishing, such as grinding on the bases. Nearly all are signed and dated (Color Plate XXXII; Ills. 206–208).

Ill. 208. DIATRETA BOWL IN BRISTOL YELLOW; satin finish. Height, 3½ inches. Signed "F. Carder 1951." *Lent to the Smithsonian Institution by the Corning Museum of Glass*

8

Steuben Trademarks
and Carder's Signatures

THE FLEUR-DE-LIS WITH THE WORD STEUBEN ON A SCROLL IS THE MOST COMMON mark used by Steuben during the time Carder was in charge (1903 to 1932). Many items are unmarked, as the acid stamped mark was applied by various employees and no strict supervision was maintained. Unmarked pieces quite often occur in stemware sets made in transparent colors, but other unmarked pieces also frequently turn up.

Aurene, Tyrian, Intarsia, and other more expensive wares were usually marked as indicated in the following pages.

STAMPED MARKS
These marks were applied with a rubber stamp and mat acid. They were used from about 1903 to 1932. (Actual size)

ETCHED MARKS
The Calcite trademark was issued June 1, 1915. Both these marks were etched in relief as part of the design or elsewhere on the object. The size varies.

PAPER STICKERS
The trademark at top was on gold paper and had the design and lettering embossed. The circular sticker was white paper with dark blue or black lettering; catalog number, price, and other information were handwritten in the center. The third sticker, white paper with a gold border, was blank; catalog number and other details were added in ink. This sticker was often used with the round sticker. All these marks are actual size.

SPECIAL MARK
The words were stamped in white enamel or mat acid on pieces made for Haviland & Co. from about 1910 to 1915.

133

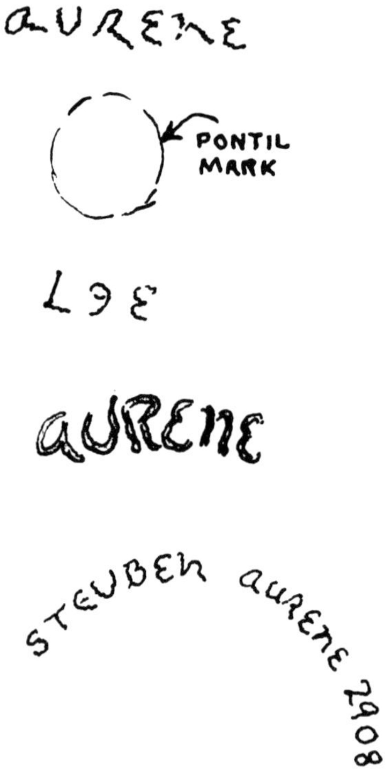

aυRεηE

← PONTIL
MARK

Lэε

aυRεηE

STEυBEη aυRεηε 2908

AURENE TRADEMARKS
Aurene pieces were marked on the
bottom with Aurene or Steuben
Aurene and the catalog number,
though the catalog number was
often omitted. There are many
variations, as these marks were
engraved by several stockroom
employees or other workers
designated as necessity demanded.
Some lettering is almost illegible
and almost all of it is shaky.

© 1929
C.G.W.

STEUBEN

Steuben

Steuben

S

LATER TRADEMARKS
The three at the top, stamped with
mat acid, were used from about
1929. The remaining two were
engraved with a diamond point,
and used after 1932.

SIGNATURES

Facsimile signature engraved on Intarsia pieces about 1930. It varied in size.

Monogram incised in models for cire perdue sculptures and other individual pieces.

Monograms used on bronze sculptures in the late nineteenth century

Typical of the signature used on Diatreta pieces. It was engraved with abrasive wheels on a flexible shaft. There are many variations in size and the date is sometimes omitted.

These signatures were engraved with abrasive wheels on a flexible shaft—with wide variations in size and placement. They are found on many pieces of all datings from 1903 to 1932, put there when collectors and dealers brought pieces to Carder for identification and signature during the last years of his life. This kind of signature could easily be forged.

9

Catalog Line Drawings

ON THE FOLLOWING PAGES APPEAR ALL KNOWN CATALOG DRAWINGS OF STEUBEN GLASS forms produced from 1903 to 1932, while Frederick Carder was in charge of the factory. The original drawings, made in India ink and pencil and placed in loose-leaf binders, were for factory use only. Carder numbered the items in the order in which he designed them for production, beginning with 1 in 1903 and ending with 7749 in about 1932. Special shapes for Marshall Field and Company, Crest Company, Art Lamp Company, and others were numbered from 8001 to 8578. Usually, these were designed for and sold exclusively to the specific companies, but occasionally regular production items appeared in this section—perhaps because a company asked for exclusive right to sell a regular production item in their area.

The drawings vary in scale, and dimensions were often omitted. Any dimensions given have been included, and items in the same numerical sequence usually have relatively the same scale.

Since the straight numerical arrangement as found in the original catalogs is rather confusing, the drawings in this book have been separated into categories to aid collectors and others interested in locating objects by category or shape. Some objects could have been placed in more than one category. For example, the categorizing of vases and bowls is often difficult. Whenever the catalog listed an object as a vase or bowl, it has been placed in that category here. Otherwise, an object has been assigned a category according to my best judgment. Large bowls and centerpieces appear in a separate category from the smaller ones. Other categories were assigned and grouped on the above guidelines.

Several hundred pages were missing, particularly from early catalogs, and so there are missing numbers. The lowest number found was the cruet, No. 97. Many of the early sketches were made by Carder himself. Later drawings in the 1920s and early 1930s were done by Bolas Manikowski, Edward Winship, and myself during the first two years I served as Carder's assistant.

Unfortunately, most of the catalog drawings are undated. From the meager references and notations on the catalog pages and other records, it is probable that Nos. 1 through about 5000 were done before the 1920s and from about 5000 on were done in the 1920s and up to about 1932.

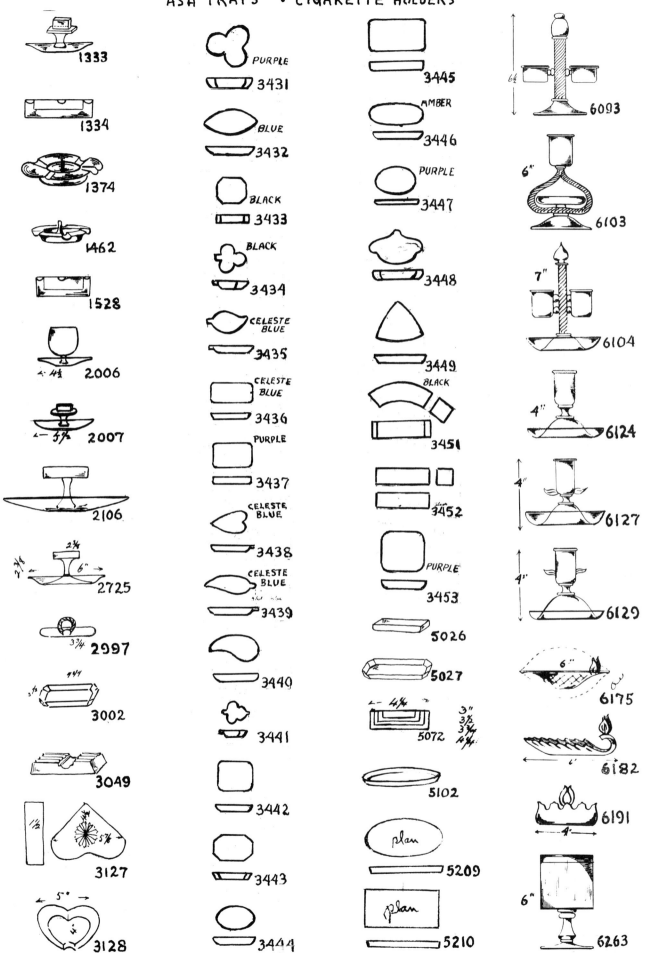

1333

1334

1374

1462

1528

2006

2007

2106

2725

2997

3002

3049

3127

3128

PURPLE
3431

BLUE
3432

BLACK
3433

BLACK
3434

CELESTE BLUE
3435

CELESTE BLUE
3436

PURPLE
3437

CELESTE BLUE
3438

CELESTE BLUE
3439

3440

3441

3442

3443

3444

3445

AMBER
3446

PURPLE
3447

3448

3449

BLACK
3451

3452

PURPLE
3453

5026

5027

5072

5102

plan
5209

plan
5210

6093

6103

6124

6127

6129

6175

6182

6191

6263

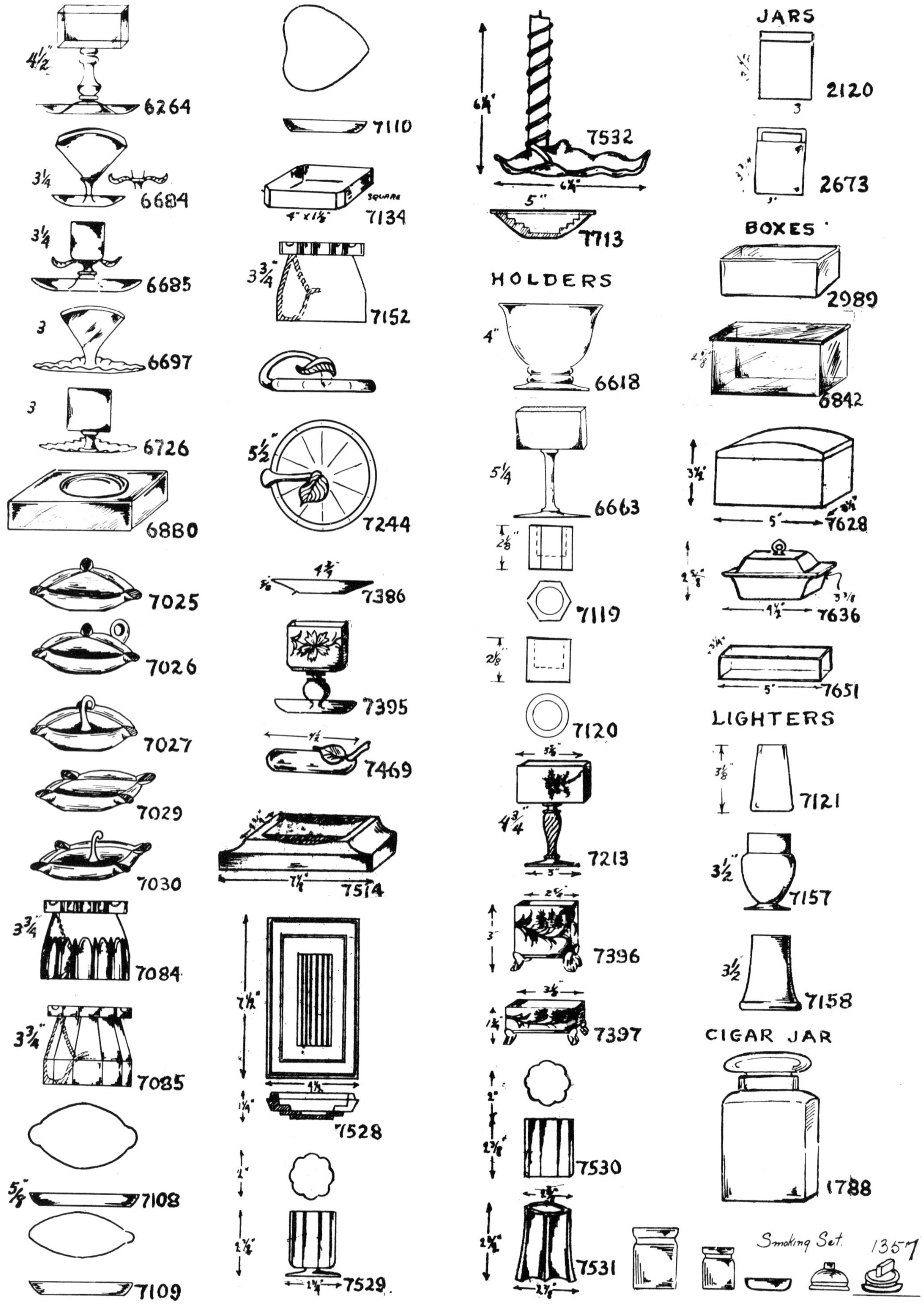
4½"
6264
3¼
6684
3¼
6685
3
6697
3
6726
6880
7025
7026
7027
7029
7030
3¾"
7084
3¾"
7085
5/8"
7108
7109
7110
SQUARE
4" x 1⅛"
7134
3¾"
7152
5½"
7244
4½"
7386
7395
4½
7469
7¼"
7514
7½"
1¼"
7528
7529
6¾"
6¾"
7532
5"
7713
HOLDERS
4"
6618
5¼
6663
2⅛"
7119
2⅛"
7120
4¾"
3"
7213
3"
7396
7397
2"
7530
7531
JARS
2120
2673
BOXES
2989
6842
3½"
5"
7628
4½"
7636
5"
7651
LIGHTERS
3⅛"
7121
3½"
7157
3½
7158
CIGAR JAR
1788
Smoking Set.
1357

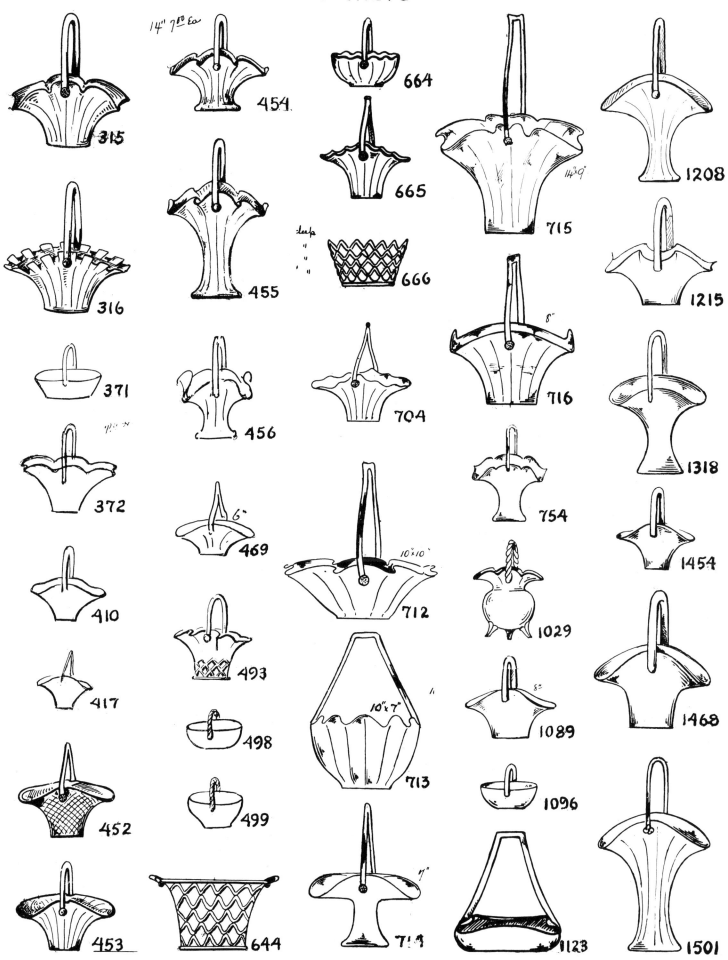

315

454

664

665

666

715

1208

316

455

716

1215

371

456

704

372

754

1318

410

469

1029

1454

417

493

712

1089

1468

452

498

1096

453

499

644

713

714

1123

1501

BASKETS

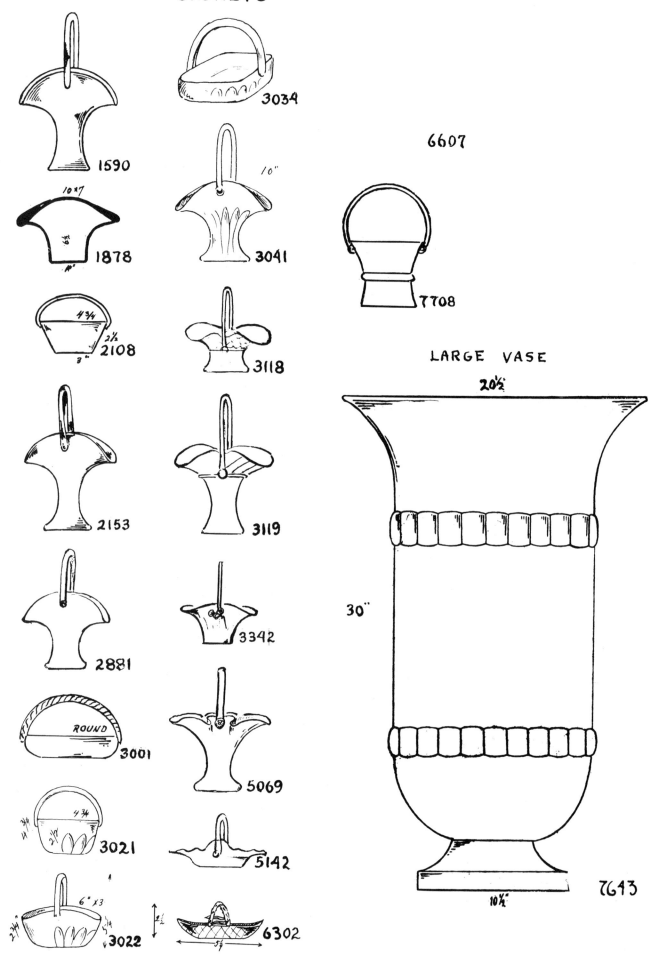

1590

10×7
1878

2108

2153

2881

ROUND
3001

3021

6"×3
3022

3034

10"
3041

3118

3119

3342

5069

5142

6302

6607

7708

LARGE VASE

20½

30"

10½

7643

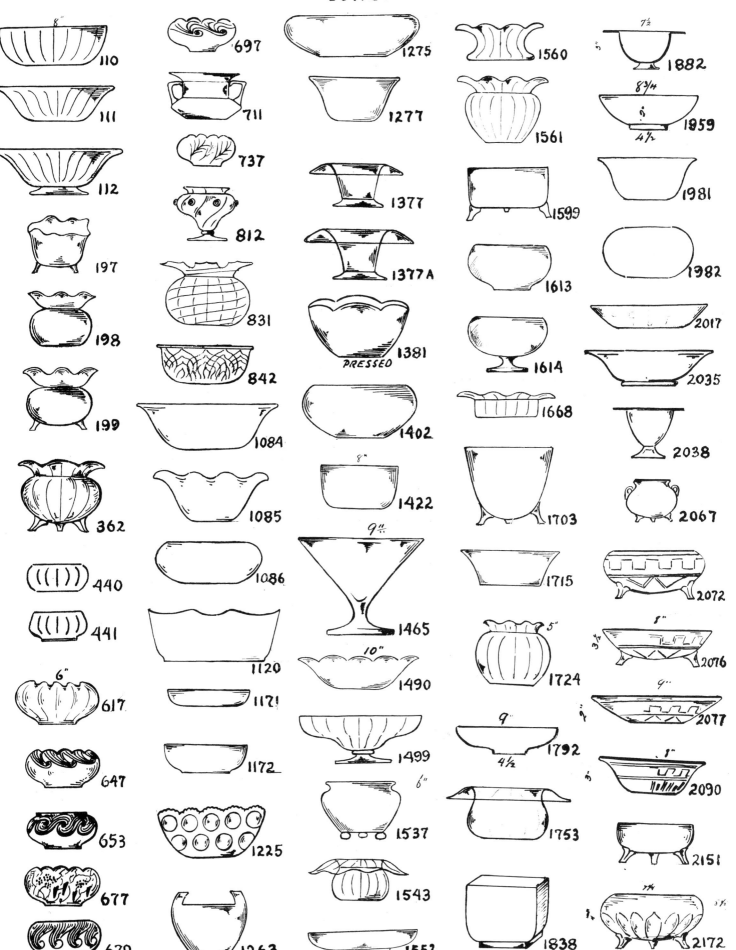

110
111
112
197
198
199
362
440
441
617
647
653
677
679
697
711
737
812
831
842
1084
1085
1086
1120
1171
1172
1225
1263
1275
1277
1377
1377A
1381 PRESSED
1402
1422 8"
1465 9"
1490 10"
1499
1537 6"
1543
1552
1560
1561
1599
1613
1614
1668
1703
1715
1724 5"
1792 9"
1753
1838
1882 7½
1959 8¾
1981
1982
2017
2035
2038
2067
2072
2076
2077 9"
2090
2151
2172

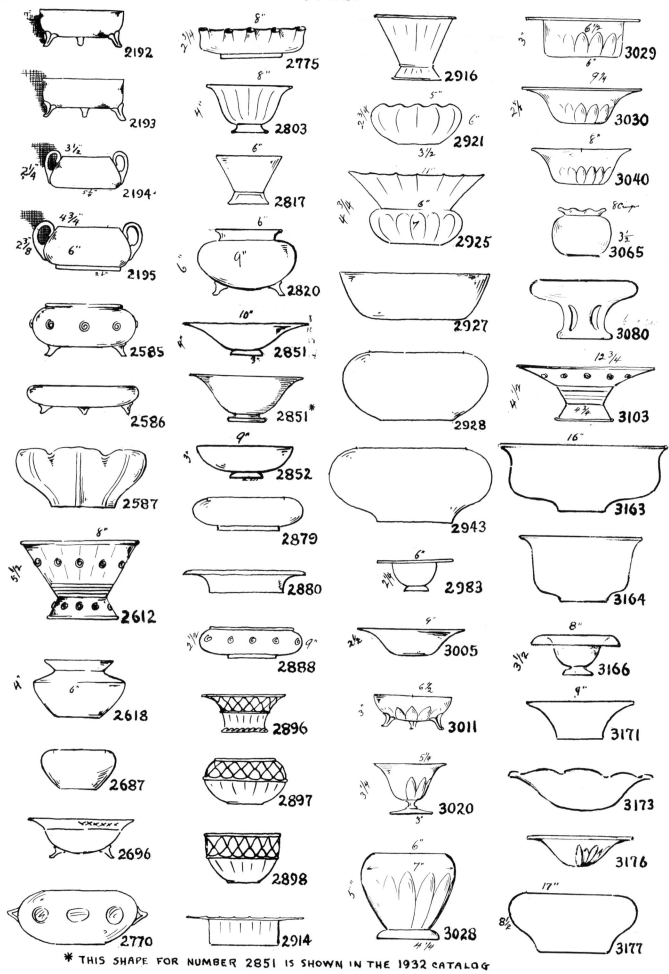

2192

2193

3½
2¼
5¼
2194

4¾
2⅜
6"
2"
2195

2585

2586

2587

8"
5½
2612

4"
6"
2618

2687

2696

2770

8"
2¾
2775

8"
4"
2803

6"
2817

6"
6"
9"
2820

10"
2851

2851 *

9"
3"
2852

2879

2880

2½
9"
2888

2896

2897

2898

2914

2916

5"
2¾
6"
2921
3½

11"
3¾
6"
4¼
7"
2925

2927

2928

2943

6"
2¼
2983

4"
3005

6½
3"
3011

5¼
3¾
3020
3"

6"
7"
5"
3028
4¼

6½
6"
3
3029

9¼
2¼
3030

8"
3040

8 cup
3½
3065

3080

12¾
4½
4¾
3103

16"
3163

3164

8"
3½
3166

9"
3171

3173

3176

17"
8½
3177

* THIS SHAPE FOR NUMBER 2851 IS SHOWN IN THE 1932 CATALOG

BOWLS

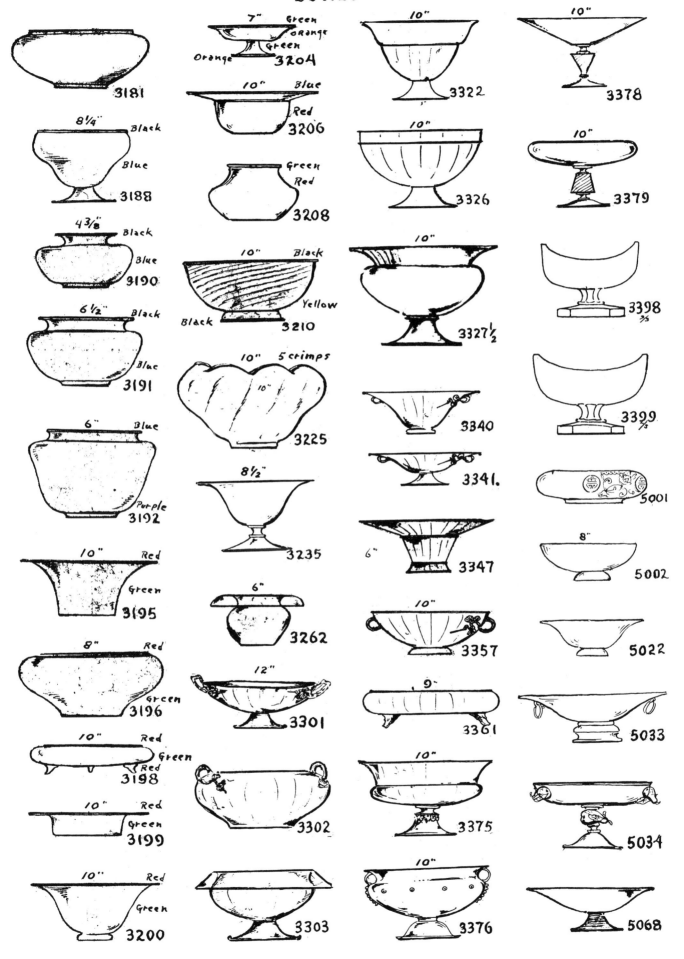

3181

7" Green
Orange
Green
Orange
3204

10" Blue
Red
3206

Green
Red
3208

8¼" Black
Blue
3188

4⅜" Black
Blue
3190

6½" Black
Blue
3191

6" Blue
Purple
3192

10" Red
Green
3195

8" Red
Green
3196

10" Red
Green
3198

10" Red
Green
3199

10" Red
Green
3200

10" Black
Yellow
Black
3210

10" 5 crimps
10"
3225

8½"
3235

6"
3262

12"
3301

3302

3303

10"
3322

10"
3326

10"
3327½

3340

3341.

6"
3347

10"
3357

9"
3361

10"
3375

10"
3376

10"
3378

10"
3379

3398 ⅔

3399 ⅔

5001

8"
5002

5022

5033

5034

5068

BOWLS

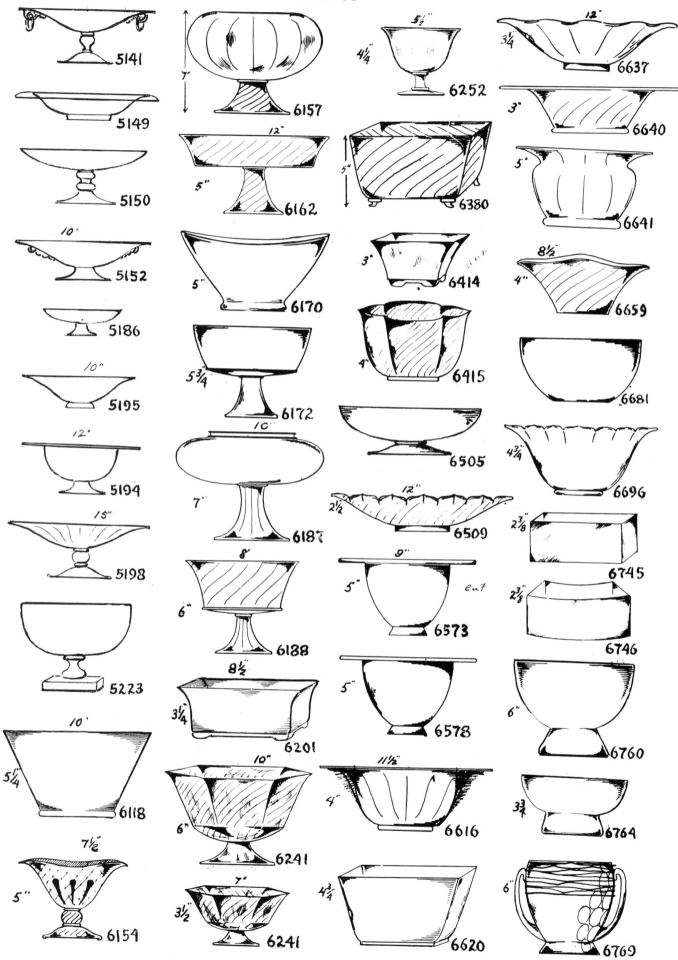

5141

5149

5150

10" 5152

5186

10" 5195

12" 5194

15" 5198

5223

10" 5¼" 6118

7½" 5" 6154

7" 6157

12" 5" 6162

5" 6170

5¾" 6172

10" 7" 6187

8" 6" 6188

8½" 3¼" 6201

10" 6" 6241

7" 3½" 6241

5½" 4¼" 6252

5" 6380

3" 6414

4" 6415

6505

12" 2½" 6509

9" 5" cut 6573

5" 6578

11½" 4" 6616

4¾" 6620

12" 3¼" 6637

3" 6640

5" 6641

8½" 4" 6659

6681

4¾" 6696

2⅜" 6745

2⅜" 6746

6" 6760

3¾" 6764

6" 6769

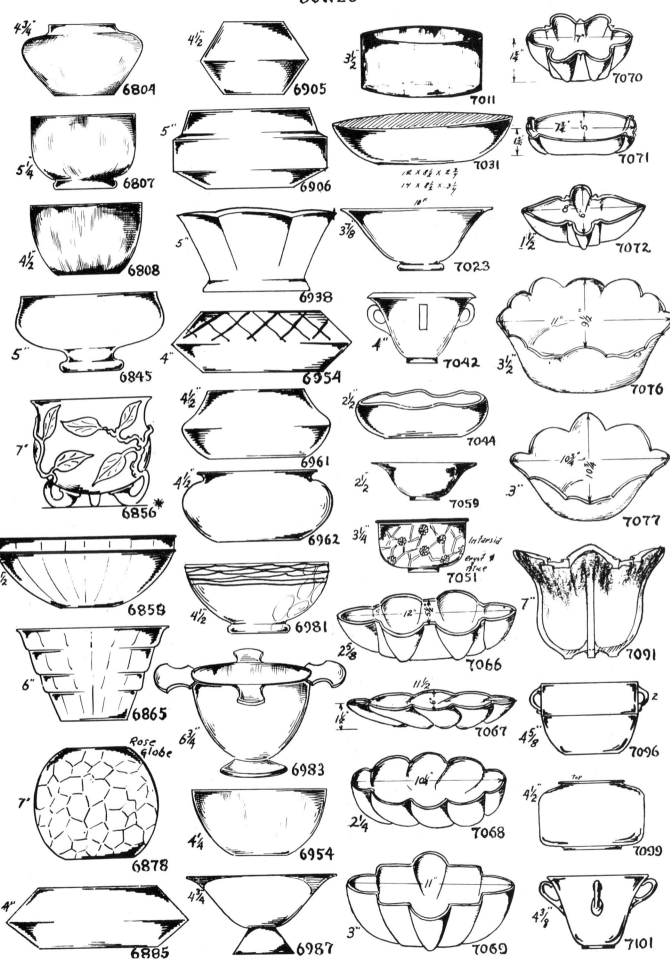

4 3/4" — 6804
4 1/2" — 6905
3 1/2" — 7011
1 1/2" — 7070

5" — 6906
5 1/4" — 6807
7031
12 x 8 1/2 x 2 7/8
14 x 8 1/2 x 3 1/2
7 1/4" — 7071

4 1/2" — 6808
5" — 6938
10"
3 7/8" — 7023
8" — 7072
1 1/2"

5" — 6845
4" — 6954
4" — 7042
11"
9 1/2"
3 1/2" — 7076

7" — 6856 *
4 1/2" — 6961
2 1/2" — 7044
10 3/4" — 7077
3"
10 1/4"

4 1/2" — 6858
4 1/2" — 6962
2 1/2" — 7059
3 1/4" — 7051
Intarsio
cryst & blue

6" — 6865
4 1/2" — 6981
12"
2 5/8" — 7066
7" — 7091

Rose Globe
7" — 6878
6 3/4" — 6983
11 1/2"
6"
1 1/2" — 7067
2" — 7096
4 5/8"

4 1/4" — 6954
10 1/4"
2 1/4" — 7068
4 1/2" — 7099
Top

4" — 6885
4 3/4" — 6987
11"
3" — 7069
4 3/8" — 7101

* ALSO LISTED AS A VASE IN THE CATALOG

BOWLS

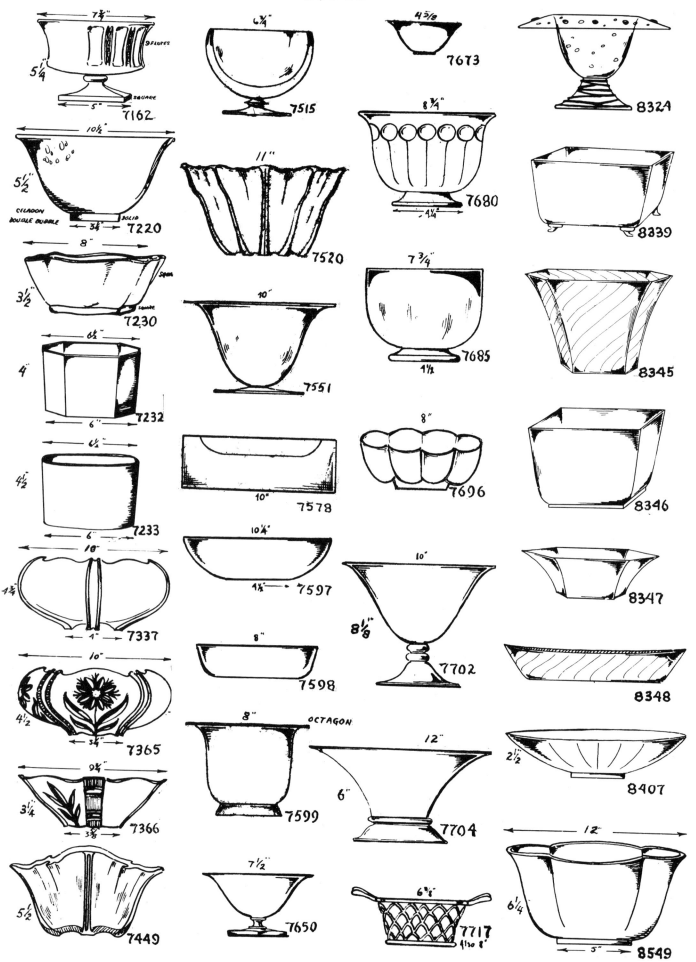

7162

7515

7673

8324

7220

7520

7680

8339

7230

7551

7685

8345

7232

7578

7696

8346

7233

7597

7347

7337

7598

7702

8348

7365

7599

7704

8407

7366

7650

7717

8549

7449

BOWLS - CENTERPIECES

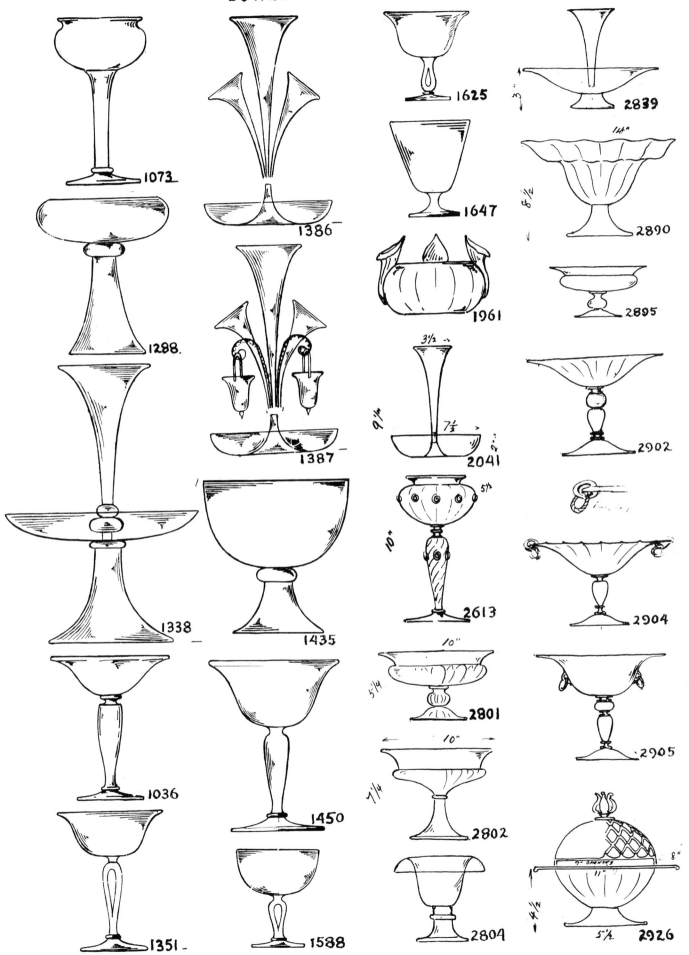

1073

1288.

1338

1036

1351

1386

1387

1435

1450

1588

1625

1647

1961

2041

2613

2801

2802

2804

2839

2890

2895

2902

2904

2905

2926

BOWLS - CENTERPIECES

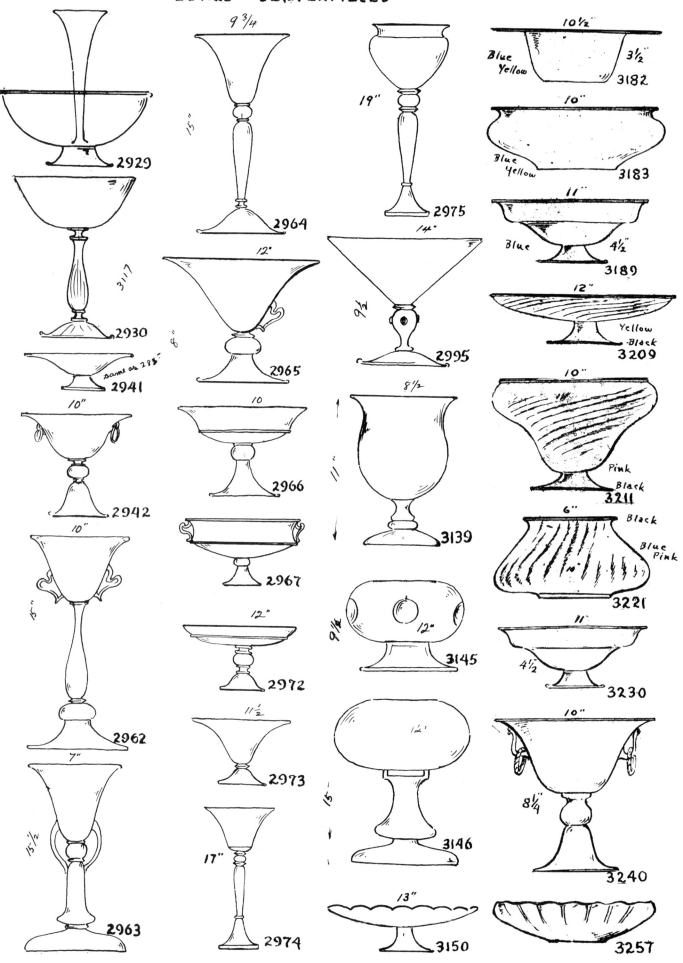

2929

9 3/4

2964

19"

2975

10 1/2
Blue
Yellow
3 1/2
3182

3117

2930

10"
Blue
Yellow
3183

same as 288
2941

12"

2965

14"
9 1/2

2995

11"
Blue
4 1/2"
3189

12"
Yellow
Black
3209

10"

2942

10

2966

8 1/2

3139

10"
Pink
Black
3211

10"

2962

2967

12"
3145

6"
Black
Blue
Pink
3221

7"

2963

12"

2972

11 1/2

2973

17"

2974

1 2

3146

11"
4 1/2
3230

10"
8 1/4"
3240

13"

3150

3257

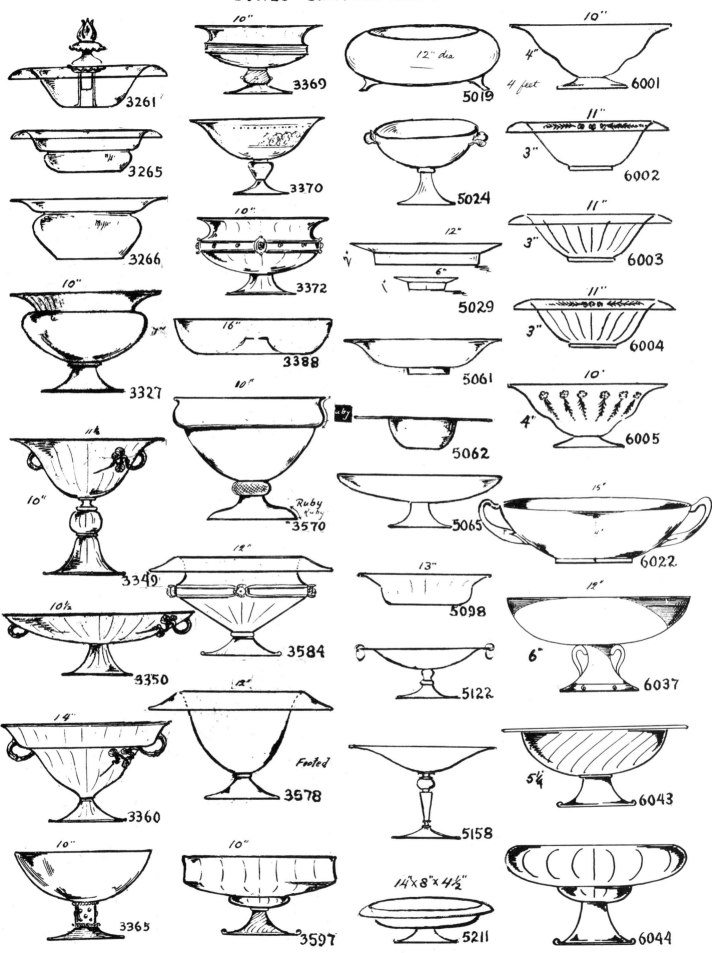

3261

3265

3266

3327

3349

3350

3360

3365

10" 3369

3370

10" 3372

16" 3388

10" Ruby Ruby 3570

12" 3584

12" Footed 3578

10" 3597

12" dia 5019

5024

12" 6" 5029

5061

5062

5065

13" 5098

5122

5158

14"x 8"x 4½" 5211

10" 4" 4 feet 6001

11" 3" 6002

11" 3" 6003

11" 3" 6004

10" 4" 6005

15" 6022

12" 6" 6037

5¼" 6043

6044

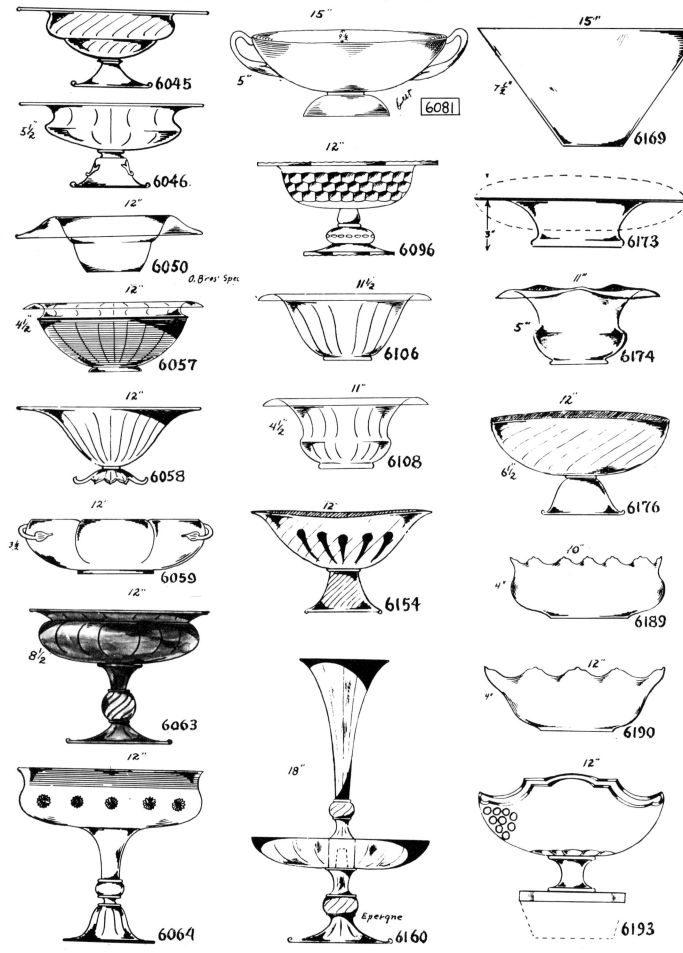

6045

6046

3½"

12"
6050

O. Bros' Spec.

12"
4½"
6057

12"
6058

12"
3¼"
6059

12"
8½"
6063

12"
6064

15"
9¼
6081
6ut

12"
6096

11½"
6106

11"
4½"
6108

12"
6154

18"
Epergne
6160

15"
7½"
6169

3"
6173

11"
5"
6174

12"
6½"
6176

10"
4"
6189

12"
4"
6190

12"
6193

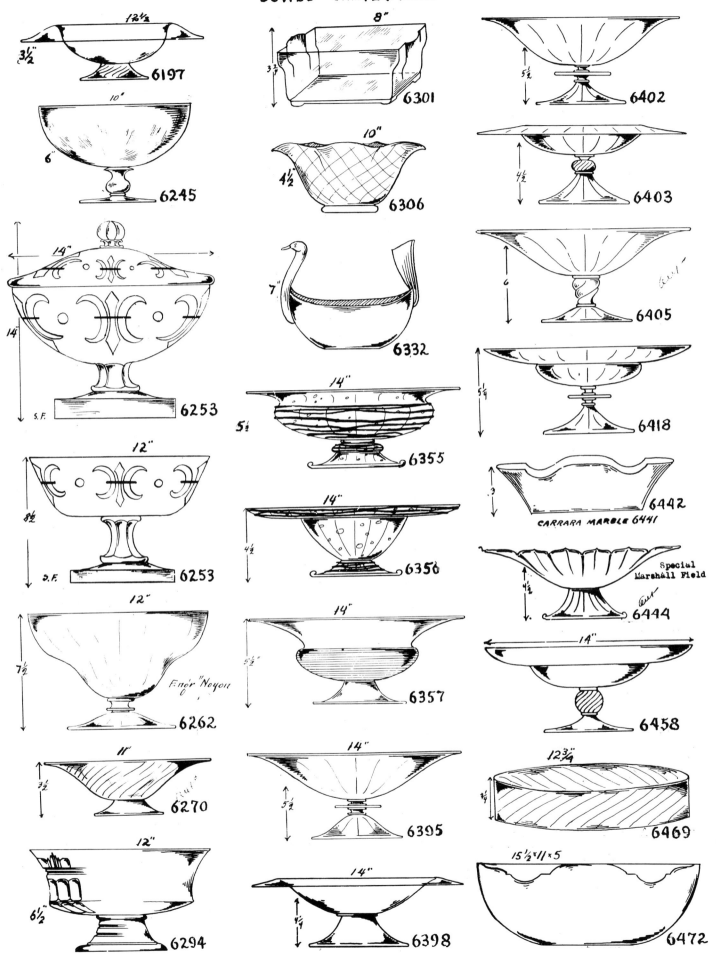

6197

6245

6253

6253

6262

6270

6294

6301

6306

6332

6355

6350

6357

6395

6398

6402

6403

6405

6418

CARRARA MARBLE 6441

6442

Special Marshall Field 6444

6458

6469

6472

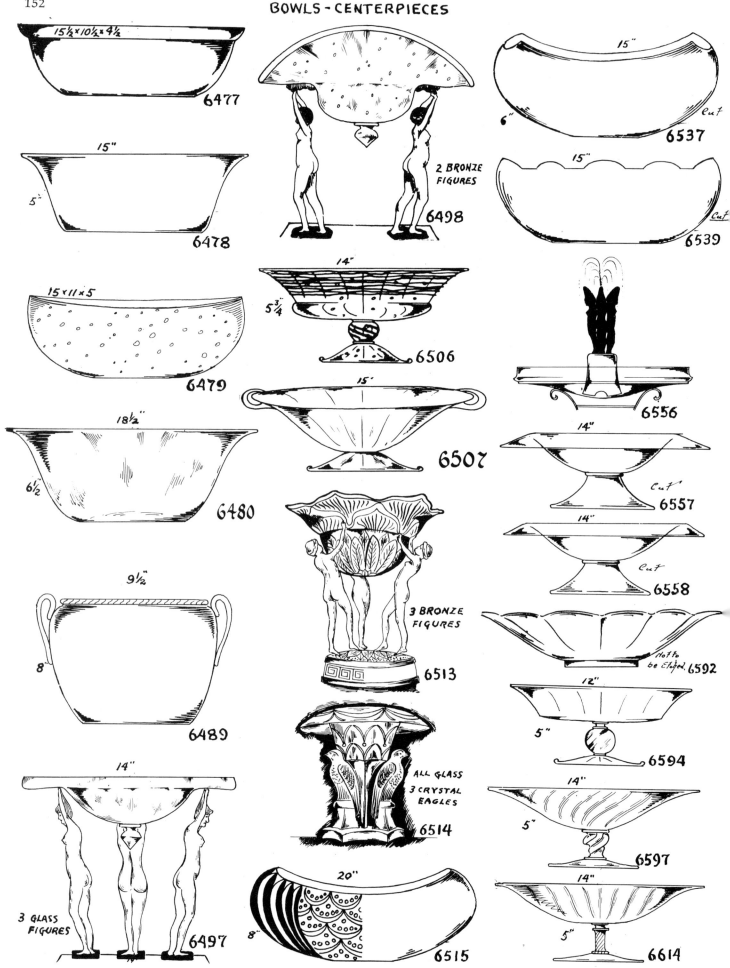

15½ × 10½ × 4½
6477

15"
5"
6478

15 × 11 × 5
6479

18½"
6½"
6480

9½"
8"
6489

14"
3 GLASS FIGURES
6497

2 BRONZE FIGURES
6498

14"
5¾"
6506

15"
6507

3 BRONZE FIGURES
6513

ALL GLASS 3 CRYSTAL EAGLES
6514

20"
8"
6515

15"
6"
Cut
6537

15"
Cut
6539

6556

14"
Cut
6557

14"
Cut
6558

Not to be Etched. 6592

12"
5"
6594

14"
5"
6597

14"
5"
6614

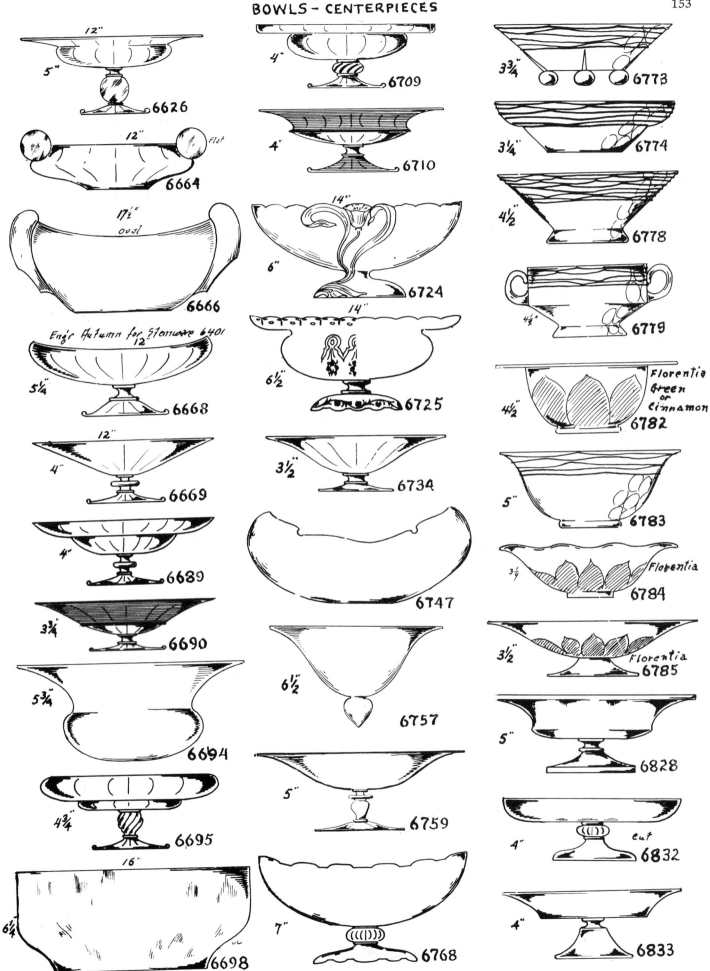

12"
5"
6626

12"
Flat
6664

17½"
oval
6666

Eng'r Autumn for Stemware 6401
12"
5¼"
6668

12"
4"
6669

4"
6689

3¾"
6690

5¾"
6694

4¾"
6695

16"
6¼"
6698

4"
6709

4"
6710

14"
6"
6724

14"
6½"
6725

3½"
6734

6747

6½"
6757

5"
6759

7"
6768

3¾"
6773

3¼"
6774

4½"
6778

4½"
6779

Florentia
Green
or
Cinnamon
4½"
6782

5"
6783

Florentia
3¼"
6784

3½"
Florentia
6785

5"
6828

cut
4"
6832

4"
6833

BOWLS - CENTERPIECES

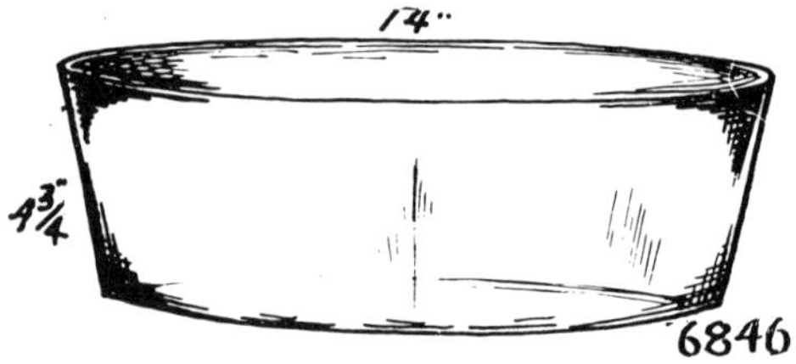

14"
4¾"
6846

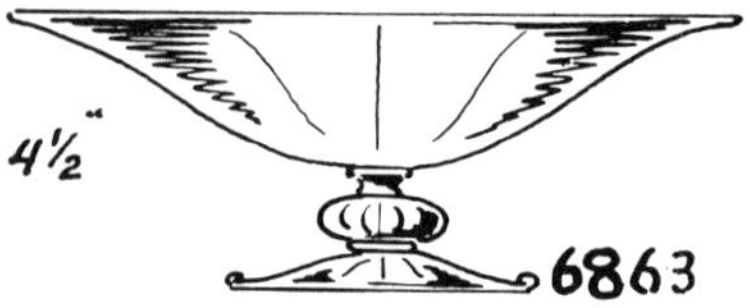

4½"
6863

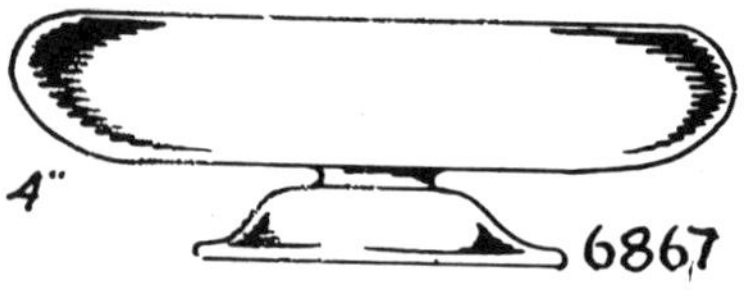

4"
6867

5½"
6868

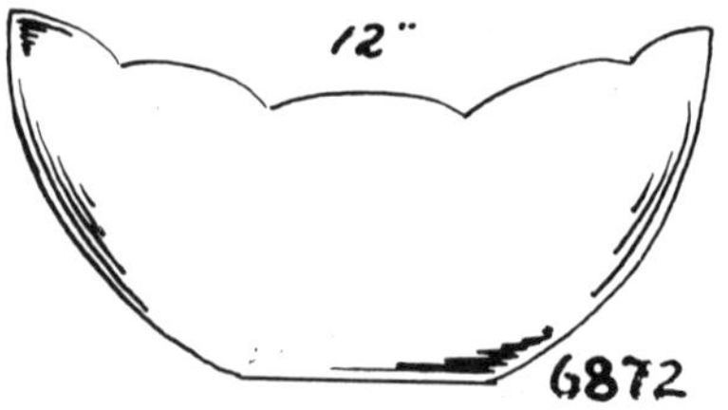

12"
6872

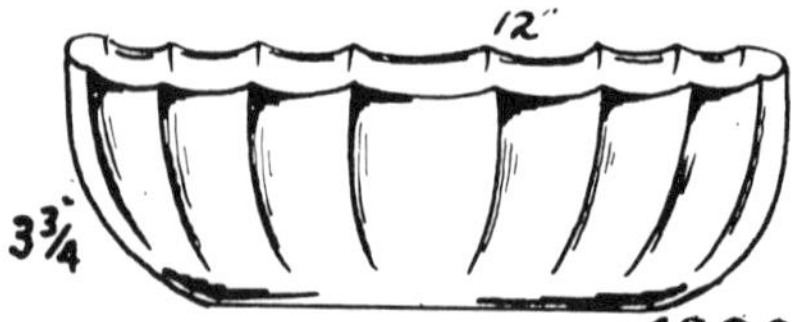

12"
3¾"
6890

13"
3¾"
6891

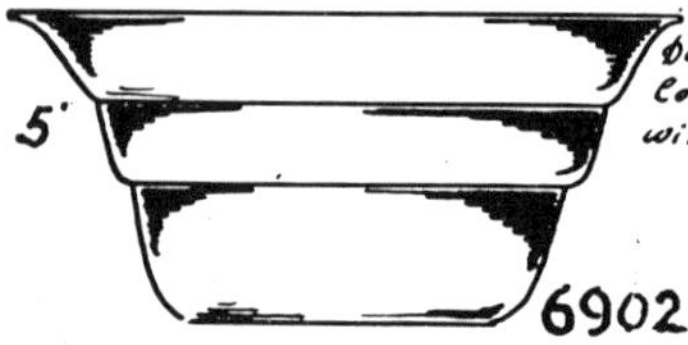

5"
Do not
Confuse
with 6865
6902

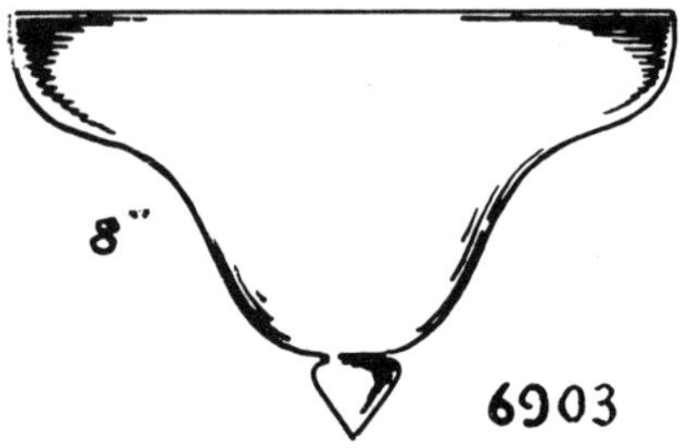

8"
6903

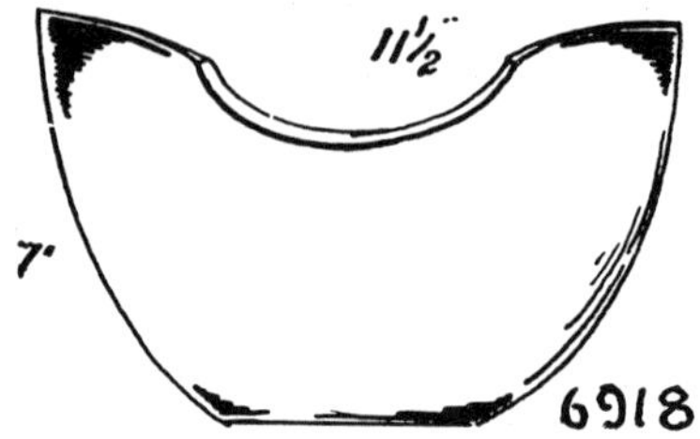

11½"
7"
6918

5"
6930

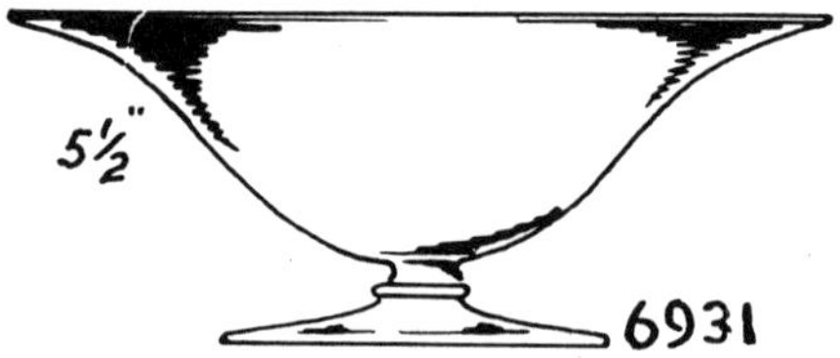

5½"
6931

5"
6967

5"
6985

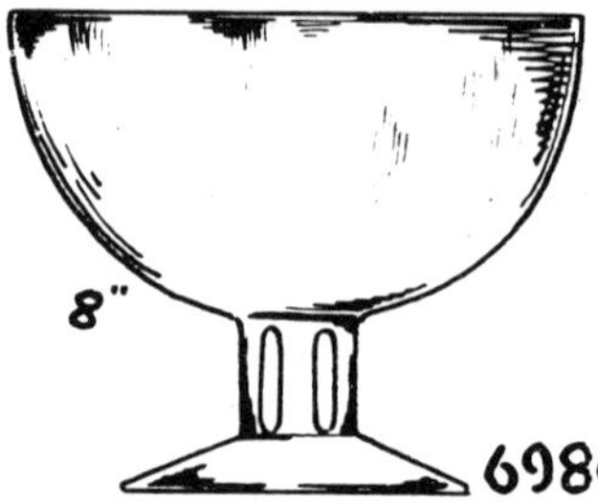

8"
6986

4½"
6995

3¼"
6996

4"
6997

5"
7003

6"
7004

6½"
7005

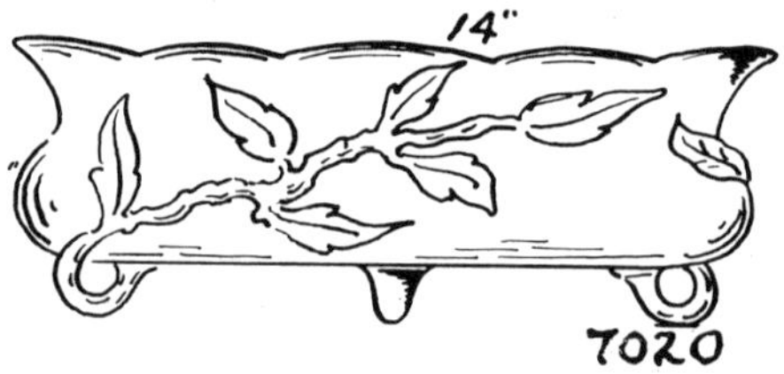

14"
7020

3½"
7049

7¼"
7057

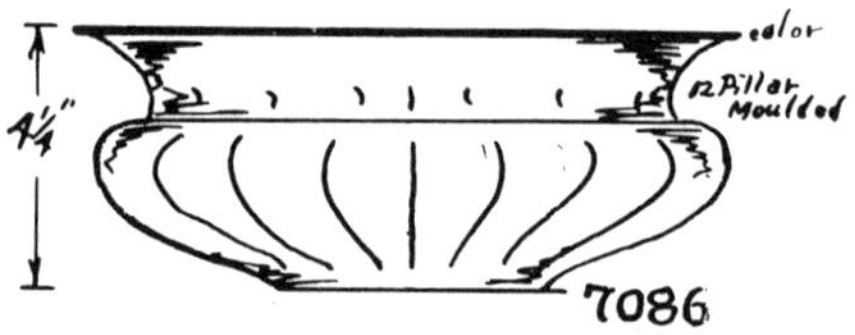

color
12 Pillar
Moulded
4¼"
7086

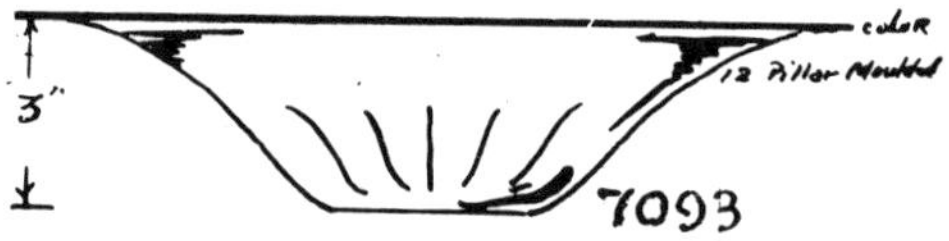

color
12 Pillar Moulded
3"
7093

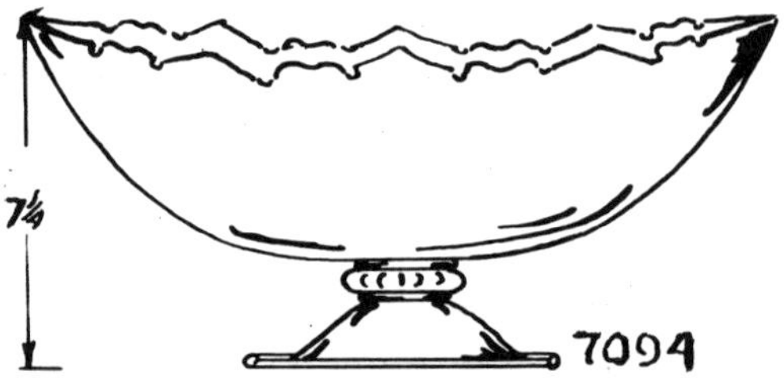

7½"
7094

BOWLS - CENTERPIECES

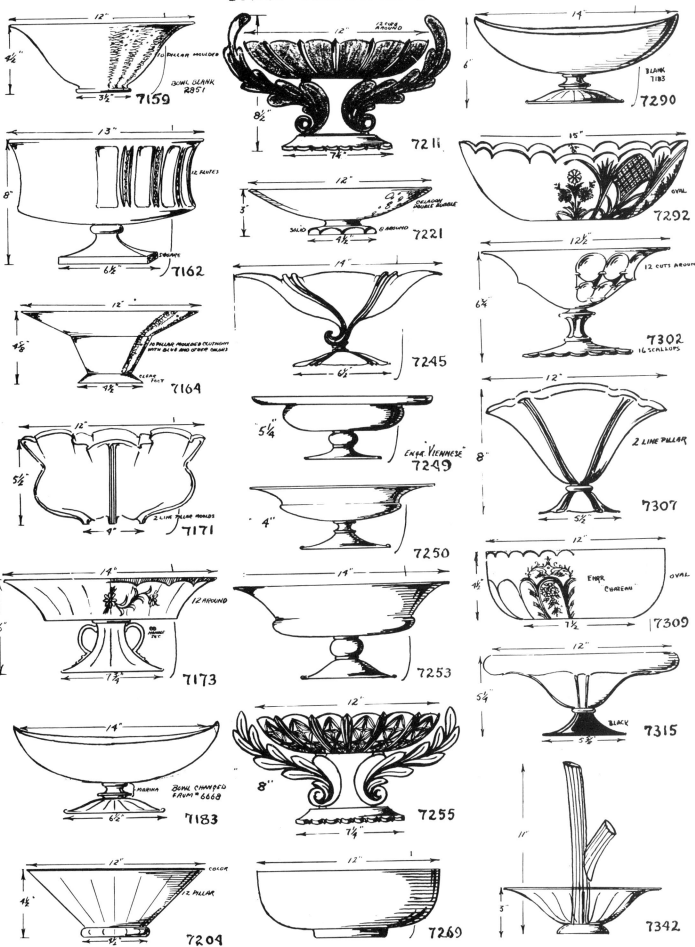

7159 — 12", 4½", 3½", 10 PILLAR MOULDED, BOWL BLANK 2851

7211 — 12", 12 CUTS AROUND, 8½", 7¼"

7290 — 14", 6", BLANK 7183

7162 — 13", 8", 12 FLUTES, 6½", SQUARE

7221 — 12", 3", CELADON DOUBLE BUBBLE, SOLID, 4½", 8 AROUND

7292 — 15", OVAL

7164 — 12", 4⅝", 4½", 10 PILLAR MOULDED CLUTHGA WITH BLUE AND OTHER COLORS, CLEAR FOOT

7245 — 14", 6½"

7302 — 12½", 12 CUTS AROUND, 6¾", 16 SCALLOPS

7171 — 12", 5½", 9", 2 LINE PILLAR MOULDS

7249 — 5¼", ENGR. VIENNESE

7307 — 12", 8", 2 LINE PILLAR, 5½"

7250 — 4"

7173 — 14", 6", 12 AROUND, 7¾"

7253 — 14"

7309 — 12", 4½", ENGR. CHATEAU, OVAL, 7½"

7183 — 14", MARINA, BOWL CHANGED FROM #6668, 6½"

7255 — 12", 8", 7¼"

7315 — 12", 5¼", BLACK, 5⅝"

7209 — 12", 4½", COLOR, 12 PILLAR, 4"

7269 — 12"

7342 — 11", 3"

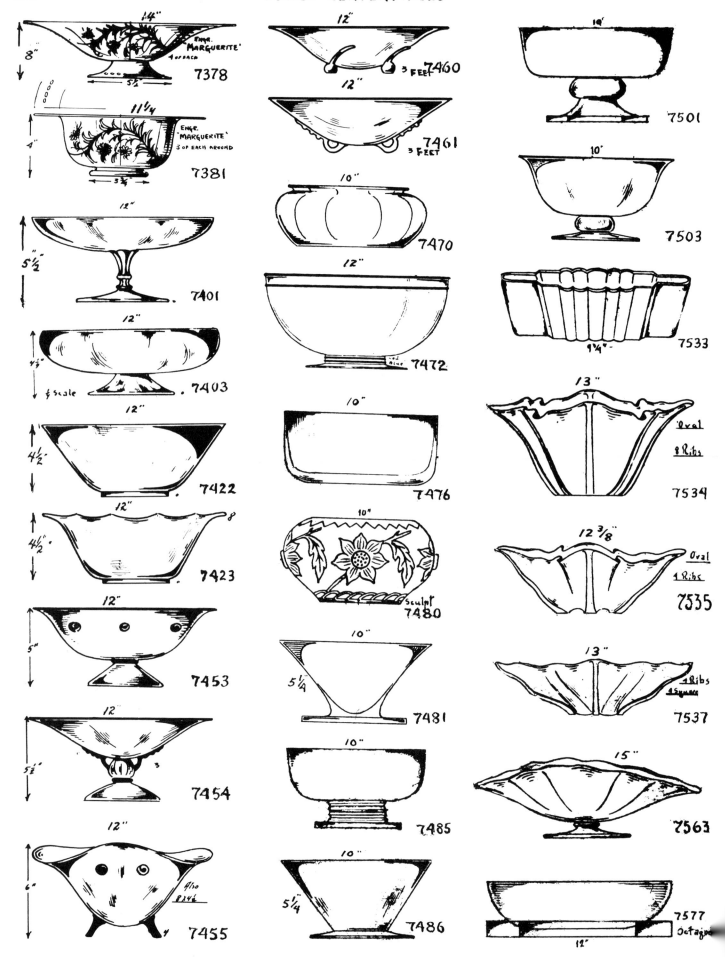

8"
14"
Engr. "MARGUERITE" 4 of each
5¼"
7378

11¼"
4"
Engr. "MARGUERITE" 3 of each around
3¾"
7381

12"
5½"
7401

12"
4½"
⅓ Scale
7403

12"
4½"
7422

12"
4½"
8
7423

12"
5"
7453

12"
5½"
3
7454

12"
6"
Also 8x4½
4
7455

12"
3 FEET
7460

12"
3 FEET
7461

10"
7470

12"
Red Blue
7472

10"
7476

10"
Sculpt
7480

10"
5¼
7481

10"
7485

10"
5¼
7486

10"
7501

10"
7503

9¾"
7533

13"
Oval
8 Ribs
7534

12⅜"
Oval
4 Ribs
7535

13"
4 Ribs
4 Square
7537

15"
7563

7577
Octagon
12"

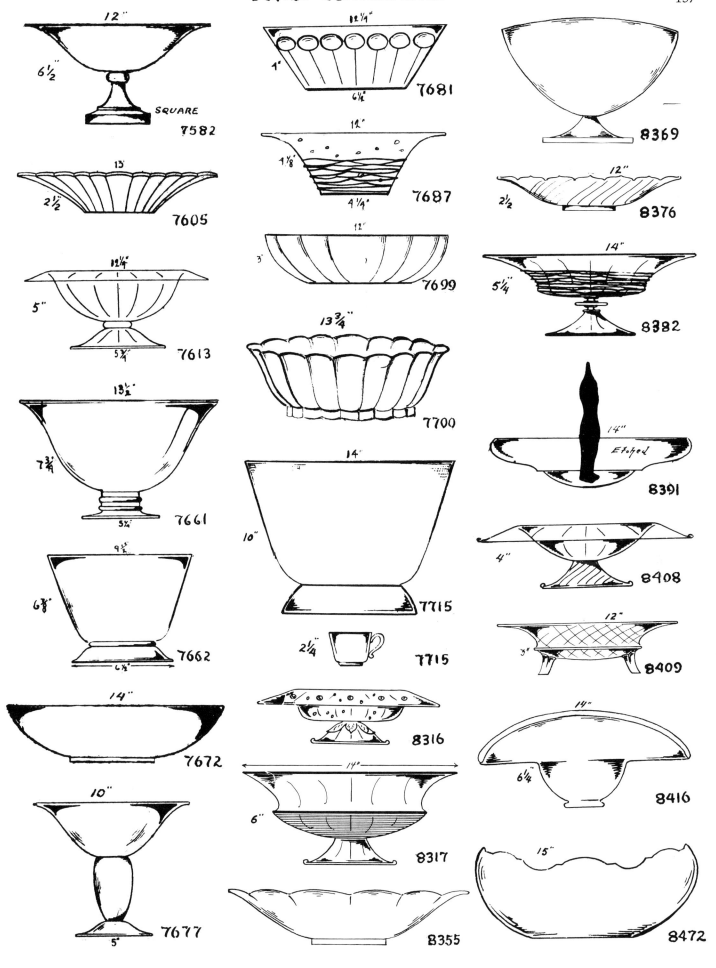

12″
6½″
SQUARE
7582

13″
2½″
7605

12¼″
5″
5¼″
7613

13½″
7¾″
5¼″
7661

9½″
6⅞″
6½″
7662

14″
7672

10″
5″
7677

12¼″
1″
6½″
7681

12″
1⅛″
4¼″
7687

12″
3″
7699

13¾″
7700

14″
10″
7715

2¼″
7715

8316

14″
6″
8317

8355

8369

12″
2½″
8376

14″
5¼″
8382

14″
Etched
8391

4″
8408

12″
3″
8409

14″
6¼″
8416

15″
8472

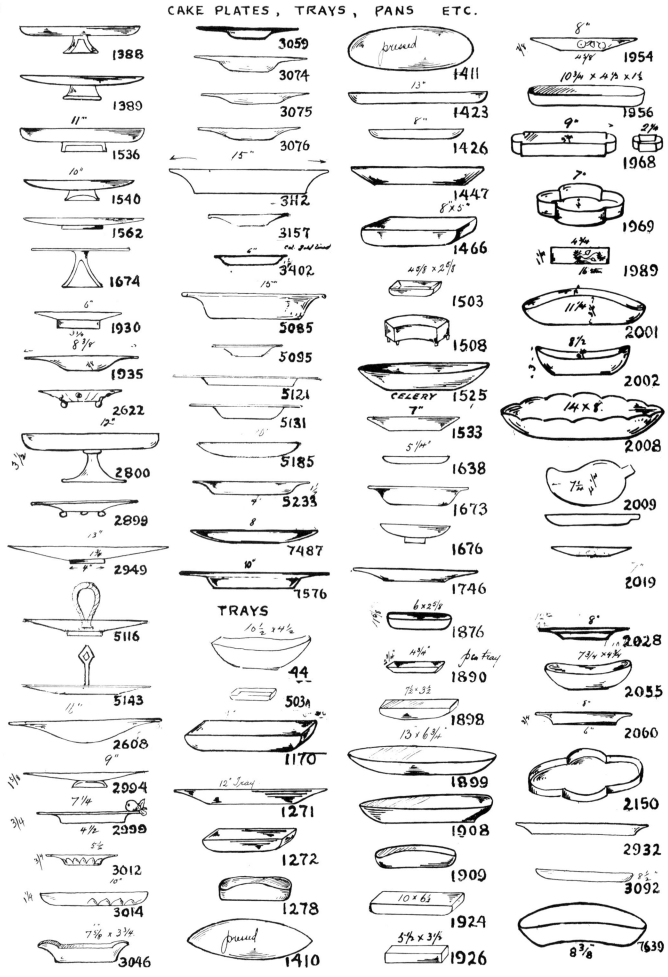

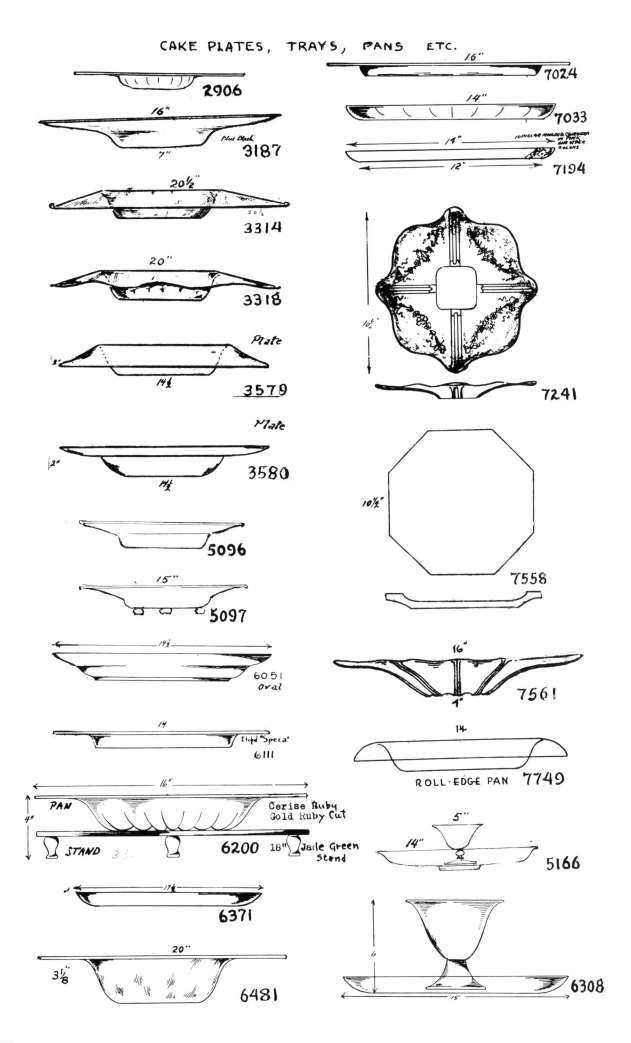

2906

16"
7"
Blue Black
3187

20½"
20½
3314

20"
3318

Plate
14½
3579

Plate
2"
14½
3580

5096

15"
5097

14½
6051
Oval

14
Etch'd "Speza"
6111

16"
PAN
4"
Cerise Ruby
Gold Ruby Cut
STAND
6200 18" *Jade Green Stand*

17½
6371

20"
3⅛"
6481

16"
7024

14"
7033

14"
10 PILLAR MOLDED OFFERED IN PINK AND OTHER COLORS
12"
7194

10½
7241

10½"
7558

16"
1"
7561

14
ROLL-EDGE PAN 7749

5"
14"
5166

6
15
6308

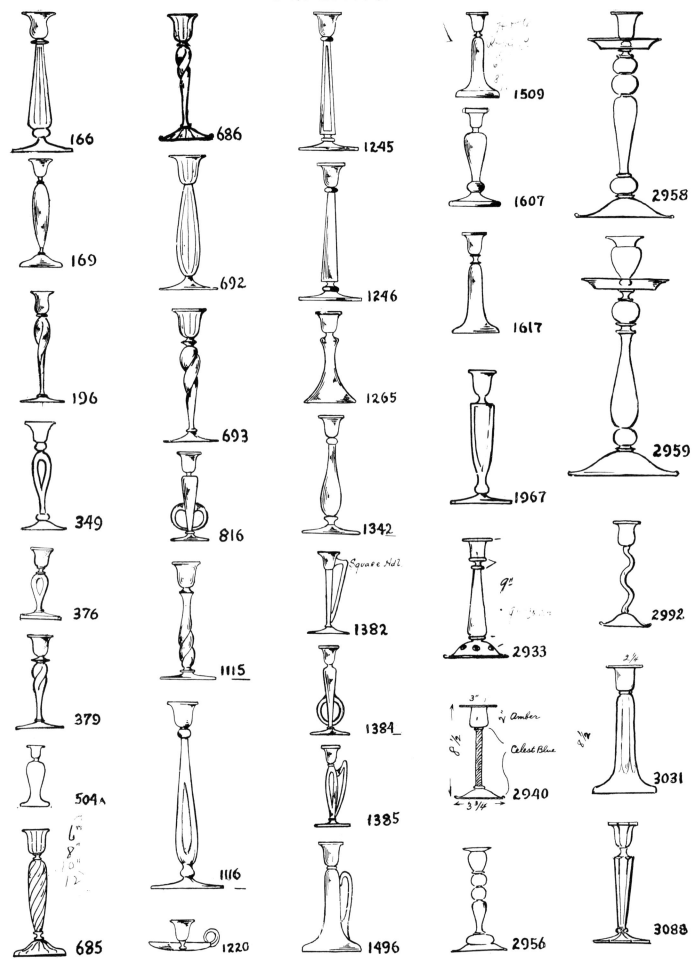

166

169

196

349

376

379

504 A

685

686

692

693

816

1115

1116

1220

1245

1246

1265

1342

1382 *Square Hdl.*

1384

1385

1496

1509

1607

1617

1967

2933 *9"*

2940 *3" ½ Amber, Celest Blue, 8½", 3¾"*

2956

2958

2959

2992

3031 *2¼ 8½"*

3088

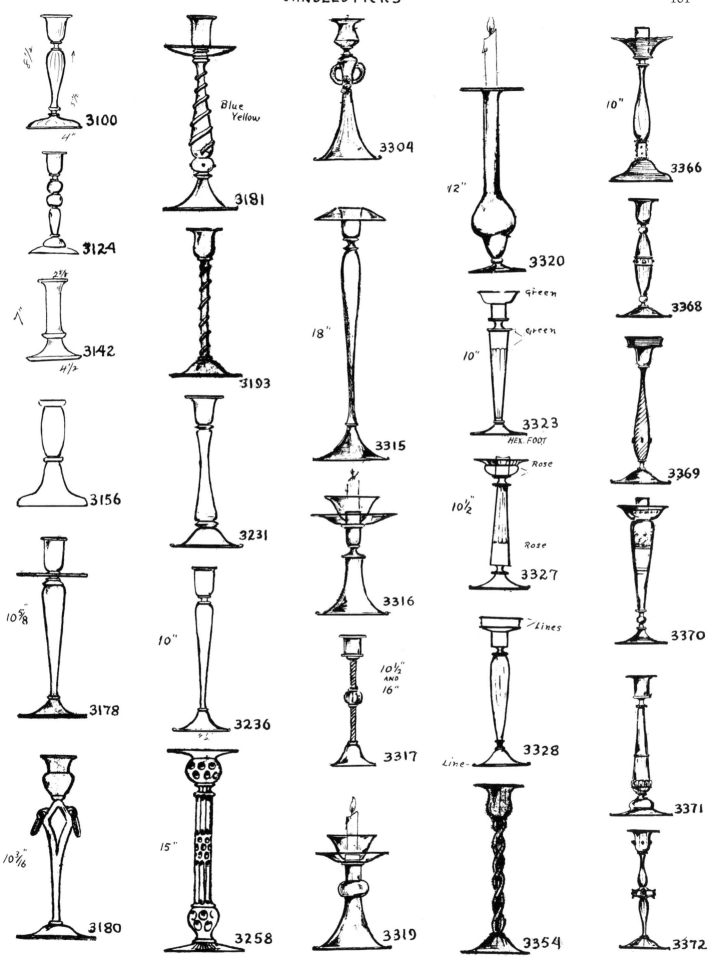

3100
8½
3½
4"

3124

3142
2⅝
7"
4½

3156

3178
10⅝"

3180
10³⁄₁₆"

3181
Blue
Yellow

3193

3231

3236
10"
4½

3258
15"

3304

3315
18"

3316

3317
10½"
AND
16"

3319

3320
12"

3323
Green
Green
10"
HEX. FOOT

3327
10½
Rose
Rose

3328
Lines
Line-

3354

3366
10"

3368

3369

3370

3371

3372

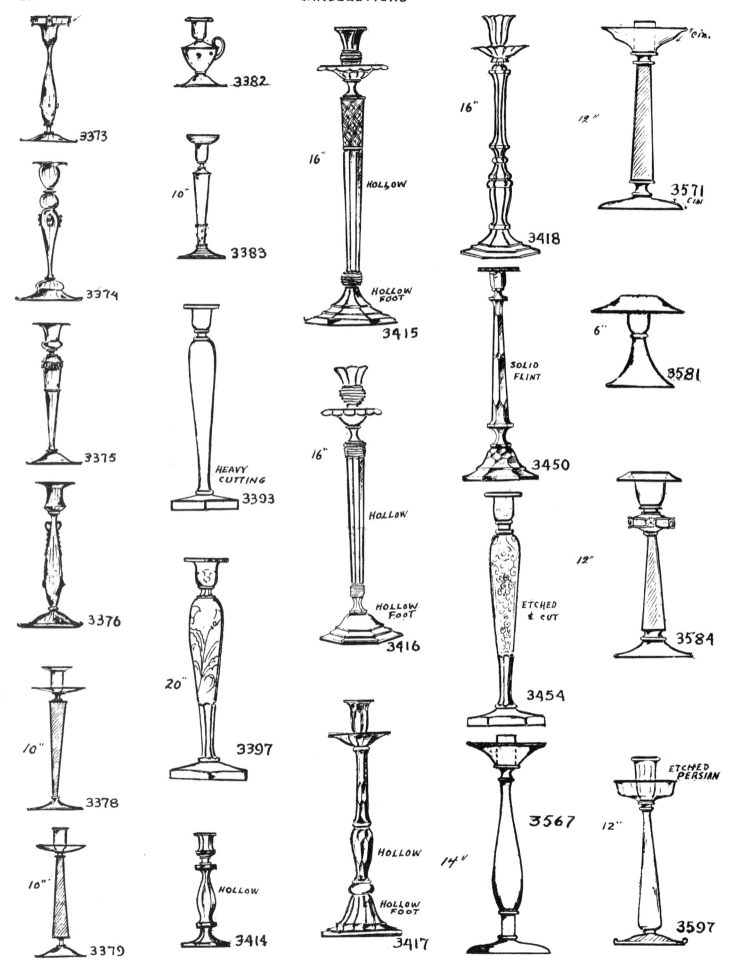

3373

3374

3375

3376

10" 3378

10" 3379

3382

10" 3383

HEAVY CUTTING 3393

20" 3397

3414 HOLLOW

16" HOLLOW

HOLLOW FOOT 3415

16" HOLLOW

HOLLOW FOOT 3416

HOLLOW

HOLLOW FOOT 3417

16" 3418

SOLID FLINT 3450

ETCHED & CUT 3454

14" 3567

12" 7 in. 3571 CIN

6" 3581

12" 3584

ETCHED PERSIAN 12" 3597

CANDLESTICKS

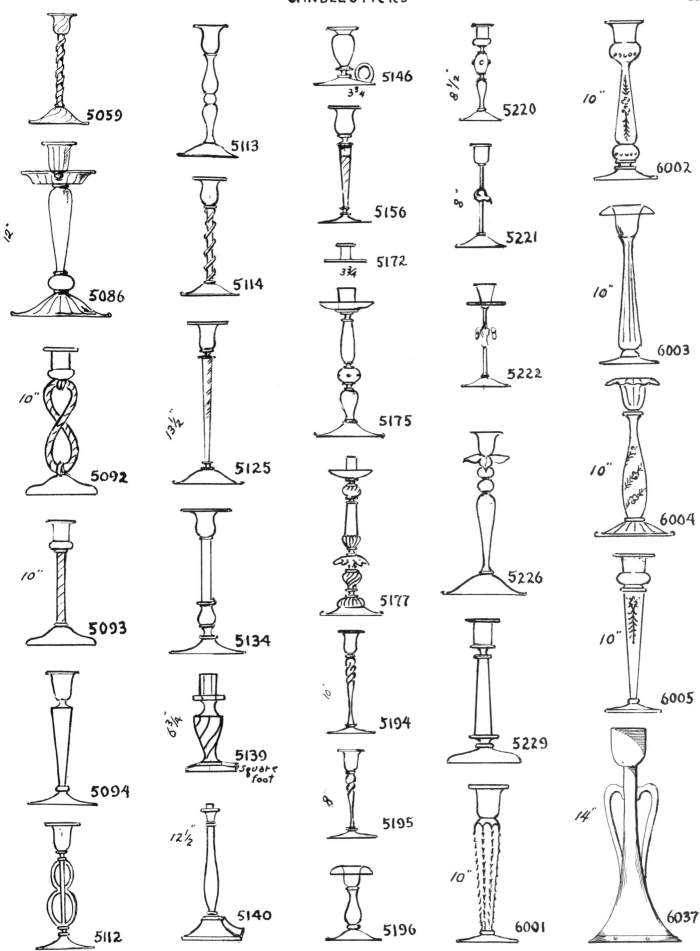

5059

5086   12″

5092   10″

5093   10″

5094

5112

5113

5114

5125   13½″

5134

5139   6¾″ square foot

5140   12½″

5146   3¾″

5156

5172   3¾″

5175

5177

5194   10″

5195   8″

5196

5220   8½″

5221   8″

5222

5226

5229

6001   10″

6002   10″

6003   10″

6004   10″

6005   10″

6037   14″

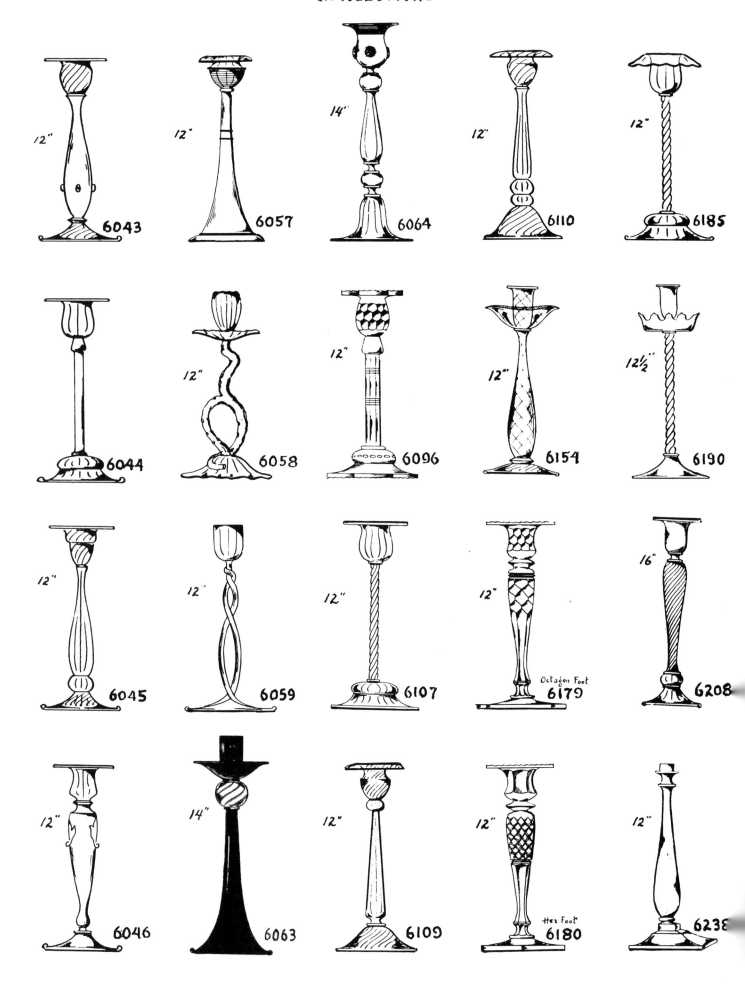

12" 6043

12" 6057

14" 6064

12" 6110

12" 6185

12" 6044

12" 6058

12" 6096

12" 6154

12½" 6190

12" 6045

12" 6059

12" 6107

12" Octagon Foot 6179

16" 6208

12" 6046

14" 6063

12" 6109

12" Hex Foot 6180

12" 6238

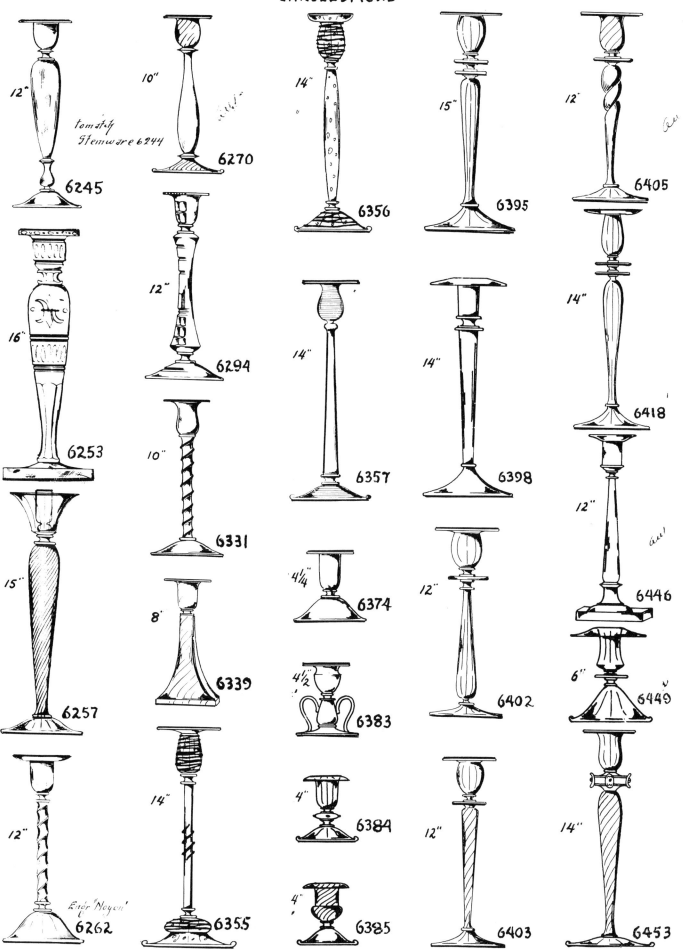

12"
to match
Stemware 6244
6245

10"
6270

14"
6356

15"
6395

12"
6405

16"
6253

12"
6294

14"
6357

14"
6398

14"
6418

15"
6257

10"
6331

4 1/4"
6374

12"
6402

12"
6446

8"
6339

4 1/2"
6383

6"
6449

12"
6262
Engr "Noyon"

14"
6355

4"
6384

4"
6385

12"
6403

14"
6453

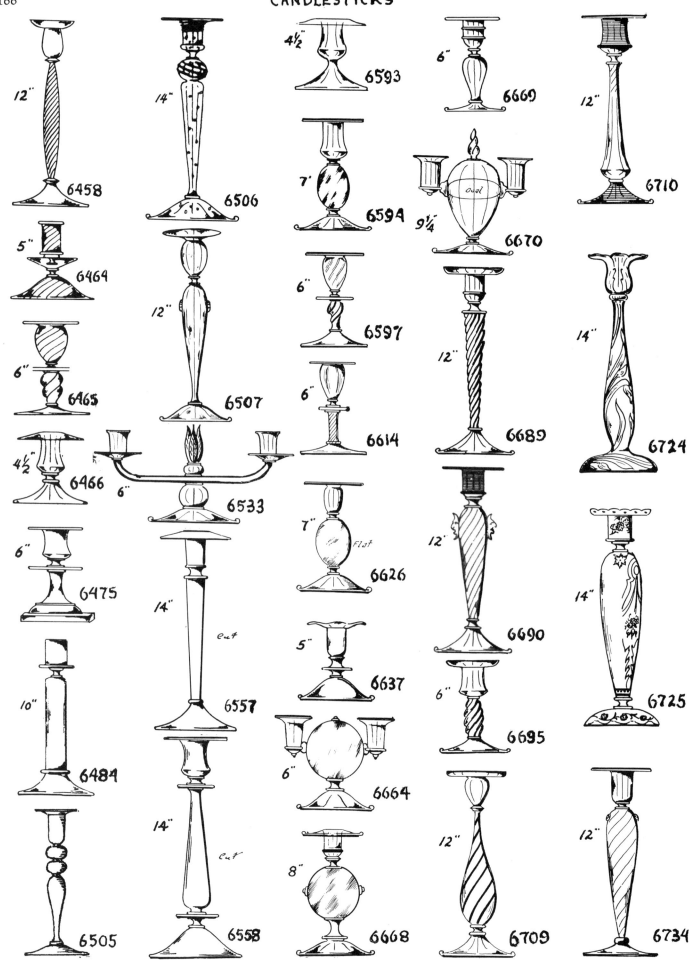

6458
12"

6464
5"

6465
6"

6466
4½"

6475
6"

6484
10"

6505

6506
14"

6507
12"

6533
6"

6557
14" Cut

6558
14" Cut

6593
4½"

6594
7"

6597
6"

6614
6"

6626
7" Flat

6637
5"

6664
6"

6668
8"

6669
6"

6670
9¼" Oval

6689
12"

6690
12"

6695
6"

6709
12"

6710
12"

6724
14"

6725
14"

6734
12"

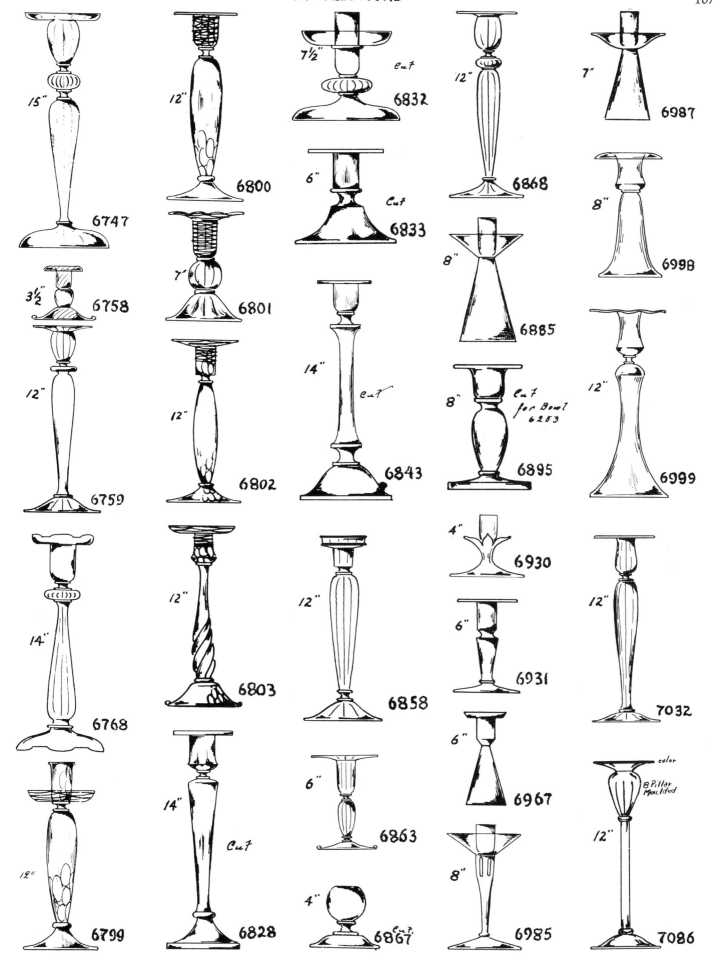

15" 6747

12" 6800

7½" 6832

6" Cut 6833

12" 6868

7" 6987

8" 6998

3½" 6758

7" 6801

14" Cut 6843

8" 6885

8" Cut for Bowl 6253 6895

12" 6999

12" 6759

12" 6802

14" 6768

12" 6803

12" 6858

4" 6930

6" 6931

12" 7032

12" 6799

14" Cut 6828

6" 6863

4" Cut 6867

6" 6967

8" 6985

color 8 Pillar Moulded 12" 7086

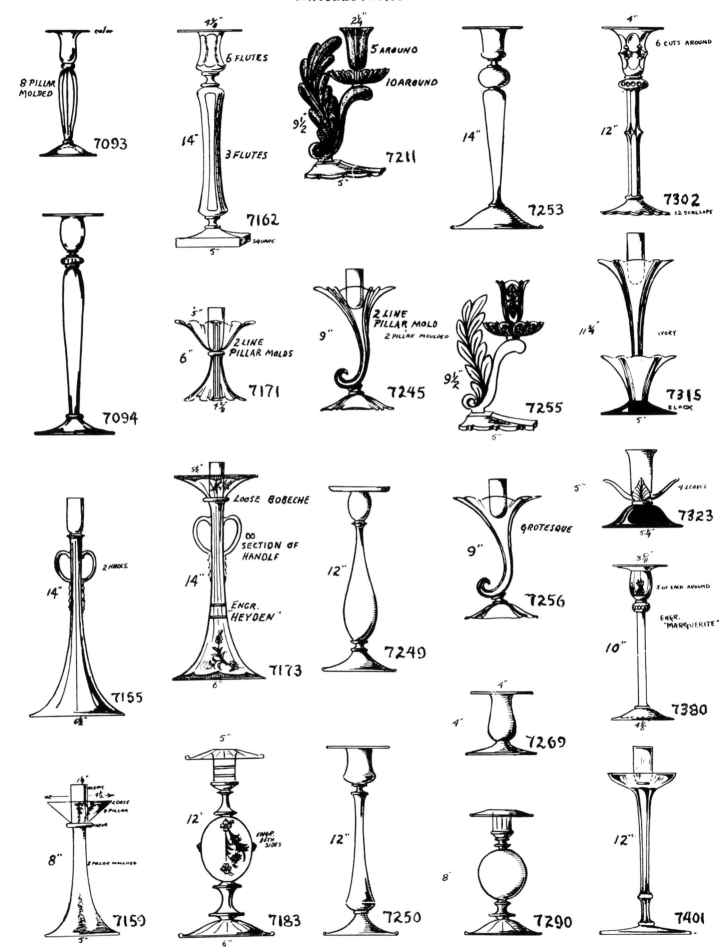

8 PILLAR MOLDED
7093

6 FLUTES
3 FLUTES
14"
5" SQUARE
7162

2¼"
5 AROUND
10 AROUND
9½"
5"
7211

14"
7253

4"
6 CUTS AROUND
12"
7302
12 SCALLOPS

7094

⅜"
2 LINE PILLAR MOLDS
6"
1⅞"
7171

9"
2 LINE PILLAR MOLD
2 PILLAR MOULDED
7245

9½"
5"
7255

11¾"
IVORY
7315
BLACK
5"

2 HNDLS.
14"
7155
6½"

5½"
LOOSE BOBECHE
∞ SECTION OF HANDLE
14"
ENGR. "HEYDEN"
7173
6"

12"
7249

9"
GROTESQUE
7256

5"
4 LEAVES
7323
5¼"

3⅝"
3 OF EACH AROUND
ENGR. "MARGUERITE"
10"
7380
4⅛"

4"
4"
7269

1½"
LOOSE 8 PILLAR
8"
8 PILLAR MOULDED
7159
5"

5"
12"
ENGR. BOTH SIDES
7183
6"

12"
7250

8"
7290

12"
7401

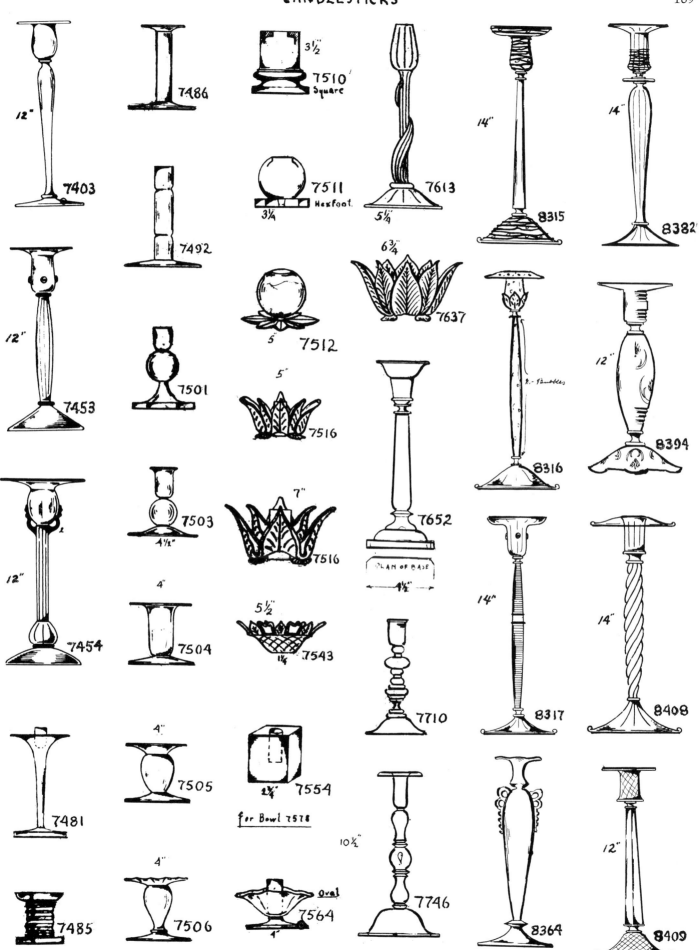

7403   12"

7486

7510   3½"   Square

7511   3¼"   Hexfoot.

7613   5½"

8315   14"

8382   14"

7492

7501

7503   4½"

7453   12"

7512   5"

7516   5"

7637   6¾"

7516   7"

7543   5½"   1¼"

7652   PLAN OF BASE   4½"

8316

8394   12"

7454   12"

7504   4"

7481

7505   4"

7554   1¼"   for Bowl 7578

7710

8317   14"

8408   14"

7485

7506   4"

7564   Oval   4"

7746   10½"

8364

8409   12"

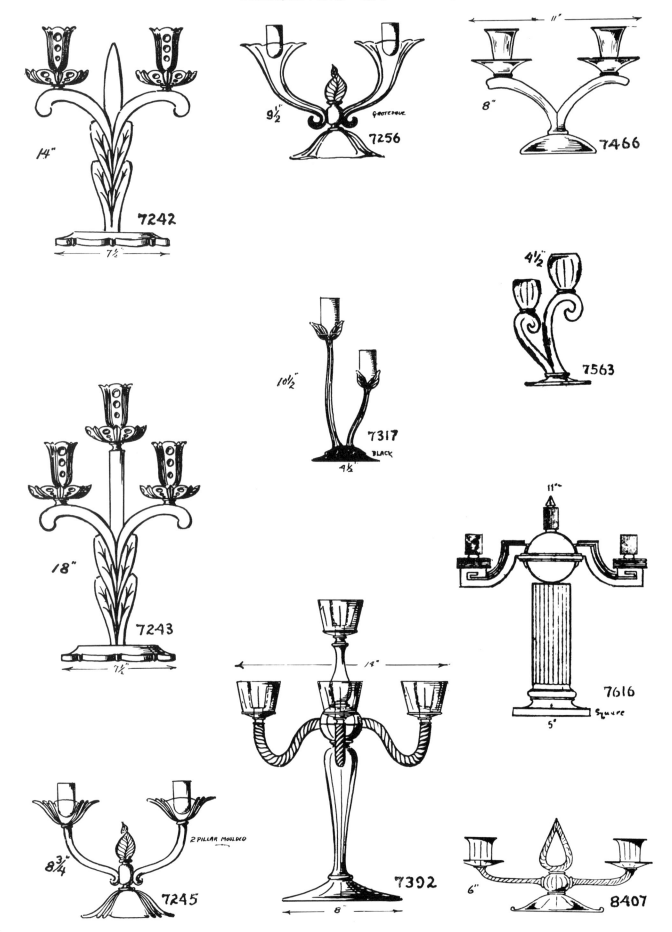

14"   7242   7½"

9½"   GROTESQUE   7256

11"   8"   7466

4½"   7563

10½"   7317   BLACK   4½"

18"   7243   7½"

11"   7616   5"   Square

8¾"   2 PILLAR MOULDED   7245

14"   7392   8"

6"   8407

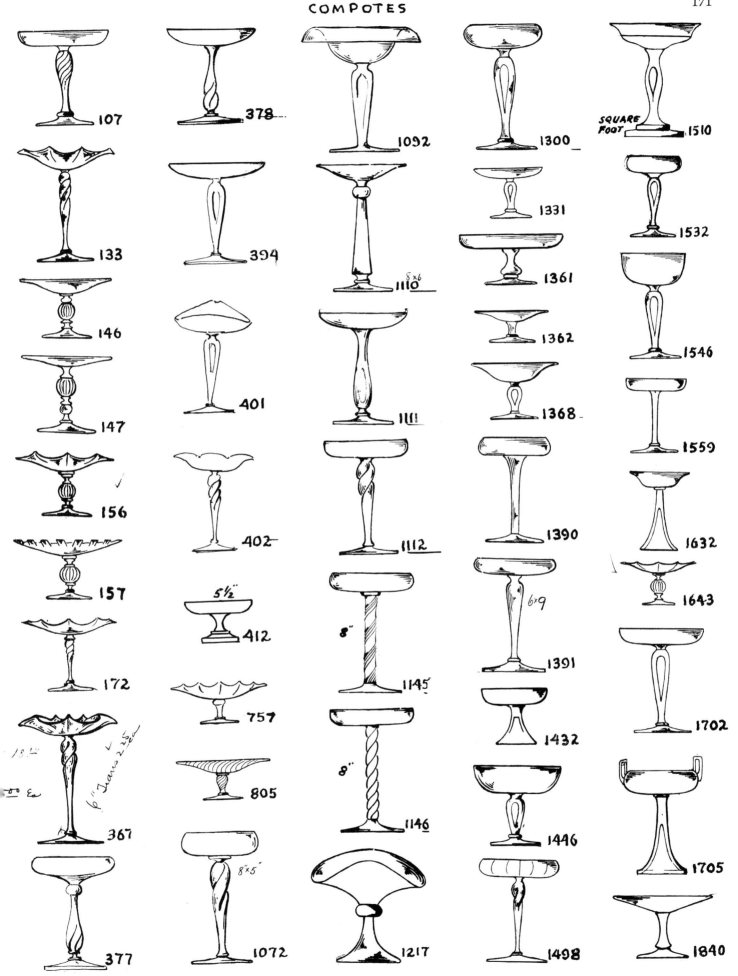

107

378

1092

1300

SQUARE FOOT 1510

133

394

1331

1532

146

401

1110 8×6

1361

1546

147

1362

1112 1112

1368

1559

156

402

1112 1112

1390

1632

157

5½" 412

1112 8"

6×9 1391

1643

172

757

1145

1432

1702

367

805

8" 1146

1446

1705

377

1072 8×5"

1217

1498

1840

172

COMPOTES

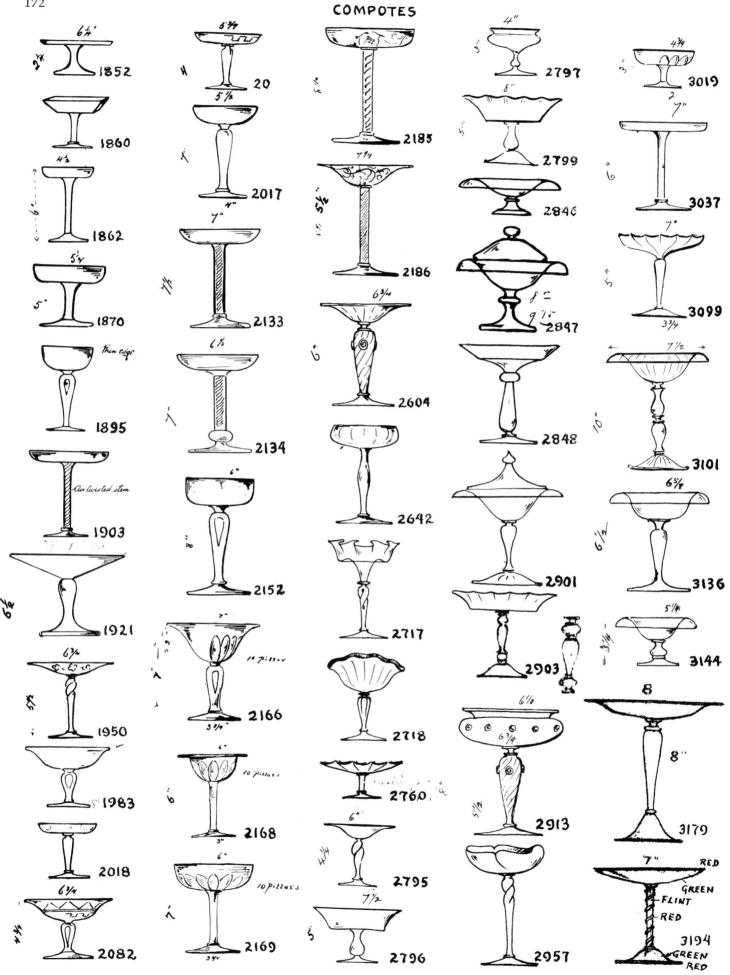

6¼"
2"
1852

6¾"
20
5½"

4"
COMPOTES
2185

4"
2797

3"
4¾"
3019

1860

7½"
2017
5½"

7¾"
2186

8"
2799

2"
7"
3037

4½"
6"
1862

4"
2133

6¾"
2604

2846

6"
3099

5¼"
5"
1870

6½"
2134

2642

8
9.75
2847

7½"
5"
3101

thin edge
1895

6"
2152

2717

2848

6½"
6⅝"
3136

Air twisted stem
1903

7"
2166

2718

2901

5¼"
3¾"
3144

6½"
1921

6"
2168

2760

2903

8

6¾"
5¼"
1950

6"
2169

6"
2795

6½"
6¾"
2913

8"
3179

1983

10 pillars
10 pillars

7½"
2796

2957

7"
RED
GREEN
FLINT
RED
3194
GREEN
RED

2018

2082

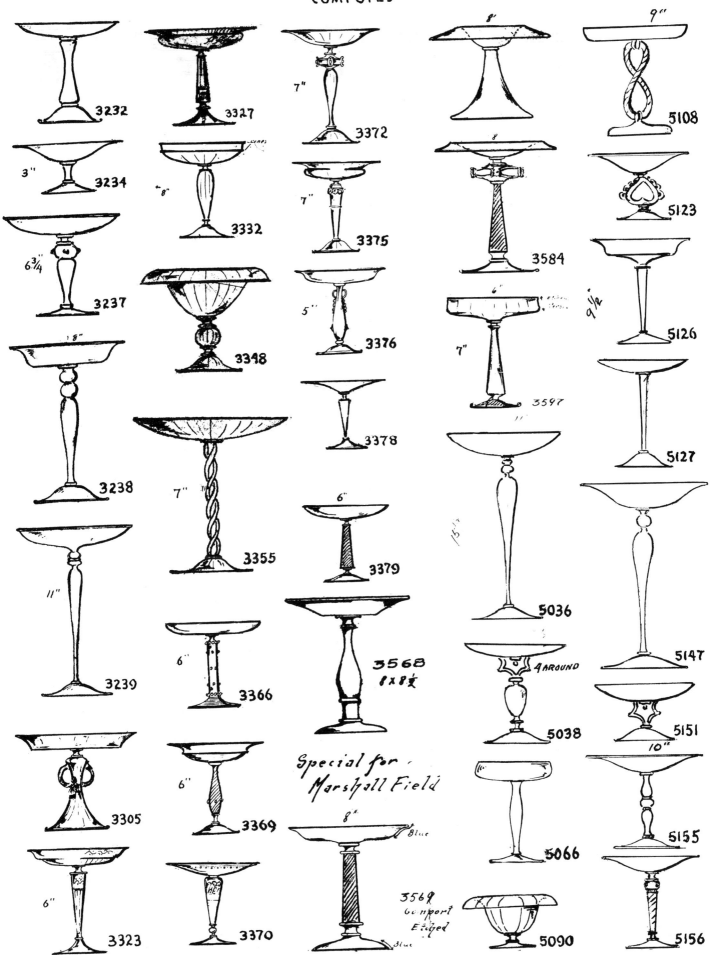

3232

3327

7" 3372

8"

9" 5108

3" 3234

8" 3332

7" 3375

5123

6¾" 3237

7" 3376

3584

5126

3348

5" 3378

6" 3597

9½"

5127

18" 3238

7" 3355

6" 3379

15"

5036

5147

11" 3239

6" 3366

3568
8 x 8½

4 AROUND

5038

5151

10"

3305

6" 3369

Special for
Marshall Field

5066

5155

6" 3323

3370

8" 3569
Comport
Etched

5090

5156

COMPOTES

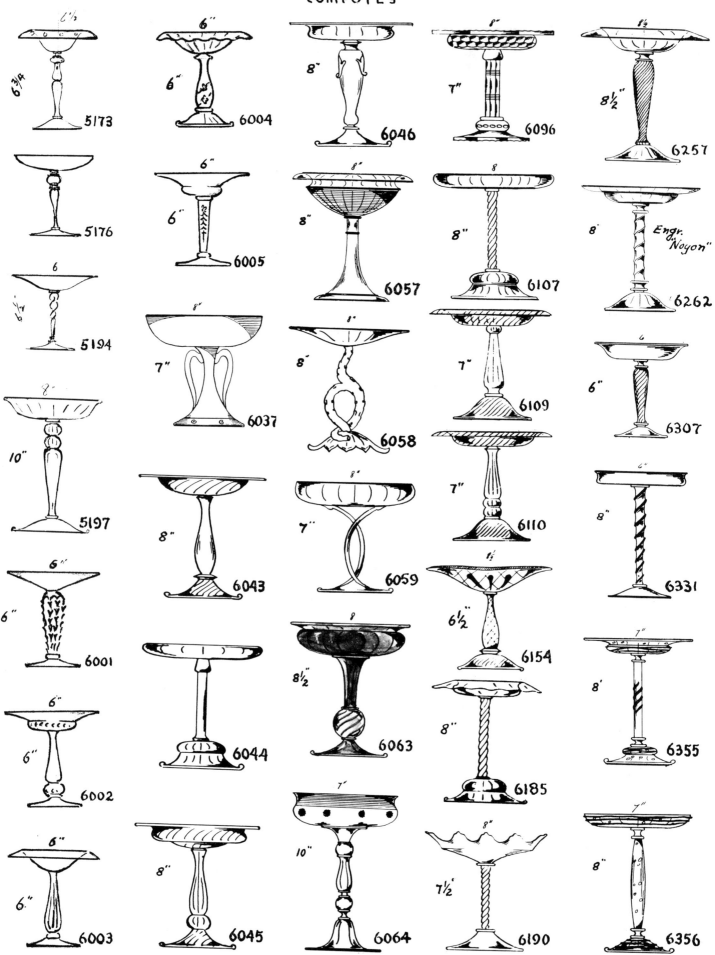

5173

6004

6046

6096

6257

5176

6005

6057

6107

6262

5194

6037

6058

6109

6307

5197

6043

6059

6110

6331

6001

6044

6063

6154

6355

6002

6045

6064

6185

6356

6003

6190

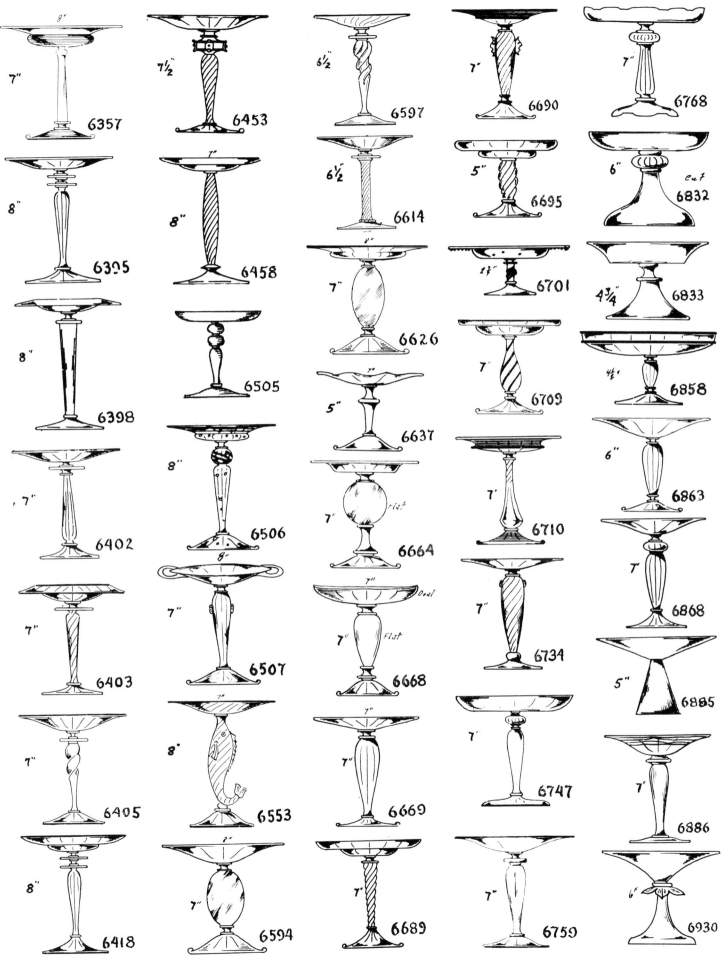

6357

6453

6597

6690

6768

6395

6458

6614

6695

6832

6398

6505

6626

6701

6833

6402

6506

6637

6709

6858

6403

6507

6664

6710

6863

6405

6553

6668

6734

6868

6418

6594

6669

6747

6885

6689

6759

6886

6930

COMPOTES

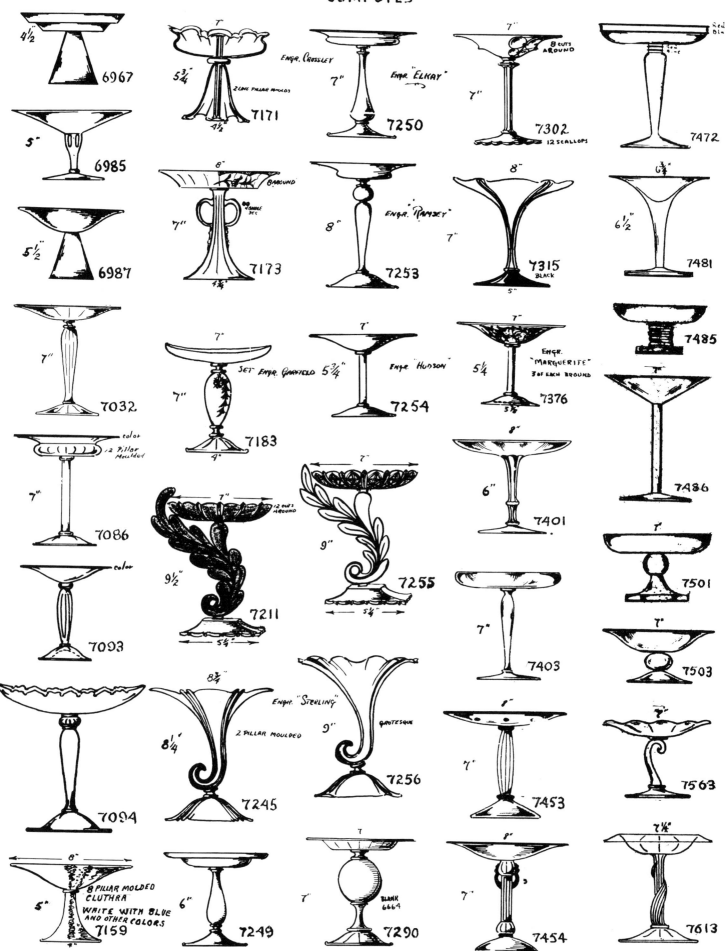

4½" 6967

5" 6985

5½" 6987

7" 7032

7" 7086 color 12 Pillar Moulded

color 7093

8" 7094

5" 8 Pillar Molded Cluthra WHITE WITH BLUE AND OTHER COLORS 7159

7" 7171 5¾" 2 LINE PILLAR MOULDS 4½"

8" 7173 8 AROUND 7" handle 3 EG 4¼"

7" 7183 SET ENGR. GARFIELD 5¾" 4"

7" 9½" 12 CUTS AROUND 7211 5¼"

8¾" 8¼" 2 PILLAR MOULDED 7245

6" 7249

7" Engr. CROSSLEY 7250

8" 8" Engr. "RAMSEY" 7253

7" 9" 7255 5¼"

Engr. "STERLING" 9" GROTESQUE 7256

7" BLANK 6664 7290

7" 8 CUTS AROUND 7302 12 SCALLOPS

8" 7" 7315 BLACK 5"

7" Engr. "HUDSON" 5¾" 7254

7" Engr. "MARGUERITE" 5¼" 3 OF EACH AROUND 7376 3⅛"

8" 6" 7401

7" 7403

7" 7453

8" 7" 7454

Red Blue 7472

6¾" 6½" 7481

7485

7486

7" 7501

7" 7503

7" 7563

7¼" 7613

COMPOTES

8"
8315

7"
8408

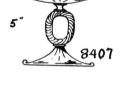
5"
8407

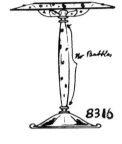
No Bubbles
8316

7"
8"
8317

8"
8382

7½"
2½"
8393

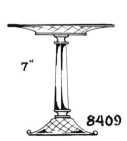
7"
8409

SPOON HOLDERS

1493

1494

MISCELLANEOUS ITEMS

1511

LEMON DISH

8370

1553

LOVING CUPS

1554½

1299

4"
5
3015
3"

9"
Also 12"
6736

3½"
5
2093
3½"

ICE TUBS

1330

1354
24 point star

1363

1372

1817

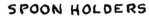
2 Handles
3
6068

4"
6831

CHAMPAGNE COOLER

7674

CRUETS

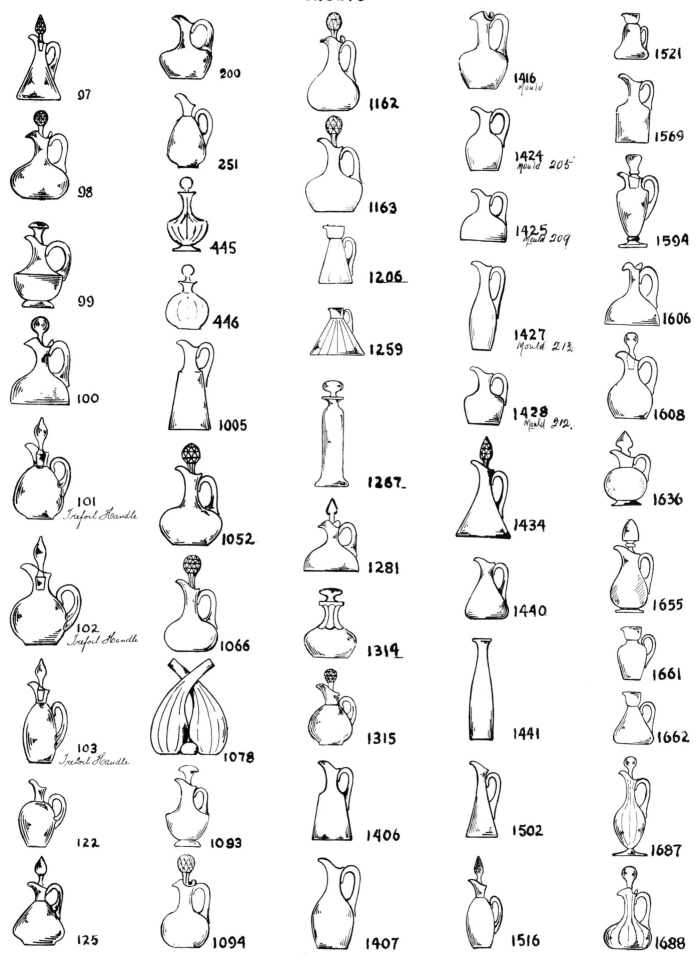

97

98

99

100

101
Trefoil Handle

102
Trefoil Handle.

103
Trefoil Handle

122

125

200

251

445

446

1005

1052

1066

1078

1093

1094

1162

1163

1206

1259

1267

1281

1314

1315

1406

1407

1416
Mould

1424
Mould 205

1425
Mould 209

1427
Mould 213

1428
Mould 212.

1434

1440

1441

1502

1516

1521

1569

1594

1606

1608

1636

1655

1661

1662

1687

1688

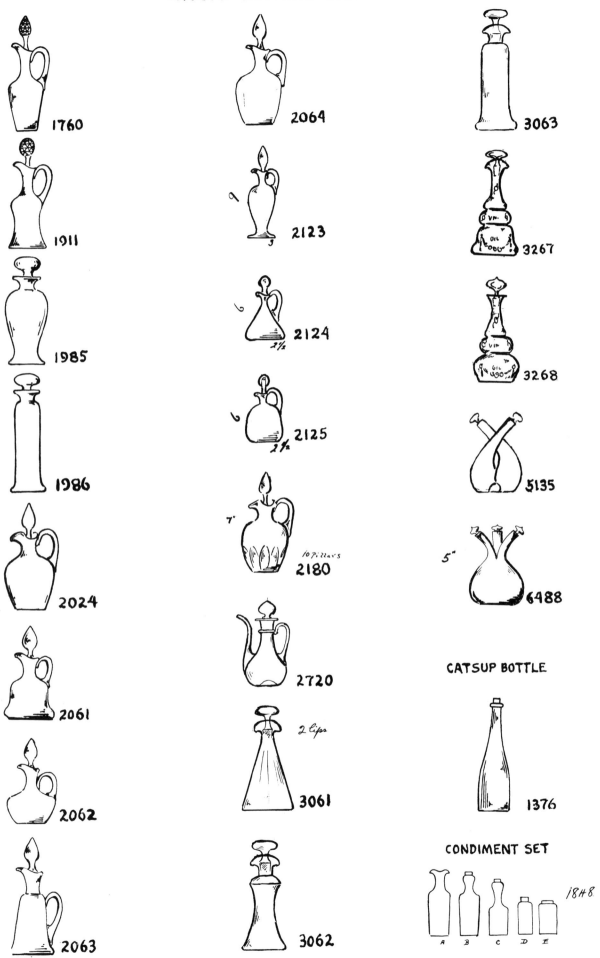

1760

1911

1985

1986

2024

2061

2062

2063

2064

2123

2124   2½

2125   2½

2180   10 Pillars

2720

3061   2 lips

3062

3063

3267

3268

5135

6488   5"

CATSUP BOTTLE

1376

CONDIMENT SET

1848

A   B   C   D   E

DECANTERS

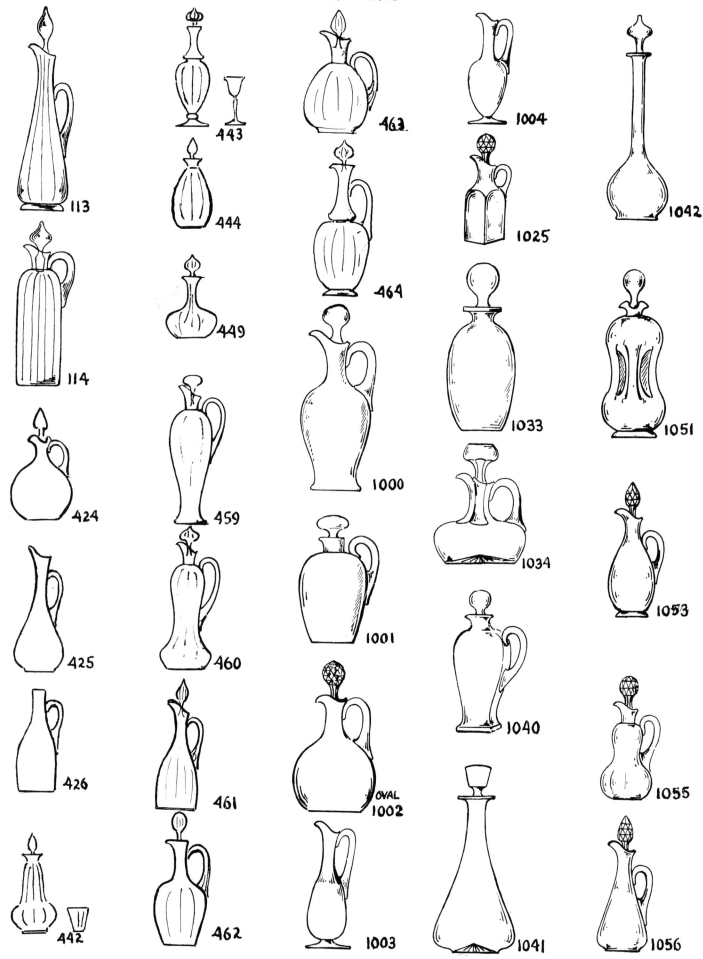

113

114

424

425

426

442

443

444

449

459

460

461

462

463

464

1000

1001

1002 OVAL

1003

1004

1025

1033

1034

1040

1041

1042

1051

1053

1055

1056

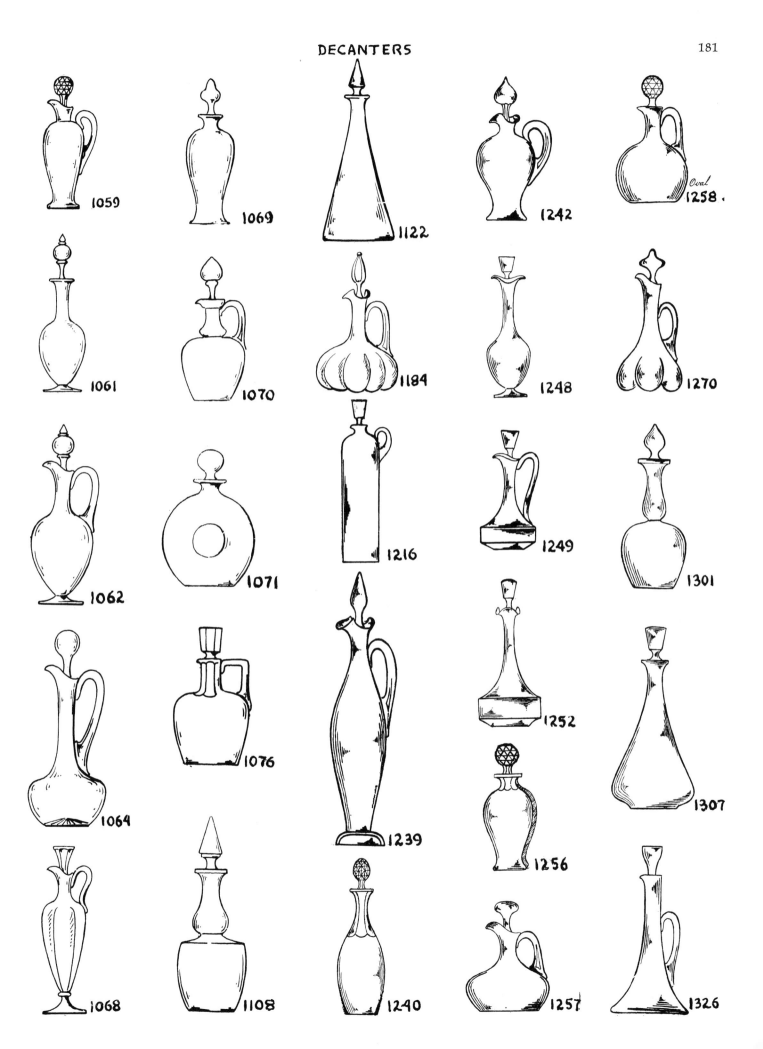

1059

1069

1122

1242

Oval
1258.

1061

1070

1184

1248

1270

1062

1071

1216

1249

1301

1064

1076

1239

1252

1256

1307

1068

1108

1240

1257

1326

DECANTERS

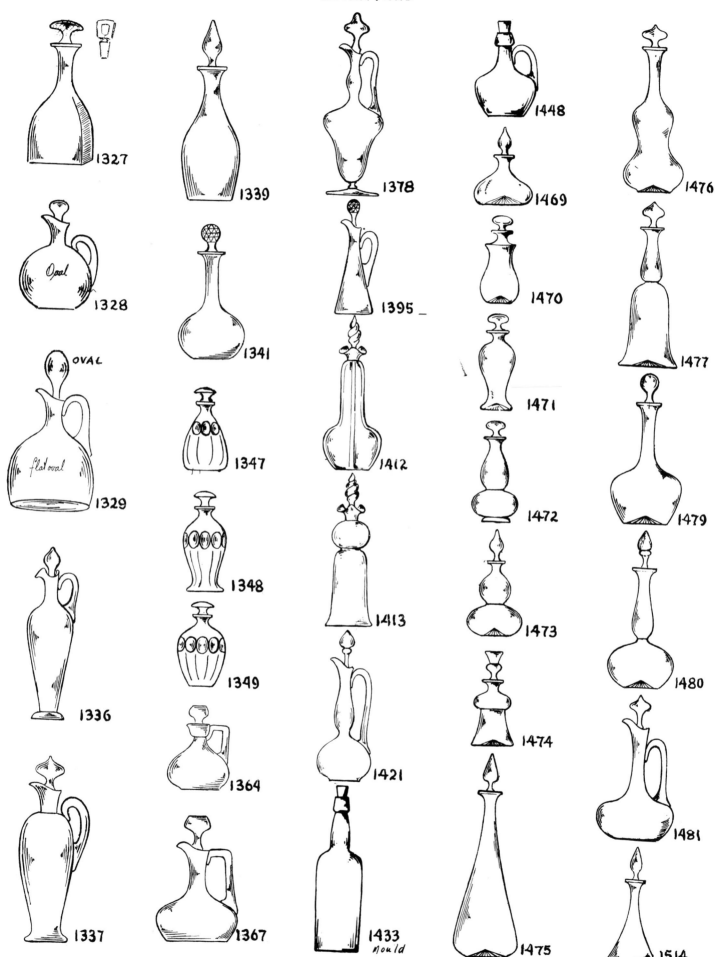

1327

1328 Oval

1329 OVAL flat oval

1336

1337

1339

1341

1347

1348

1349

1364

1367

1378

1395

1412

1413

1421

1433 Mould

1448

1469

1470

1471

1472

1473

1474

1475

1476

1477

1479

1480

1481

1514

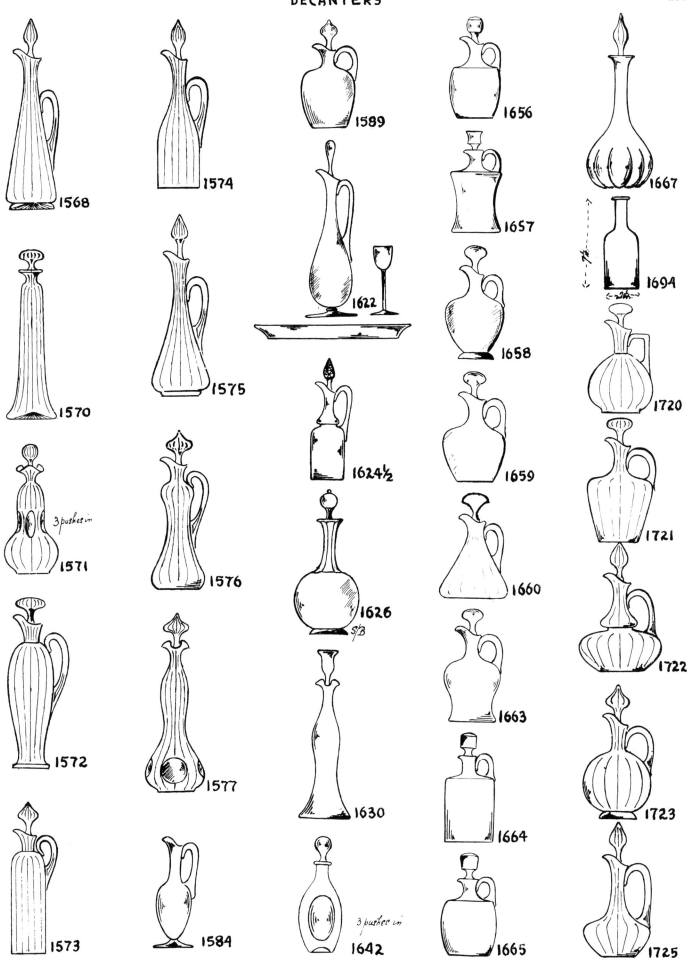

1568

1574

1589

1656

1667

1570

1575

1622

1657

1694

1571   3 pushes in

1576

1624½

1658

1720

1572

1577

1626   S/B

1659

1721

1573

1584

1630

1660

1722

1642   3 pushes in

1663

1723

1664

1665

1725

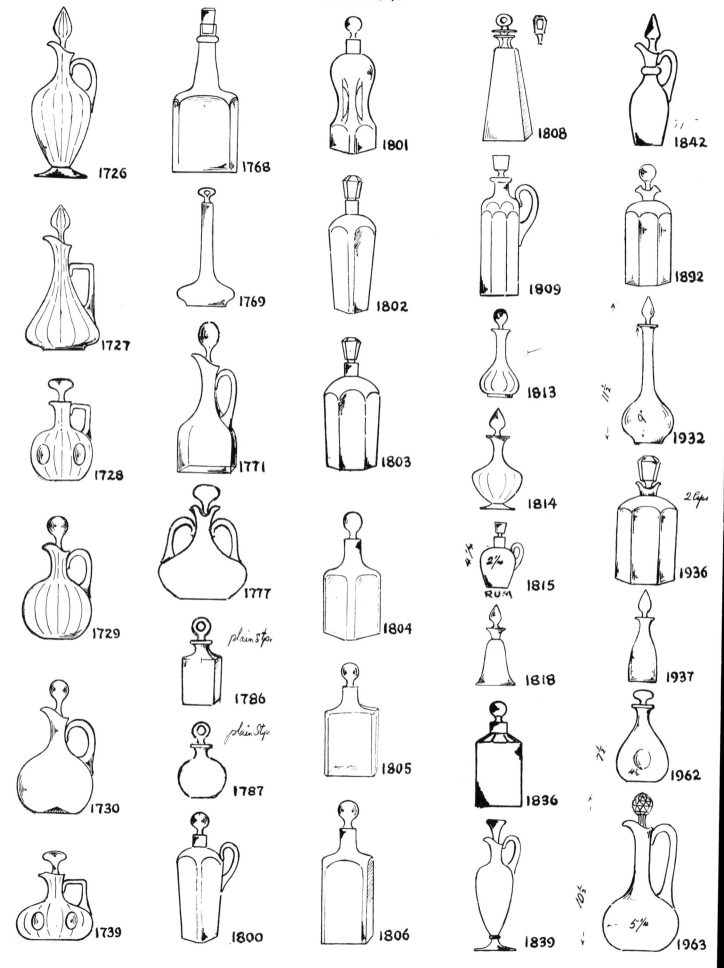

1726

1768

1801

1808

1842

1727

1769

1802

1809

1892

1728

1771

1803

1813

1932

1729

1777

1804

1814

2 Cups

1936

1786   plain stp.

1815
RUM
2¾
4¾

1937

1730

1787   plain stp.

1805

1818

7½
4½
1962

1739

1800

1806

1836

1839   10½

1963
5-¼

DECANTERS

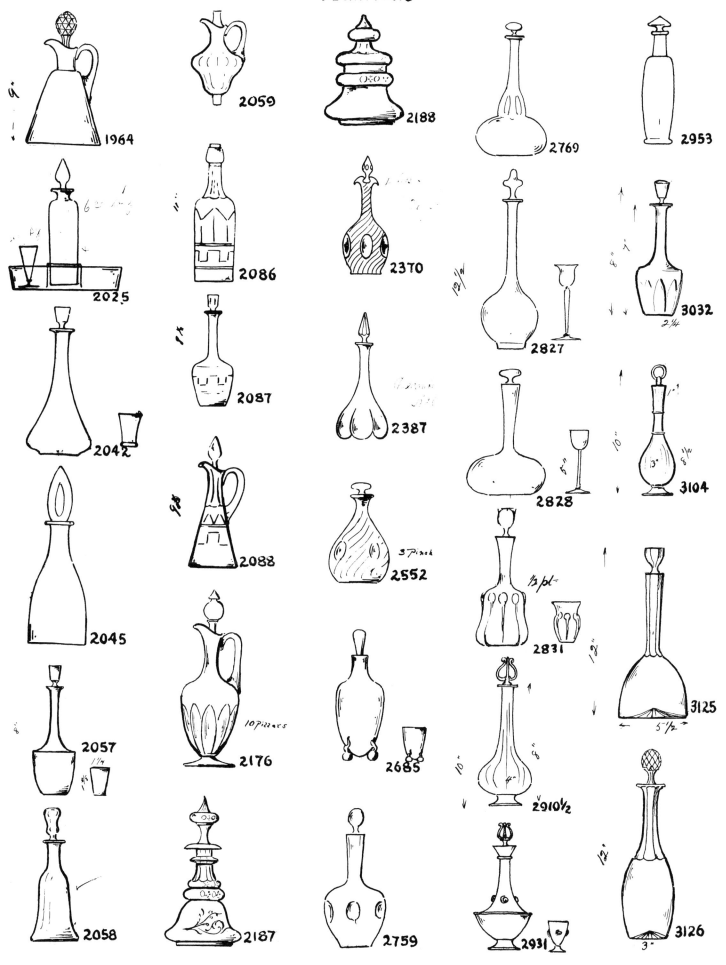

185

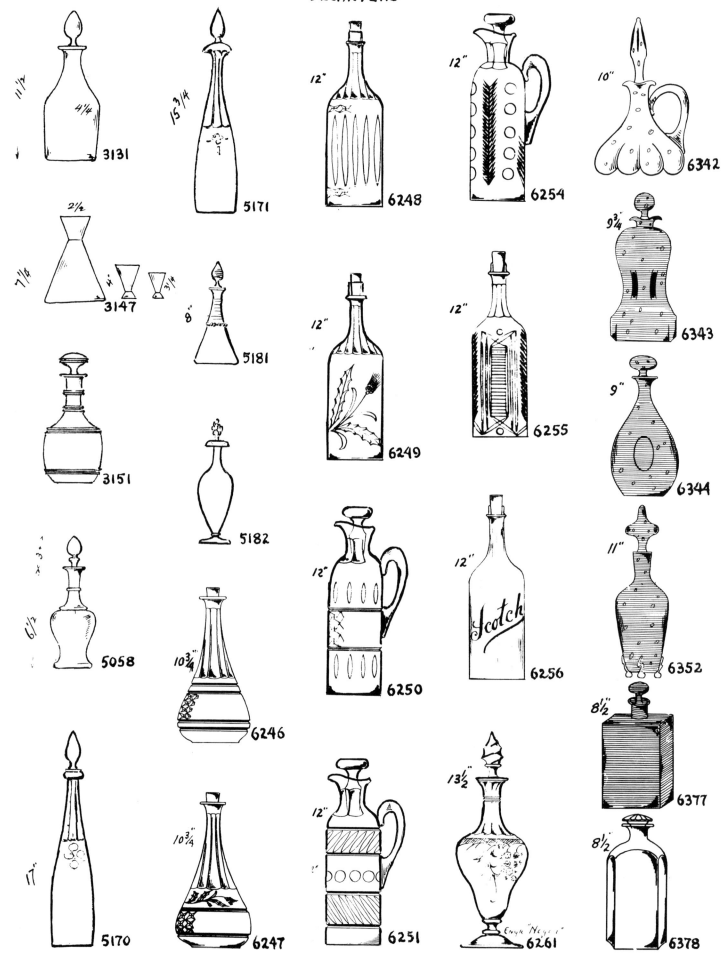

11½   4¼   3131

15¾   5171

2½   7¼   4"   3¾"   3147

8"   5181

3151

5182

6½   x 3"   5058

10¾"   6246

17"   5170

10¾"   6247

12"   6248

12"   6249

12"   6250

12"   6251

12"   6254

12"   6255

12"   6256

Scotch   12"   6256

13½   6261

10"   6342

9¾"   6343

9"   6344

11"   6352

8½"   6377

8½"   6378

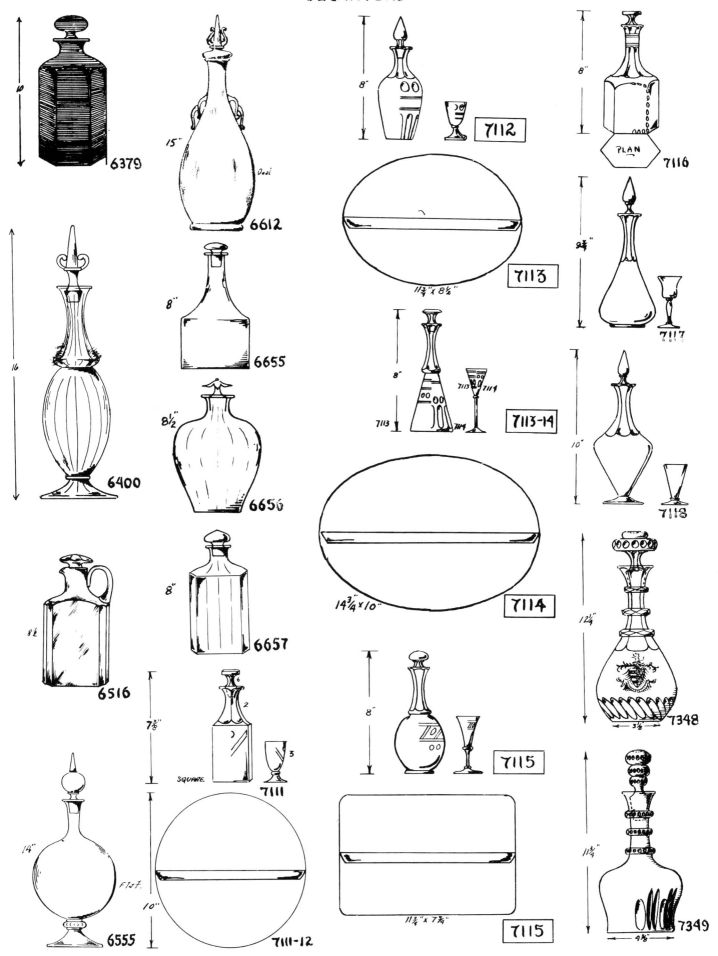

6379

15"
6612
Oval

8"
7112

PLAN
7116
8"

11¾" x 8½"
7113

16
6400

8"
6655

8½"
6656

8"
7113
7114
7113-14

9¾"
7117

8½"
6516

8"
6657

14¾" x 10"
7114

10"
7118

7⅜"
SQUARE
7111
2
6
3

8"
7115

12¼"
3⅜"
7348

14"
F.T.J.F.
6555
10"
7111-12

11¾" x 7¾"
7115

11¾"
4⅜"
7349

DECANTERS

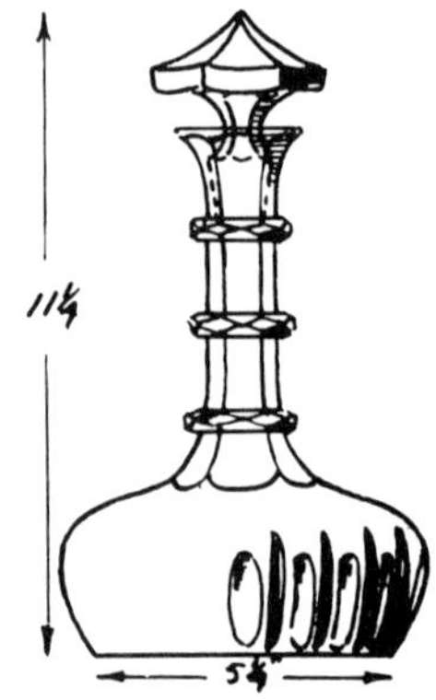
11¼
5¼"

7350

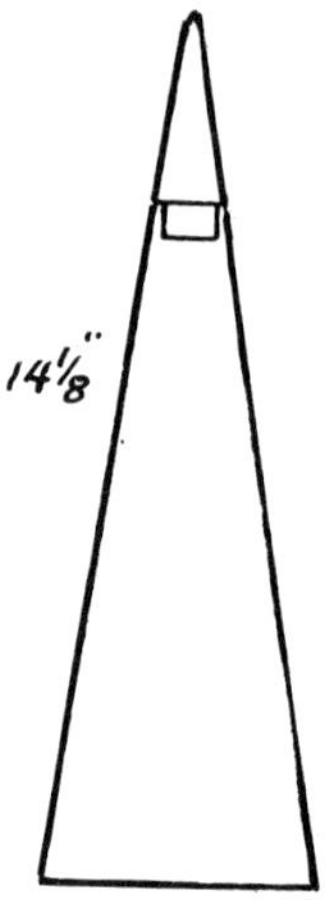
14⅛"

7625

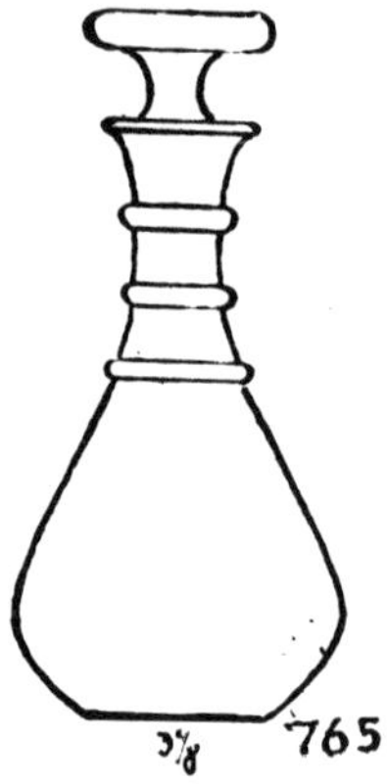
3⅞

7655

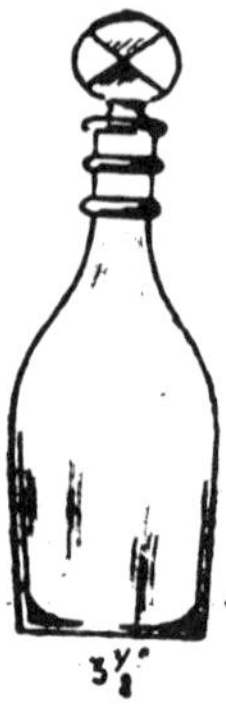
3⅛"

7665

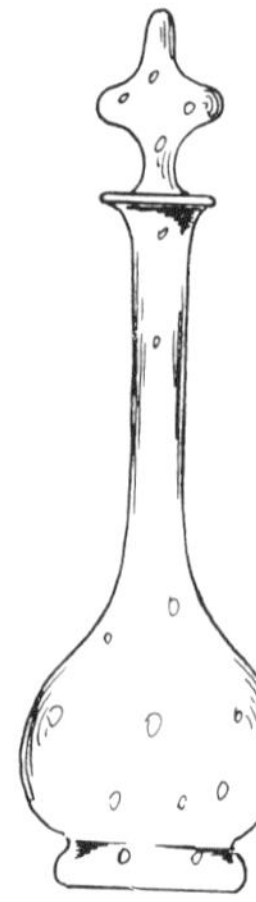

8341

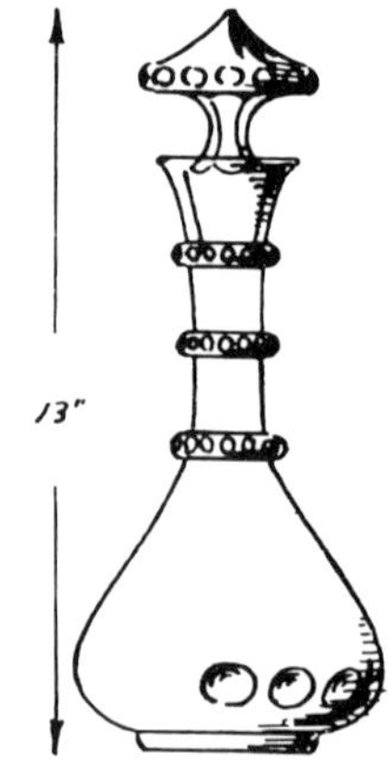
13"

7351

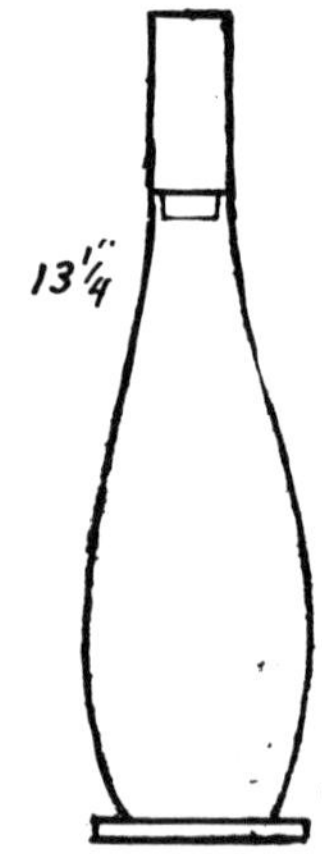
13¼"

7626

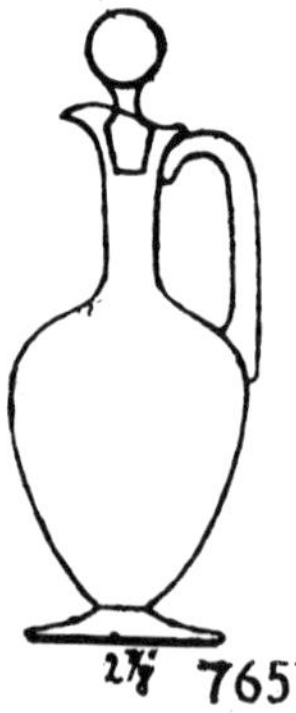
2⅞

7657

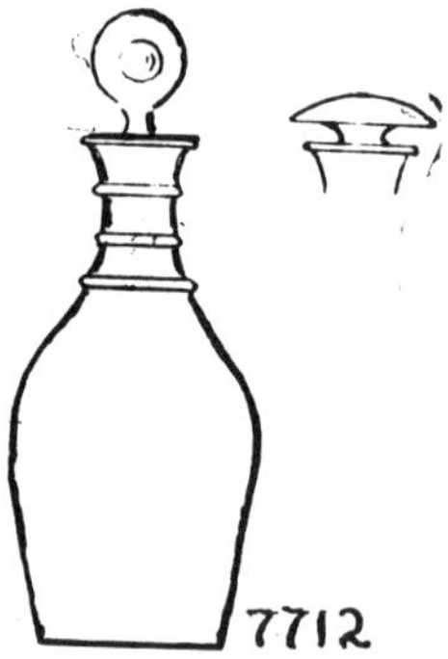

7712

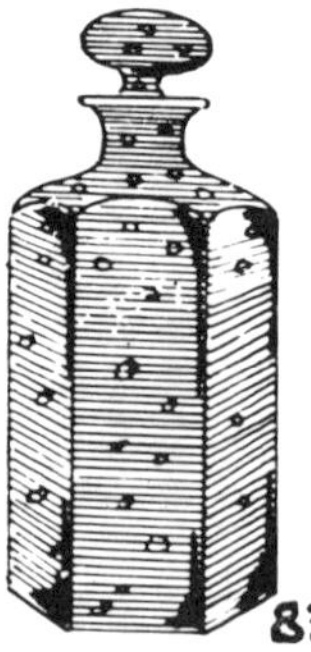

8349

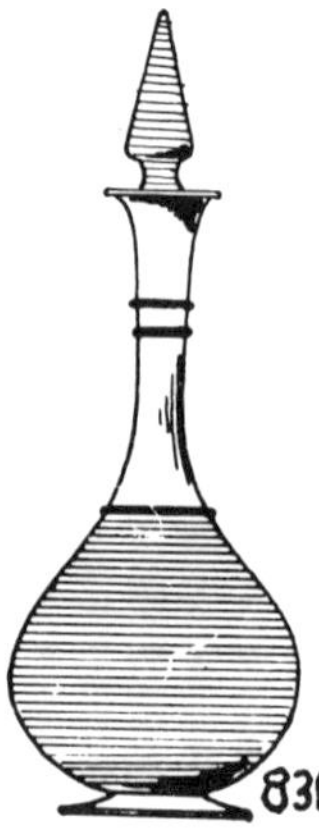

8317

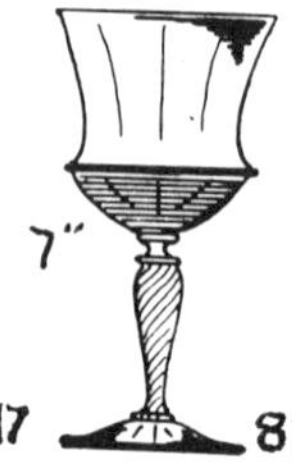
7"

8317

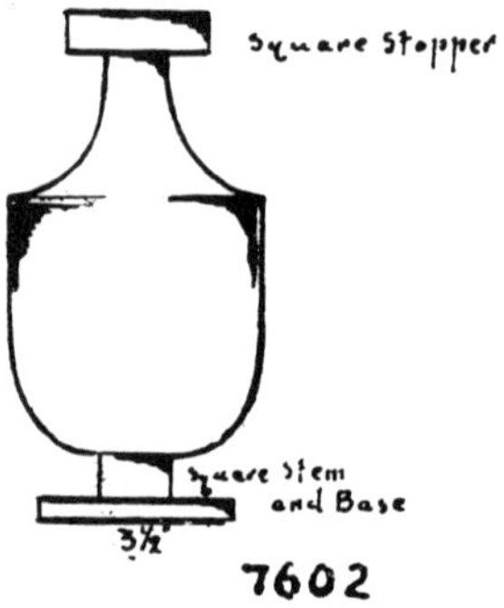
Square Stopper
Square Stem and Base
3½"

7602

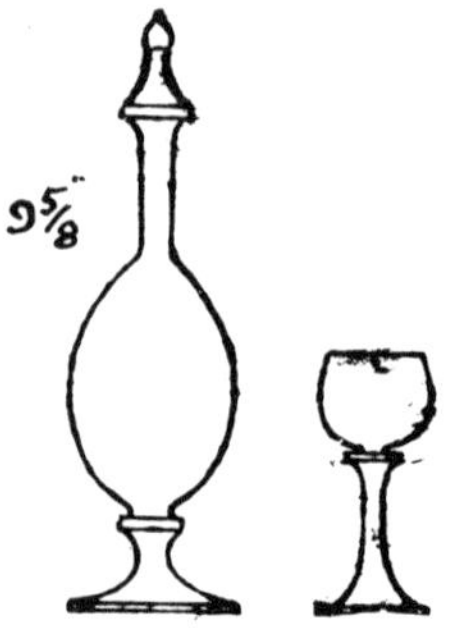
9⅝"

7627

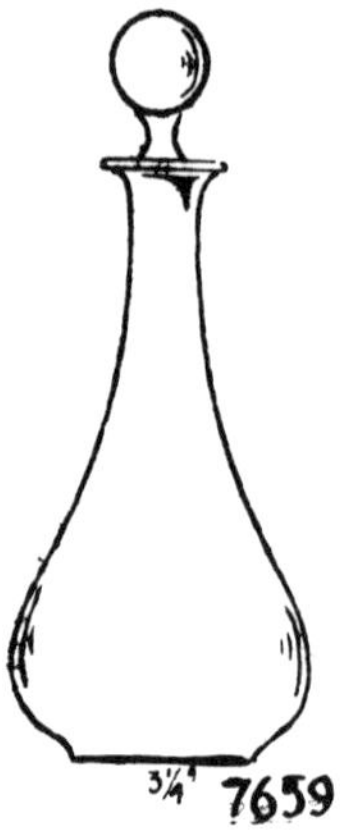
3¼"

7659

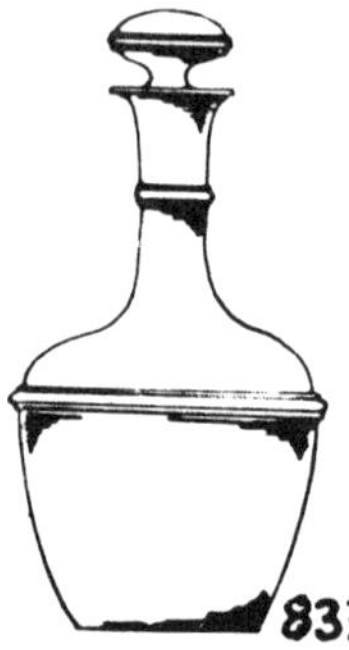

8336

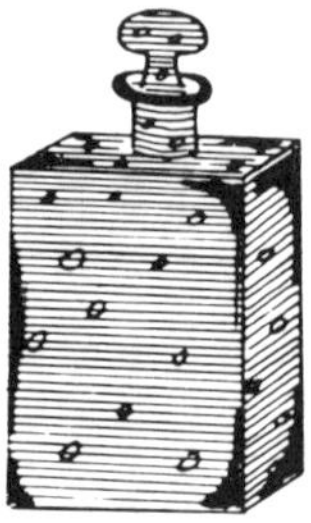

8350

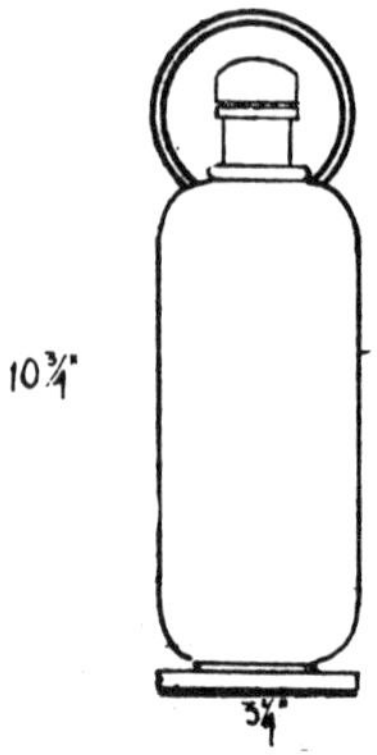
10¾"
3¼"

7624

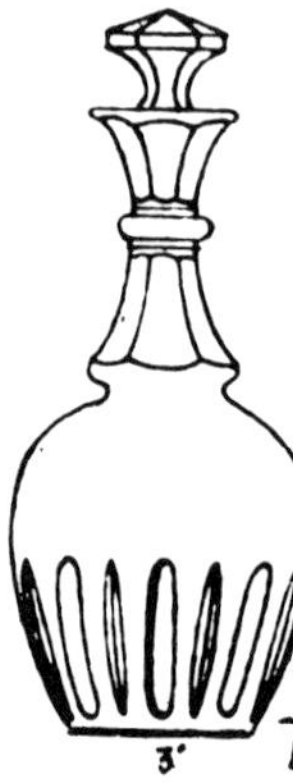
3"

7654

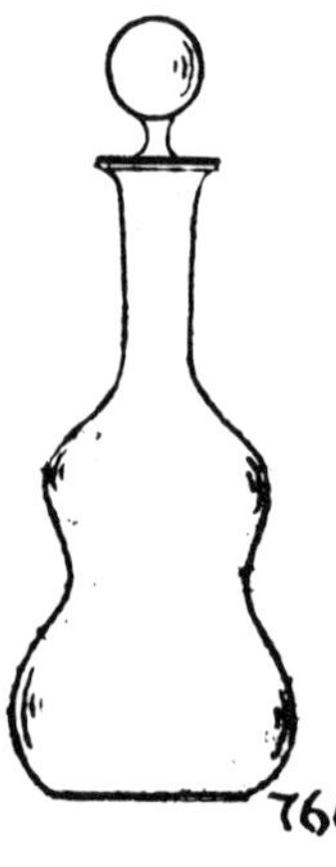

7660

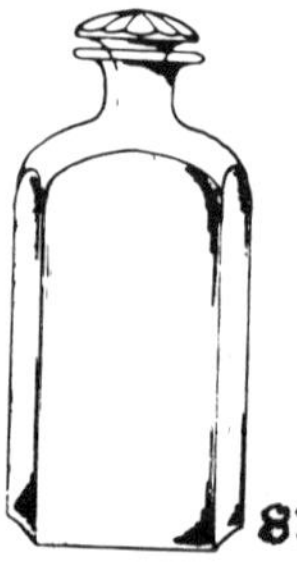

8337

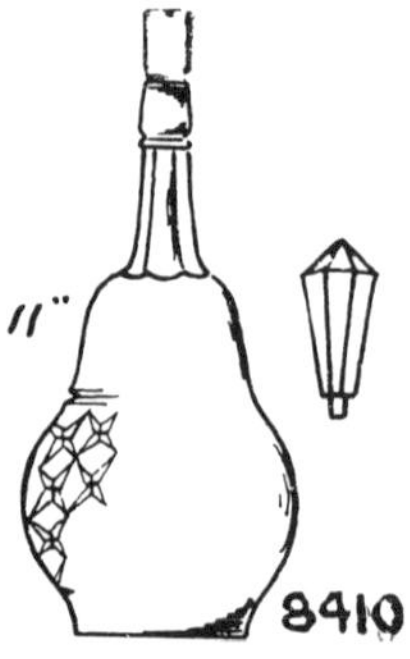
11"

8410

FINGER BOWLS AND PLATES

171

204

6/3   Style A

620   Style "A"

818

1820

1984

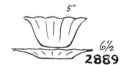
5"   6½
2889

2¼
3321

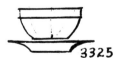
3325

3550

4"
5067

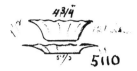
4¾"
5110

3"
6682

BOUILLION CUPS

3⅝"
2½   2175

2700

3½"
3291

2½   6737

2½   6738

2½   6739

2½   6740

WINE GLASS COOLERS

6475

5½"
7716

1758

5¾
1957

3298

3299

TOOTHPICK HOLDERS

1580

1583

1596

1708

MISCELLANEOUS ITEMS

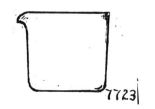
11¼   2¼
2772   4"

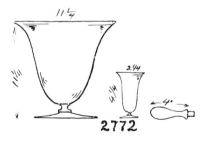
7723

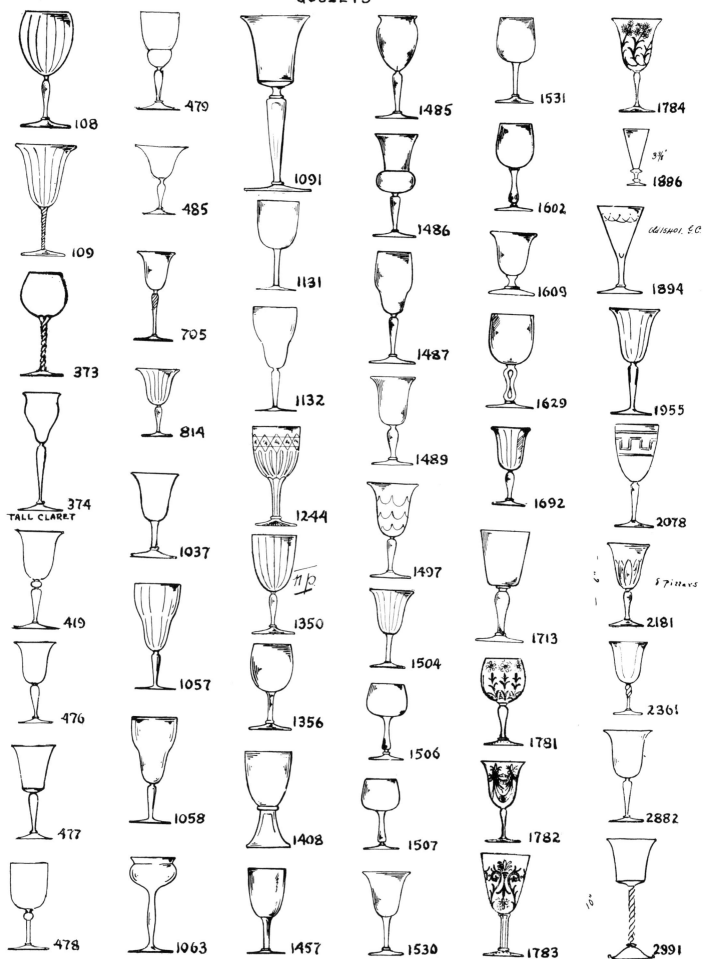

108

479

1091

1485

1531

1784

109

485

1486

1602

1886   3¾"

373

705

1131

1609

Old 15 Aol, E.C.

374
TALL CLARET

814

1132

1487

1629

1894

419

1037

1244   *11 p.*

1489

1692

1955

476

1057

1350

1497

1713

2078

477

1058

1356

1504

1781

2181   *8 Pillars*

478

1063

1408

1506

1782

2361

1457

1530

1783

2882

1507

2991

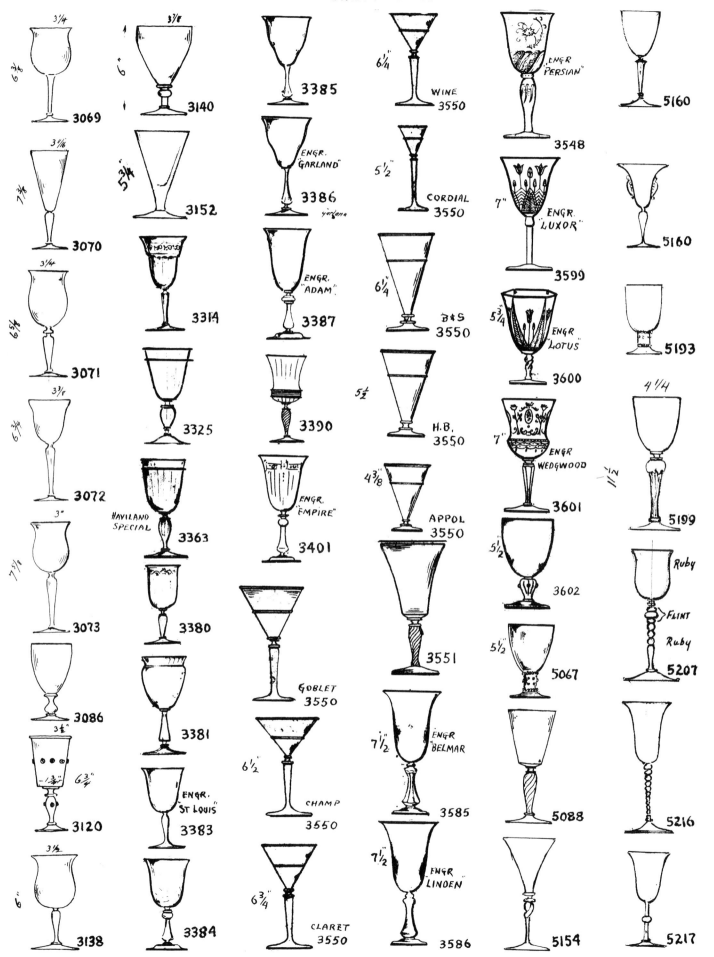

$7\frac{3}{4}$ 6052

$7\frac{7}{8}$ 6062

$6\frac{1}{2}$ 6067

$7''$ 6073 Engr "Beaumont"

$7''$ 6074 Engr "Chelsea"

$7\frac{3}{4}$ to match 6001 6080

$5\frac{3}{4}$ 6087

6113

6114

6115 Hex Foot.

$6\frac{1}{4}$ 6116 Octagon Foot

$7''$ 6121

$7''$ Etched "Persian" to match Set 3597 6125

$10''$ 6126 Engr "Noyon"

$8\frac{1}{4}$ 6131

$6\frac{1}{2}$ 6132

$5\frac{1}{2}$ 6134

$5\frac{1}{2}$ 6183 Sq Foot

$5\frac{3}{4}$ cut 10035 10036 10037 6192

$6''$ 6220

$6\frac{1}{4}$ 6225

$6''$ 6231

$5\frac{1}{2}$ 6242 Hex.

$5\frac{3}{4}$ 6244

$5\frac{1}{2}$ 6268 Cut Queen Anne

$10''$ 6269

6277

6278

$8''$ 6279

$8''$ 6280

$7''$ 6281

$4\frac{5}{8}$ 6282

$7\frac{1}{2}$ 6285

$8''$ 6303

$8''$ 6330

$6\frac{1}{2}$ 6333

$8''$ 6334

$6\frac{1}{2}$ 6338

$7''$ 6354

$7\frac{1}{2}$ 6358

$7\frac{1}{2}$ 6359

$7''$ 6360

$6''$ cut 6361

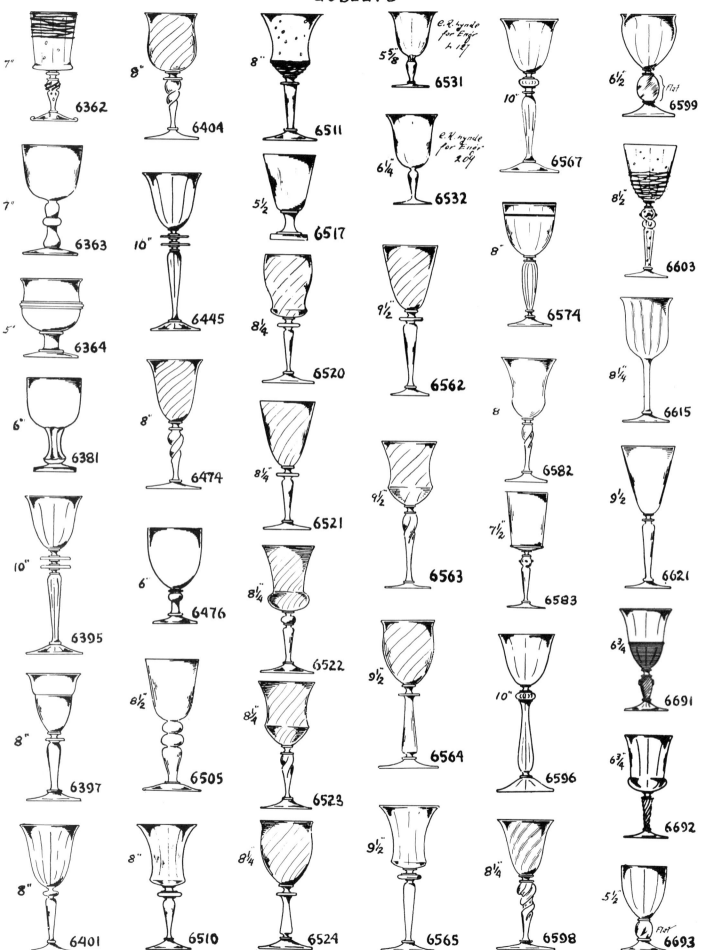

7" 6362

8" 6404

8" 6511

5 5/8" 6531 *e.R. hynde for Eng'r h. 187*

6 1/4" 6532 *e.R. hynde for Eng'r 204*

10" 6567

6 1/2" 6599 *flat*

7" 6363

10" 6445

5 1/2" 6517

9 1/2" 6562

8" 6574

8 1/2" 6603

5" 6364

8" 6474

8 1/4" 6520

8" 6582

8 1/4" 6615

6" 6381

6 1/4" 6521

9 1/2" 6563

7 1/2" 6583

9 1/2" 6621

10" 6395

6" 6476

8 1/4" 6522

9 1/2" 6564

10" 6596

6 3/4" 6691

8" 6397

8 1/2" 6505

8 1/4" 6523

6 3/4" 6692

8" 6401

8" 6510

8 1/4" 6524

9 1/2" 6565

8 1/4" 6598

5 1/2" 6693 *flat*

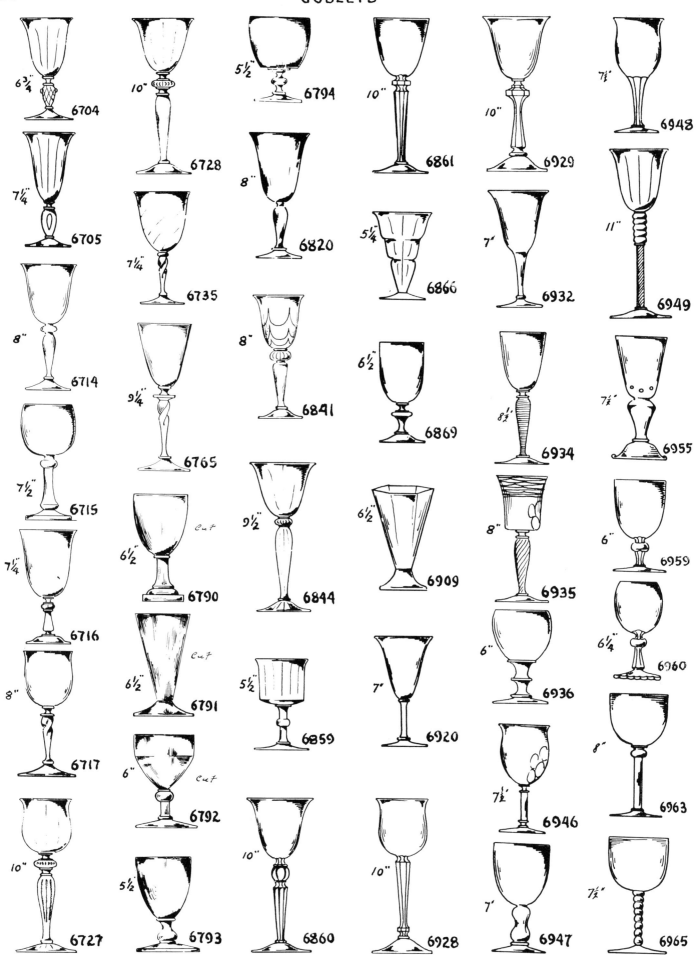

6 3/4" 6704

7 1/4" 6705

8" 6714

7 1/2" 6715

7 1/4" 6716

8" 6717

10" 6727

10" 6728

7 1/4" 6735

9 1/4" 6765

6 1/2" Cut 6790

6 1/2" Cut 6791

6" Cut 6792

5 1/2" 6793

5 1/2" 6794

8" 6820

8" 6841

9 1/2" 6844

5 1/2" 6859

10" 6860

10" 6861

5 1/4" 6866

6 1/2" 6869

6 1/2" 6909

7" 6920

10" 6928

10" 6929

7" 6932

8 1/2" 6934

8" 6935

6" 6936

7 1/2" 6946

7" 6947

7 1/4" 6948

11" 6949

7 1/2" 6955

6" 6959

6 1/4" 6960

8" 6963

7 1/2" 6965

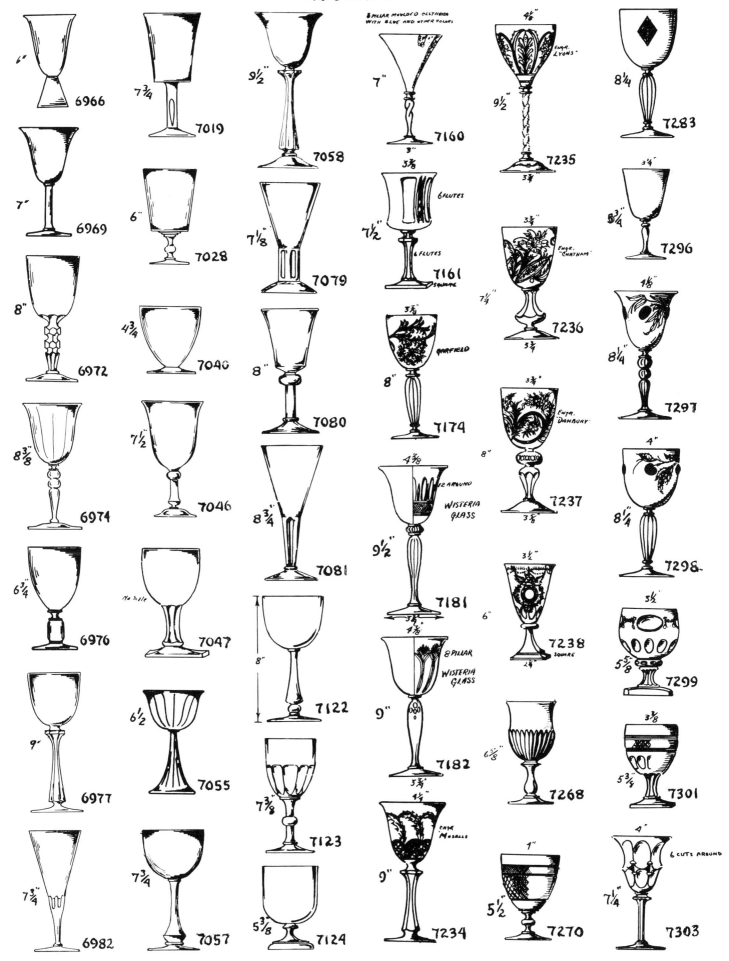

6966
7019
7058
7160
7235
7283

6969
7028
7079
7161
7236
7296

6972
7040
7080
7174
7237
7297

6974
7046
7081
7181
7238
7298

6976
7047
7122
7182
7268
7299

6977
7055
7123
7234
7268
7301

6982
7057
7124
7234
7270
7303

3¼"
6⅝"
7332

4"
8"
3⅜"
7336

4"
7"
STEM MADE IN TWO STYLES
7338

5¾"
7⅛"
3¾"
7339

7¾"
7341

10⅛"
7343
BLACK OVER CRYSTAL ENGR. "GOBELIN"

10¼"
7344
BLACK OVER CRYSTAL ENGR. "ALPINE"

10"
7345
BLACK OVER CRYSTAL ENGR. "FLORIAN"

5⅞"
7346

3⅜"
6⅛"
3¼"
7353

4"
8"
7382

3⅝"
7⅜"
6 CUTS AROUND
7383

3¼"
24 cuts
6⅛"
7384

3⅜"
6¼"
7385

3½"
IVORY
5¾"
BLACK
7390

7½"
7401

8"
7402

8"
7403

6"
4"
7462

7481

7485

7486

7501

7522
3"

8"
7527

3¼"
7555

3½"
7585
Water

3"
3"
Square Stem and Base
7602
Water

6¹³⁄₁₆"
7611

6"
7623

7¾"
7629

6⅝"
7634

7644
3"

3¼"
7666

7667

8"
8315

8316

8336

10"
8351

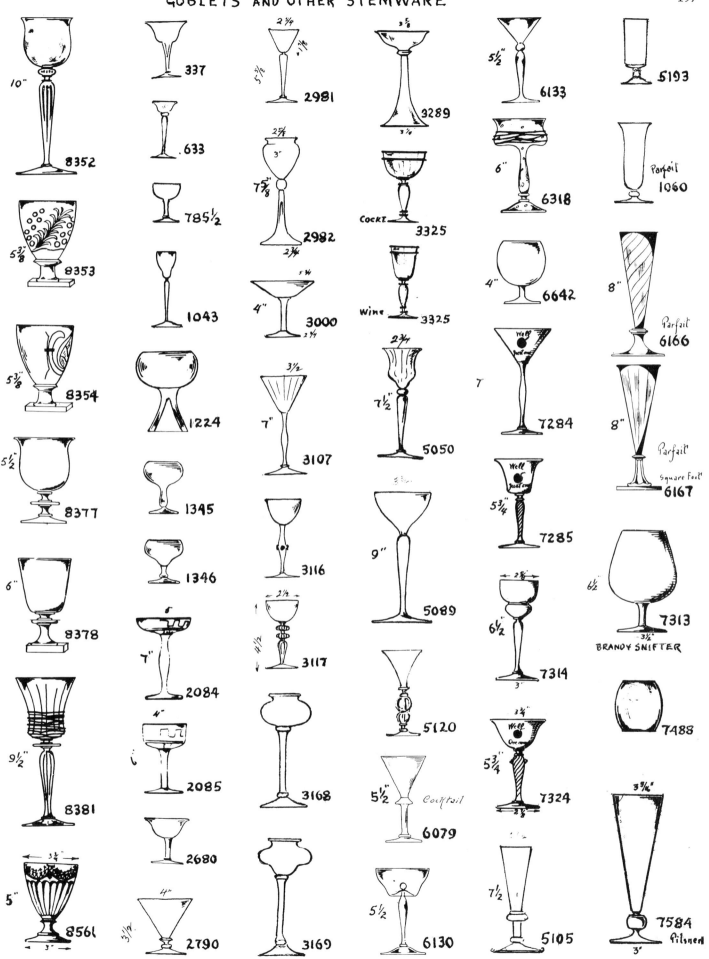

8352 — 10"
8353 — 5 3/8"
8354 — 5 3/8"
8377 — 5 1/2"
8378 — 6"
8381 — 9 1/2"
8561 — 5"

337
633
785 1/2
1043
1224
1345
1346
2084
2085
2680
2790 — 4"

2981 — 2 3/4, 5 5/8, 7/8
2982 — 2 5/8, 3, 7 5/8, 2 3/4
3000 — 4", 5 1/4, 2 1/4
3107 — 3 1/2, 7"
3116
3117 — 2 1/2, 4 1/2
3168
3169

3289 — 5 5/8, 3 1/4
3325 — Cockt.
3325 — Wine
5050 — 2 3/4, 7 1/2
5089 — 9"
5120
6079 — Cocktail, 5 1/2"
6130 — 5 1/2

6133 — 5 1/2"
6318 — 6"
6642 — 4"
7284 — 7, Well just one
7285 — 5 3/4", Well just one
7314 — 2 5/8, 6 1/2, 3"
7324 — 3 3/4, Well one more, 5 3/4, 2 3/8
5105 — 7 1/2

5193
1060 — Parfait
6166 — 8", Parfait
6167 — 8", Parfait, Square Foot
7313 — 6 1/2, 3 1/2, BRANDY SNIFTER
7488
7584 — 3 3/16", Pilsner, 3"

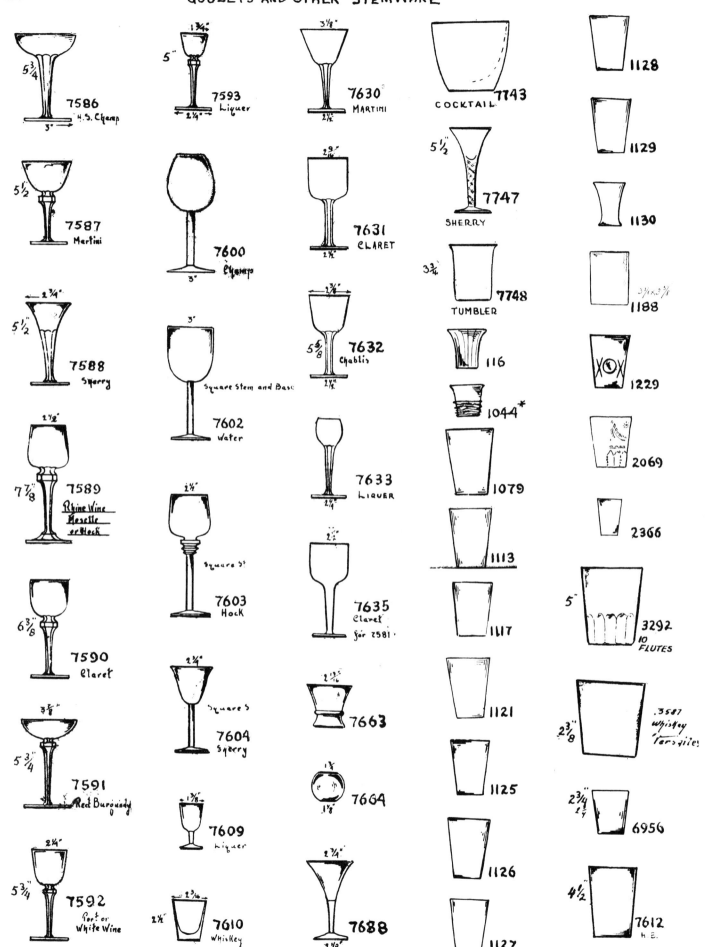

7586 H.S. Champ
7593 Liquer
7630 Martini
7743 Cocktail
1128
7587 Martini
7600 Champ
7631 Claret
7747 Sherry
1129
7588 Sherry
7632 Chablis
7748 Tumbler
1130
7589 Rhine Wine Moselle or Hock
7602 Square Stem and Base Water
116
1188
7590 Claret
7603 Square St Hock
7633 Liquer
1044*
1079
1229
7591 Red Burgundy
7604 Square S Sherry
7635 Claret for 7581
1113
2069
1117
2366
7592 Port or White Wine
7609 Liquer
7663
1121
3292 10 FLUTES
7664
1125
.3581 Whiskey Tarantiles
7610 Whiskey
7688
1126
6956
7612 H.E.
1127

* THIS COCKTAIL GLASS IS *1044 IN THE 1932 CATALOG. IN EARLIER CATALOGS NUMBER 1044 IS A VASE.

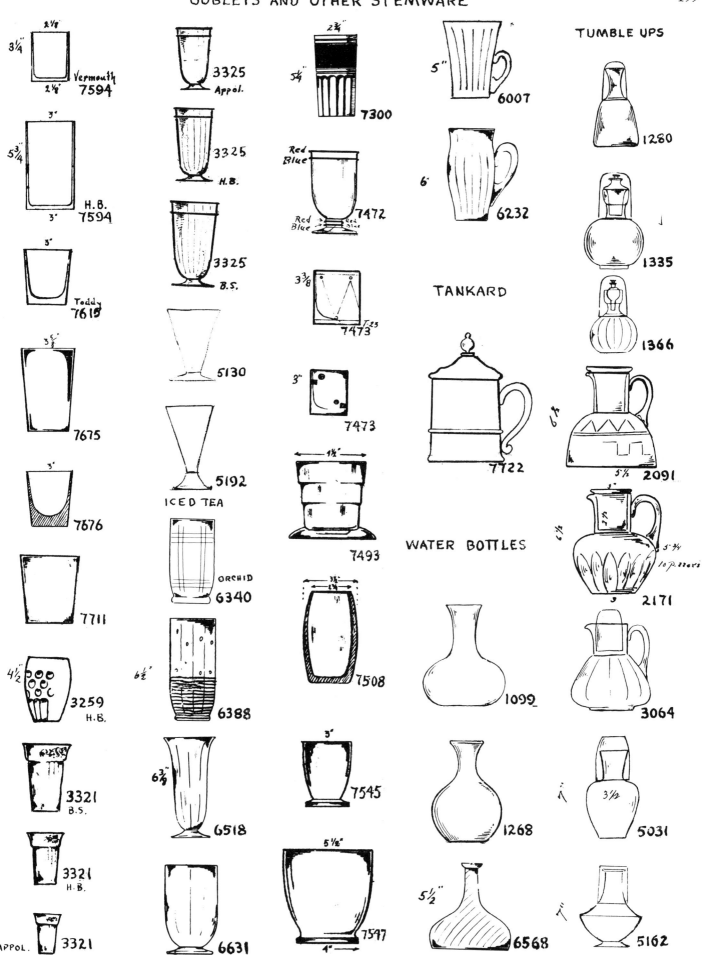

TUMBLE UPS

TANKARD

WATER BOTTLES

ICED TEA

LAMPS

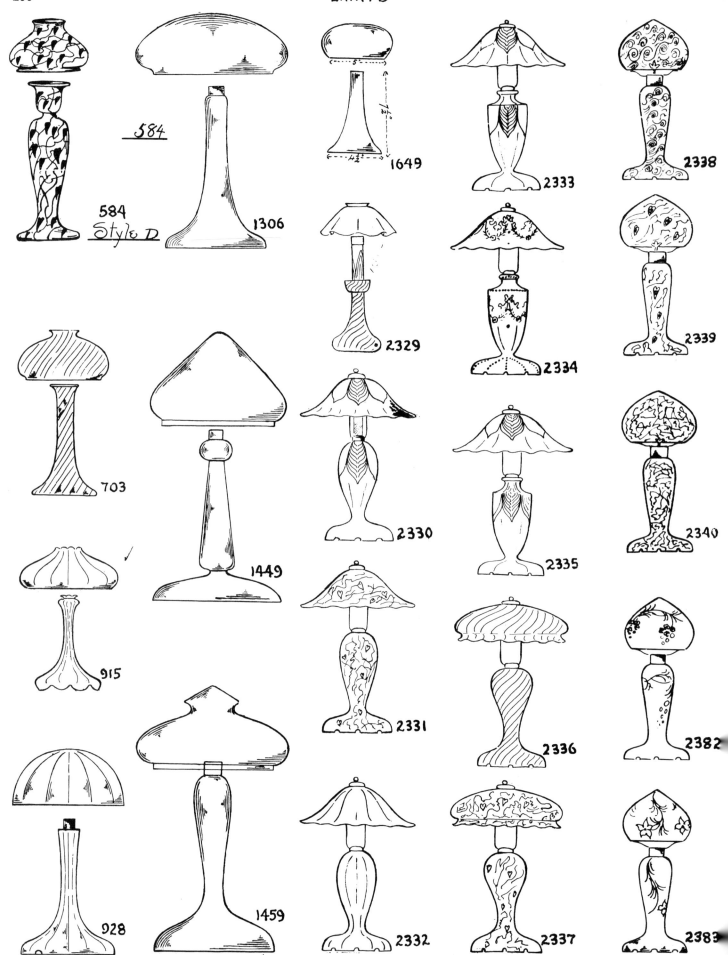

584

584
Style D

1306

1649

1306

2333

2338

703

1449

2329

2334

2339

915

2330

2335

2340

2331

2336

2382

928

1459

2332

2337

2383

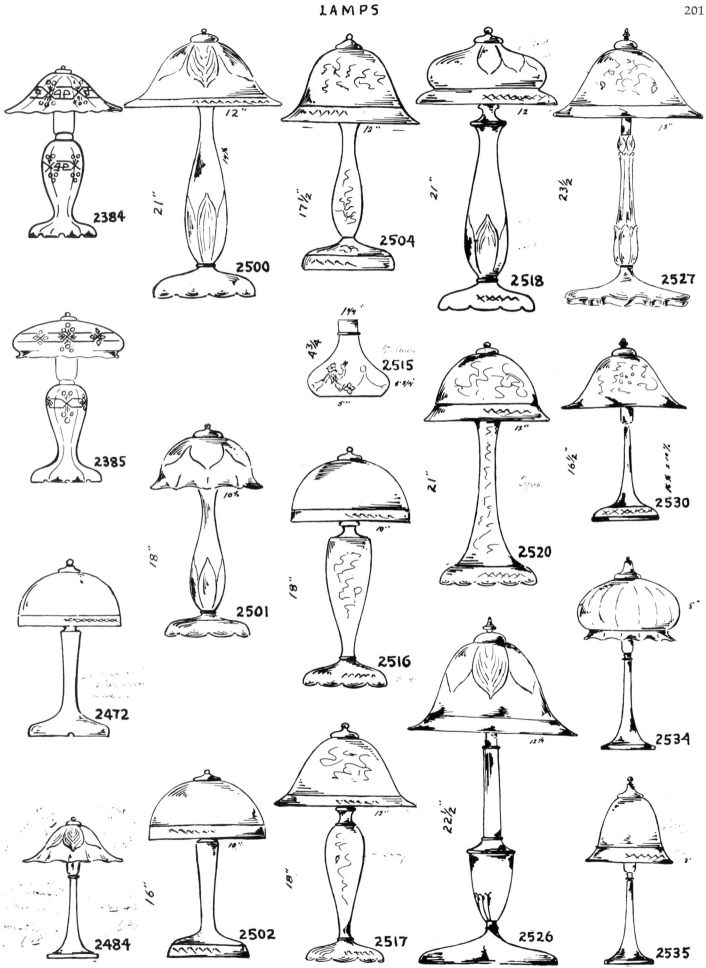

2384

2500 12" 21"

2504 12" 17½"

2518 12 21"

2527 13" 23½"

2385

2515 4¾" 1¼" 5"

2501 10½" 18"

2516 10" 18"

2520 12" 21"

2530 16½"

2472

2534

2484 16"

2502 10" 16"

2517 13" 18"

2526 22½"

2535

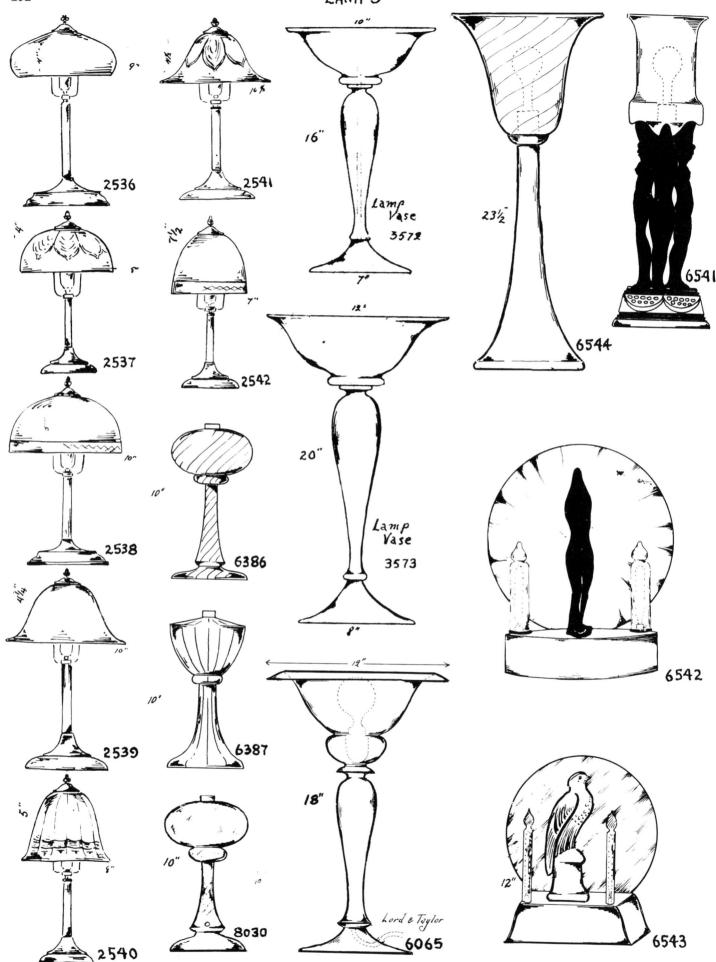

2536

2541

2537

2542

2538

6386

2539

6387

2540

8030

Lamp Vase 3572

Lamp Vase 3573

6065

Lord & Taylor

6544

6541

6542

6543

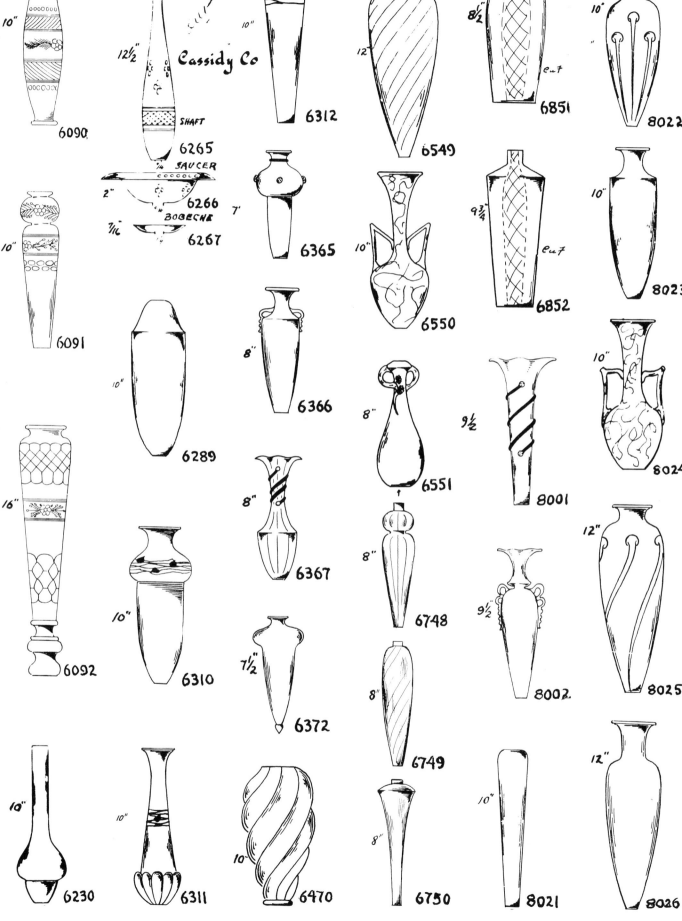

10"
6090.

12½"
Cassidy Co
SHAFT
6265
SAUCER
2"
6266
7/16
BOBECHE
6267
7"

10"
6091

16"
6092

10"
6289

10"
6310

10"
6230

10"
6311

10"
6312

6365

8"
6366

8"
6367

7½"
6372

6470
10"

12"
6549

10"
6550

8"
6551

8"
6748

8"
6749

6750
8"

8½"
6851
cut

9¾"
6852
cut

9½"
8001

9½"
8002

10"
8021

10"
8022

10"
8023

10"
8024

12"
8025

12"
8026

204

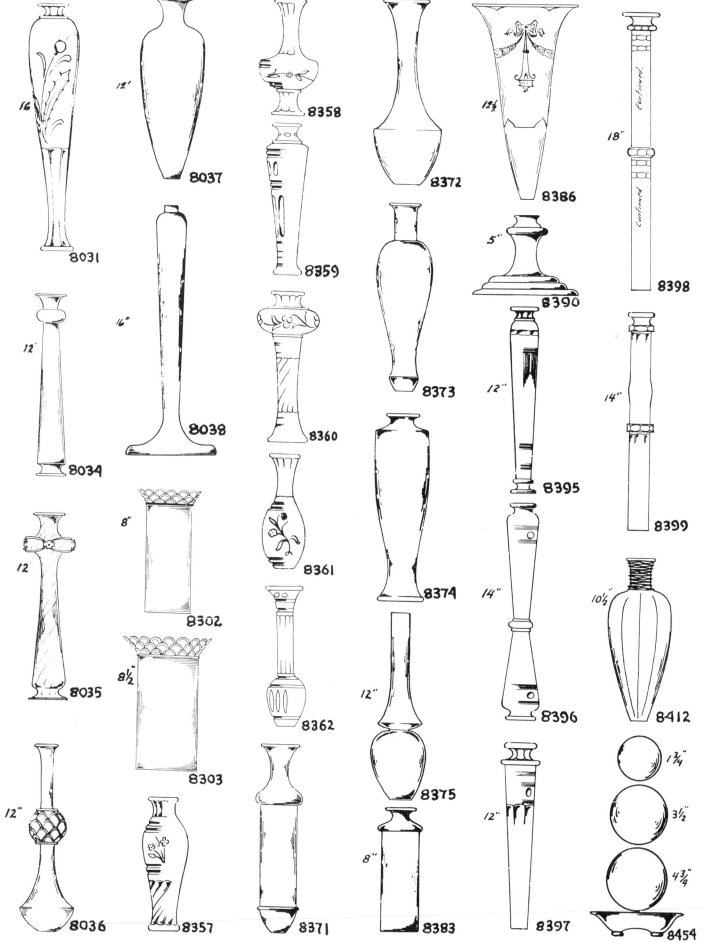

16

12'

8358

8372

12¼

Perfumed.

18"

8386

8031

8037

Confined

8398

12'

16"

5"

8390

8359

14"

8034

8038

8360

8373

12"

8395

8399

8302

8361

12

8303

8362

14"

8035

8374

10½"

8412

12

1¾"

12"

8375

3½"

12"

8036

8357

8371

8383

8397

4¾"

8454

8"

8"

5¼"   #269

7150

2⅜"

7151

10"

8466

6½"

8470

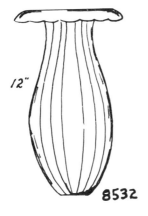

3¾"

8516

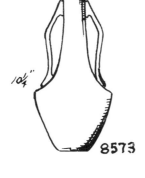

12"

8532

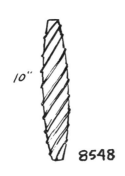

10"

8548

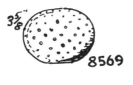

3⅝"

8569

7"

8490

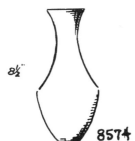

10¼"

8573

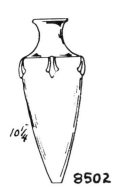

10¼"

8502

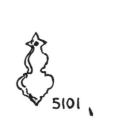

8½"

8574

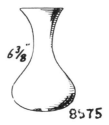

6⅜"

8575

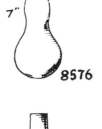

7"

8576

6½"

8577

7"

8578

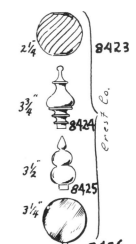

2¼"   8423

3¾"   8424

3½"   8425

3¼"   8426

Crest Co.

8427   3½"

4¼"   Flat   8428

4¼"   8429

HOUR GLASS

7"   Art hight Special

6591

PENDANT

5101

975

976½

980½

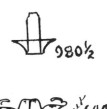

6447

LIMOUSINE VASES · TORCHÈRES AND OTHER SHAPES USED IN METAL MOUNTS

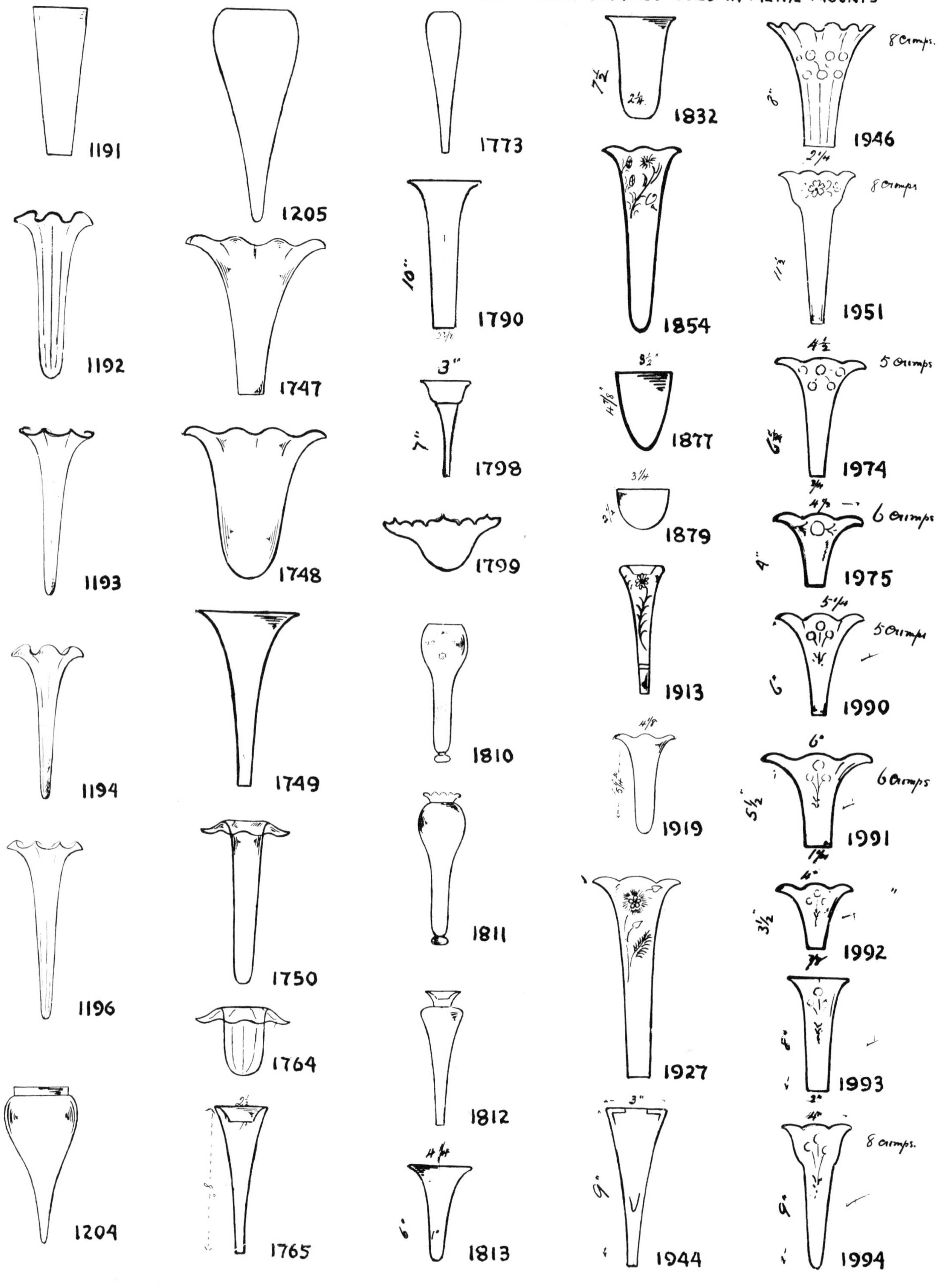

1191

1205

1192

1747

1193

1748

1194

1749

1196

1750

1764

1204

1765

1773

1790 — 10"

1798 — 3"

1799

1810

1811

1812

1813

1832 — 7½ — 2¼

1854

1877 — 3½" — 4⅞"

1879 — 3¼ — 2½

1913

1919 — 4/8

1927

1944 — 3"

1946 — 8 Crmps. — 8"

1951 — 8 Crmps — 1⅓

1974 — 4½ — 5 Crimps — 6¾

1975 — 4½ — 6 Crimps — 4"

1990 — 5-¾ — 5 Crimps — 6"

1991 — 6° — 6 Crimps — 5½" — 1¾

1992 — 4° — 3½ — ¾

1993 — 2"

1994 — 4° — 8 Crimps — 9°

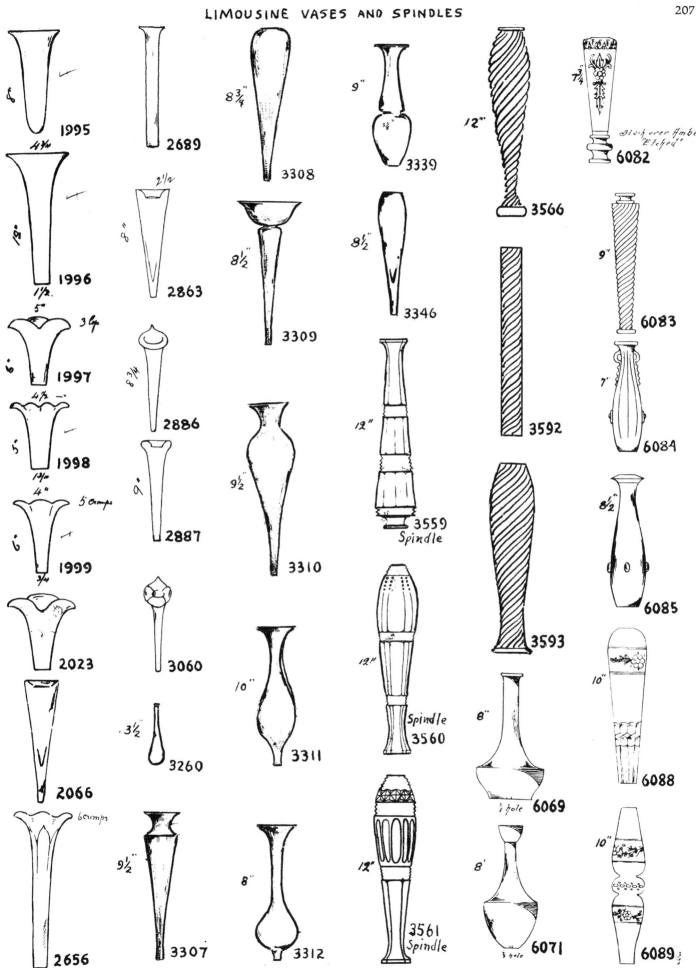

1995

4¾

1996

8"

1½

5"

3¼

1997

6"

4½

1998

5"

1¾

4"

5 Crimps

1999

6"

¾

2023

2066

6 crimps

2656

2689

2½

2863

8"

6¼

2886

9"

2887

3060

3½

3260

9½

3307

8¾

3308

8½

3309

9½

3310

10"

3311

8"

3312

9"

3339

¾

8½

3346

12"

3559
Spindle

12"

3560
Spindle

12"

3561
Spindle

12"

3566

3592

3593

7¼

6082

Black over Amber
"Etched"

9"

6083

7"

6084

8½

6085

8"

6069

½ hole

8'

6071

¾ hole

10"

6088

10"

6089

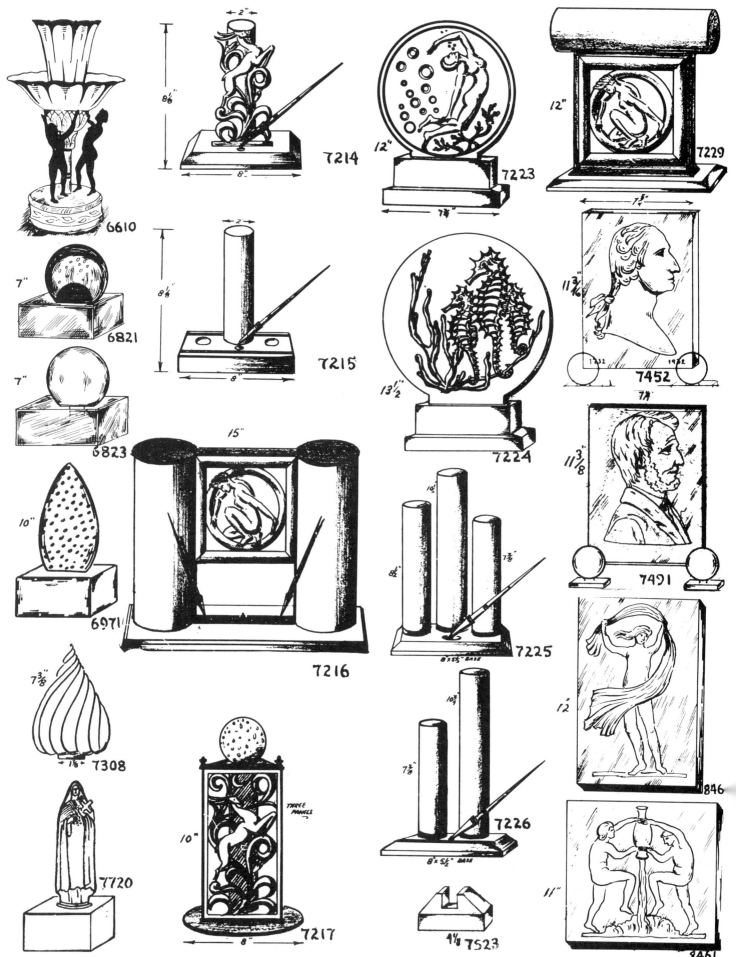

6610

7214

7223

12"

7229

6821

7215

7452

6823

7224

7491

6971

7216

7225

7308

7720

7217

7226

7523

846

8461

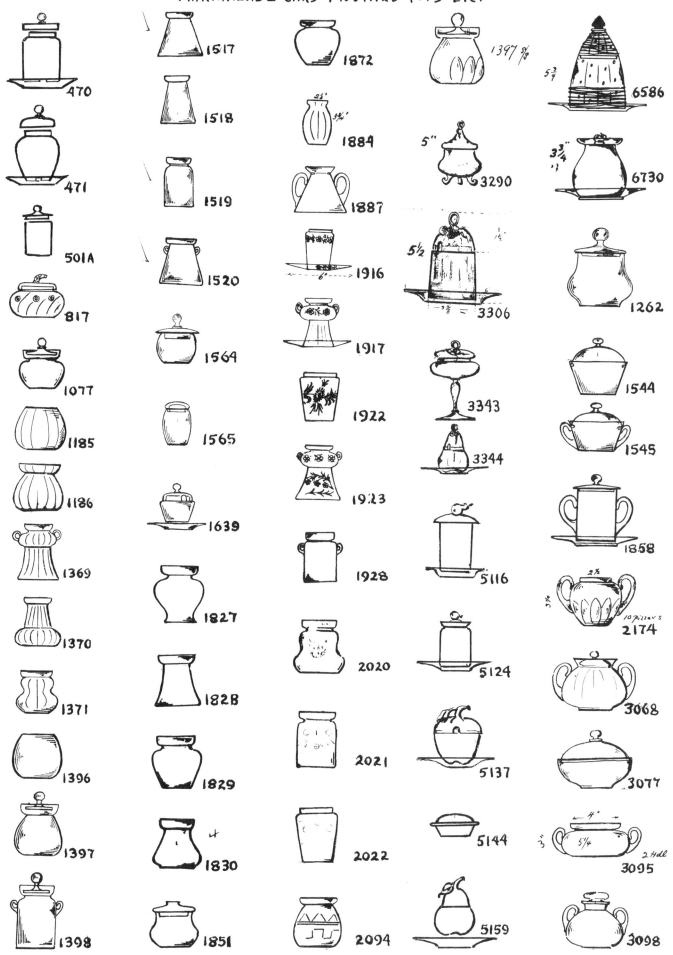

470

471

501A

817

1077

1185

1186

1369

1370

1371

1396

1397

1398

1517

1518

1519

1520

1564

1565

1639

1827

1828

1829

1830 +

1851

1872

1884 2¼" 3¾"

1887

1916 6"

1917

1922

1923

1928

2020

2021

2022

2094

1397 ⅝

3290 5"

3306 5½ ½ ⅜

3343

3344

5116

5124

5137

5144

5159

6586 5¾

6730 3¾ ·⅞

1262

1544

1545

1858

2174 3¾ 2⅜ 10 pieces

3068

3077

3095 4" 5¼ 3 2 Hdl

3098

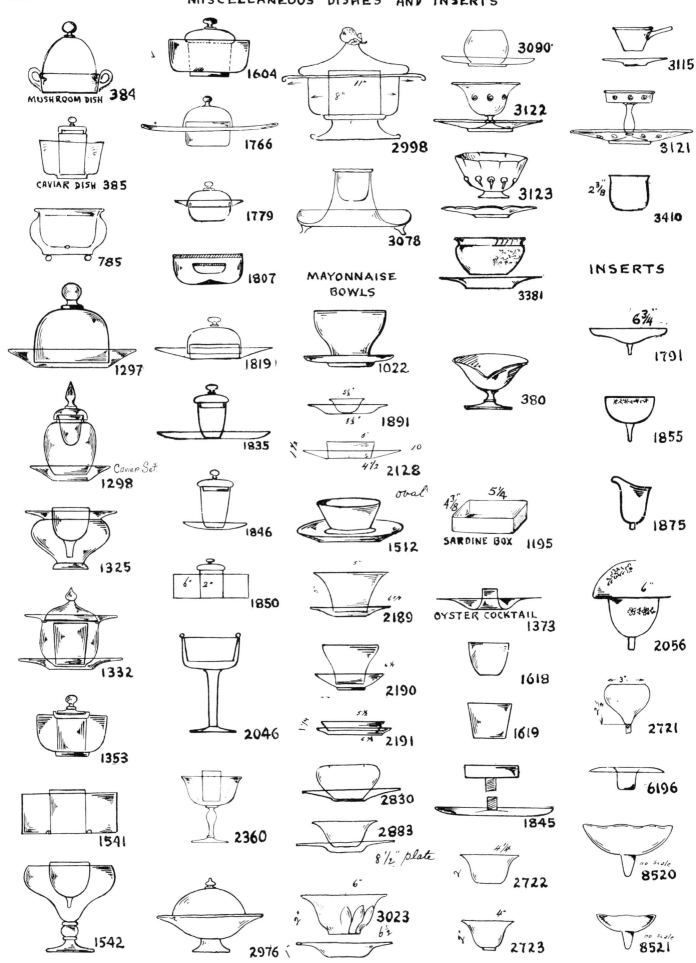

MUSHROOM DISH 384

CAVIAR DISH 385

785

1297

Cavier Set.
1298

1325

1332

1353

1541

1542

1604

1766

1779

1807

1819

1835

1846

1850

2046

2360

2976

MAYONNAISE BOWLS

2998

3078

1022

1891

2128

oval
1512

2189

2190

2191

2830

2883

8½" plate

3023

3090

3122

3123

3381

380

SARDINE BOX 1195

OYSTER COCKTAIL 1373

1618

1619

1845

2722

2723

3115

3121

3410

INSERTS

1791

1855

1875

2056

2721

6196

8520

8521

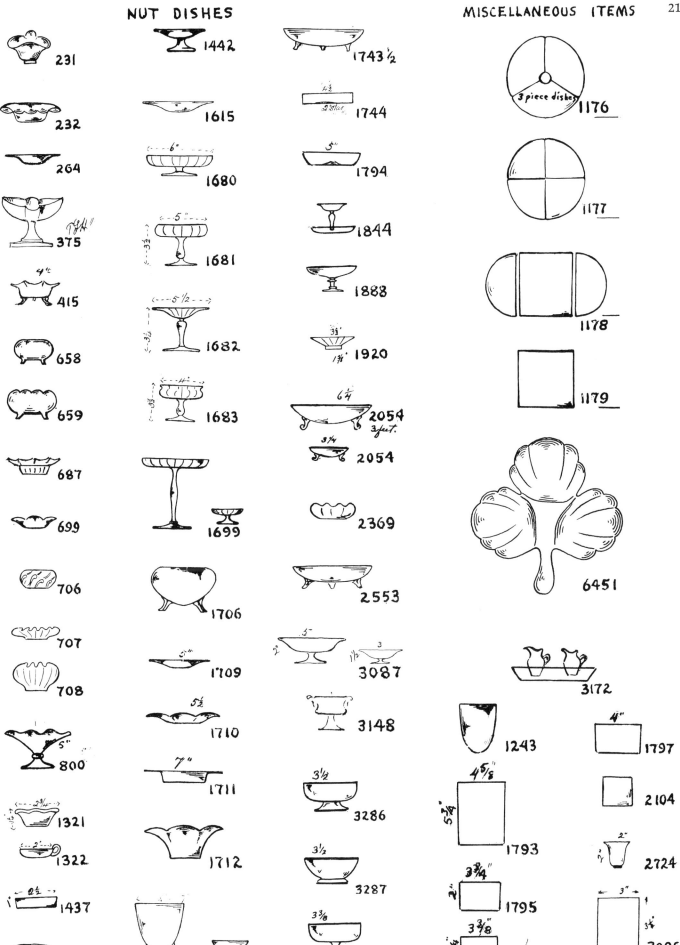

NUT DISHES

MISCELLANEOUS ITEMS 211

231

232

264

375

415

658

659

687

699

706

707

708

800

1321

1322

1437

1439 oval

1442

1615

1680 6"

1681 5"

1682 5½"

1683 4"

1699

1706

1709

1710 5½

1711 7"

1712

1714

1743½

1744

1794 5"

1844

1888

1920

2054 6¼ 3 feet.

2054

2369

2553

3087

3148

3286 3½

3287 3½

3288 3⅜

1176 3 piece dishes

1177

1178

1179

6451

3172

1243

1793

1795

1796

1797 4"

2104

2724

3096

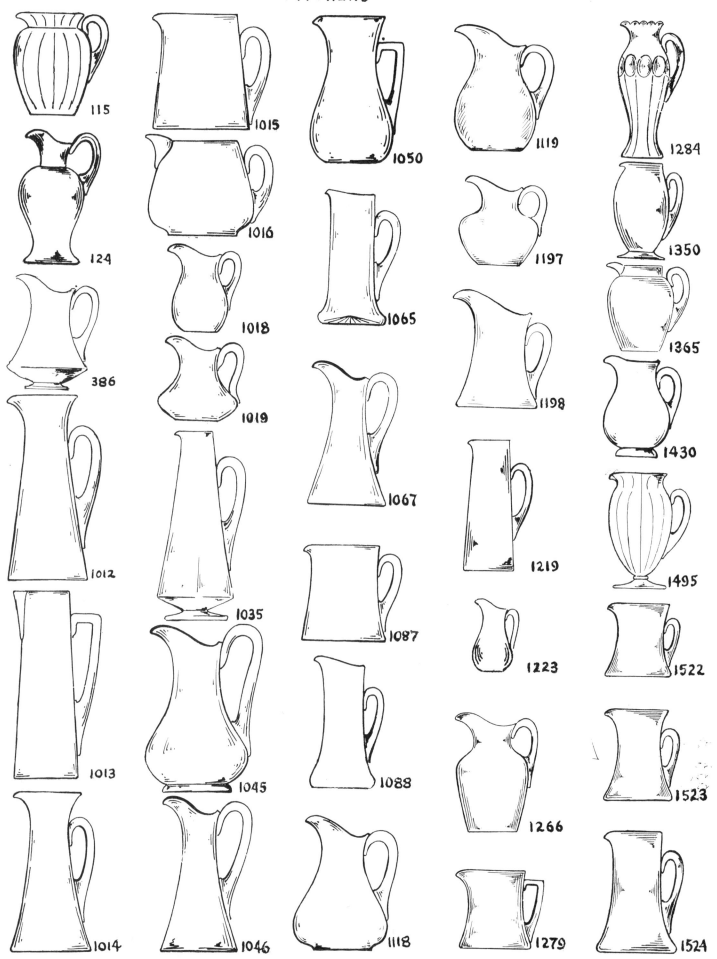

115

1015

1050

1119

1284

124

1016

1197

1350

386

1018

1065

1365

1019

1067

1198

1430

1012

1035

1219

1495

1013

1045

1087

1223

1522

1088

1266

1523

1014

1046

1118

1279

1524

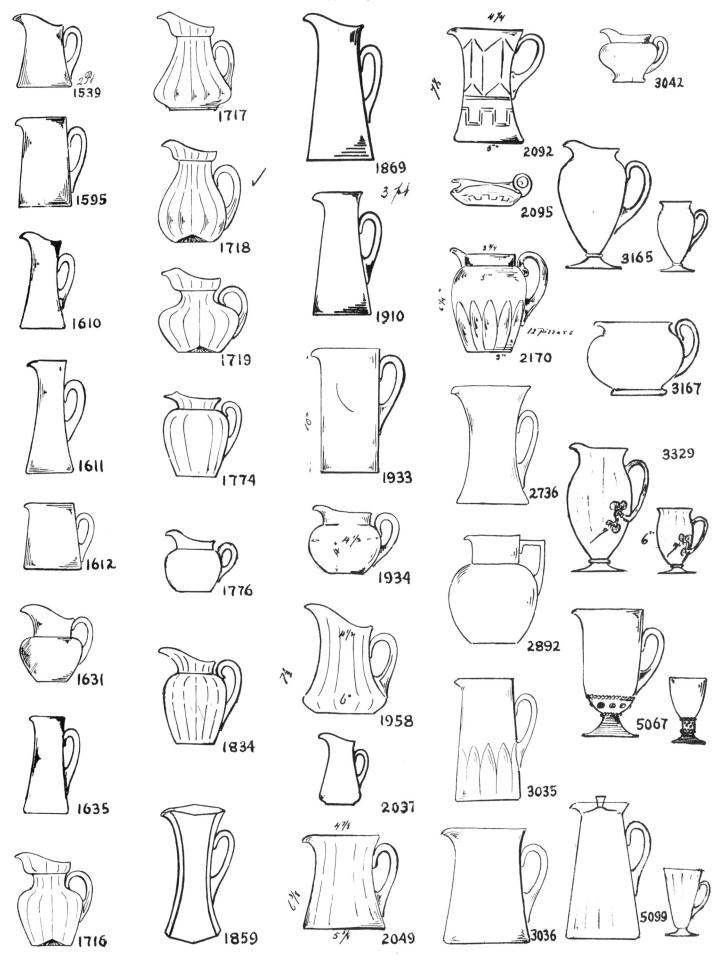

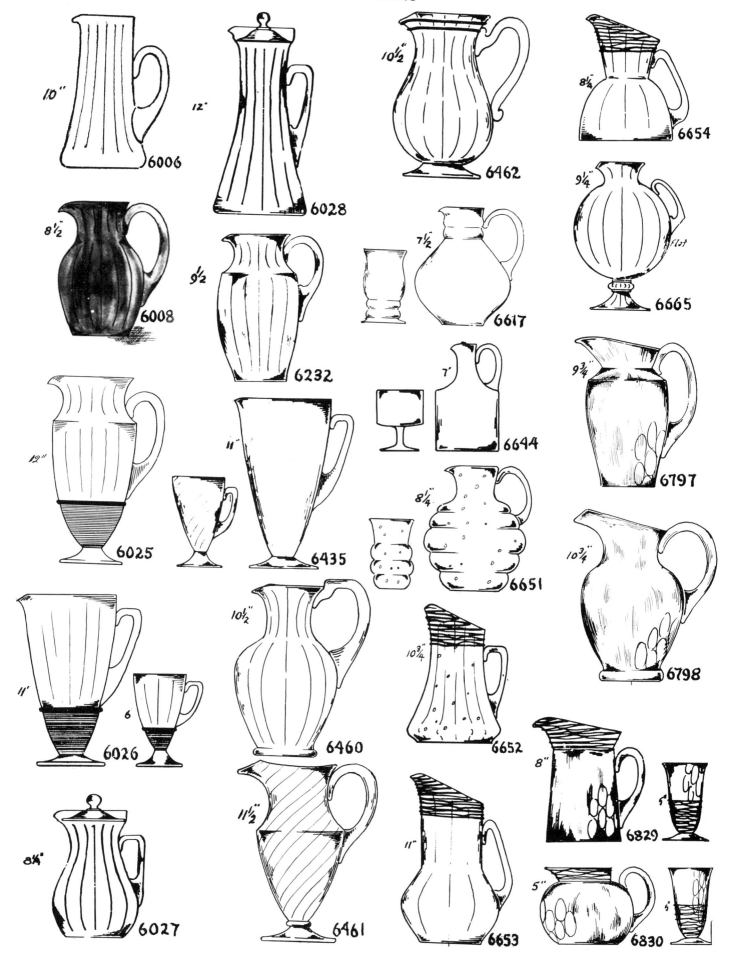

10"   6006

12"   6028

10½"   6462

8¼"   6654

8½"   6008

9½"   6232

7½"   6617

9¼"   Flat   6665

12"   6025

11"   6435

7"   6644

9¾"   6797

8¼"   6651

11'   6   6026

10½"   6460

10¾"   6652

10¾"   6798

8¼"   6027

11½"   6461

11"   6653

8"   5"   6829

5"   5"   6830

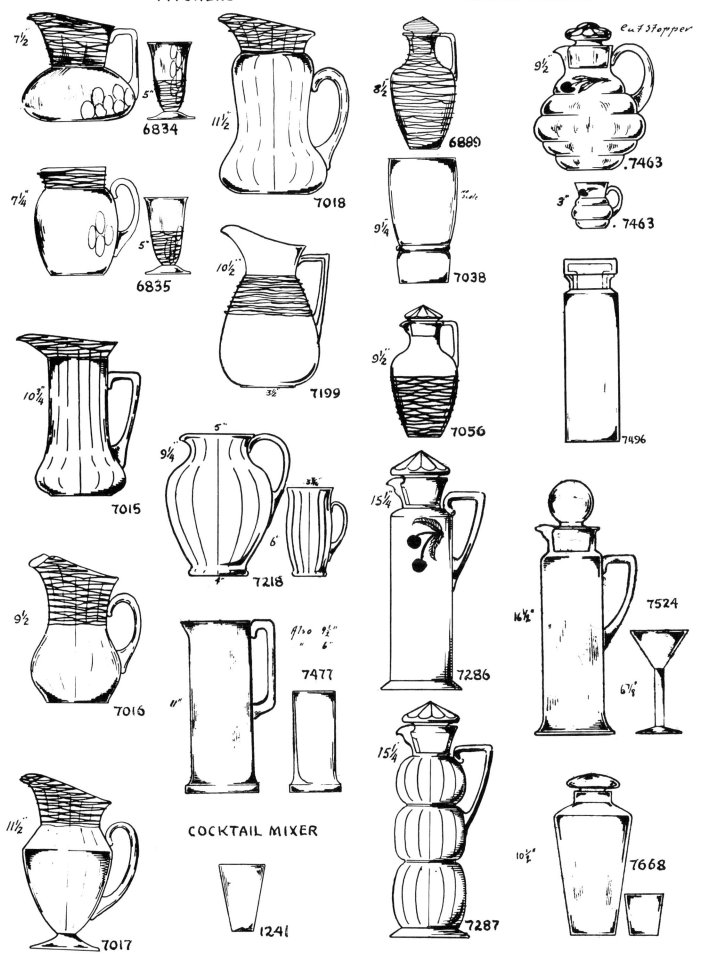

PITCHERS

7½" — 6834 (5")

7¼" — 6835 (5")

11½" — 7018

10½" — 7199 (3½)

10¾" — 7015

9¼" 5" 3¼" 6" 4" — 7218

9½" — 7016

11" Also 9½" 6" — 7477

11½" — 7017

COCKTAIL MIXER

1241

COCKTAIL SHAKERS

8½" — 6889

9¼" scale — 7038

9½" — 7056

15¼" — 7286

15¼" — 7287

9½" cut stopper — 7463

3" — 7463

7496

7524

16½" 6⅞" — 7524

10½" — 7668

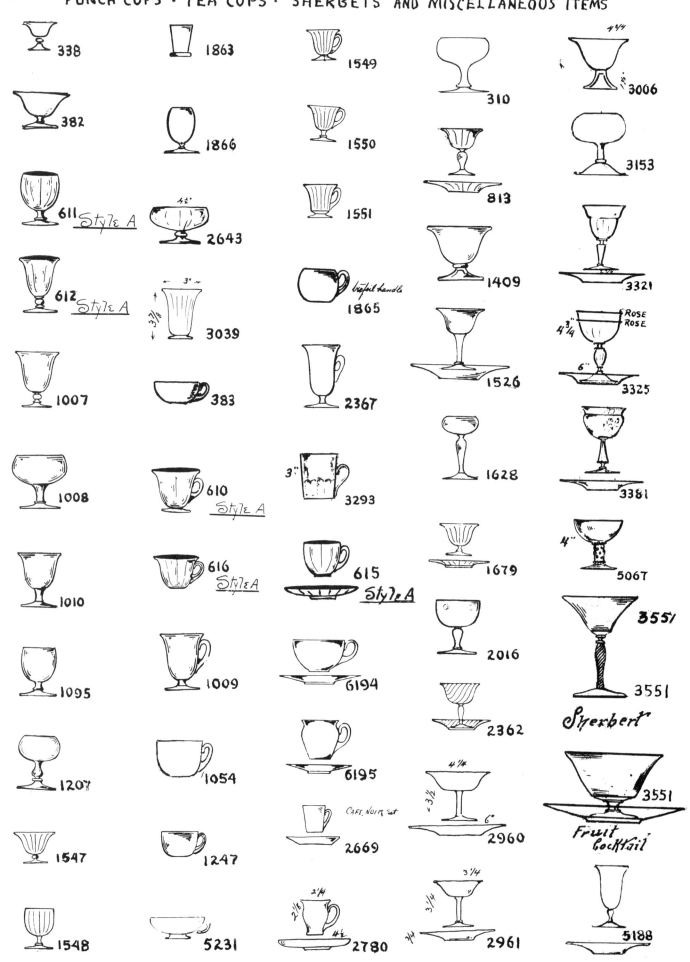

338

1863

1549

310

4 1/4
3006

382

1866

1550

3153

611 Style A

4 1/2
2643

1551

813

612 Style A

3"
3 7/8
3039

trefoil handle
1865

1409

3321

1007

383

2367

1526

4 3/4
ROSE
ROSE
6"
3325

1008

610
Style A

3"
3293

1628

3381

1010

616
Style A

615
Style A

1679

4"
5067

1095

1009

6194

2016

3551

1207

1054

6195

2362

3551
Sherbert

1547

1247

CAFE NOIR Set
2669

4 1/4
3 1/2
6"
2960

3551
Fruit
Cocktail

1548

5231

2 1/4
2 1/8
4 1/2
2780

3 1/4
3/4
3/4
2961

5188

SALTS, CELERY DIPS, ETC.

SALT AND PEPPER SHAKERS

SUGAR SHAKERS

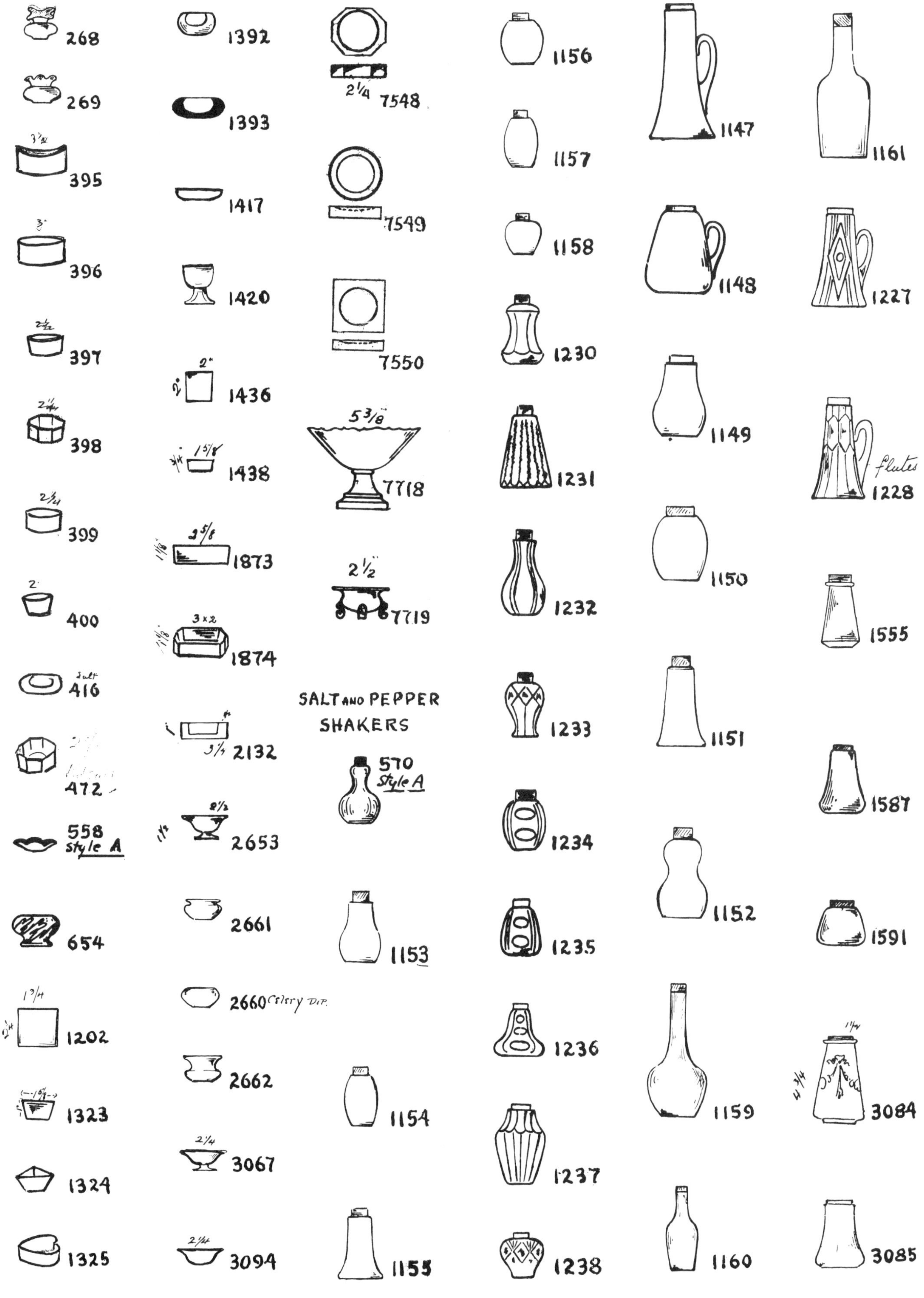

268
269
395
396
397
398
399
400
416
472
558 style A
654
1202
1323
1324
1325
1392
1393
1417
1420
1436
1438
1873
1874
2132
2653
2661
2660 Celery Dip
2662
3067
3094
7548
7549
7550
5 3/8"
7718
2 1/2"
7719
SALT AND PEPPER SHAKERS
570 Style A
1153
1154
1155
1156
1157
1158
1230
1231
1232
1233
1234
1235
1236
1237
1238
1147
1148
1149
1150
1151
1152
1159
1160
1161
1227
flutes
1228
1555
1587
1591
3084
3085

SHADES

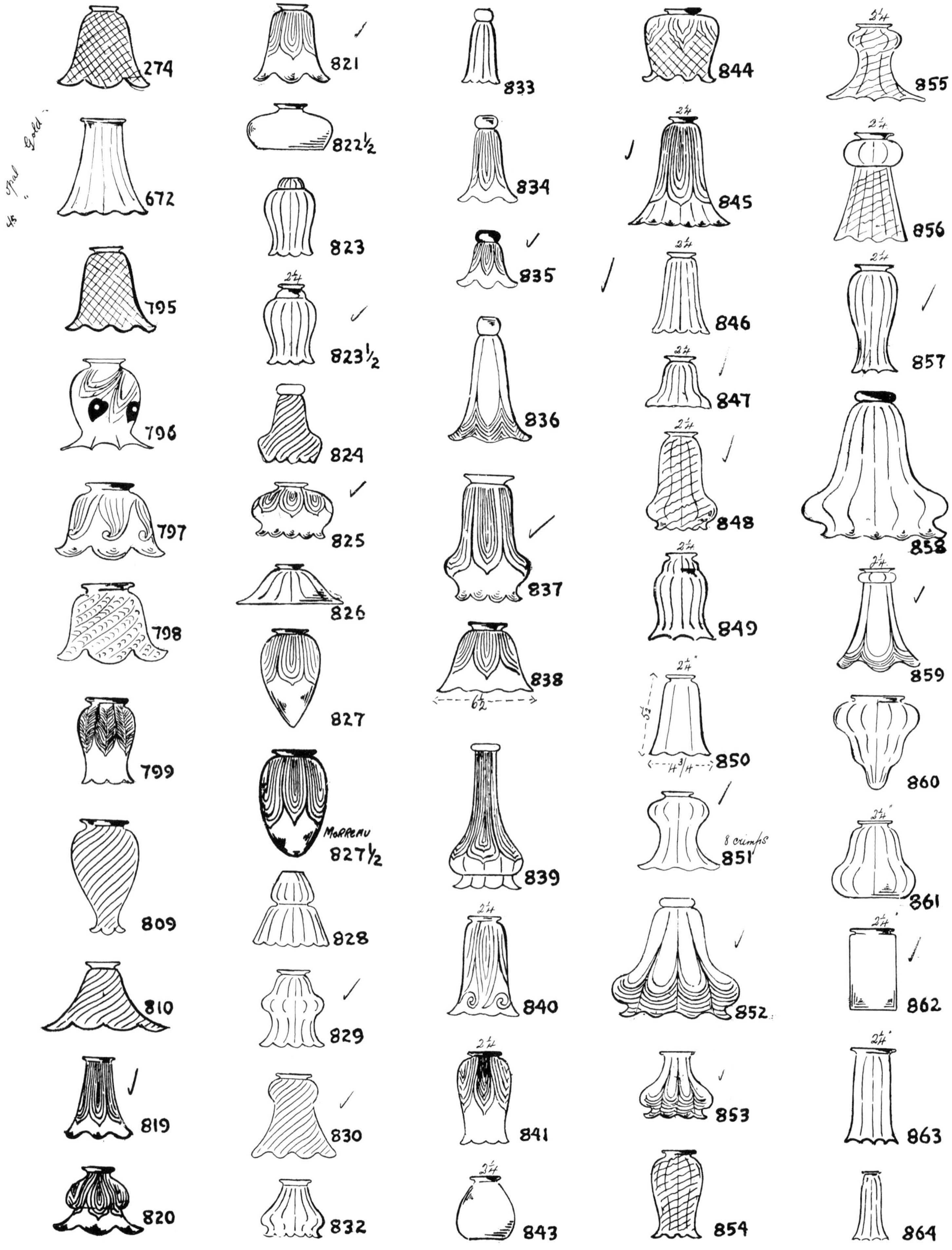

274

821

833

844

855

45 "Mat Gold .
45 " Gold .

672

822½

834

845

856

795

823

835

846

857

796

823½

836

847

798

824

837

848

858

797

825

838
‹------ 6½ ------›

849

859

798

826

850
2¼"
5½
4¾

860

799

827

839

851
8 crimps

861

809

827½
MoRREAU

828

840

852

862

810

829

841

853

863

819

830

854

864

820

832

843

854

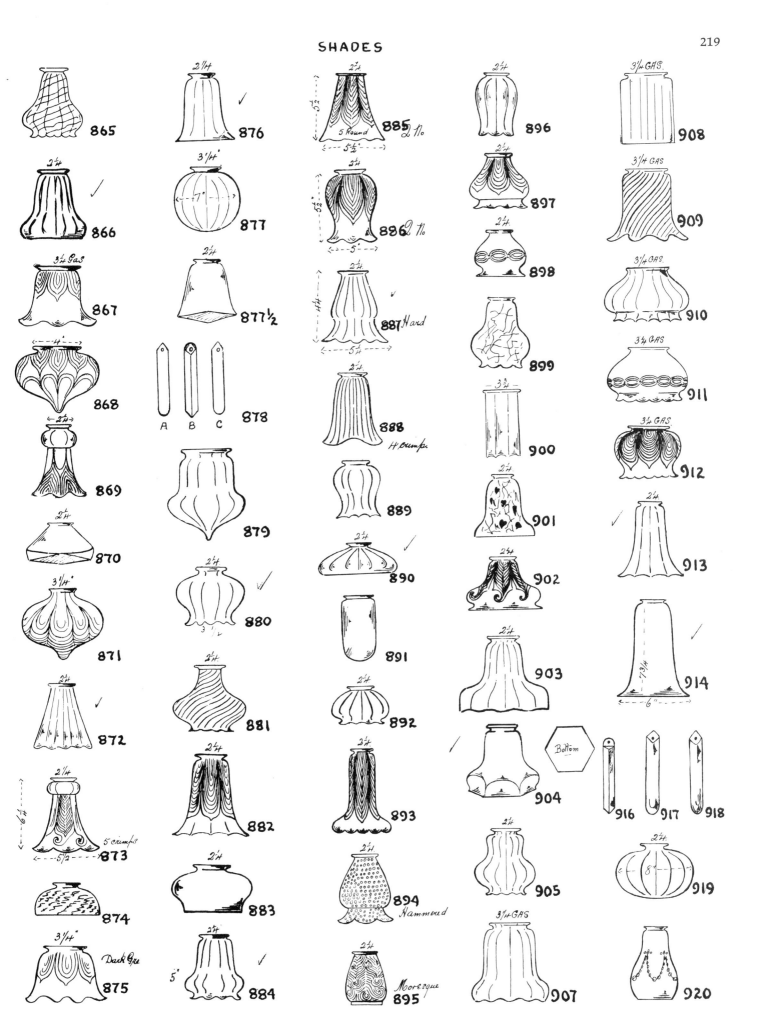

865

2¼" 876 ✓

866 2¼" ✓

3¼" 877 ←7"→

3¼ Gas 867

2¼" 877½

868 ←4"→

A B C 878

869 ←2¼"→

879

870 2¼" H

871 3¼"

880 2¼" ✓ 3½"

872 2¼" ✓

881 2¼"

873 2¼" H ←6¼"→ 5 crimps ←5½"→

882 2¼"

874

883 2¼"

875 3¼" Dark Gre

884 2¼" ✓ 5"

885 2½" 2 No. ←5½"→ 5 Round ←5½"→

886 2½" 2 No. ←5½"→ ←5"→

887 2¼" ✓ Hard ←4¼"→ ←5¾"→

888 2¼" H. Crimps

889 2¼"

890 2¼" ✓

891 2¼"

892 2¼"

893 2¼"

894 2¼" Hammered

895 2¼" Moresque

896 2¼"

897 2¼"

898 2¼"

899 2¼"

900 3¾"

901 2¼"

902 2½"

903 2¼"

904 Bottom

905 2¼"

907 3¼" GAS

908 3¼" GAS

909 3¼" GAS

910 3¼" GAS

911 3¼ GAS

912 3¼ GAS

913 2¼"

914 2¼" 7¾" ←6"→ ✓

916 917 918

919 2¼" ←8"→

920

SHADES

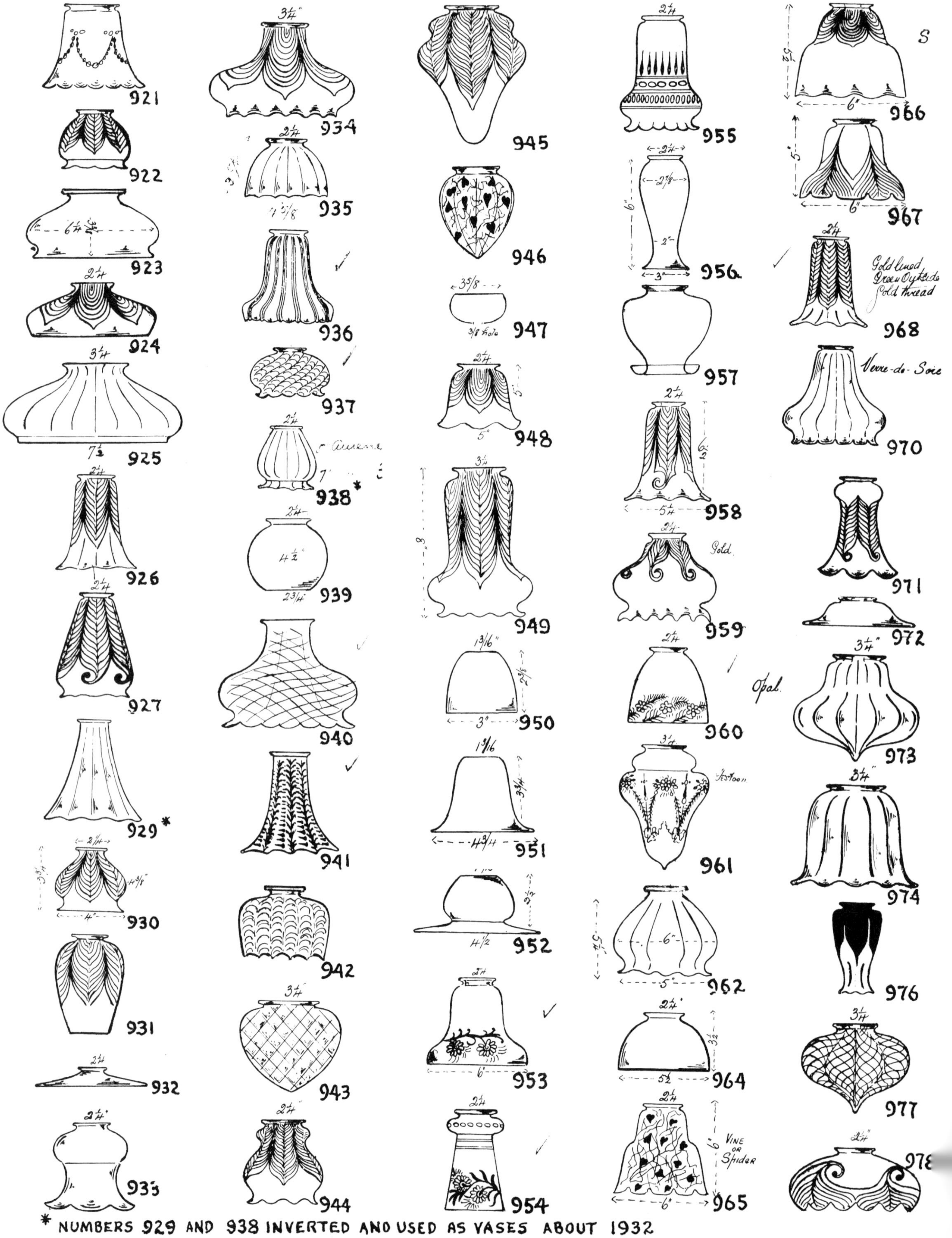
921
922
923
924
925
926
927
929 *
930
931
932
933
934
935
936
937
938 *
939
940
941
942
943
944
945
946
947
948
949
950
951
952
953
954
955
956
957
958
959
Gold.
960
Opal.
961
962
964
965
VINE OR Spider
966
S
967
968
Gold lined
Verre-de-Soie
970
971
972
973
974
976
977
978

* NUMBERS 929 AND 938 INVERTED AND USED AS VASES ABOUT 1932

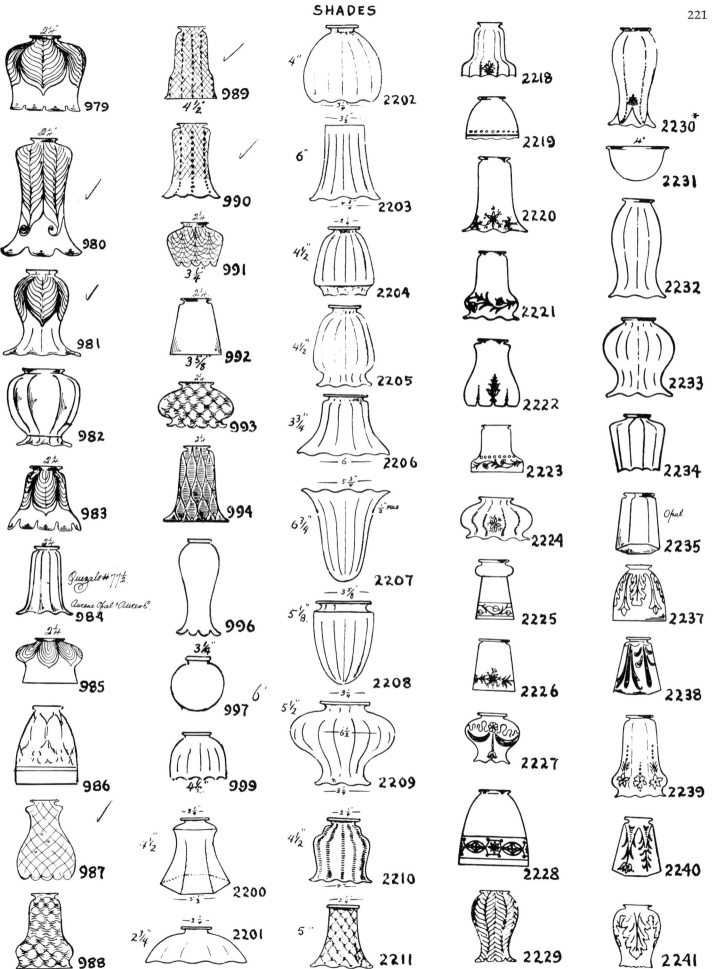

979
989 4½
990
980
991 3¼
981
992 3⅝
982
993
983
994
984 Quezale # 77½
Aurene Opal + Aurene E.
996
985 3¼
997 6
986
999 4½
987
2200 4½
988
2201 2¾

4" 2202 3¾ 3½
6" 2203 4¾
4½" 2204 2¼
4½" 2205
3¾" 2206 6
6¾" 2207 5¾ ½ HOLE
5⅛" 2208 3⅝
2209 5½ 3¼ 6½ 3¼
4½" 2210 2⅛ 4
5" 2211 2¼

2218
2219
2220
2221
2222
2223
2224
2225
2226
2227
2228
2229

2230*
2231 4"
2232
2233
2234
2235 Opal
2237
2238
2239
2240
2241

* NUMBER 2230 INVERTED AND USED AS A VASE ABOUT 1932

SHADES

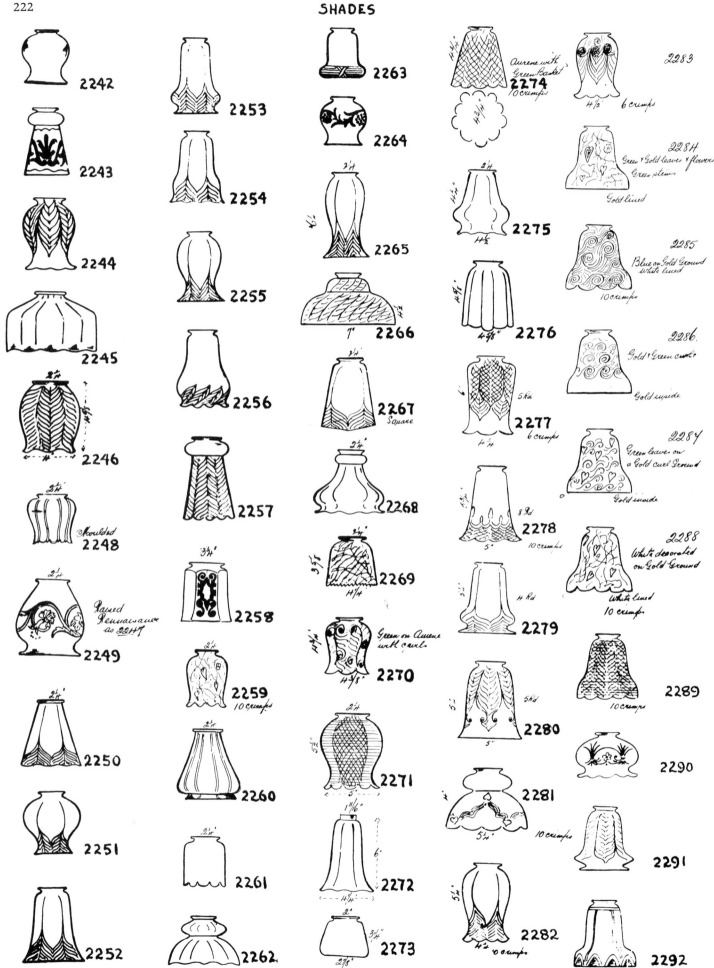

2242

2243

2244

2245

2246 2½" 4½" 4"

2248 3½" Moulded

2249 2½" Raised Renaissance as 22H7

2250 2½"

2251

2252

2253

2254

2255

2256 3"

2257

2258 3¾"

2259 2½" 10 crimps

2260 2½"

2261 2½"

2262

2263

2264

2265 2½" 4½"

2266 1" 4½"

2267 3" Square

2268 2½"

2269 3¾" 2½" 4¼"

2270 4½" Green on Aurene with curls 4¾"

2271 5½" 2¾" 5"

2272 1"1/6 6" 4¼"

2273 2" 3¾" 2⅜"

2274 4¾" Aurene with Green Basket 10 crimps 4¾"

2275 2¾" 4½" 4½"

2276 4¾" 4⅝"

2277 1" 5Rd 6 crimps 4¼"

2278 3½" 8Rd 10 crimps 5"

2279 5" 4 Rd

2280 5" 5Rd 5"

2281 4" 5¾" 10 crimps

2282 5½" 4¾" 10 crimps

2283 4½" 6 crimps

228H Green & Gold leaves & flowers Green stems Gold lined

2285 Blue on Gold Ground White lined 10 crimps

2286 Gold & Green curls Gold inside

2287 Green leaves on a Gold curl Ground Gold inside

2288 White decorated on Gold Ground White lined 10 crimps

2289 10 crimps

2290

2291

2292

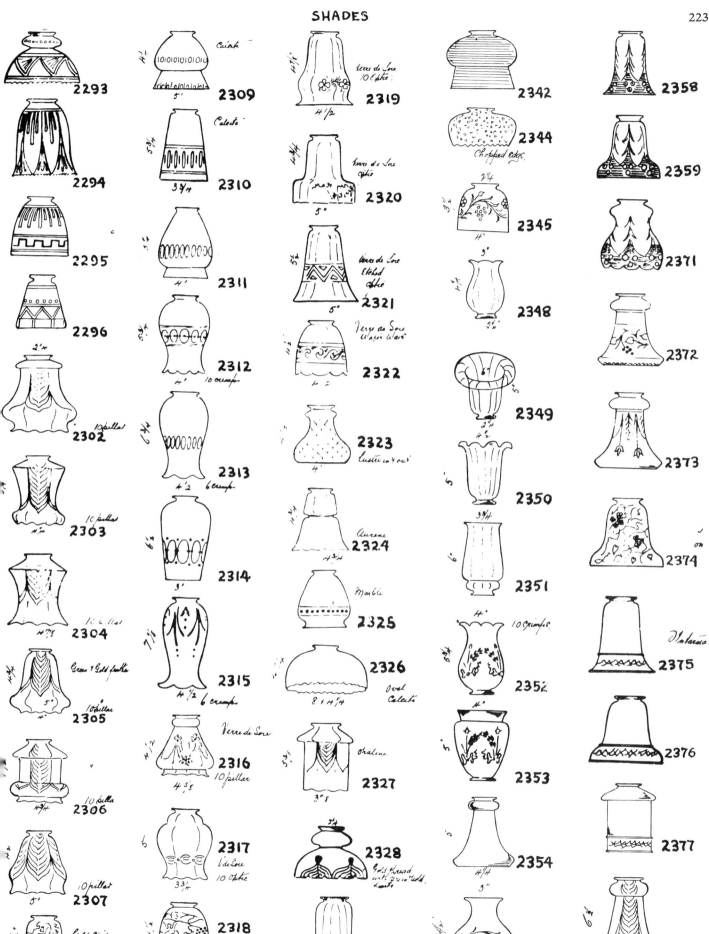

2293

2294

2295

2296

2302

2303

2304

Green & Gold feather
2305

10 bella
2306

10 pillar
2307

Gold Spider
2308

Caieta
2309

Calista
2310

2311

2312
10 crimps

2313
6 crimp

2314

2315
6 crimp

Verre de Soie
2316
10 pillar

V de Soie
2317
10 Optic

Verre de Soie Optic
2318
10 crimp

Verre de Soie 10 Optic
2319

Verre de Soie Optic
2320

Verre de Soie Etched Optic
2321

Verre de Soie Water Wave
2322

2323
lustre in 4 out

Aurene
2324

Marble
2325

2326
Oval Calista

Opaline
2327

Gold thread with green Gold hearts
2328

2341

2342

2344
Chopped edge

2345

2348

2349

2350

2351

2352
10 crimps

2353

2354

2355

2358

2359

2371

2372

2373

2374

Intarsia
2375

2376

2377

2378

SHADES

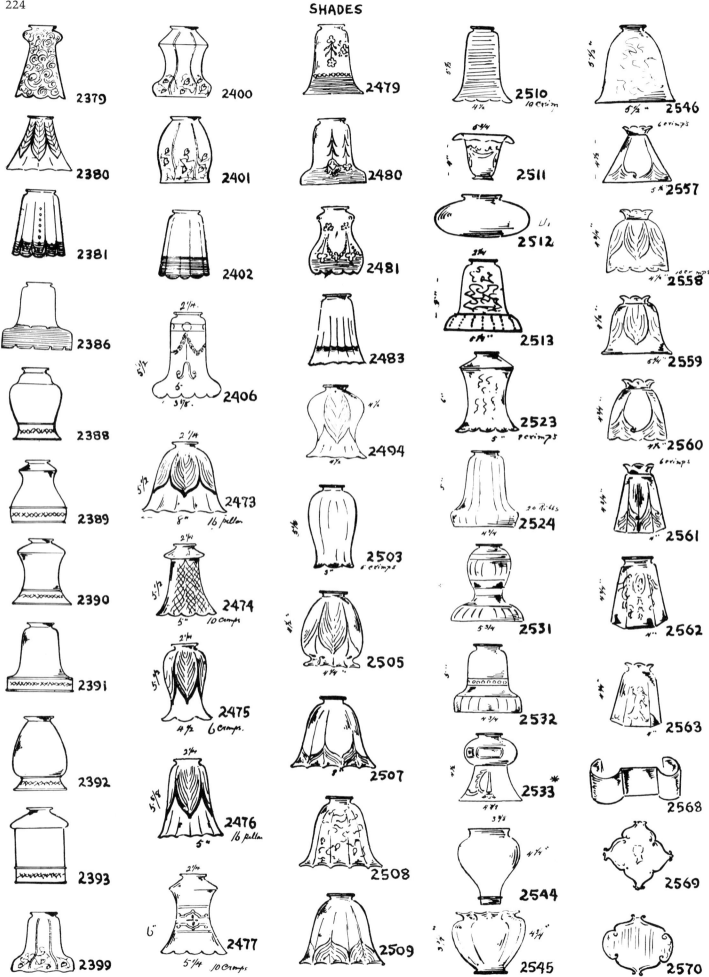

2379

2380

2381

2386

2388

2389

2390

2391

2392

2393

2399

2400

2401

2402

2 1/4
5 1/2
6"
3 5/8
2406

2 1/4
5 1/2
8"   16 pillar
2473

5 1/2
5"   10 Crimps
2474

2 1/4
5 1/2
4 1/2   6 Crimps.
2475

2 1/4
5 1/4
2476
5"   16 pillar

2 1/4
6"
2477
5 1/4   10 Crimps

2479

2480

2481

2483

4 1/2
2494
4 1/2

2503
3"   6 crimps

2505
4 1/2

2507
5"

2508

2509

5 1/8
2510
4 1/2   10 Crimp

5 1/4
2511

2512

3 1/4
5 1/4
2513

2523
5"   6 crimps

20 Ribbs
4 1/4
2524

5 3/4
2531

4 3/4
2532

2533 ✱
4 1/8
3 7/8

4 1/4
2544

4 3/4
2545

5 1/2
2546

6 crimps
4 1/8
5"   2557

4 1/4
4 1/4   10 crimps
2558

4 1/4
5 1/4   2559

4 1/4
4 1/8   2560

6 crimps
4 1/4
4"   2561

4 3/4
4"   2562

4 1/8
2563

2568

2569

2570

✱ NUMBER 2533 INVERTED AND USED AS A VASE ABOUT 1932

SHADES

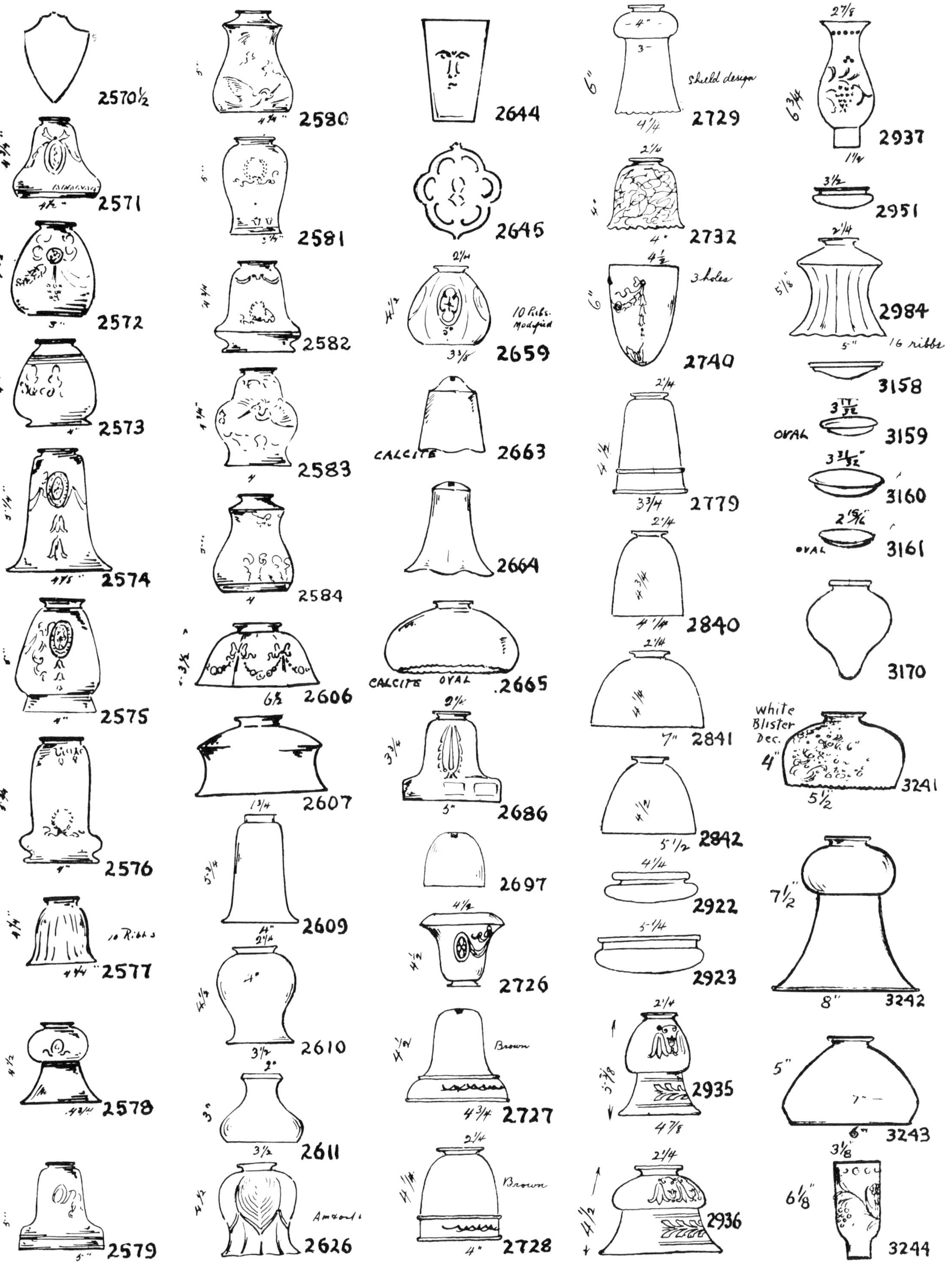
2570½
4 3/4"
2571
4½"
2572
3"
2573
4"
5 1/4"
2574
4½"
2575
4"
2576
4"
4 1/4"
10 Ribbs
2577
4 1/4
4½
2578
4 3/4"
2579
5"
2580
4 1/4"
2581
3 1/4"
2582
4 1/4
2583
4
2584
4
3¾
6½
2606
2607
1 3/4
5 3/4
2609
4"
2¼
4"
2610
3½
2"
2611
3½
4½
Amond
2626
2644
2645
2¼
4½
10 Ribs. Modified
3 3/8
2659
CALCITE
2663
2664
CALCITE OVAL
2665
2¼
3 3/4
5"
2686
2697
4½
4½
2726
4 1/4
Brown
4 3/4
2727
2¼
4 1/4
Brown
4"
2728
4"
3-
6"
Shield design
4 1/4
2729
2¼
4"
4"
2732
4½
3 holes
6"
2740
2¼
4½
3 3/4
2779
2¼
3 1/4
4 1/4
2840
2¼
4 1/4
7"
2841
4½
5½
2842
4 1/4
2922
5 1/4
2923
2¼
5 3/8
4 7/8
2935
2¼
4½
2936
2 7/8
6 3/4
1½
2937
3½
2951
2¼
5 7/8
2984
5"
16 ribbs
3158
3 11/32
OVAL
3159
3 31/32"
3160
2 15/16
OVAL
3161
3170
White Blister Dec.
6"
4"
5½
3241
7½"
8"
3242
5"
7"
6"
3243
3 1/8
6 1/8"
3244

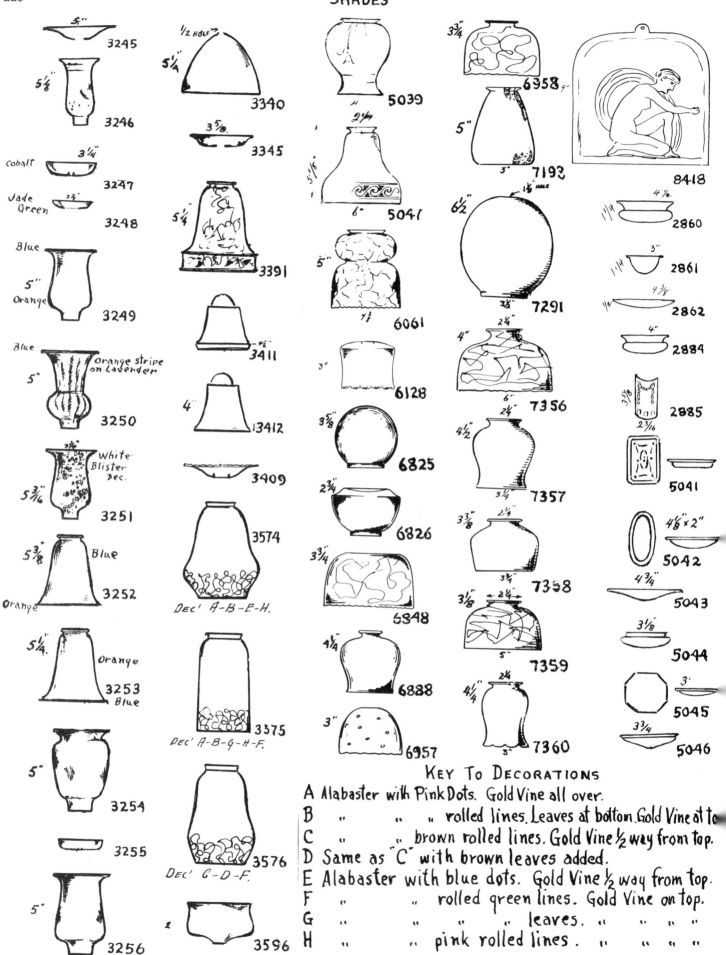

3245
5"

3246
5⅛"

3247
Cobalt   3¼"

3248
Jade Green   3¼"

3249
Blue   5"
Orange

3250
Blue   5"
Orange stripe on Lavender

3251
Blue   5⅜"
White Blister Dec.

3252
5⅜"   Blue
Orange

3253
5¼"   Orange
Blue

3254
5"

3255

3256
5"

3340
½ HOLE→
5¼"

3345
3⅝"

3391
5¼"

3411

13412
4"

3409

3574

3575
Dec' A-B-E-H.

3576
Dec' A-B-G-H-F.

3596
Dec' G-D-F.

5039
3¾"

5041
2¾"
6"

6061
5"
1¼

6128
3"

6825
3⅝"

6826
2¾"

6848
3¾"

6888
4¼"

6957
3"

6958
3¾"

7193
5"
3"

7291
6½"   1½" HOLE
3½"

7356
4"   2¼"
6"

7357
4½"   2¼"
3¾"

7358
3⅜"   2¼"
3¾"

7359
3⅛"   ←2¼"→
5"

7360
4¼"   2¼"
3"

8418

2860
1¼"   4½

2861
1¼   3"

2862
1¼   4⅜

2884
4"

2885
3⅝"
2 3/16

5041
3⅛

5042
4⅛" x 2"

5043
4¾"

5044
3⅛"

5045
3"

5046
3¾

KEY TO DECORATIONS

A Alabaster with Pink Dots. Gold Vine all over.
B   "   "   " rolled lines. Leaves at bottom. Gold Vine at top.
C   "   "   " brown rolled lines. Gold Vine ½ way from top.
D Same as "C" with brown leaves added.
E Alabaster with blue dots. Gold Vine ½ way from top.
F   "   "   " rolled green lines. Gold Vine on top.
G   "   "   "   "   "   " leaves. "   "   " "
H   "   "   " pink rolled lines . "   "   "   "

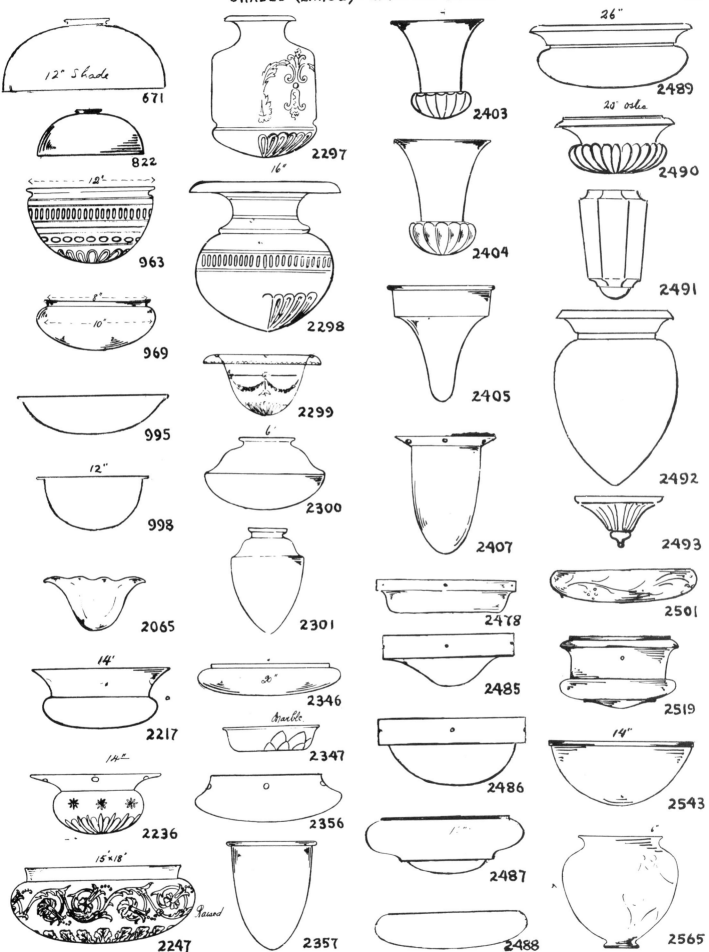

12" Shade 671

822

12" 963

8" 10" 969

995

12" 998

2065

14' 2217

14" 2236

15"x18" Raised 2247

16" 2297

2298

2299

6' 2300

2301

20" 2346

Marble 2347

2356

2357

2403

2404

2405

2407

2478

2485

2486

1" 2487

2488

26" 2489

20" osha 2490

2491

2492

2493

2501

2519

14" 2543

6' 2565

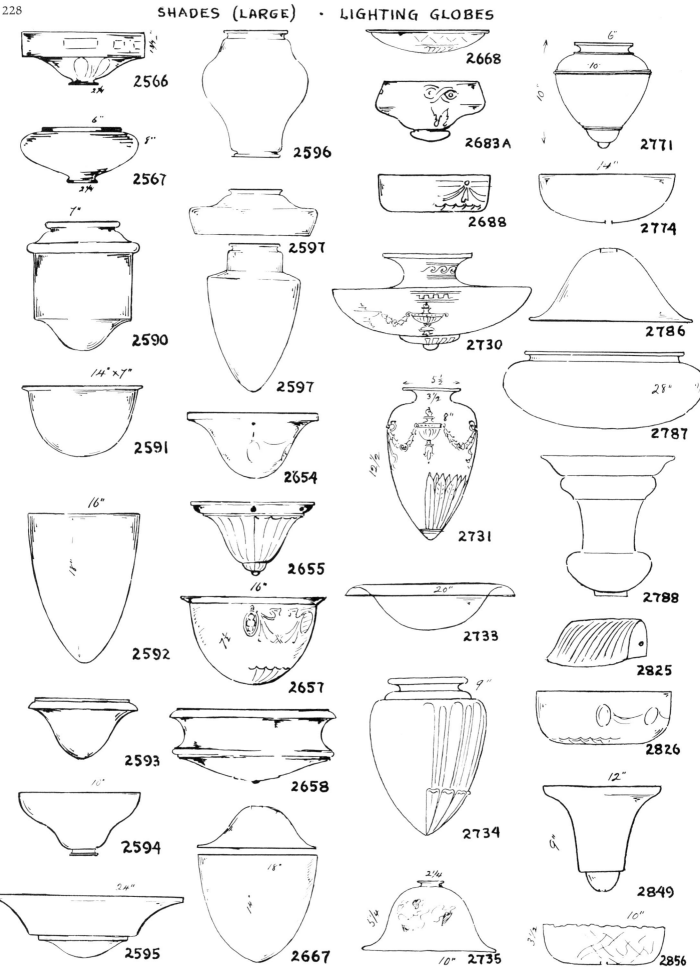

2566

2567

6"
8"

7"
2590

14" x 7"
2591

16"
2592

2593

10"
2594

24"
2595

2596

2597

2597

2654

2655

16"
7½
2657

2658

18"
2667

2668

2683A

2688

2730

5½
3½
8"
12½
2731

20"
2733

9"
2734

2¼
5¼
10" 2735

6"
10"
10"
2771

14"
2774

2786

28"
2787

2788

2825

2826

12"
9"
2849

10"
3½
2856

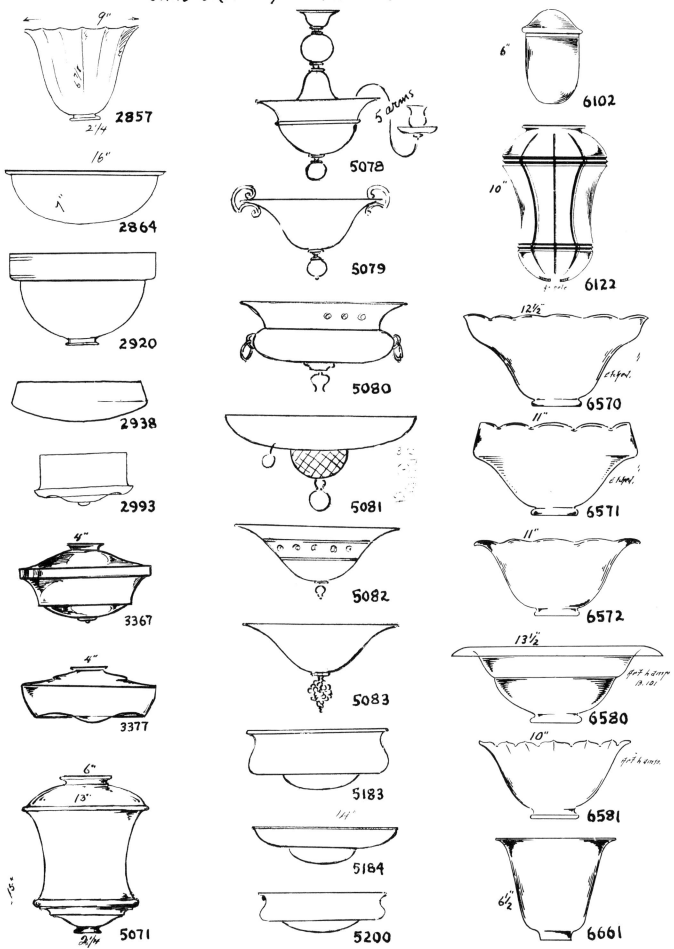

2857

2864

2920

2938

2993

3367

3377

5071

5078

5079

5080

5081

5082

5083

5183

5184

5200

6102

6122

6570

6571

6572

6580

6581

6661

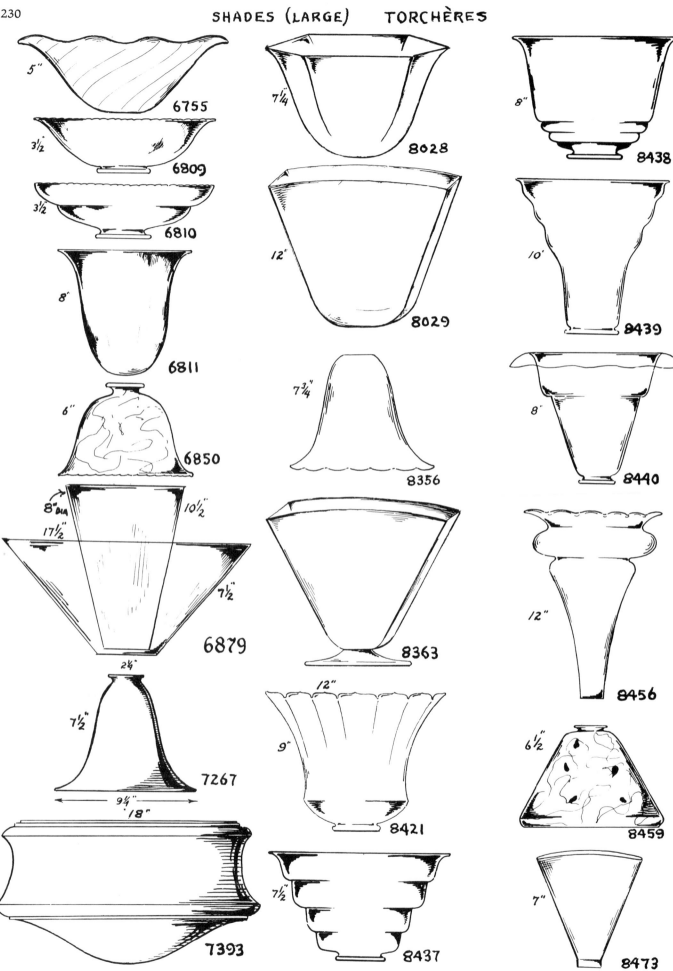

5" 6755

3½" 6809

3½" 6810

8" 6811

6" 6850

8" DIA
17½"
10½"
7½"
6879

2¼"
7½"
7267
9¼"
18"
7393

7¼" 8028

12" 8029

7¾" 8356

8363

12"
9"
8421

7½" 8437

8" 8438

10" 8439

8" 8440

12" 8456

6½" 8459

7" 8473

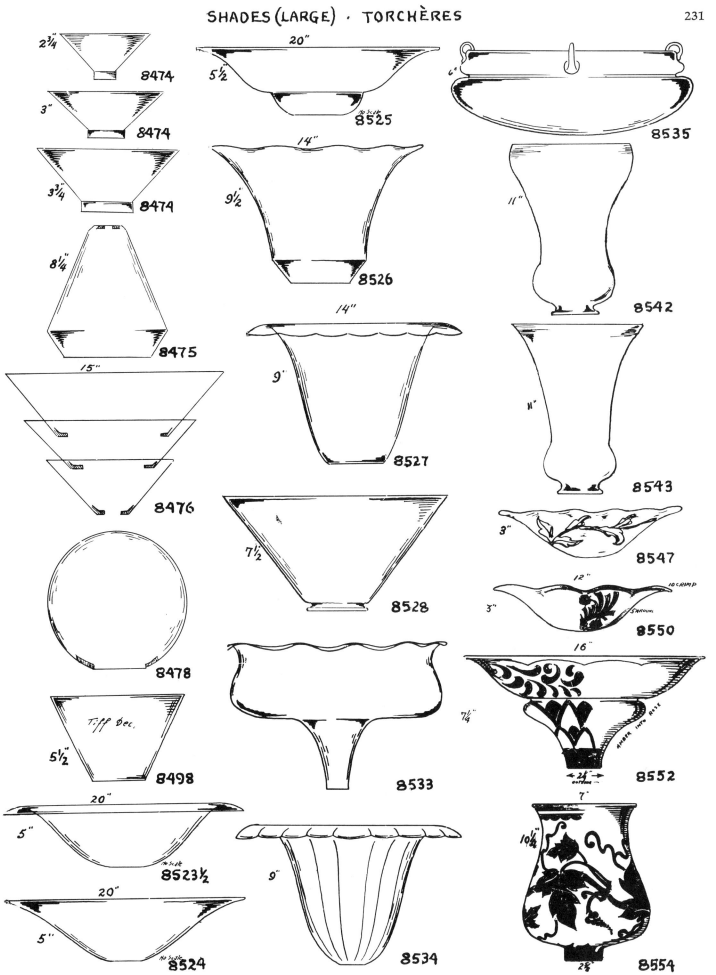

2¾" 8474

3" 8474

3¾" 8474

8¼" 8475

15" 8476

8478

Tiff Dec.
5½" 8498

20"
5" No Scale 8523½

20"
5" No Scale 8524

20"
5½" No Scale 8525

14"
9½" 8526

14"
9" 8527

7½" 8528

8533

9" 8534

6" 8535

11" 8542

11" 8543

3" 8547

12"
3" 10 CRIMP
5 AROUND 8550

16"
7¼" AMBER INTO ROSE
←2¼"→ OUTSIDE 8552

7"
10½" 2⅝" 8554

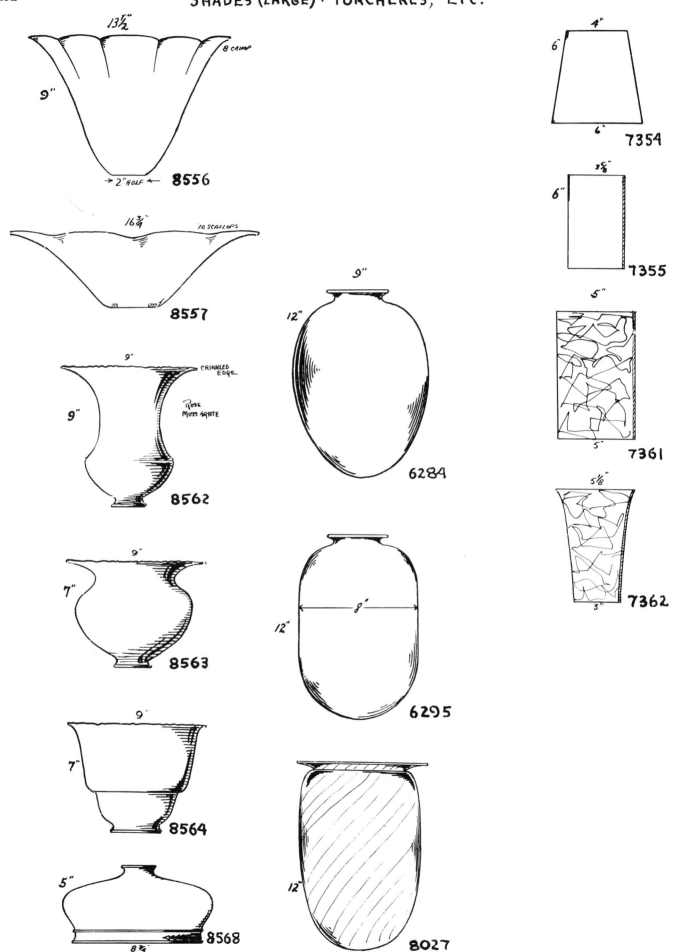

13½"
8 CRIMP
9"
2" HOLE
8556

16¾"
10 SCALLOPS
8557

9"
CRINKLED EDGE
ROSE MOSS AGATE
9"
8562

9"
7"
8563

9"
7"
8564

5"
8568
8¾"

9"
12"
6284

12"
8"
6295

12"
8027

4"
6"
6"
7354

3⅝"
6"
7355

5"
5"
7361

5⅛"
3"
7362

SPOONERS

117

118

119

120

All sizes 1529

NAPPIES

106

121

126

127

191

205

287

6"
466

Style A
510

807

1030

1031

NAPPIES

1226

1273

1403

5"
1533

4½"
1534

4½"
1535

6"
2080

6"
10 pillars
2173

6"
2605
3 gal.

2670

3½
2671

7"x5"
2955

BON BONS ETC.

393

138

139

192

228

6 x 3½
317

5"
318

5¼ x 3
319

320

321

322

323

324

325

326

327

328

329

330

390

403

404

BON BONS ETC.

-4 ¢
405

4½ x 5
2½
406

5½ x 3½
407

6"
408

6 x 3
409

7¼ x 6½
414

509
Style A

529
Style A

530
Style A

531
Style A

532
Style A

564
Style A

565
style A

709

738

739

740

1090

5"
1133

5¼
1134

6"
1135

6½
1136

5½
1137

4"
1138

5¼
1139

6"
1140

5¼
1141

5¼
1142

1144

½
1189

3¼
1190

1290

1291

1292

PRESSED
1404

PRESSED
1405

3"
1579

SUGAR BOWLS AND CREAMERS

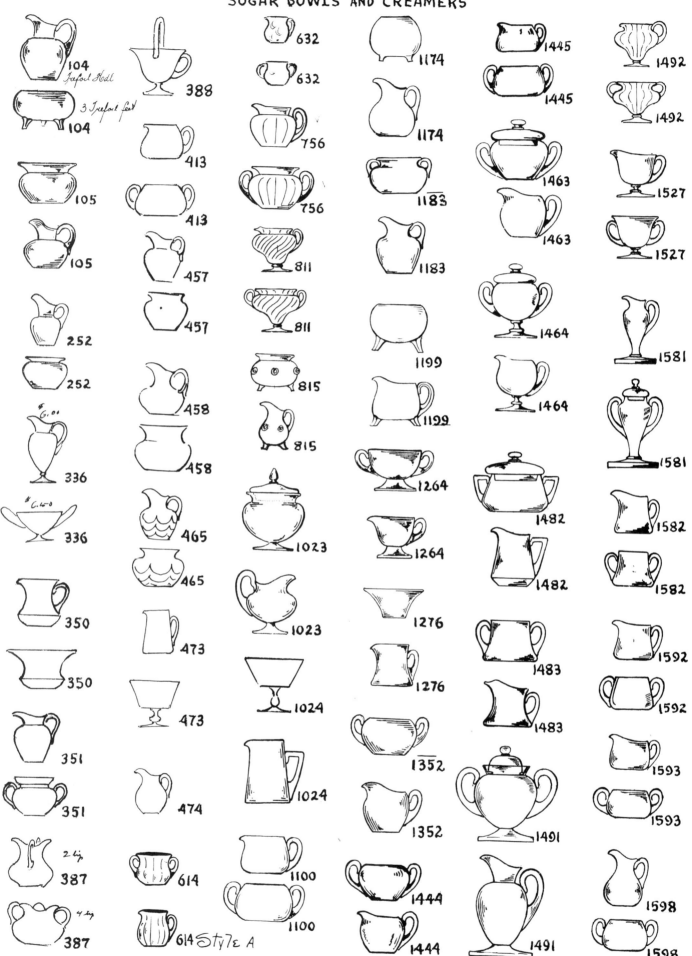

104
Trefoil Hdl.

104
3 Trefoil feet

105

105

252

252

336
#C,01

336
#C,4-0

350

350

351

351

387
2 Lip

387
4 Lip

388

413

413

457

457

458

458

465

465

473

473

474

614

614 *Style A*

632

632

756

756

811

811

815

815

1023

1023

1024

1024

1024

1100

1100

1174

1174

1183

1183

1199

1199

1264

1264

1276

1276

1352

1352

1444

1444

1445

1445

1463

1463

1464

1464

1482

1482

1483

1483

1491

1491

1492

1492

1527

1527

1581

1581

1582

1582

1592

1592

1593

1593

1598

1598

SUGAR BOWLS AND CREAMERS

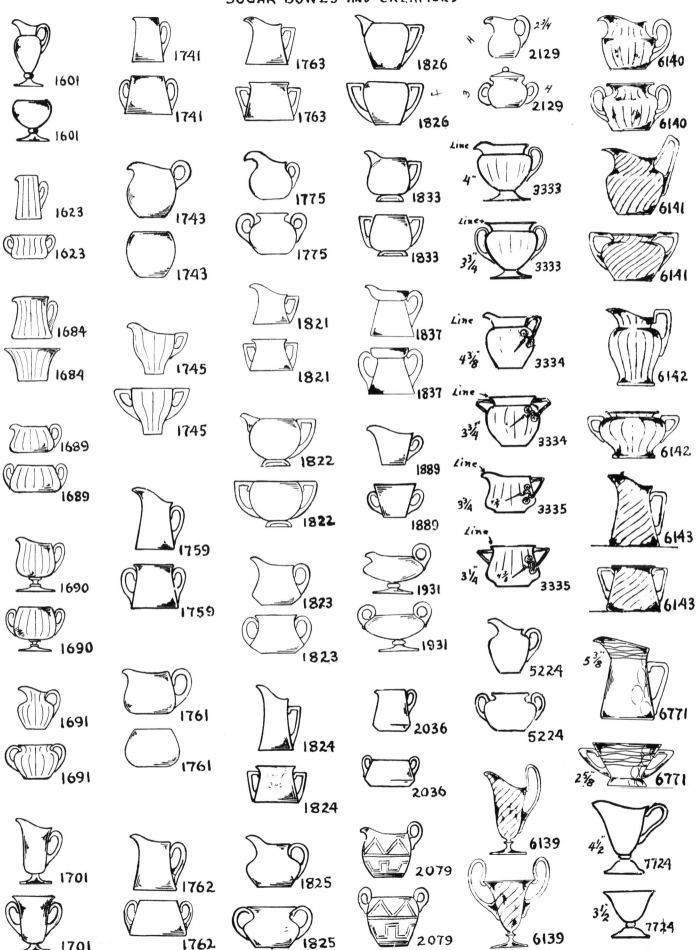

236

TABLE DECORATIONS and ACCESSORIES

EAGLE

8" cut

6502

PHEASANT

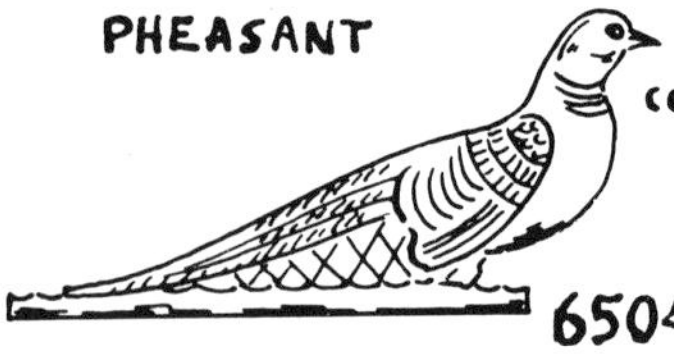

cut

6504

PIGEON

6"

6822

PIGEON
cut

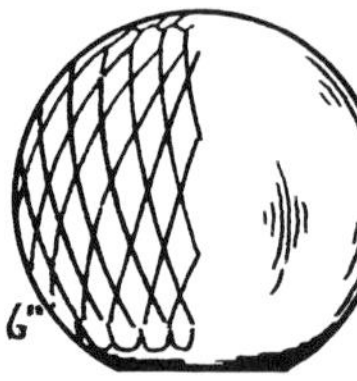

6"

6824

PEGASUS
cut

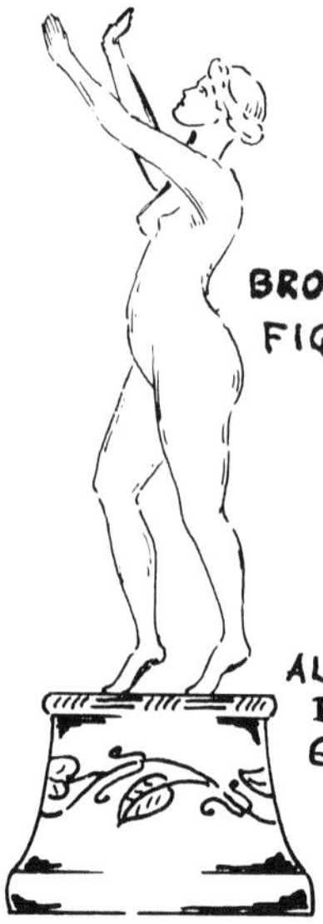

6½"

7010

PEACOCK
cut

7½"

7398

GAZELLE

7"

7399

DUCK
cut

5½"

7400

12"

6927

8"

7133

17"

7638

10½"

7698

6"

6"

8"

also 8"
cut Warwick

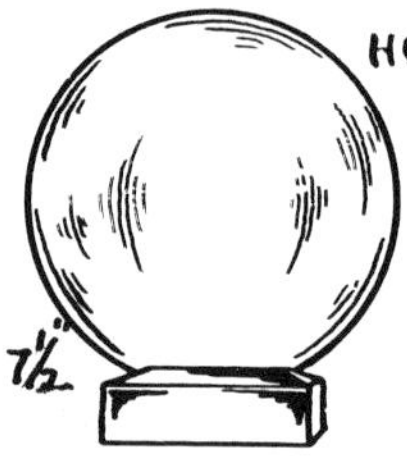

7448

3"

cut Warwick

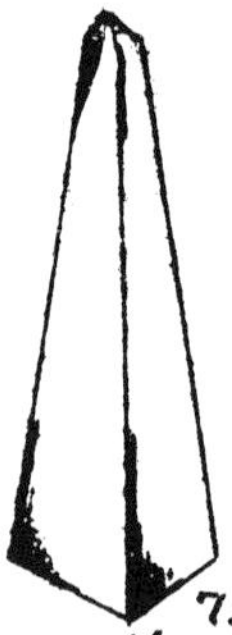

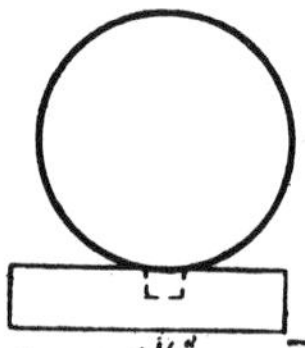

7448

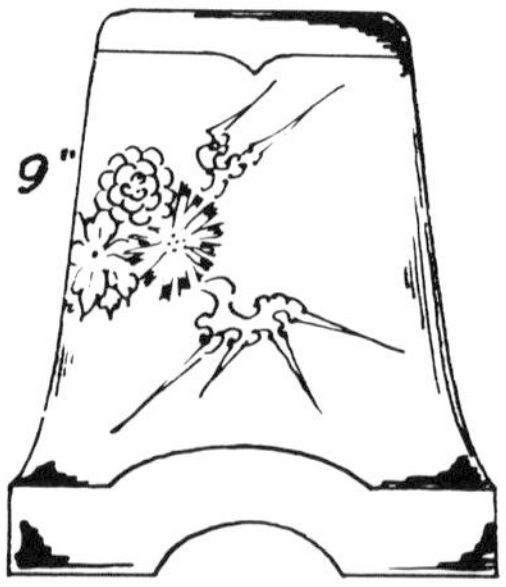

HOLLOW
BALL

7½"

7450

4½"

4¼

7641

4¼"

SOLID
BALL

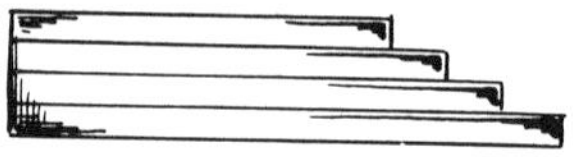

8462

7556

3¼"

6486

7474

7474

6"

BRONZE
FIGURE

16"

ALABASTER
ETCHED
GLASS
BASE

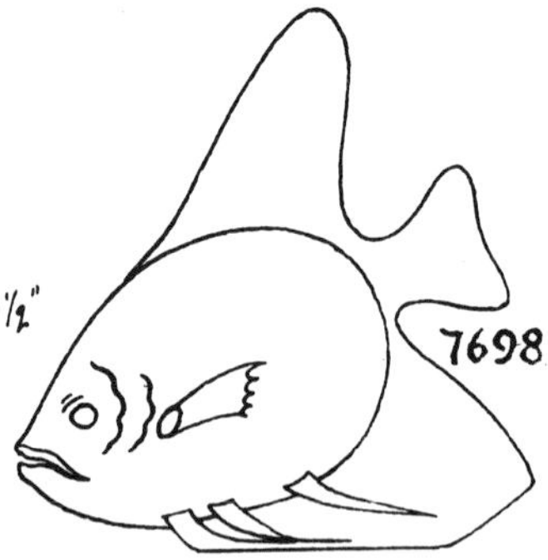

6609

9"

6711

2"

6973

6274

DOOR STOP

4"

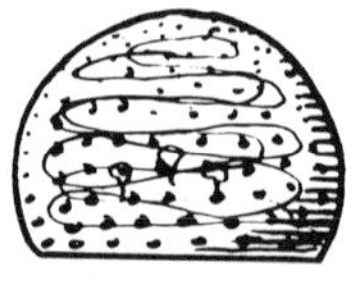

7257

 **TABLE DECORATIONS** and **ACCESSORIES**  237

FLOWER BLOCKS

3269

NO NUMBER

4¾"
6448

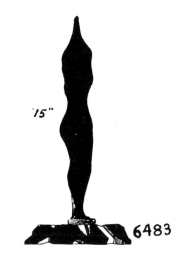
15"
6483

7½"
6495

6662

12"
6721

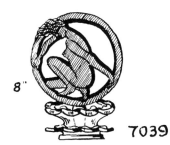
6937

8"
7039

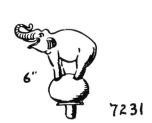
7½"
7064

6"
7231

FLOWER POTS AND STANDS

1415

1669

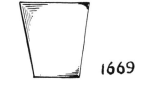
1672
10 crimps

6¼"
6676

FERN BOWLS

1640

1641

BELLS

4½ 3½ 5¼ 3⅞ 3¾ b
1970

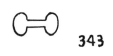
2368

5035

KNIFE RESTS

343

1221

1222

PLACE SETTING

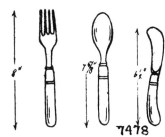
8" 7⅞" 6¼"
7478

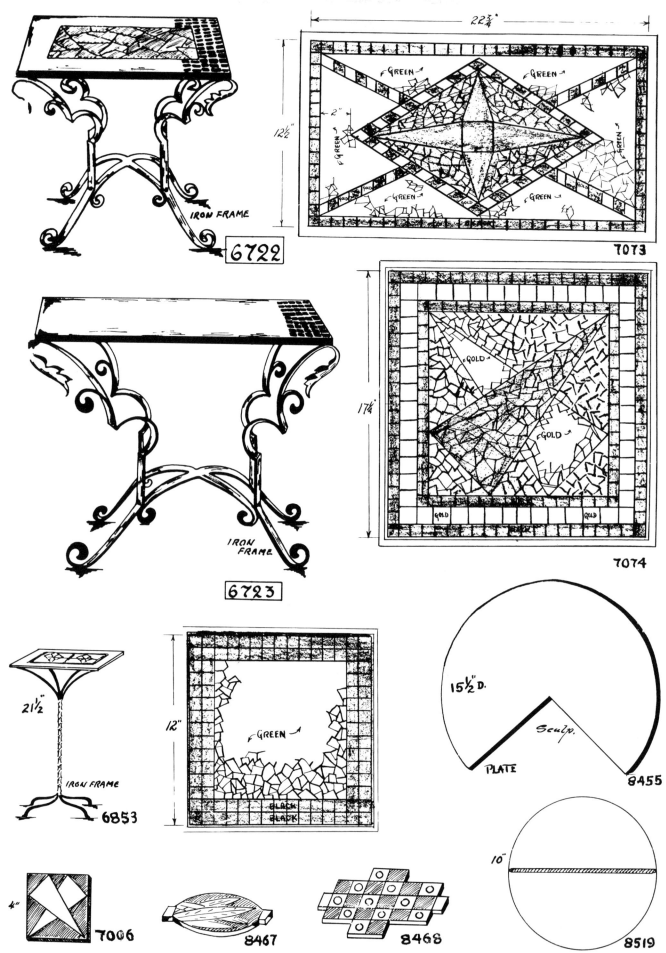

6722

IRON FRAME

7073

22¾"

12½"

2"

GREEN

GREEN

GREEN

GREEN

GREEN

GOLD

GOLD

GOLD

GOLD

6723

IRON FRAME

7074

17¼"

GOLD

GOLD

GOLD

GOLD

6853

21½

IRON FRAME

12"

GREEN

BLACK
BLACK

15½" D.

Sculp.

PLATE

8455

10"

8519

4"

7006

8467

8468

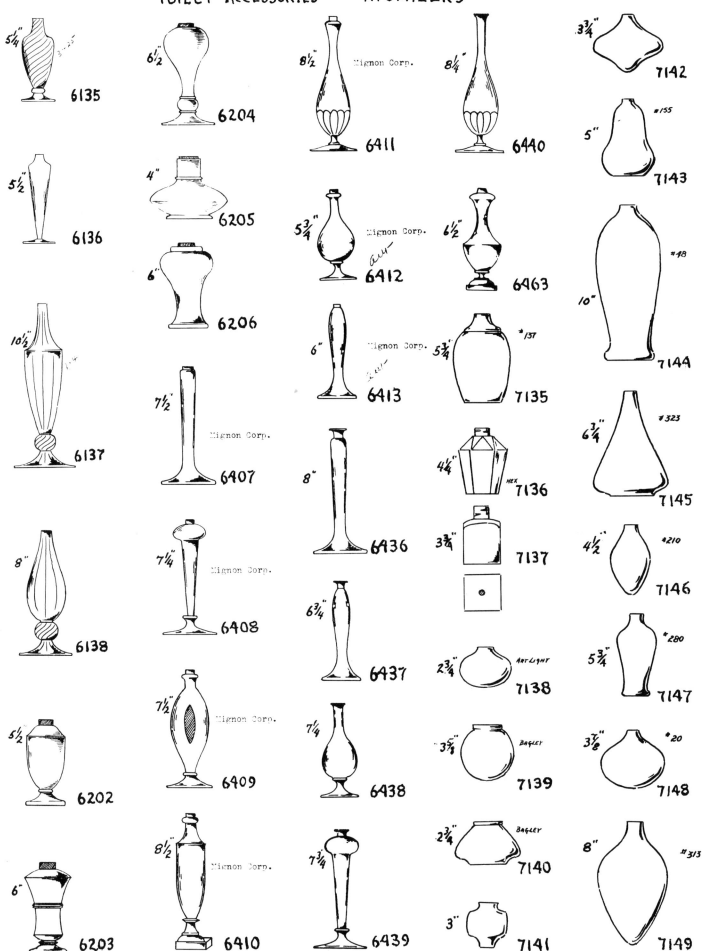

5 1/4" 6135

6 1/2" 6204

8 1/2" Mignon Corp. 6411

8 1/4" 6440

3 3/4" 7142

5 1/2" 6136

4" 6205

5 3/4" Mignon Corp. 6412

6 1/2" 6463

5" #155 7143

6" 6206

10 1/2" 6137

7 1/2" Mignon Corp. 6407

6" Mignon Corp. 6413

5 3/4" #137 7135

10" #18 7144

8" 6436

4 1/4" HEX 7136

6 3/4" #323 7145

8" 6138

7 1/4" Mignon Corp. 6408

6 3/4" 6437

3 3/4" 7137

4 1/2" #210 7146

5 1/2" 6202

7 1/2" Mignon Corp. 6409

7 1/4" 6438

2 3/4" ART LIGHT 7138

5 3/4" #280 7147

6" 6203

8 1/2" Mignon Corp. 6410

7 3/4" 6439

3 5/8" BAGLEY 7139

3 7/8" #20 7148

2 3/4" BAGLEY 7140

3" 7141

8" #313 7149

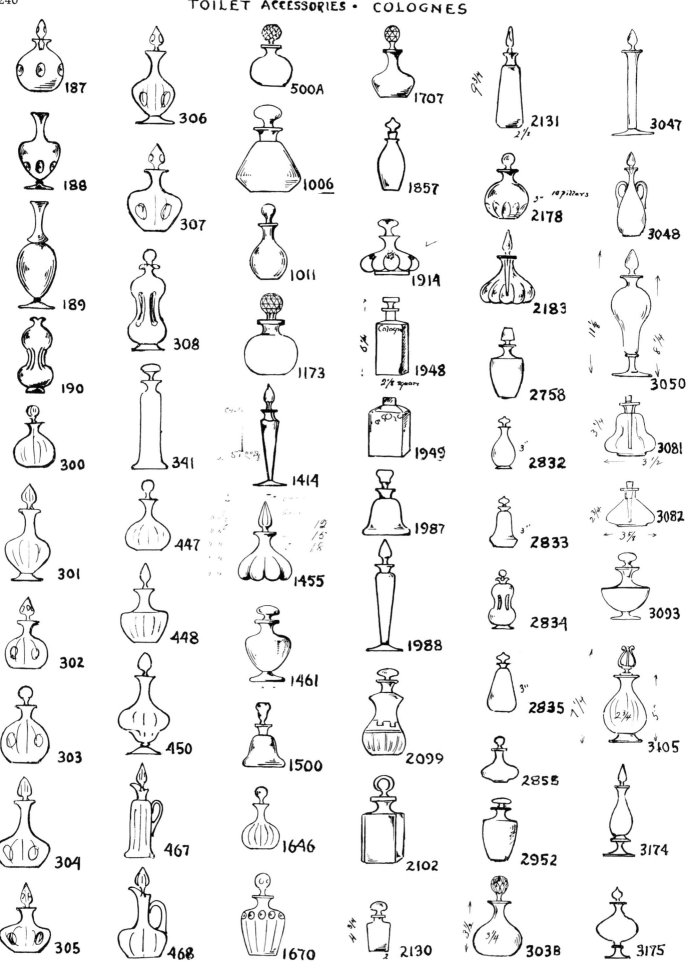

187
188
189
190
300
301
302
303
304
305

306
307
308
341
447
448
450
467
468

500A
1006
1011
1173
1414
1455
1461
1500
1646
1670

1707
1857
1914
1948
1949
1987
1988
2099
2102
2130

2131
2178
2183
2758
2832
2833
2834
2835
2855
2952
303B

3047
3048
3050
3081
3082
3093
3405
3174
3175

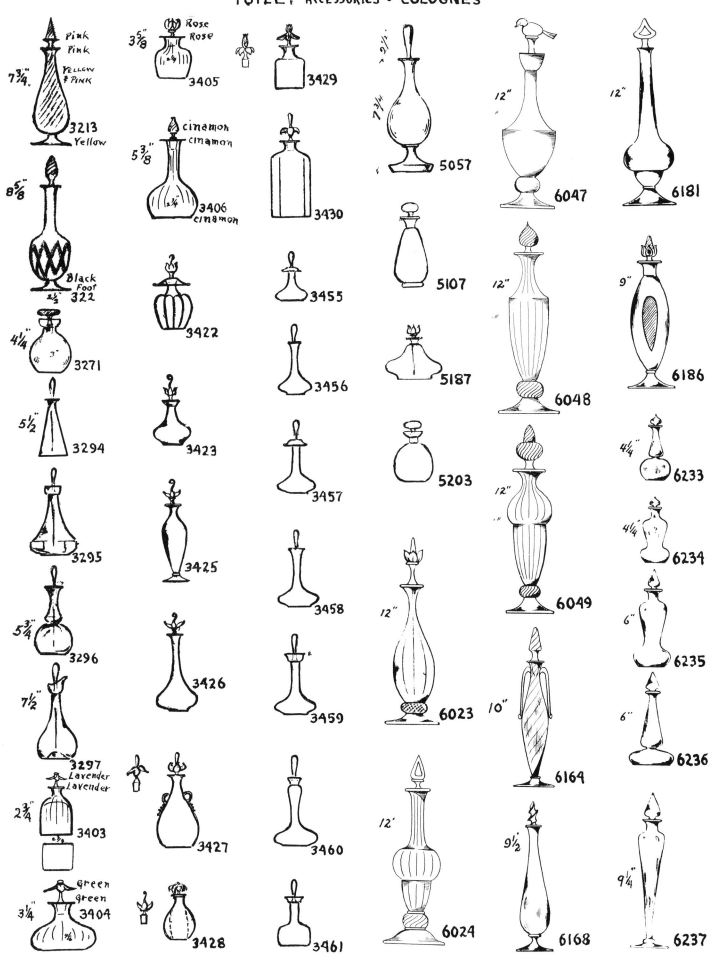

Pink
Pink

YELLOW & PINK

7 3/4" 3213
Yellow

8 5/8" 322
Black Foot
4 1/2"

4 1/4" 3271
3"

5 1/2 3294

3295

5 3/4" 3296

7 1/2 3297
Lavender
Lavender

2 3/4" 3403

Green
green
3 1/4 3404

3 5/8" 3405
Rose
Rose

5 3/8 3406
cinamon
cinamon
2 1/4
cinamon

3422

3423

3425

3426

3427

3428

3429

3430

3455

3456

3457

3458

3459

3460

3461

> 9 1/2"
7 3/4 5057

5107

5187

5203

12" 6023

12' 6024

12" 6047

12" 6048

12" 6049

6164

10" 6164

9 1/2 6168

12" 6181

9" 6186

4 1/4" 6233

4 1/4 6234

6" 6235

6" 6236

9 1/4" 6237

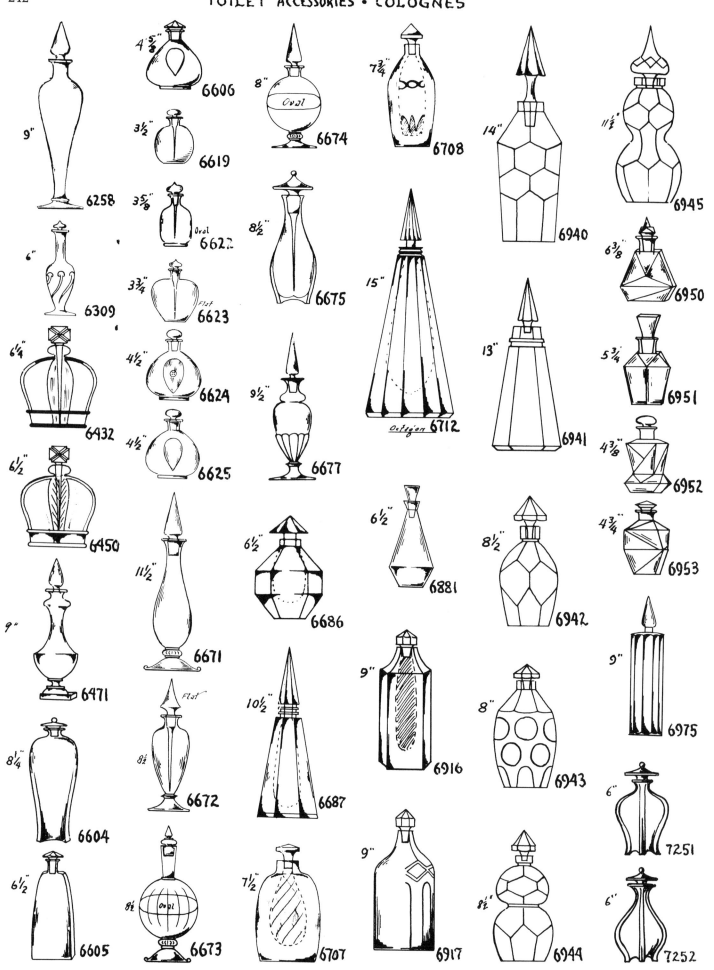

9" 6258

4 5/8" 6606

3 1/2" 6619

8" Oval 6674

7 3/4" 6708

14" 6940

11 1/4" 6945

6" 6309

3 5/8" Oval 6622

3 3/4" Flat 6623

4 1/2" 6624

8 1/2" 6675

6 3/8" 6950

6 1/4" 6432

4 1/2" 6625

9 1/2" 6677

15" Octagon 6712

13" 6941

5 3/4" 6951

6 1/2" 6450

11 1/2" 6671

6 1/2" 6686

6 1/2" 6881

8 1/2" 6942

4 3/8" 6952

4 3/4" 6953

9" 6471

9" 6916

8" 6943

9" 6975

8 1/4" 6604

8 1/2" 6672

10 1/2" 6687

6 1/2" 6605

8 1/2" Oval 6673

7 1/2" 6707

9" 6917

8 1/2" 6944

6" 7251

6" 7252

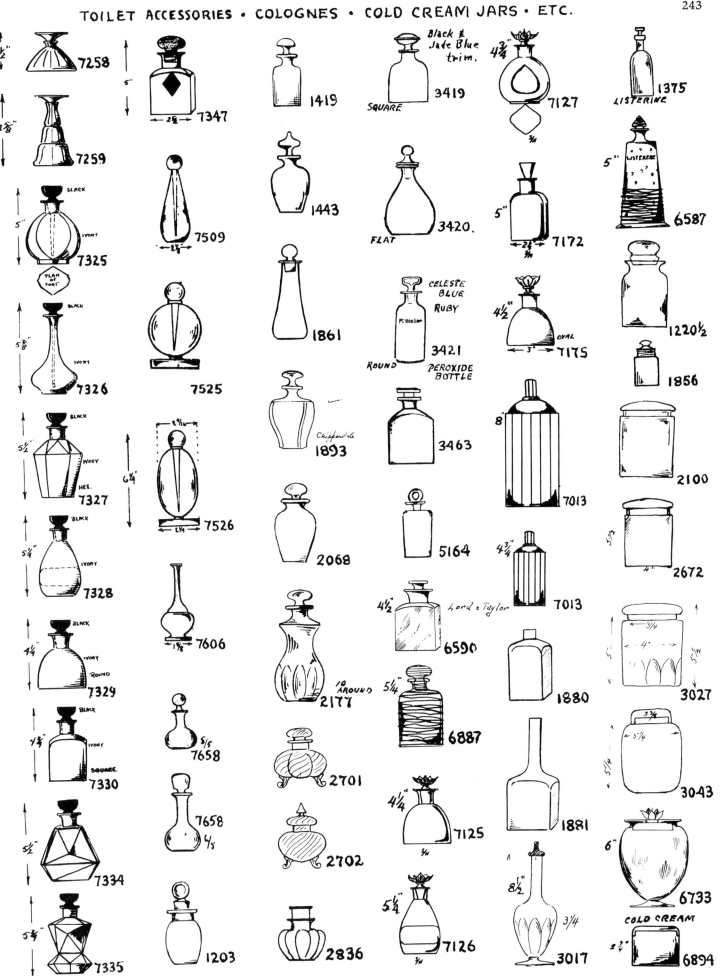

TOILET ACCESSORIES · PUFF BOXES* ETC.

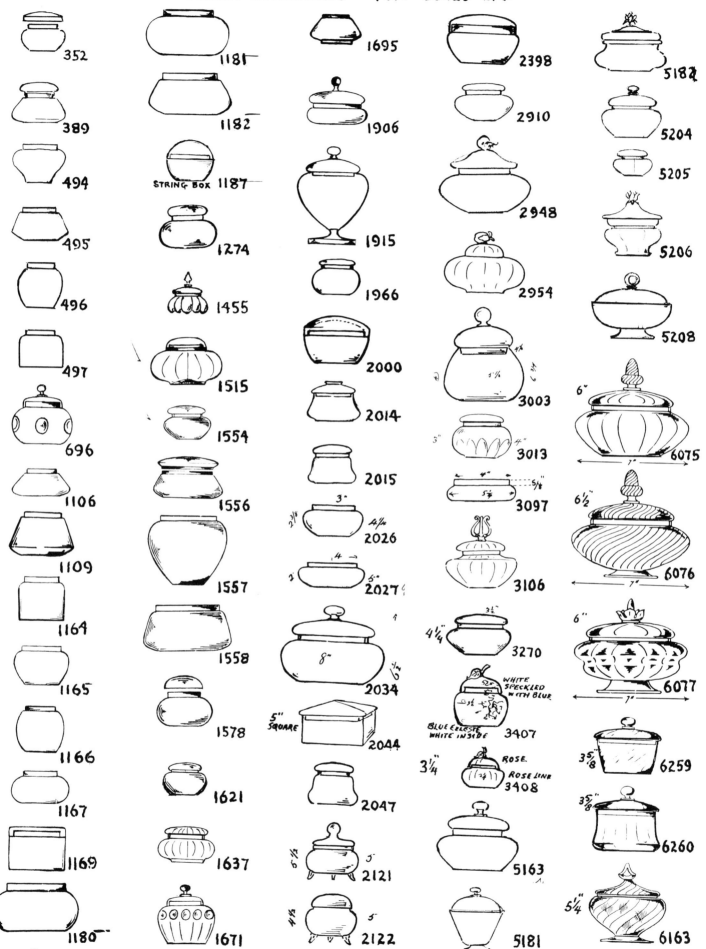

352

1181

1695

2398

5182

389

1182

1906

2910

5204

494

STRING BOX 1187

1915

2948

5205

495

1274

1966

2954

5206

496

1455

2000

3003

5208

497

1515

2014

3013

6" 6075

696

1554

2015

3097

6½" 6076

1106

1556

2026

3106

1109

1557

2027

3270

6" 6077

1164

1558

2034

WHITE SPECKLED WITH BLUE 3407

3⅝" 6259

1165

1578

5" SQUARE 2044

BLUE CELESTE WHITE INSIDE

1166

1621

2047

3¼" ROSE. ROSE LINE 3408

3⅝" 6260

1167

1637

2121

5163

1169

1671

2122

5181

5¼" 6163

1180

*SOME PUFF BOXES ARE ALSO USED AS CANDY BOXES

TOILET ACCESSORIES

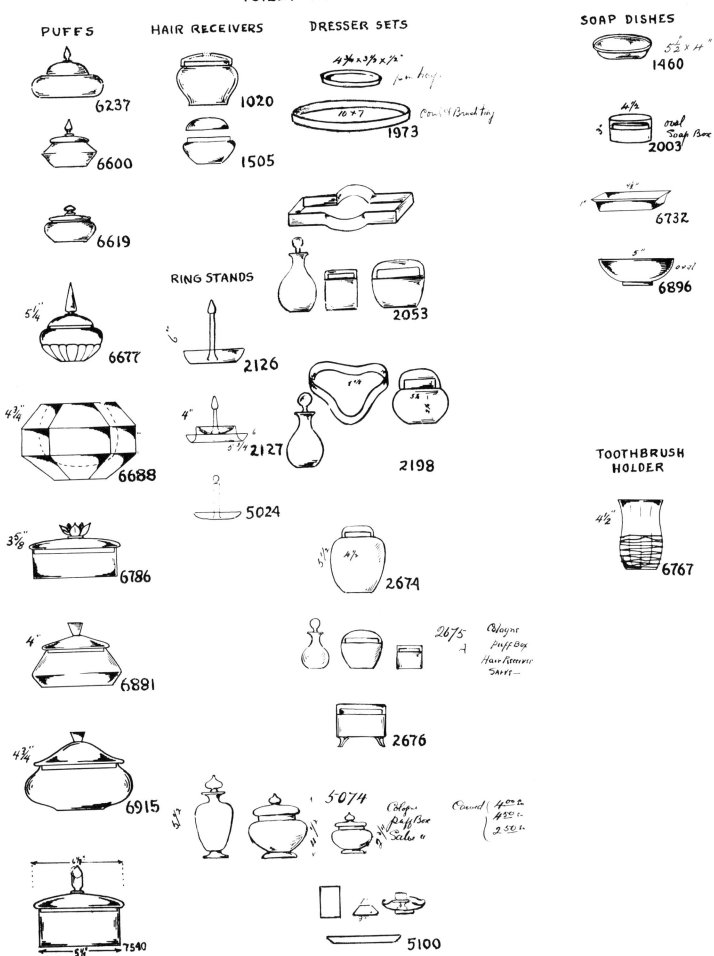

PUFFS

6237

6600

6619

5 1/4"
6677

4 3/4"
6688

3 5/8"
6786

4"
6881

4 3/4"
6915

6 1/2"
5 1/2"
7540

HAIR RECEIVERS

1020

1505

RING STANDS

6"
2126

4"
5 1/4"
6"
2127

5024

DRESSER SETS

4 3/8 x 3 1/3 x 1/2"
jam tray

10 x 7
Comb & Brush tray
1973

2053

1 3/8"
5 3/8
2198

5 1/2
4 1/2
2674

2675
A

Cologne
Puff Box
Hair Receiver
Salve —

2676

5-074

Cologne
Puff Box
Salve "

Oued { 4.00 s.
4.50 s.
2.50 s.

5100

SOAP DISHES

5 1/2" x 4"
1460

3"
4 1/2
oval
Soap Box
2003

4 1/2"
1"
6732

5"
oval
6896

TOOTHBRUSH
HOLDER

4 1/2"
6767

VASES

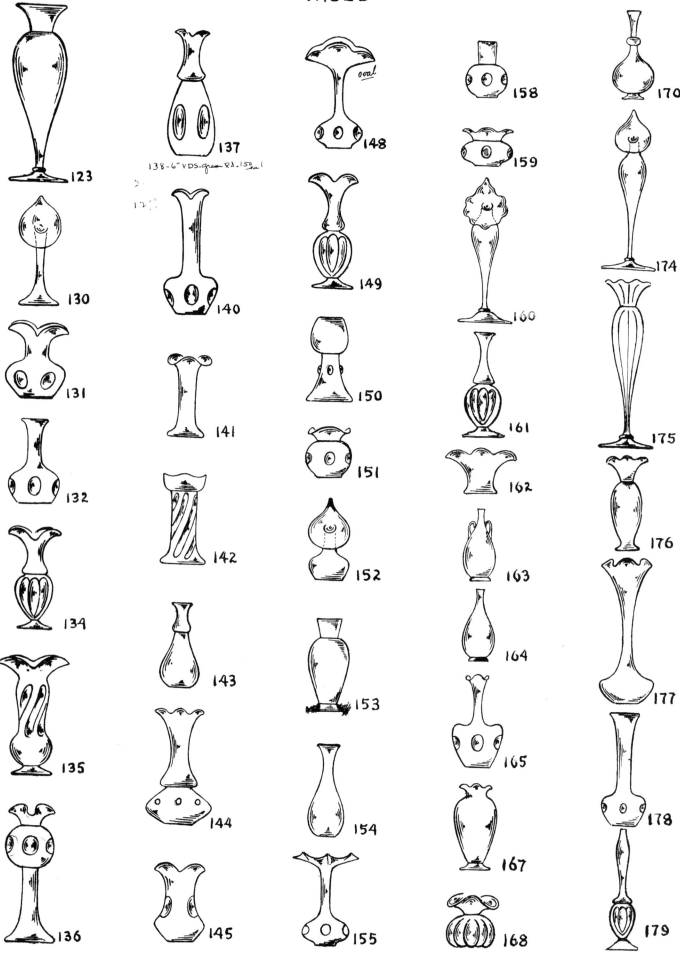

123

130

131

132

134

135

136

137

138-6" VDS-green Rd. 15° ea 1

140

141

142

143

144

145

148 oval

149

150

151

152

153

154

155

158

159

160

161

162

163

164

165

167

168

170

174

175

176

177

178

179

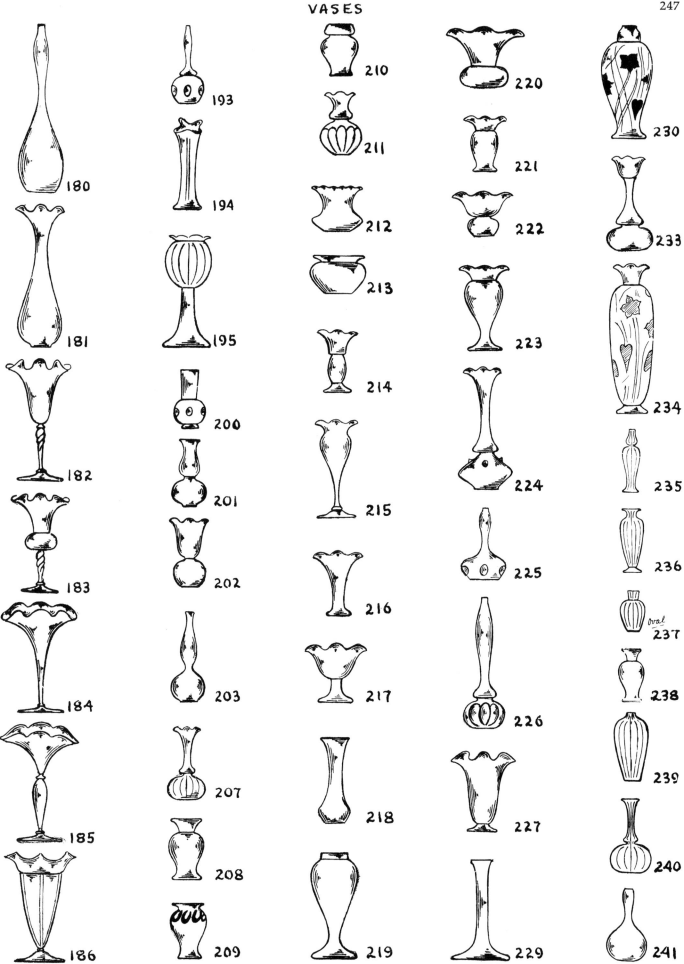

VASES

242

243

244

2'

3¼

1½

3¾

245

246

247

248

249

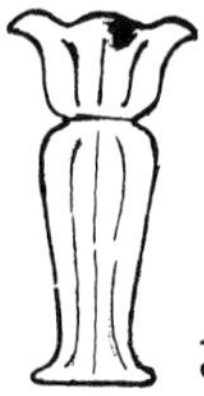

250

253

254

255

256

257

258

259

260

261

262

263

265

266

267

270

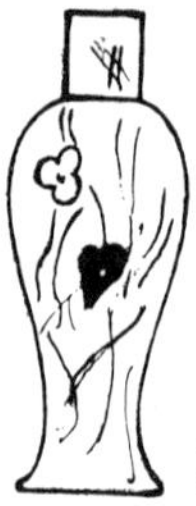

271

272

273

275

276

277

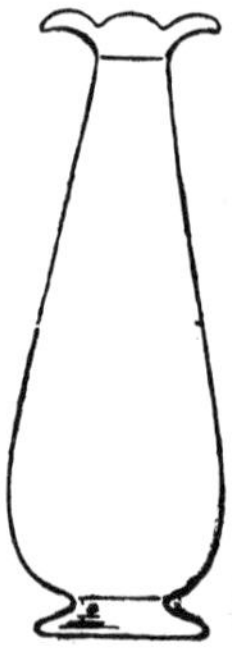

278

279

280

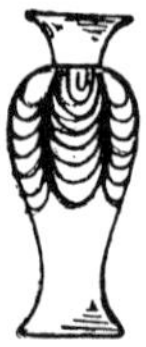

281

282

283

284

285

286

VASES

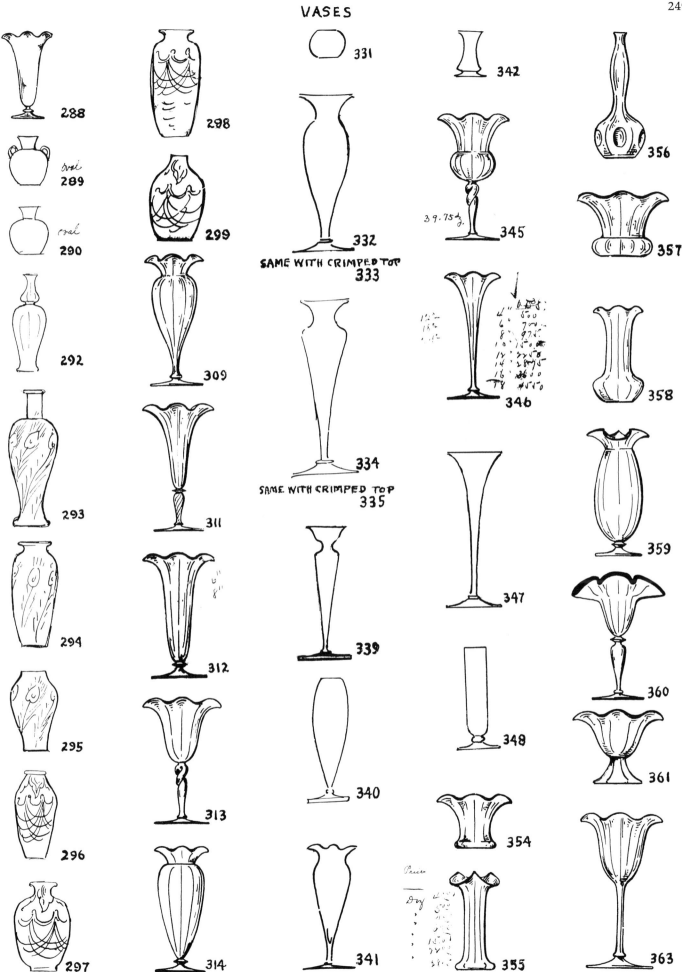

288

289 oval

290 oval

292

293

294

295

296

297

298

299

309

311

312

313

314

331

332

SAME WITH CRIMPED TOP
333

334

SAME WITH CRIMPED TOP
335

339

340

341

342

39.75 J.
345

346

347

348

354

355

356

357

358

359

360

361

363

250

VASES

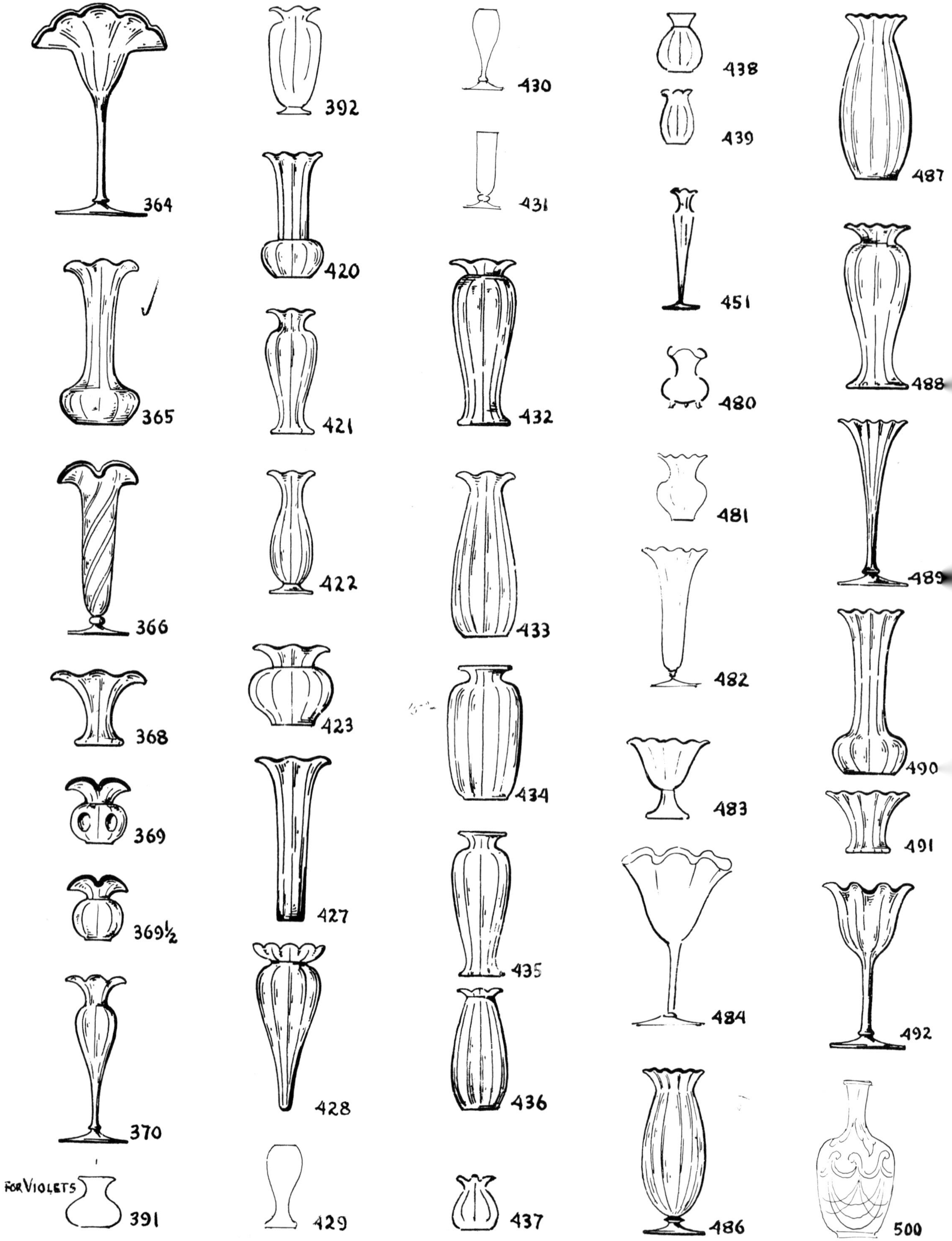

364

365

366

368

369

369½

370

FOR VIOLETS
391

392

420

421

422

423

427

428

429

430

431

432

433

434

435

436

437

438

439

451

480

481

482

483

484

486

487

488

489

490

491

492

500

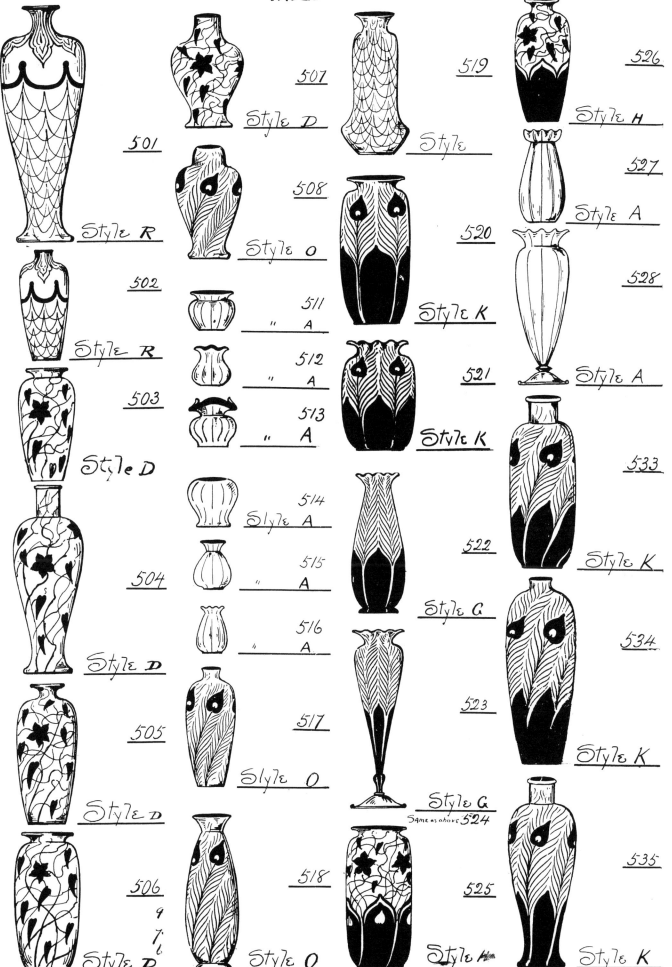

501

Style **R**

502

Style **R**

503

Style **D**

504

Style **D**

505

Style **D**

506

9

Style **D**

507

Style **D**

508

Style **O**

511
" **A**

512
" **A**

513
" **A**

514

Style **A**

515
" **A**

516
" **A**

517

Style **O**

518

Style **O**

519

Style

520

Style **K**

521

Style **K**

522

Style **G**

523

Style **G**
Same as above **524**

525

Style **A**

526

Style **H**

527

Style **A**

528

Style **A**

533

Style **K**

534

Style **K**

535

Style **K**

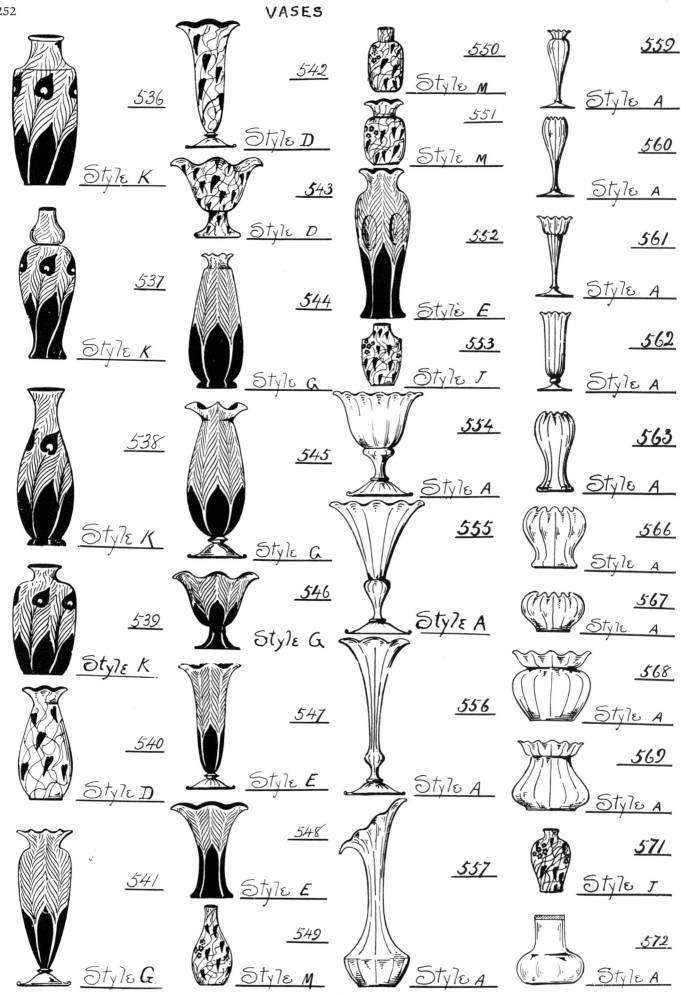

536
Style K

537
Style K

538
Style K

539
Style K

540
Style D

541
Style G.

542
Style D

543
Style D

544
Style G

545
Style G

546
Style G

547
Style E

548
Style E

549
Style M

550
Style M

551
Style M

552
Style E

553
Style J

554
Style A

555
Style A

556
Style A

557
Style A

559
Style A

560
Style A

561
Style A

562
Style A

563
Style A

566
Style A

567
Style A

568
Style A

569
Style A

571
Style J

572
Style A

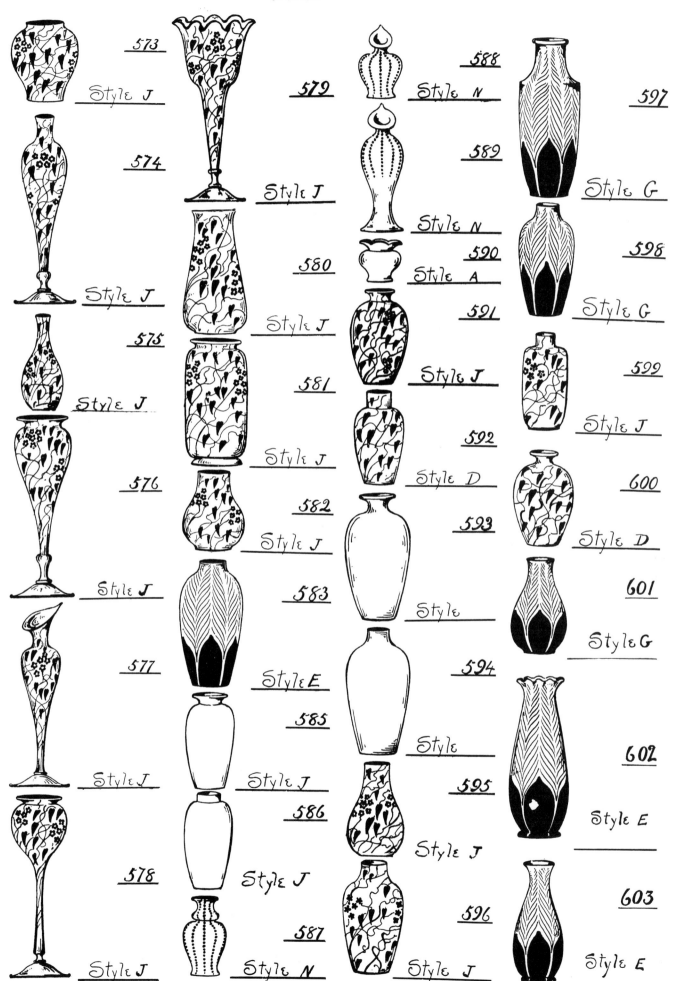

573 Style J

574 Style J

575 Style J

576 Style J

577 Style J

578 Style J

579 Style J

580 Style J

581 Style J

582 Style J

583 Style E

585 Style J

586 Style J

587 Style N

588 Style N

589 Style N

590 Style A

591 Style J

592 Style D

593 Style

594 Style

595 Style J

596 Style J

597 Style G

598 Style G

599 Style J

600 Style D

601 Style G

602 Style E

603 Style E

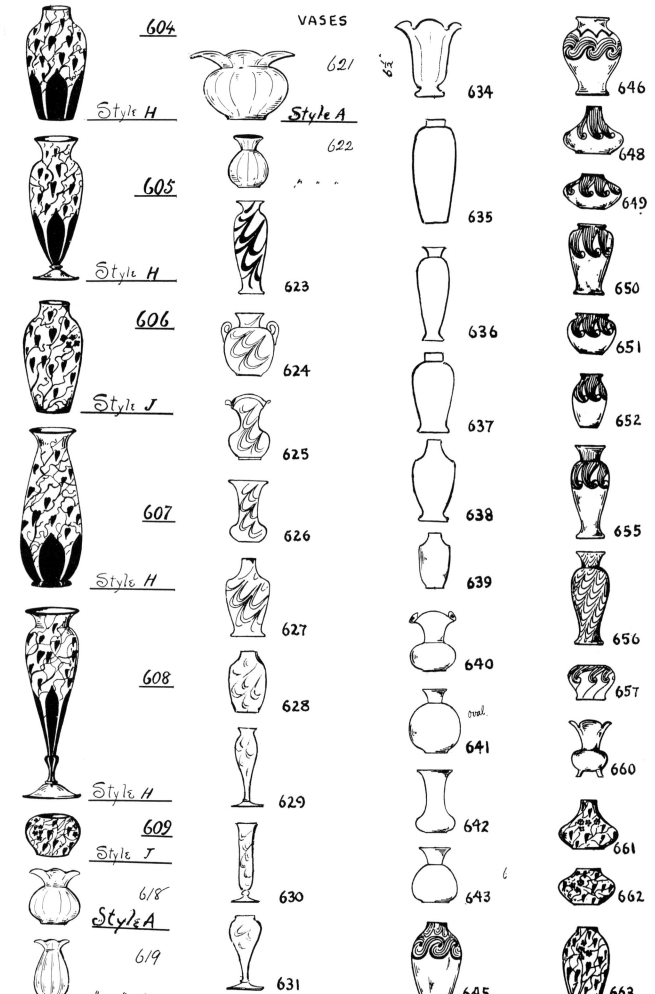

254

VASES

604
Style H

605
Style H

606
Style J

607
Style H

608
Style H

609
Style J

618
Style A

619
" " "

621
Style A

622
" " "

623

624

625

626

627

628

629

630

631

634

635

636

637

638

639

640

641
oval.

642

643

645

646

648

649

650

651

652

655

656

657

660

661

662

663

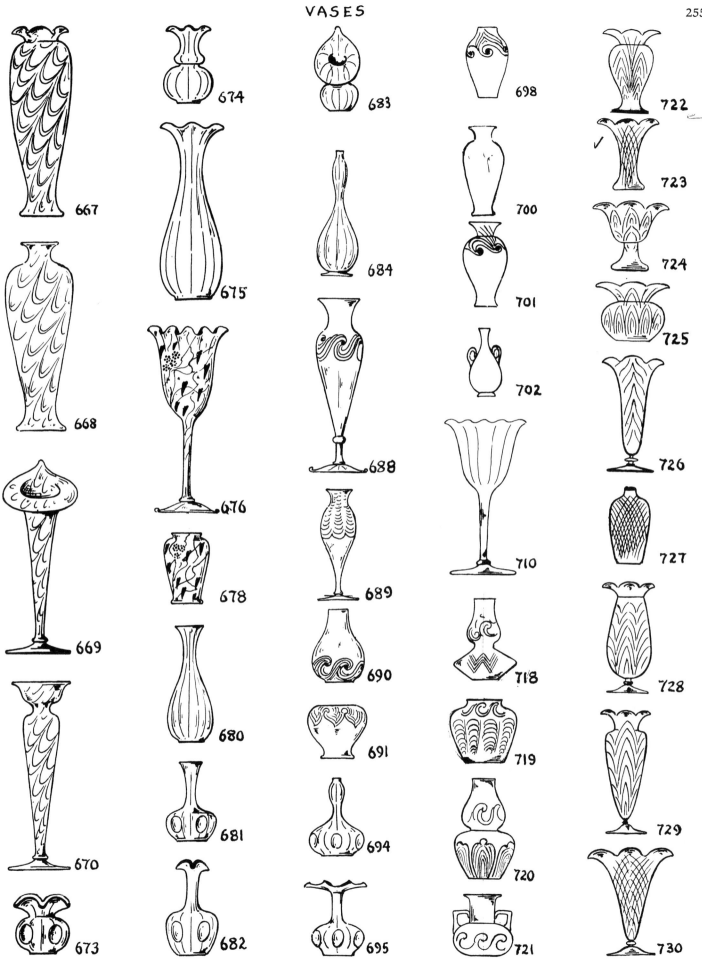

667
668
669
670
673
674
675
676
678
680
681
682
683
684
688
689
690
691
694
695
698
700
701
702
710
718
719
720
721
722
723
724
725
726
727
728
729
730

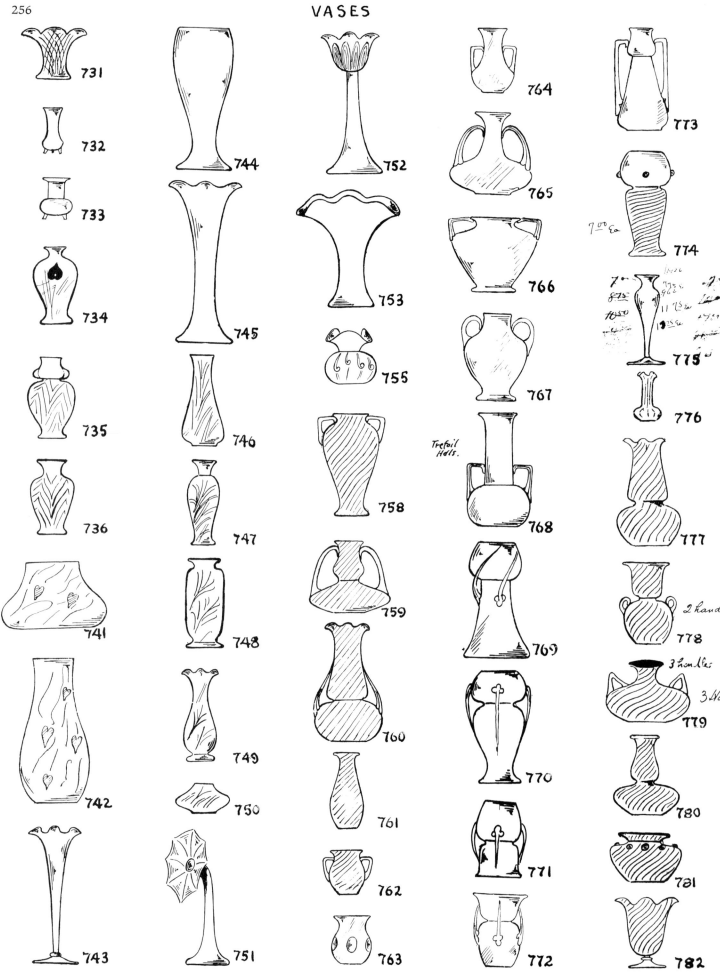

731
732
733
734
735
736
741
742
743

744
745
746
747
748
749
750
751

752
753
755
758
759
760
761
762
763

764
765
766
767
Trefoil Hdls.
768
769
770
771
772

773
774
775
776
777
2 hand
778
3 handles
3 Hd.
779
780
781
782

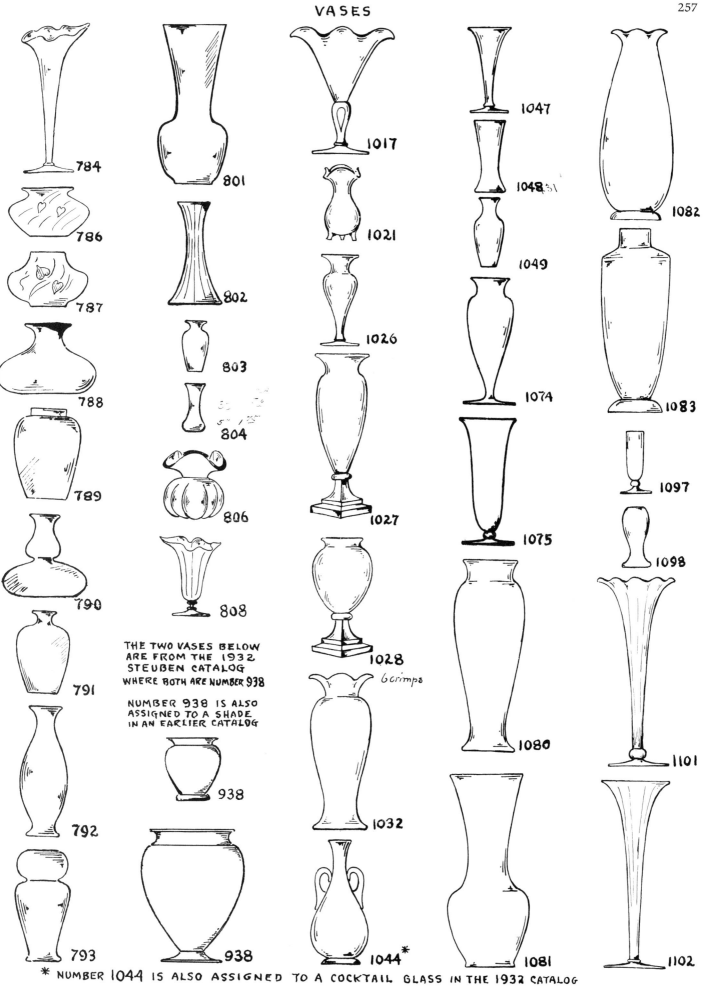

784

786

787

788

789

790

791

792

793

801

802

803

804

806

808

THE TWO VASES BELOW
ARE FROM THE 1932
STEUBEN CATALOG
WHERE BOTH ARE NUMBER 938

NUMBER 938 IS ALSO
ASSIGNED TO A SHADE
IN AN EARLIER CATALOG

938

938

1017

1021

1026

1027

1028

6 crimps

1032

1044 *

1047

1048

1049

1074

1075

1080

1081

1082

1083

1097

1098

1101

1102

* NUMBER 1044 IS ALSO ASSIGNED TO A COCKTAIL GLASS IN THE 1932 CATALOG

258

VASES

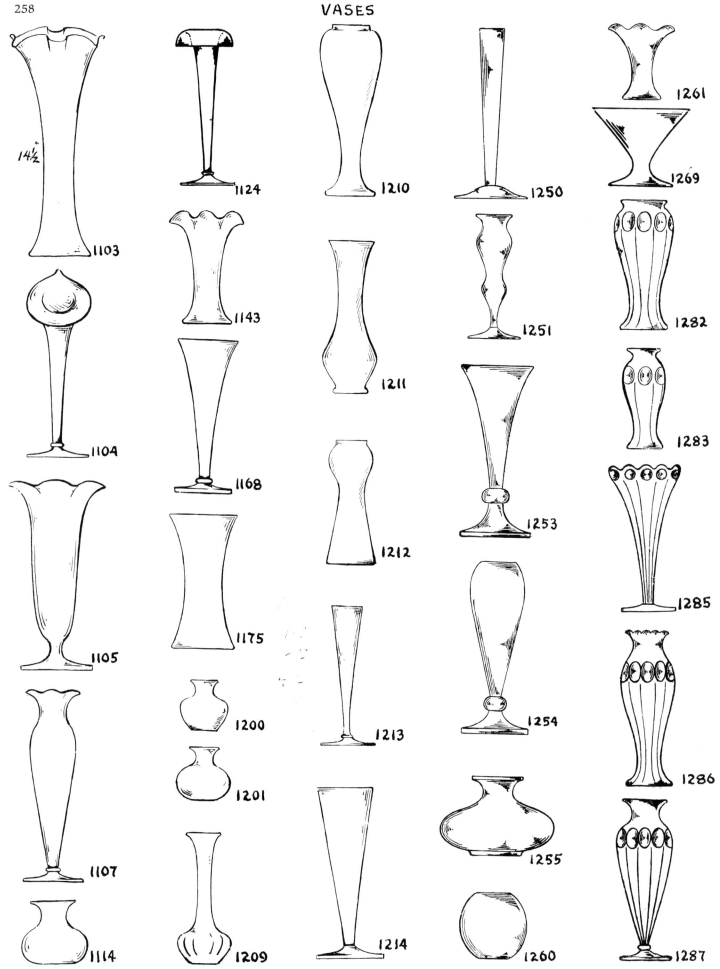

14½"

1103

1104

1105

1107

1114

1124

1143

1168

1175

1200

1201

1209

1210

1211

1212

1213

1214

1250

1251

1253

1254

1255

1260

1261

1269

1282

1283

1285

1286

1287

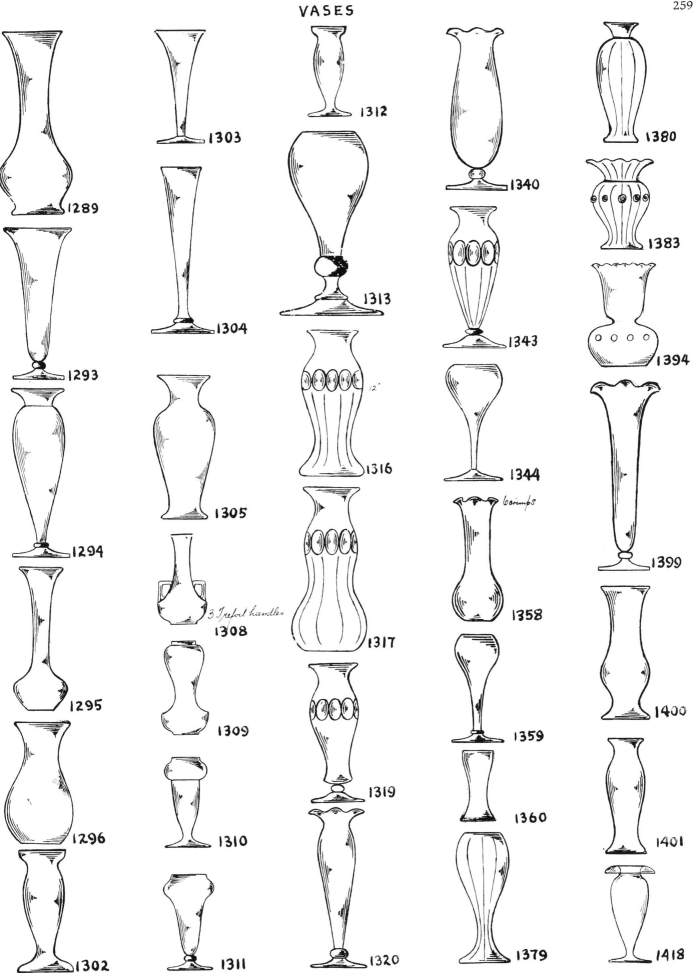

1289

1293

1294

1295

1296

1302

1303

1304

1305

3 Trefoil handles

1308

1309

1310

1311

1312

1313

1316

1317

12˝

1319

1320

1340

1343

1344

6 crimps

1358

1359

1360

1379

1380

1383

1394

1399

1400

1401

1418

VASES

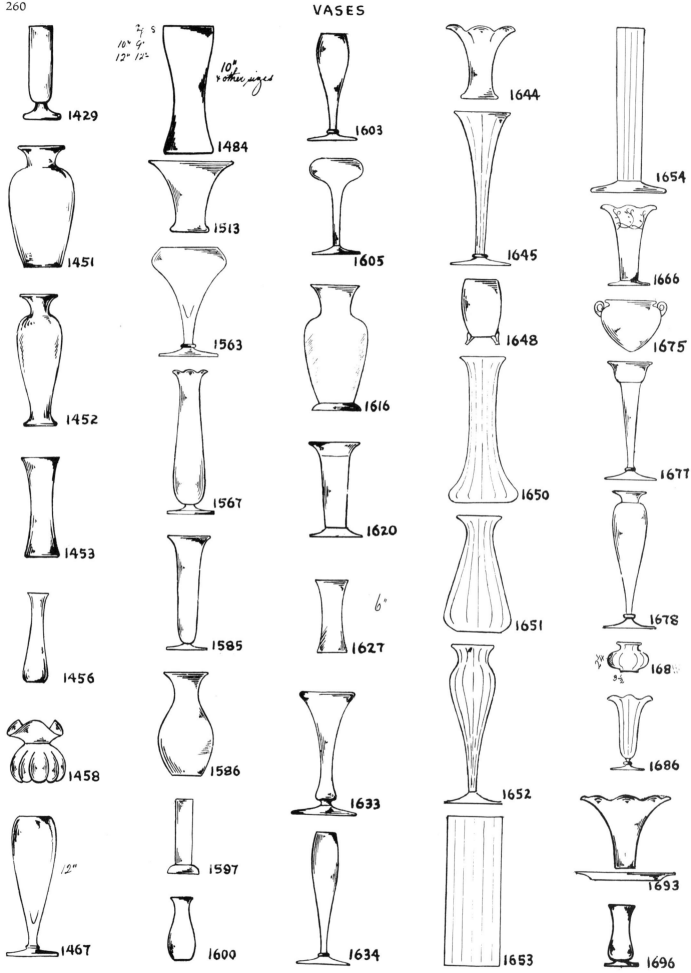

1429

1484

2⅞ S
10″ 9″
12″ 12″

10″
& other sizes

1513

1563

1567

1585

1586

1597

1600

1451

1452

1453

1456

1458

12″

1467

1603

1605

1616

1620

1627

6″

1633

1634

1644

1645

1648

1650

1651

1652

1653

1654

1666

1675

1677

1678

168⸬

2″×″
9½

1686

1693

1696

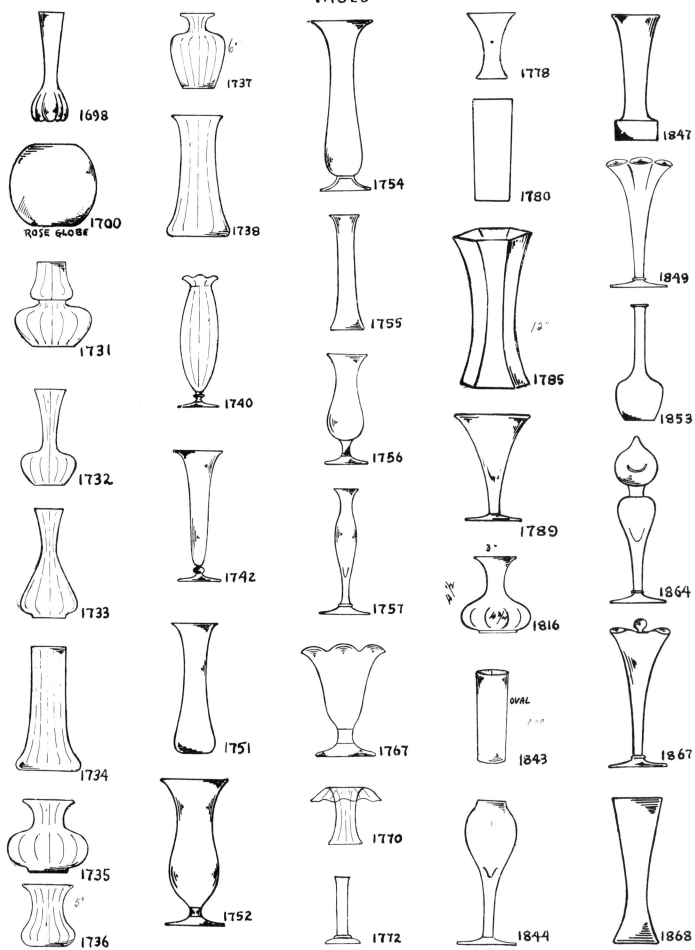

1698

1700 ROSE GLOBE

1731

1732

1733

1734

1735

1736 5"

1737 6"

1738

1740

1742

1751

1752

1754

1755

1756

1757

1767

1770

1772

1778

1780

1785 12"

1789

1816 3" 4½"

1843 OVAL

1844

1847

1849

1853

1864

1867

1868

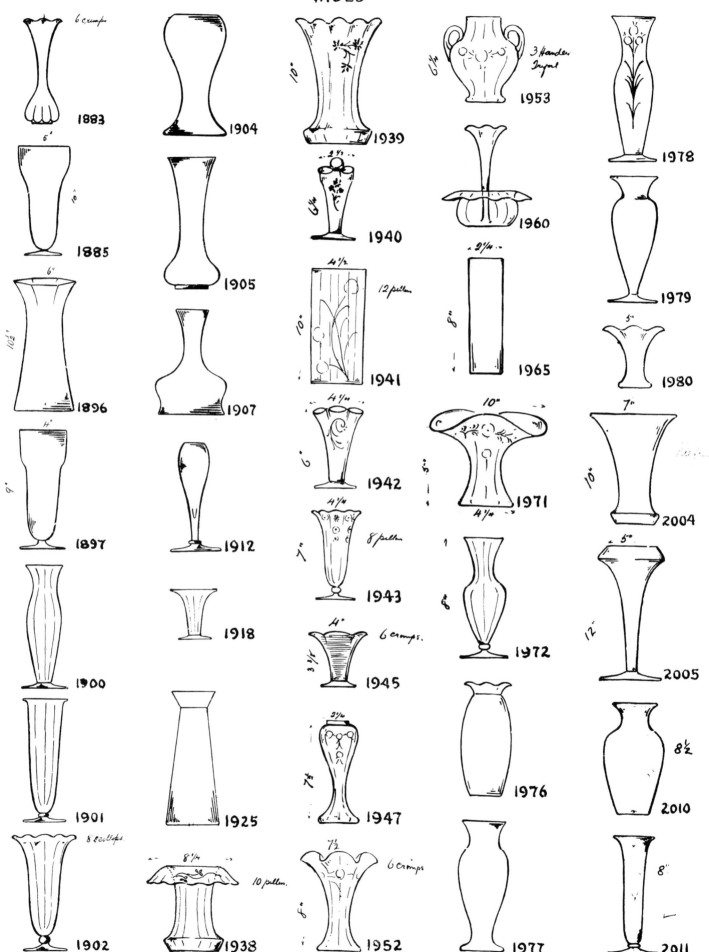

1883

1885

1896

1897

1900

1901

1902

1904

1905

1907

1912

1918

1925

1938

1939

1940

1941

1942

1943

1945

1947

1952

1953

1960

1965

1971

1972

1976

1977

1978

1979

1980

2004

2005

2010

2011

VASES

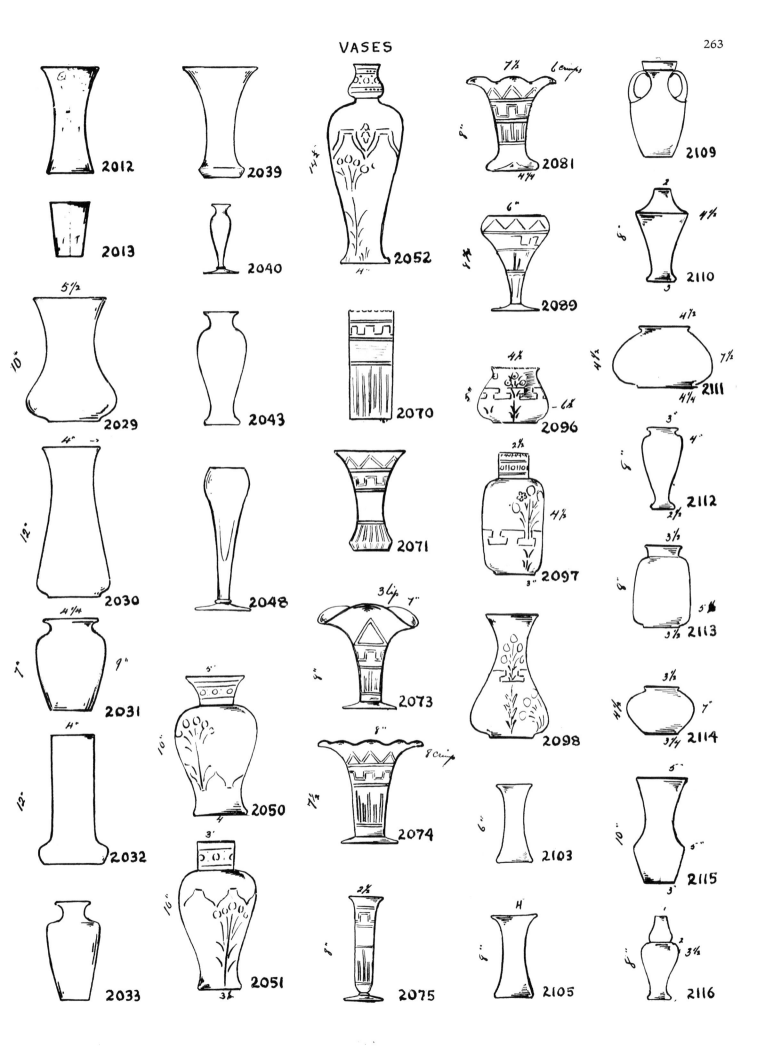

2012

2013

2029

2030

2031

2032

2033

2039

2040

2043

2048

2050

2051

2052

2070

2071

2073

2074

2075

2081

2089

2096

2097

2098

2103

2105

2109

2110

2111

2112

2113

2114

2115

2116

VASES

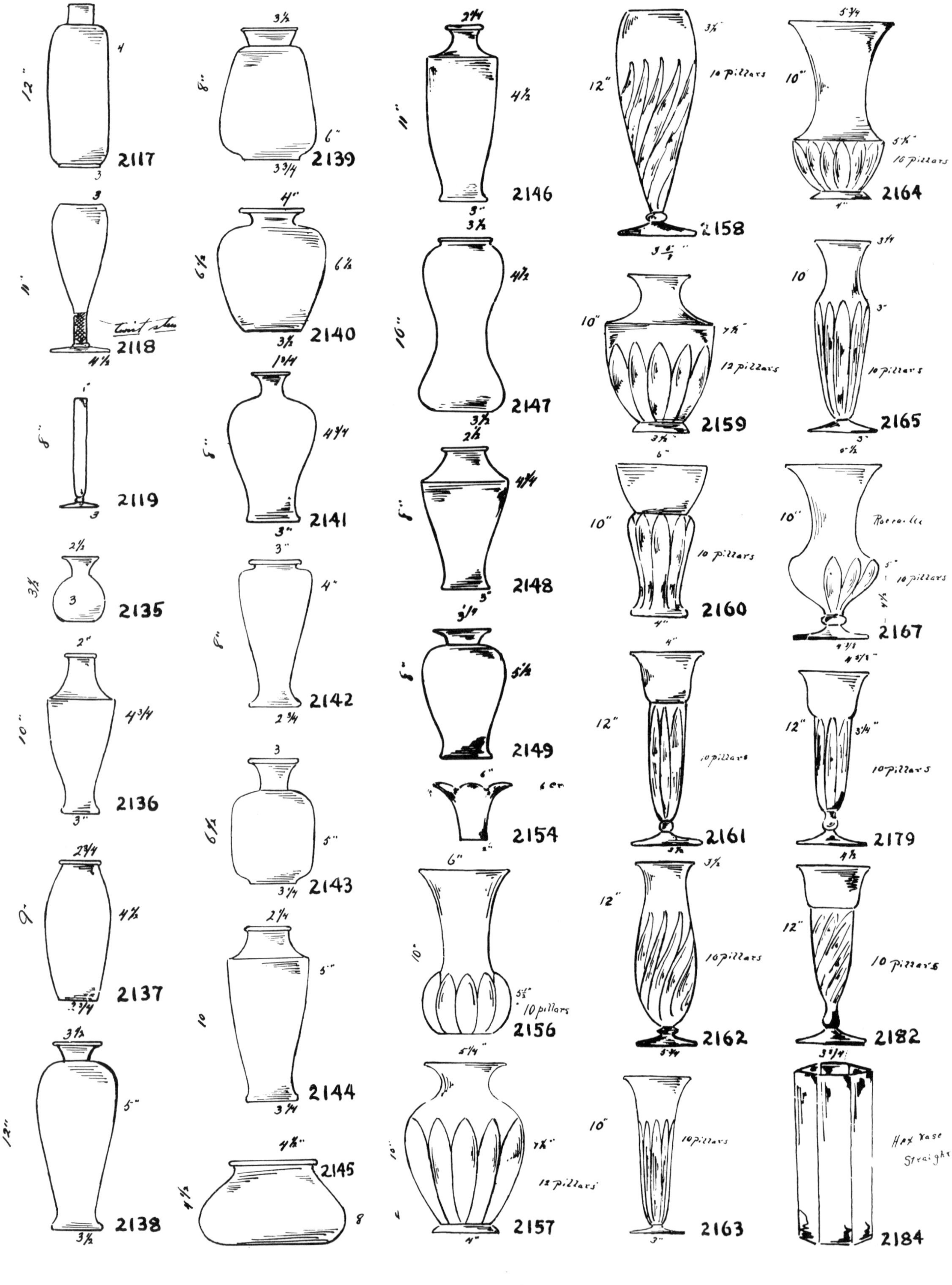

2117
2118
2119
2135
2136
2137
2138
2139
2140
2141
2142
2143
2144
2145
2146
2147
2148
2149
2154
2156
2157
2158
2159
2160
2161
2162
2163
2164
2165
2167
2179
2182
2184

Twist stem

Rosaville

Hex Vase Straight

VASES

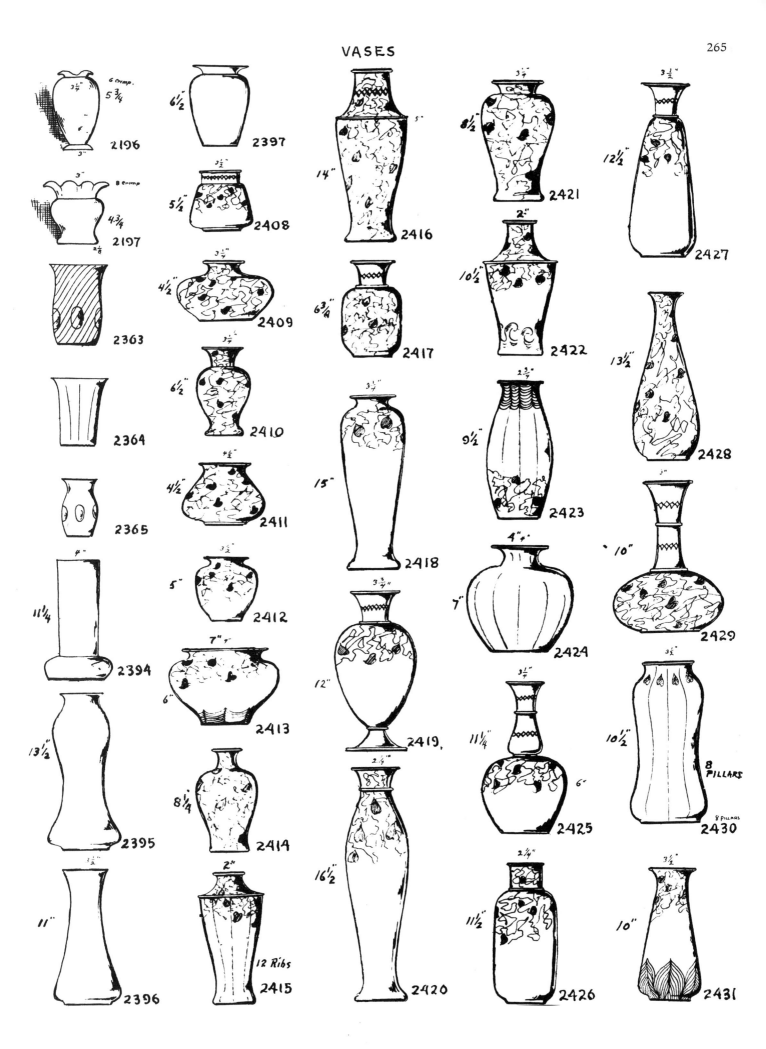

3¾"
6 crimp.
5¾"
3"
2196

3"
8 crimp
4¾"
2⅛"
2197

2363

2364

2365

4"
11¼"
2394

13½"
2395

3½"
11"
2396

6½"
2397

3½"
5½"
2408

3½"
4½"
2409

3½"
6½"
2410

4½"
4½"
2411

3½"
5"
2412

7"
6"
2413

8¼"
2414

2"
12 Ribs
2415

14"
5"
2416

6¾"
2417

3½"
15"
2418

3¾"
12"
2419

2½"
16½"
2420

3½"
8½"
2421

2"
10½"
2422

2¾"
9½"
2423

4"
7"
2424

3½"
11¼"
6"
2425

2¼"
11½"
2426

3½"
12½"
2427

13½"
2428

3"
10"
2429

3½"
10½"
8 PILLARS
8 PILLARS
2430

3½"
10"
2431

VASES

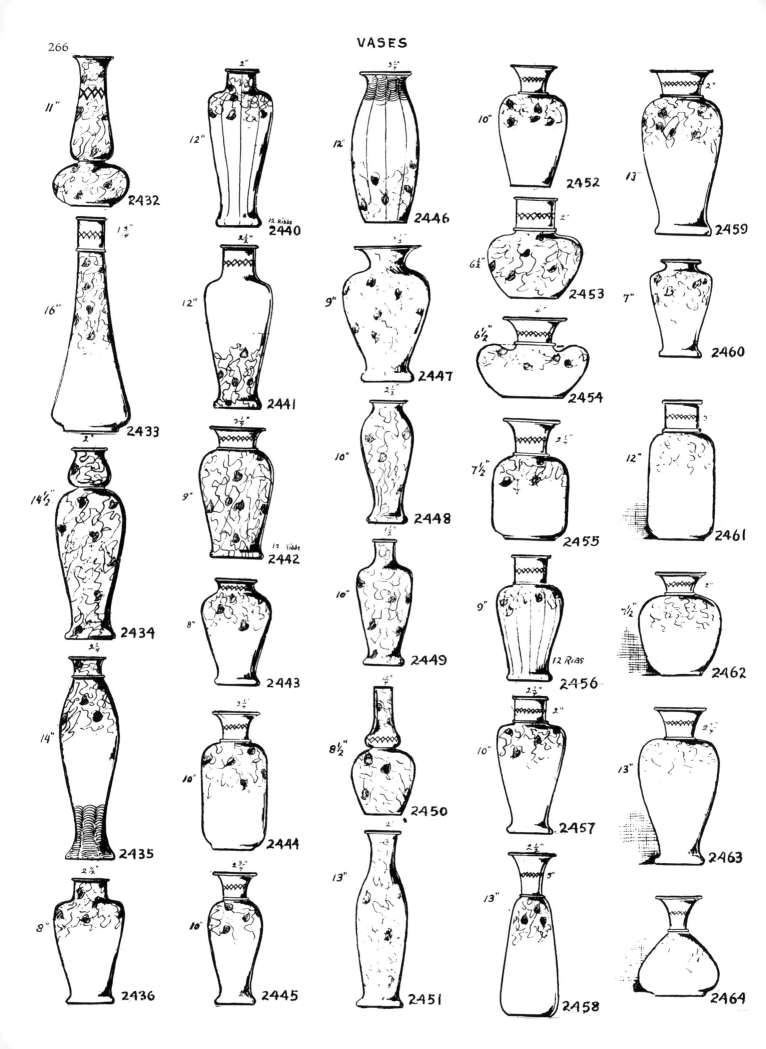

11" 2432

12" 2440 (12 Ribbs)

12" 2446

10" 2452

13" 2459

1¾" 16" 2433

2½" 12" 2441

9" 2447

2" 6½" 2453

7" 2460

14½" 2434

3½" 9" 2442 (12 Ribbs)

2½" 10" 2448

4" 6½" 2454

12" 2461

14" 2435

8" 2443

10" 2449

2½" 7½" 2455

7½" 2462

2½" 8" 2436

3½" 10" 2444

¼" 8½" 2450

2" 9" 2456 (12 Ribs)

2½" 2" 10" 2457

13" 2463

2¾" 10" 2445

13" 2451

2½" 5" 13" 2458

2464

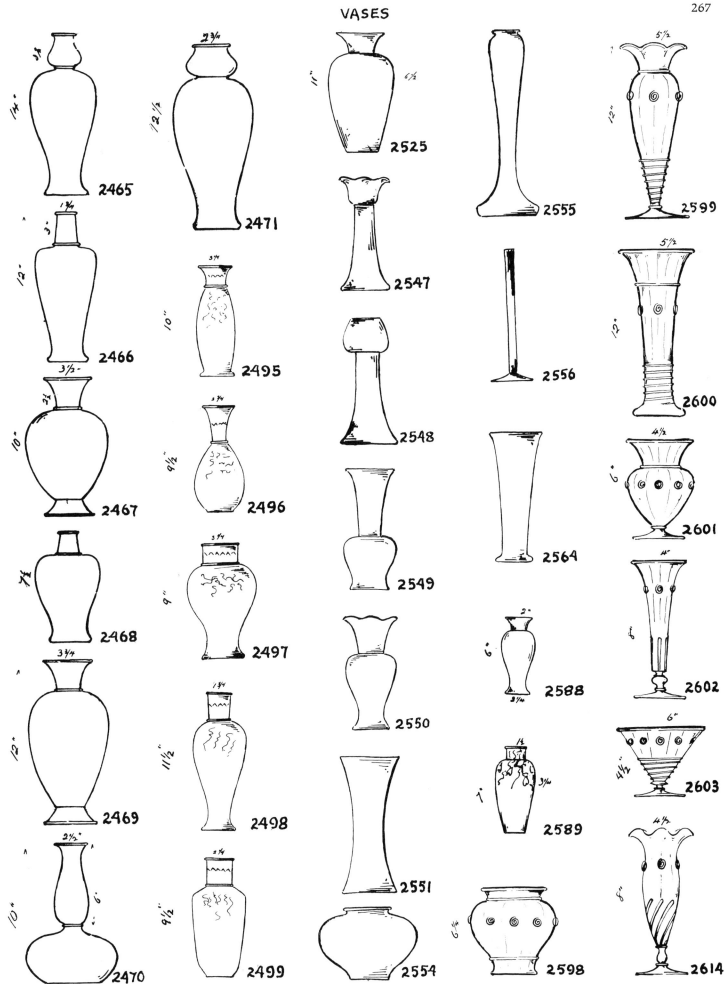

2465

2471

2525

2555

2599

2466

2495

2547

2556

2600

2467

2496

2548

2564

2601

2468

2497

2549

2588

2602

2469

2498

2550

2589

2603

2470

2499

2551

2554

2598

2614

VASES

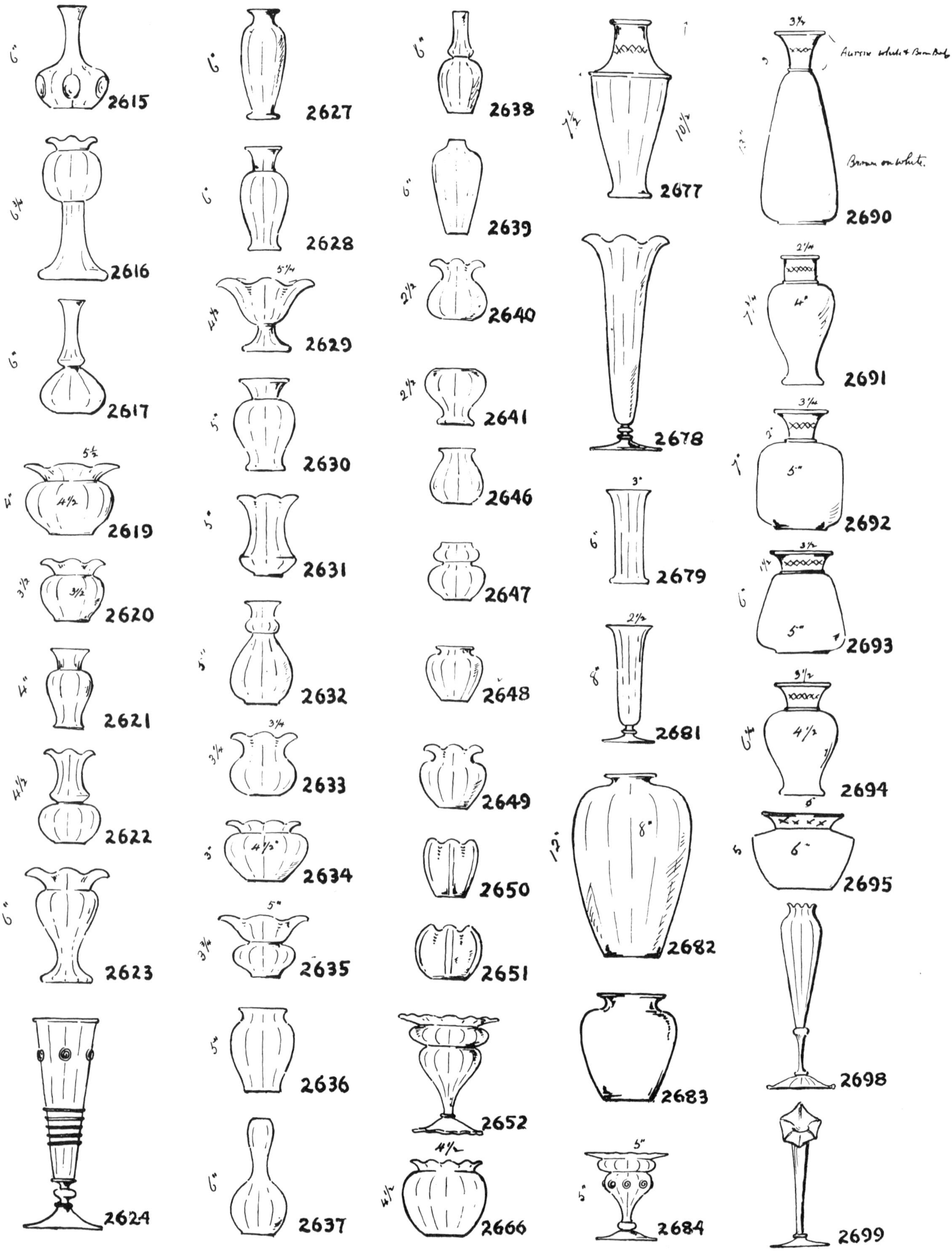

6" 2615

6¼" 2616

6" 2617

5½" 4" 4½" 2619

3½" 3½" 2620

4" 2621

4½" 2622

6" 2623

2624

6" 2627

6" 2628

4⅛" 5¼" 2629

5" 2630

5" 2631

5" 2632

3¾" 3¾" 2633

3" 4½" 2634

3¾" 5" 2635

5" 2636

6" 2637

6" 2638

6" 2639

2½" 2640

2½" 2641

2646

2647

2648

2649

2650

2651

2652

4½" 4½" 2666

7½" 10½" 2677

2678

3" 6" 2679

2½" 8" 2681

12" 8" 2682

2683

5" 5" 2684

3¾" 3" 2690

Brown on white.

2¼" 7¼" 4" 2691

3¼" 2" 5" 2692

3¼" 1¼" 6" 5" 2693

3½" 6¼" 4½" 6" 2694

6" 5 2695

2698

2699

VASES

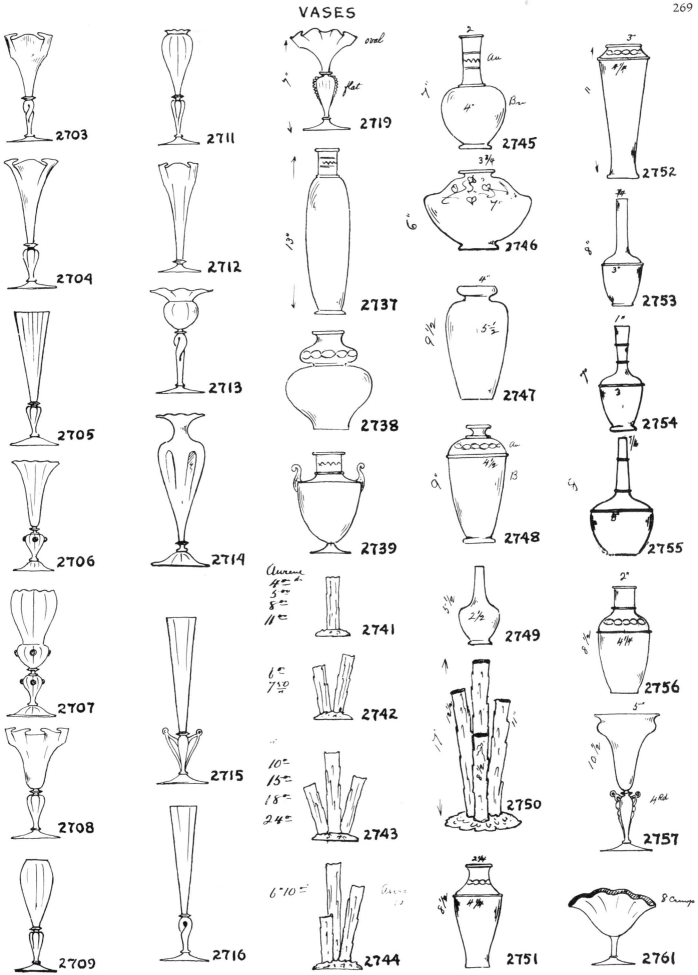

2703

2711

2719 oval flat

2745 2 au 4" Br

3 3/4 2746 6" 7"

3" 2752 4 1/2

2704

2712

2737 13"

2747 4" 9 1/2 5 1/2

2753 8" 3"

2705

2713

2738

2748 au 9 4 1/2 B

2754 1" 7" 3

2706

2714

2739

2749 5 1/2 2 1/2

2755 1 1/6 4 8

2707

2715

Aurene 4" d. 5" 8" 11"

2741

2750 17" 8 1/2

2756 2" 8 1/2 4 1/4

2708

6" 7 1/2"

2742

2757 5" 10 1/2 4 Rd

2709

2716

10" 15" 18" 24"

2743

2751 2 1/4 8 1/4 4 1/4

2761 8 Crimps

6"-10"

2744

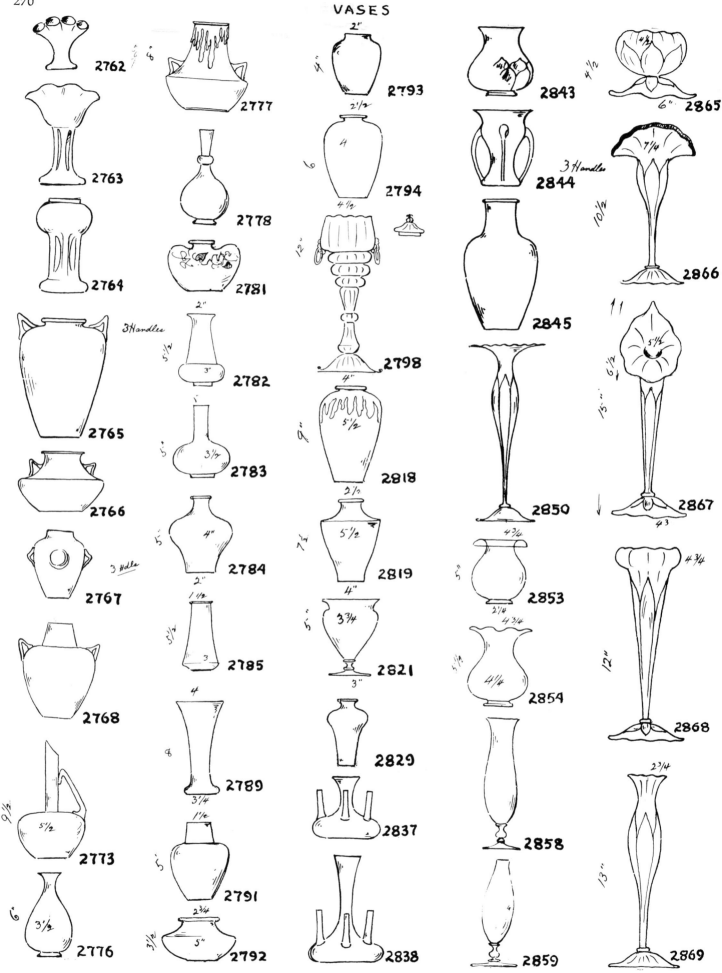

270

VASES

2762

2763

2764

2765

3 Handles

2766

2767 3 Hdls

2768

2773 9½ 5½

2776 6" 3½

2777 6"

2778

2781

2782 2" 5½ 3"

2783 5" 3½

2784 5" 4"

2785 5¼ 2" 3

2789 4" 8 3¼

2791 1½ 5"

2792 2¾ 3½ 5"

2793 2" 4"

2794 2½ 4 4½ 6

2798 12" 4"

2818 9" 5½

2819 7½ 2½ 5½

2821 5" 5" 3¾ 3"

2829 4"

2837

2838

2843 4½

2844 3 Handles

2845

2850 4¾

2853 5" 2¼

2854 4¾ 5½ 4¼

2858

2859

2865 4½ 6"

2866 7¼ 10½

2867 11 5½ 6½ 15" 4 3

2868 4¾ 12"

2869 2¾ 13"

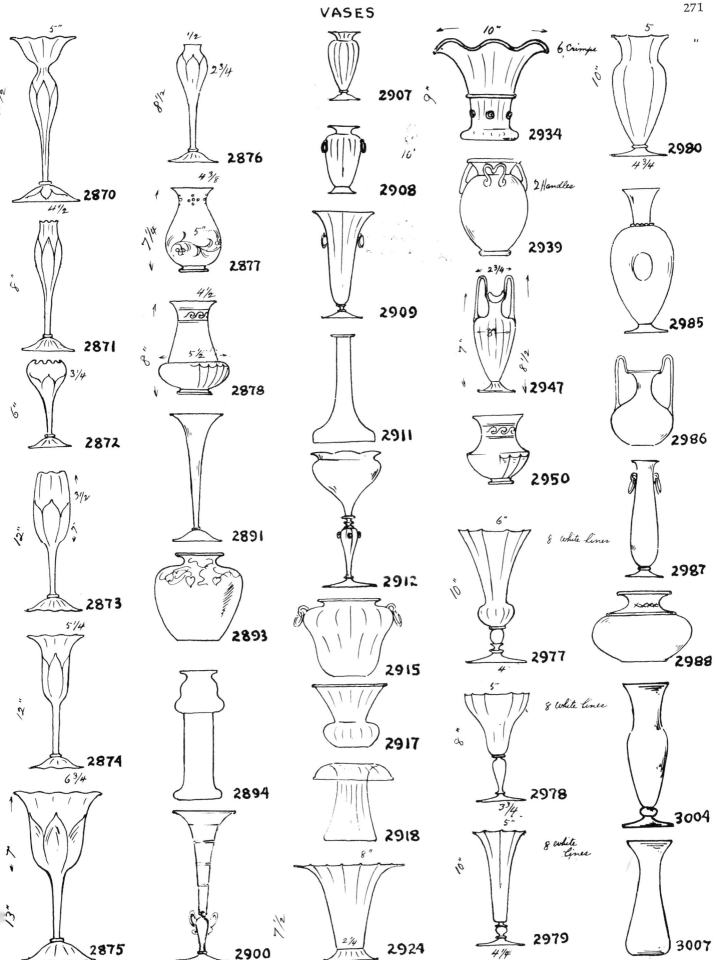

5"
11½
2870
4½

½
2876
8½
2¾

4⅜
2877
7¼
5"

4½
2878
8"
5½

2891

2893

2894

2900
7½

2907
9"

2908
10"

2909

2911

2912

2915

2917

2918

8"
2924
2¼

10"
2934
6 Crimpe

2 Handles
2939

2¾
7"
8½
2947
8"

2950

6"
10"
2977
4"

5"
8"
2978
3¾

5"
10"
2979
4¼

8 white lines

8 white lines

8 white lines

5"
10"
2980
4¾

2985

2986

2987

2988

3004

3007

6"
2871

6"
3¾
2872

3½
7"
12"
2873

5¼
12"
2874
6¾

13"
2875
7

VASES

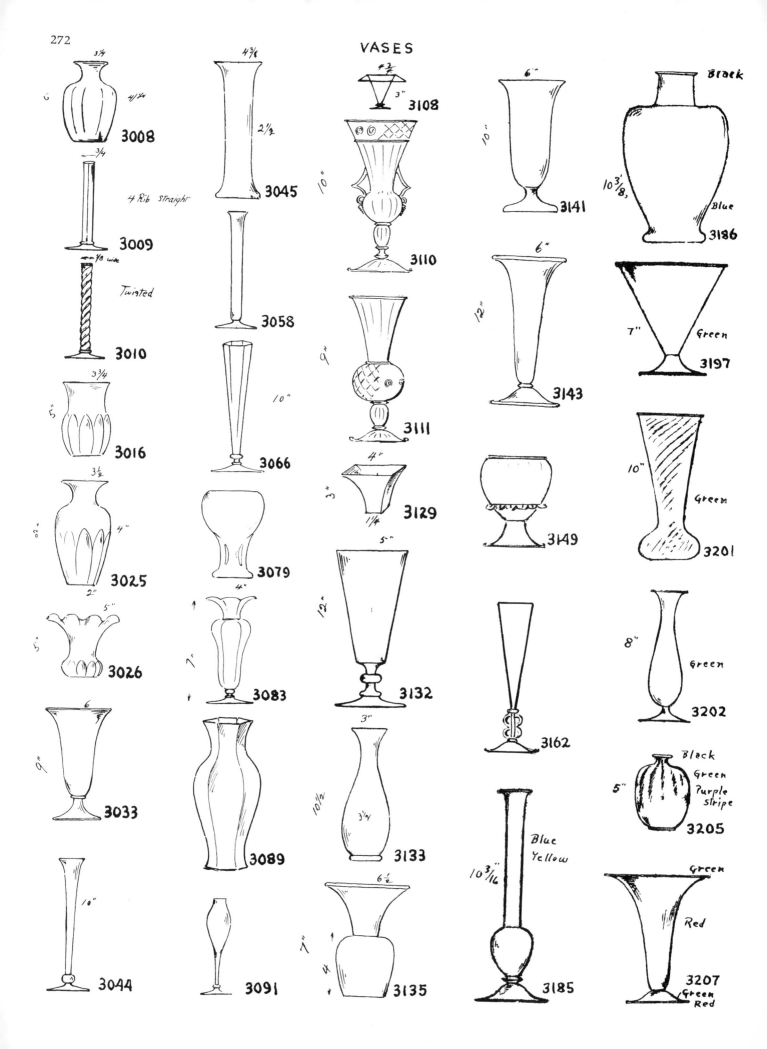

3/4

4 1/4

6"

3008

3/4

4 Rib Straight

3009

1/8 wide

Twisted

3010

3 3/4

5"

3016

3 1/2

6"

4"

3025

2"

5"

5"

3026

6"

9"

3033

10"

3044

4 3/8

2 1/2

3045

3058

10"

3066

3079

4"

4"

7"

3083

3089

3091

4 1/2

3"

3108

10"

3110

9"

3111

4"

3"

1 1/4

3129

5"

12"

3132

3"

10 1/2

3 3/4

3133

6 1/2

7"

4"

3135

6"

10"

3141

6"

12"

3143

3149

3162

Blue
Yellow

10 3/16"

3185

Black

10 3/8,

Blue

3186

7"

Green

3197

10"

Green

3201

8"

Green

3202

Black
Green
Purple
Stripe

5"

3205

Green

Red

3207
Green
Red

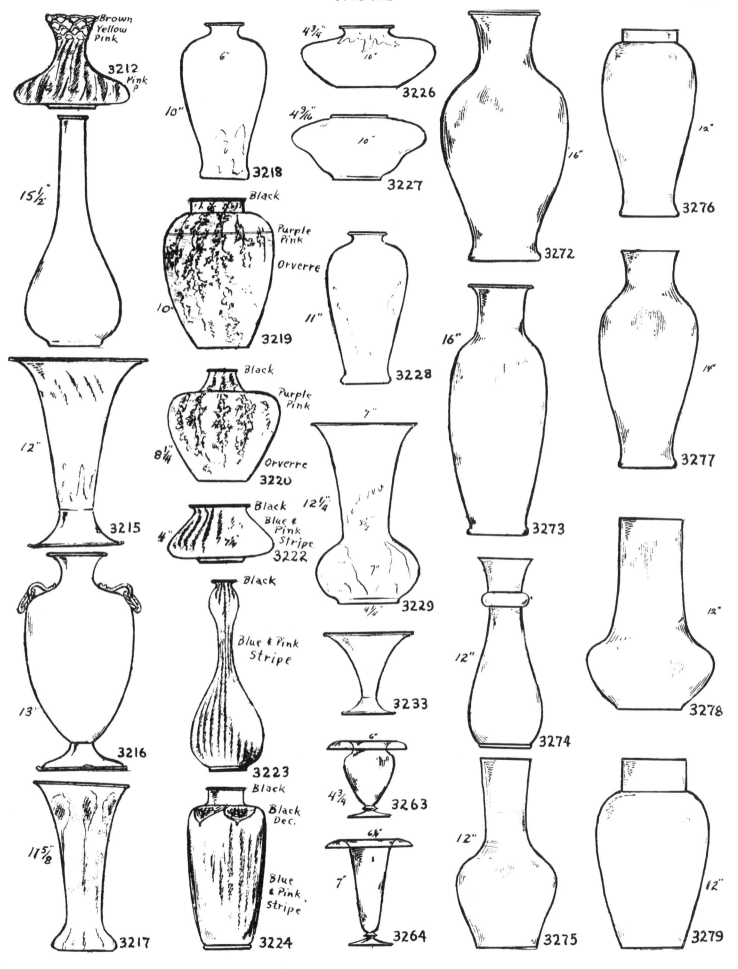

Brown Yellow Pink — 3212 — Pink P — 15½"

6" — 3218 — 10"

4¾" — 3226 — 10"

4³⁄₁₆" — 3227 — 10"

3272 — 16"

3276 — 12"

12" — 3215

Black — Purple Pink — Orverre — 3219 — 10"

Black — Purple Pink — Orverre — 3220 — 8¼"

11" — 3228

7" — 12¼" — 3½" — 7" — 4¾" — 3229

16" — 3273

14" — 3277

13" — 3216

11⅝" — 3217

Black — Blue & Pink Stripe — 4" — 7½" — 3222

Black — Blue & Pink Stripe — 3223

Black — Black Dec. — Blue & Pink Stripe — 3224

3233

6" — 4¾" — 3263

6¼" — 7" — 3264

12" — 3274

12" — 3275

12" — 3278

12" — 3279

VASES

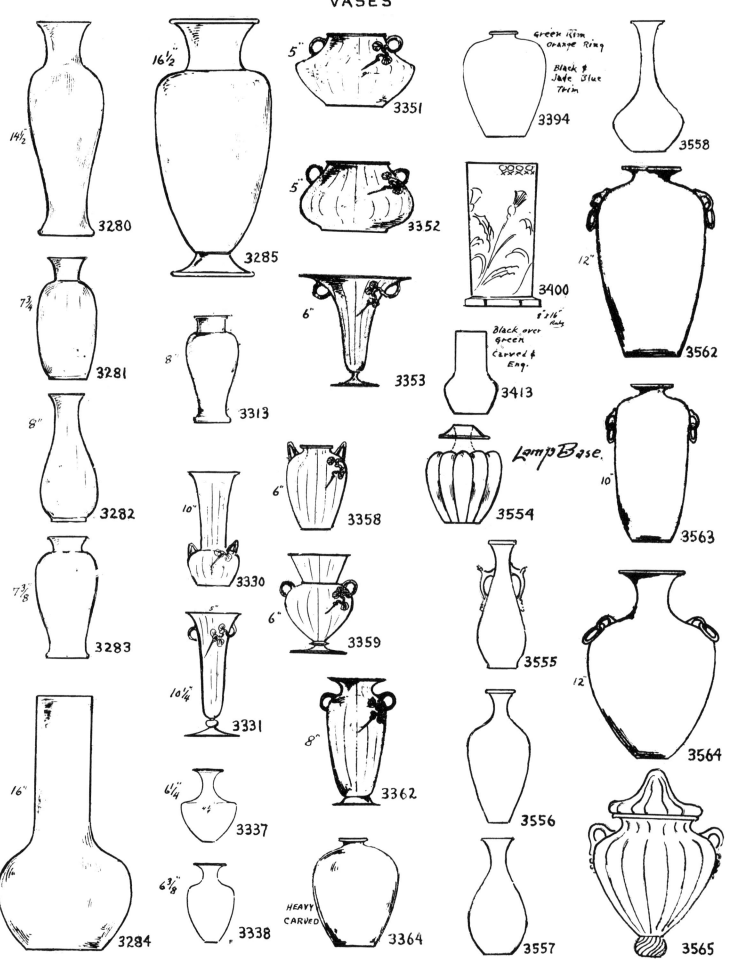

14½" 3280

16½" 3285

5" 3351

5" 3352

6" 3353

Green Rim Orange Ring

Black & Jade Blue Trim

3394

3558

12" 3562

7¾" 3281

8" 3282

7⅜" 3283

16" 3284

8" 3313

10" 3330

10¼" 3331

6¼" 3337

6⅜" 3338

6" 3358

6" 3359

8" 3362

HEAVY CARVED 3364

3400 8"x16" Ruby

Black over Green Carved & Eng. 3413

Lamp Base. 3554

3555

3556

3557

10" 3563

12" 3564

3565

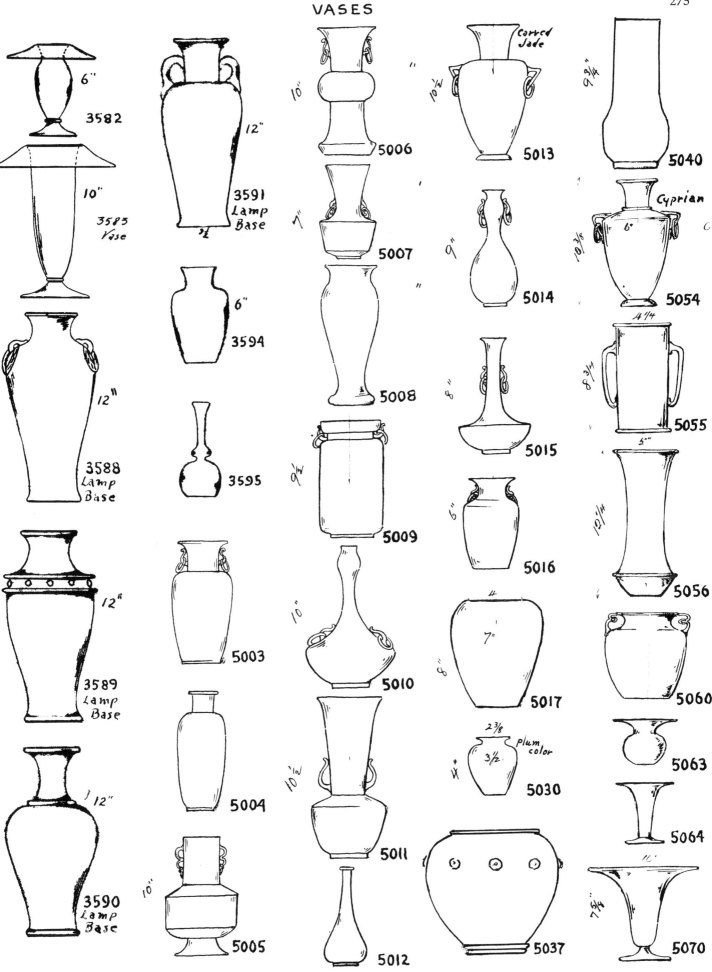

VASES

6"
3582

10"
3585 Vase

12"
3588 Lamp Base

12"
3589 Lamp Base

12"
3590 Lamp Base

12"
3591 Lamp Base

6"
3594

3595

5003

5004

10"
5005

10"
5006

7"
5007

"
5008

9½
5009

10"
5010

10½
5011

5012

10½
5013 Carved Jade

9"
5014

8"
5015

6"
5016

7"
4
8"
5017

2⅜
3½
plum color
5030

5037

9¾
5040

Cyprian
10⅜   6"
5054

4¼
8¾
5"
5055

5"
10¼
5056

5060

5063

5064

7¾
5070

VASES

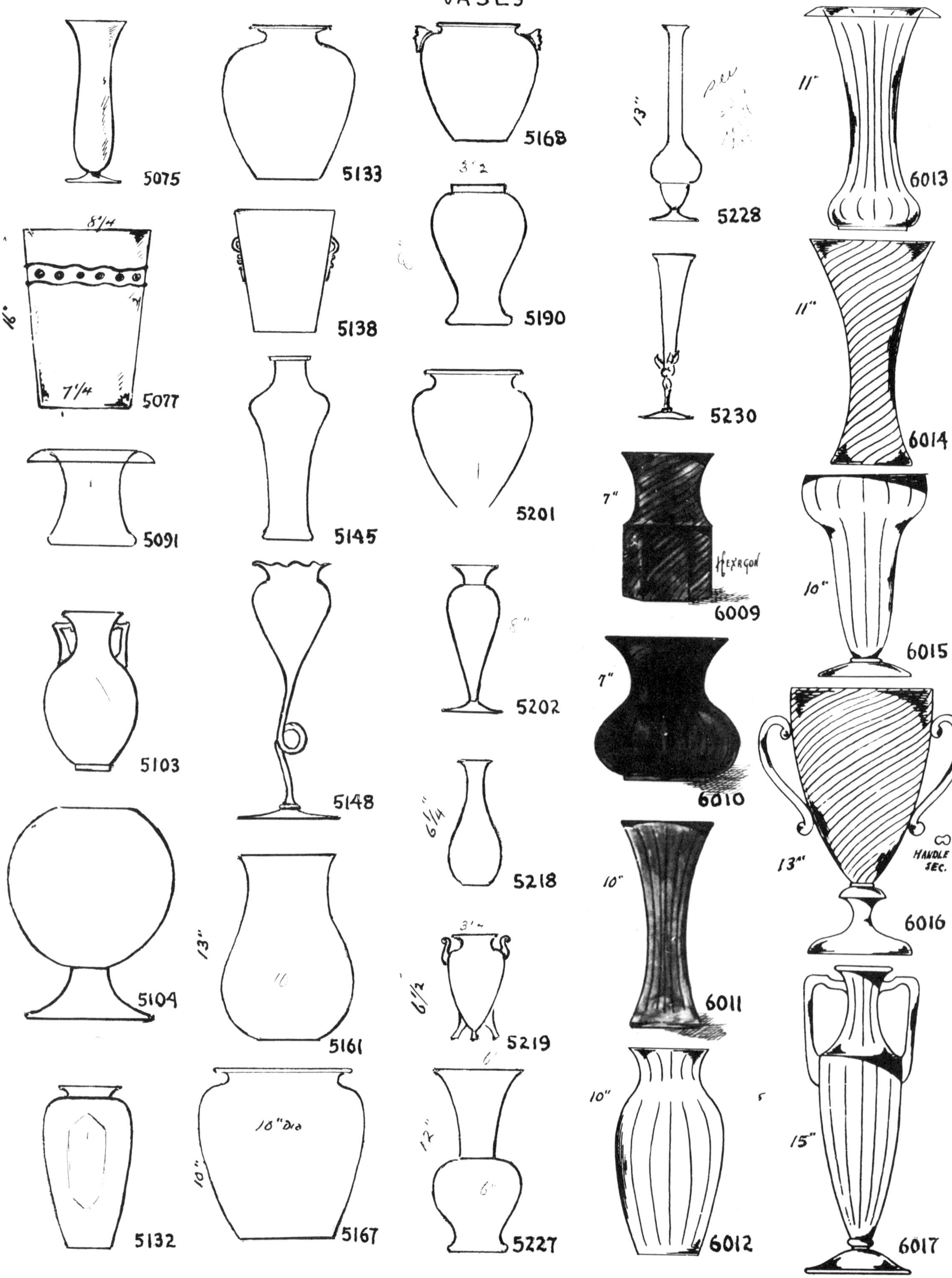

5075

5133

5168

3'2

5190

5138

8'/4

16°

7'/4

5077

5145

5201

5091

5103

5148

5202

8"

5104

5161

6'/4

5218

13"

5132

10"

5167

10"Dia

3'~

5219

6'/2

12"

6"

5227

6"

5228

13"

5230

6009

7"

HEXAGON

6010

7"

6011

10"

6012

10"

5

6013

11"

6014

11"

6015

10"

6016

13"

HANDLE SEC.

6017

15"

VASES

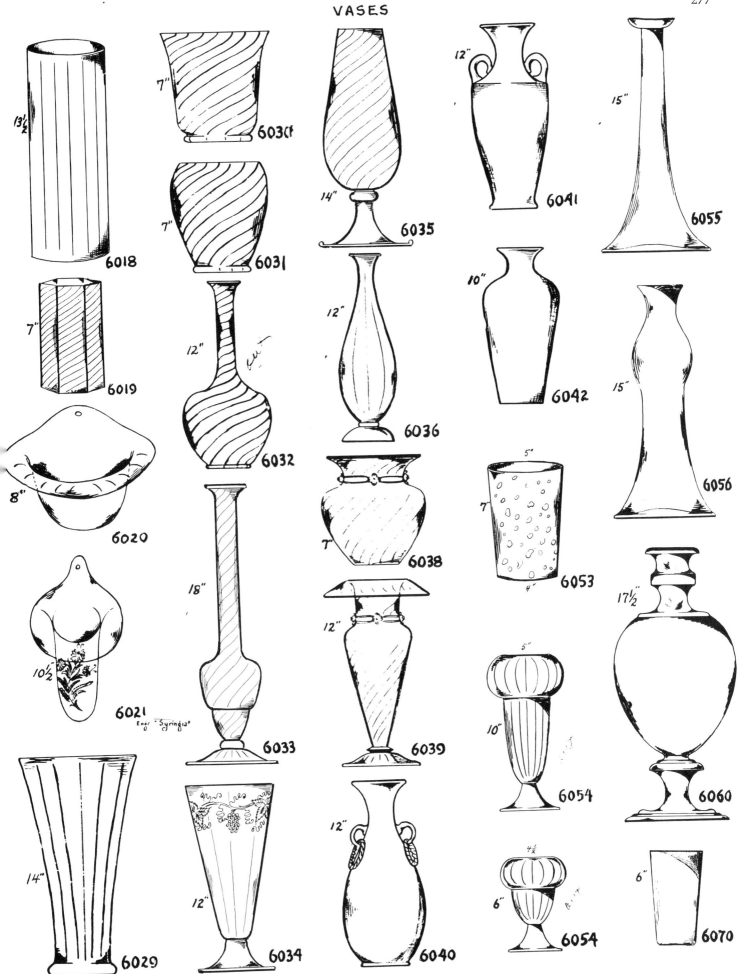

13½" 6018

7" 6019

8" 6020

10½" 6021

14" 6029

7" 6030

7" 6031

12" 6032

18" 6033
Engr "Syringa"

12" 6034

12" 6035

12" 6036

7" 6038

12" 6039

12" 6040

12" 6041

10" 6042

5" 7" 4" 6053

5" 10" 6054

4½" 6" 6054

17½" 6060

15" 6055

15" 6056

6" 6070

VASES

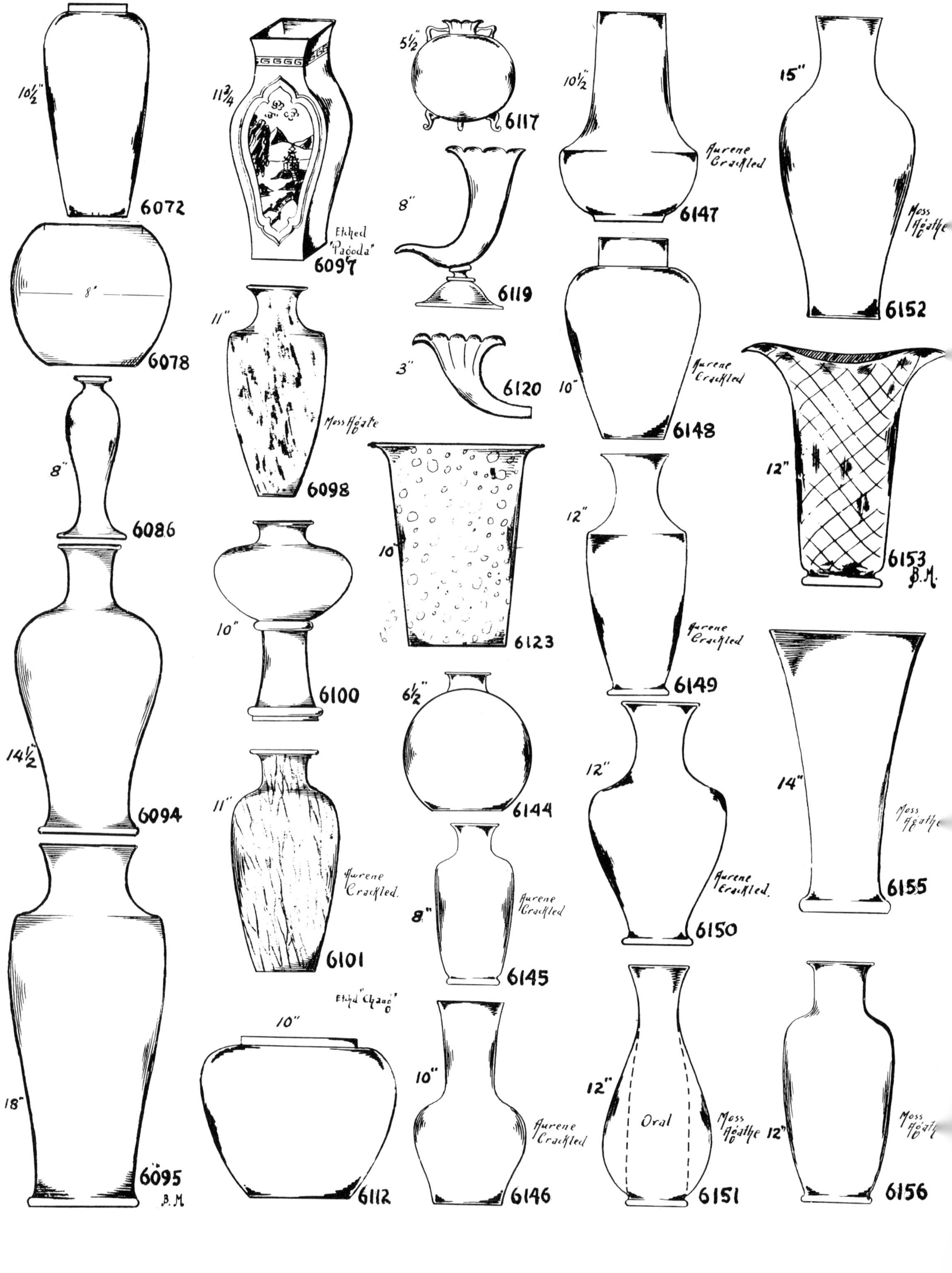

10½" 6072

8" 6078

8" 6086

14½" 6094

18" 6095 B.M.

11¾" 6097 Etched "Pagoda"

11" 6098 Moss Agate

10" 6100

11" 6101 Etd "Chang"

10" 6112

5½" 6117

8" 6119

3" 6120

10" 6123

6½" 6144

8" 6145 Aurene Crackled

10" 6146 Aurene Crackled

10½" 6147 Aurene Crackled

10" 6148 Aurene Crackled

12" 6149 Aurene Crackled

12" 6150 Aurene Crackled.

12" Oral 6151 Moss Agathe

15" 6152 Moss Agathe

12" 6153 B.M.

14" 6155 Moss Agathe

12" 6156 Moss Agath

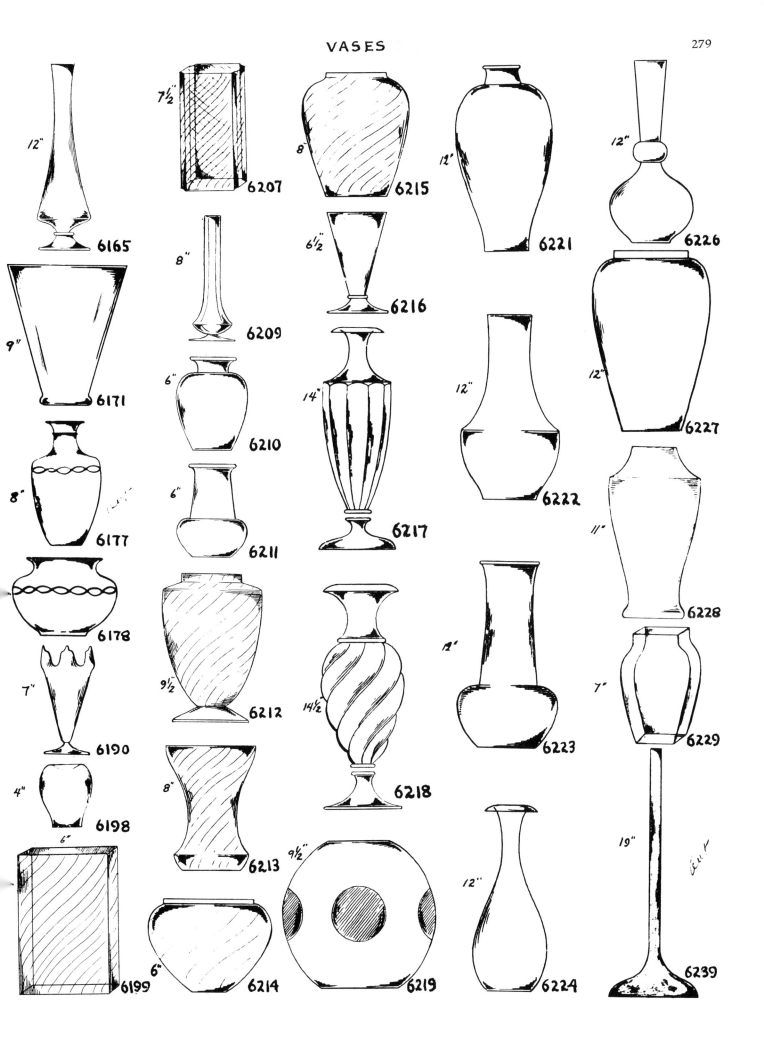

12" 6165

7½" 6207

8" 6215

12" 6221

12" 6226

9" 6171

8" 6209

6½" 6216

12" 6222

12" 6227

8" 6177

6" 6210

14" 6217

11" 6228

6" 6211

12" 6223

6178

9½" 6212

12" 6218 14½"

7" 6229

7" 6190

8" 6213

4" 6198

6" 6199

6" 6214

9½" 6219

12" 6224

19" 6239

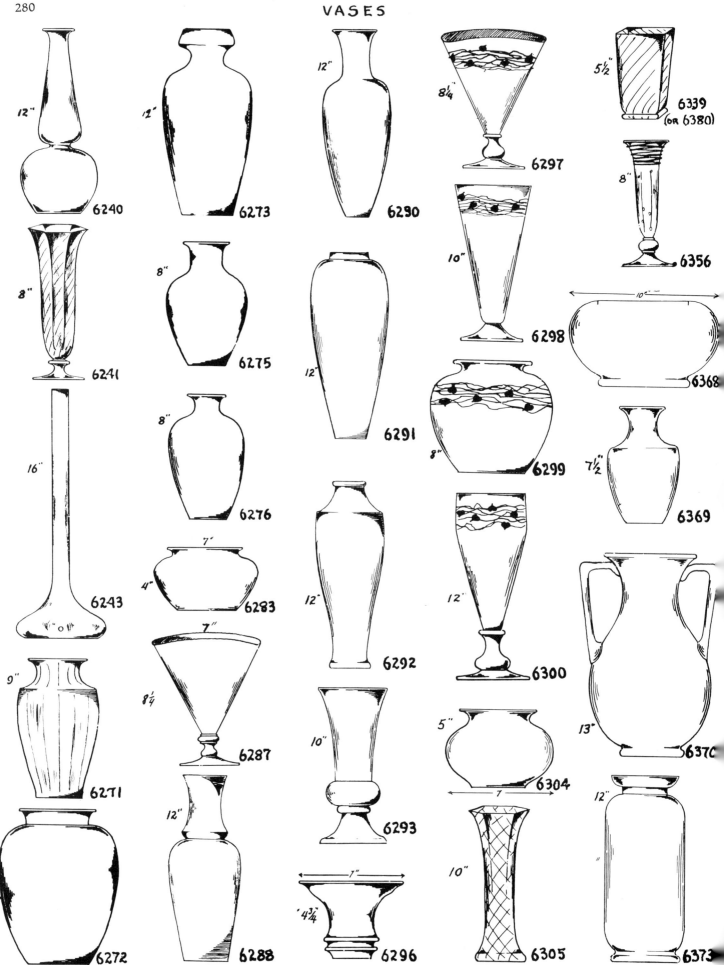

12" 6240

12" 6273

12" 6290

8¼" 6297

5½" 6339 (OR 6380)

8" 6241

8" 6275

8" 6276

10" 6298

8" 6356

16" 6243

8" 6276

7" 6283

12" 6291

8" 6299

10" 6368

9" 6271

4" 6283

7" 6287

12" 6292

12" 6300

7½" 6369

12" 6272

12" 6288

10" 6293

1" 6296 4¾"

5" 6304 7

10" 6305

13" 6370

12" 6373

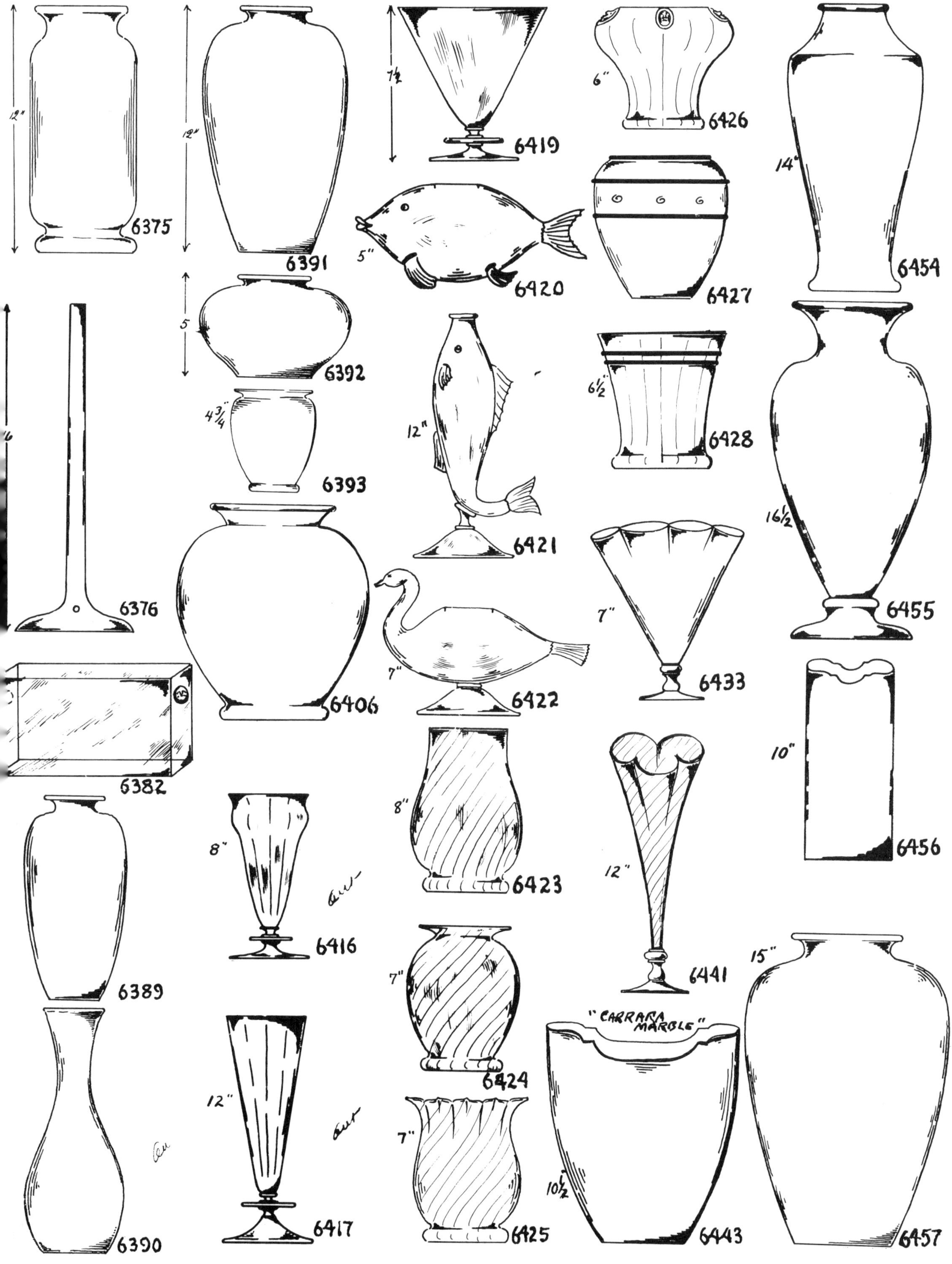

6375

12"

6391

12"

7½ 6419

6" 6426

6427

14" 6454

5" 6420

5 6392

4¾" 6393

12" 6421

6½" 6428

6433 7"

16½" 6455

6376

6 6382

6406

7" 6422

8" 6423

12" 6441

10" 6456

6389

8" 6416

7" 6424

"CARRARA MARBLE"

15" 6457

6390

12" 6417

7" 6425

10½" 6443

VASES

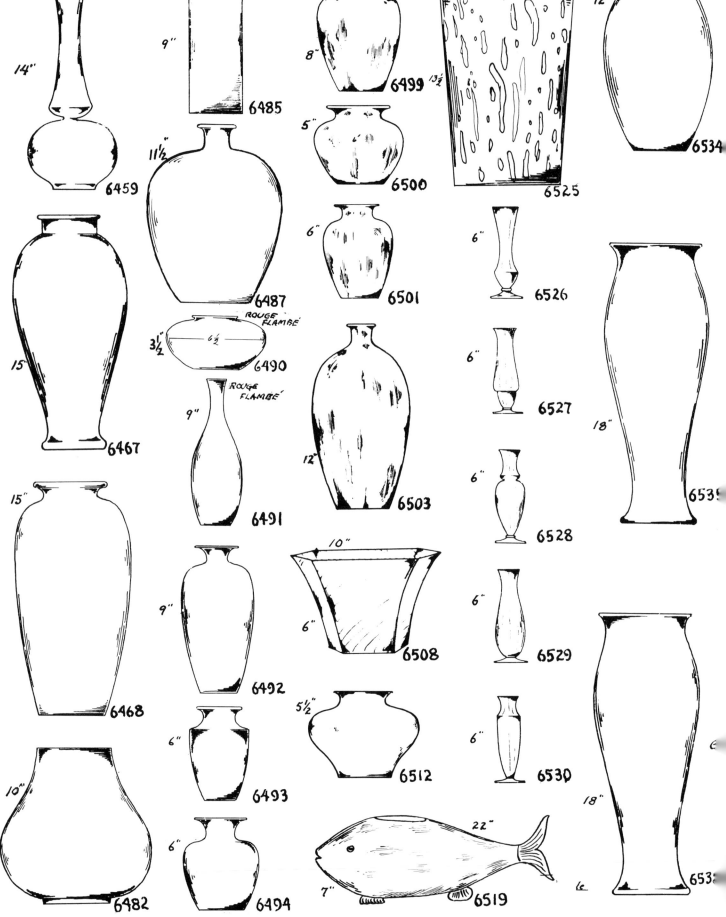

14" 6459

9" 6485

11½" 6487

ROUGE FLAMBÉ
3½" 6½" 6490

9" ROUGE FLAMBÉ 6491

15" 6467

15" 6468

9" 6492

6" 6493

6" 6494

10" 6482

8" 6499

5" 6500

6" 6501

12" 6503

10" 6508

5½" 6512

7" 6519

13½" 6525

6" 6526

6" 6527

6" 6528

6" 6529

6" 6530

12" 6534

18" 6539

18" 653

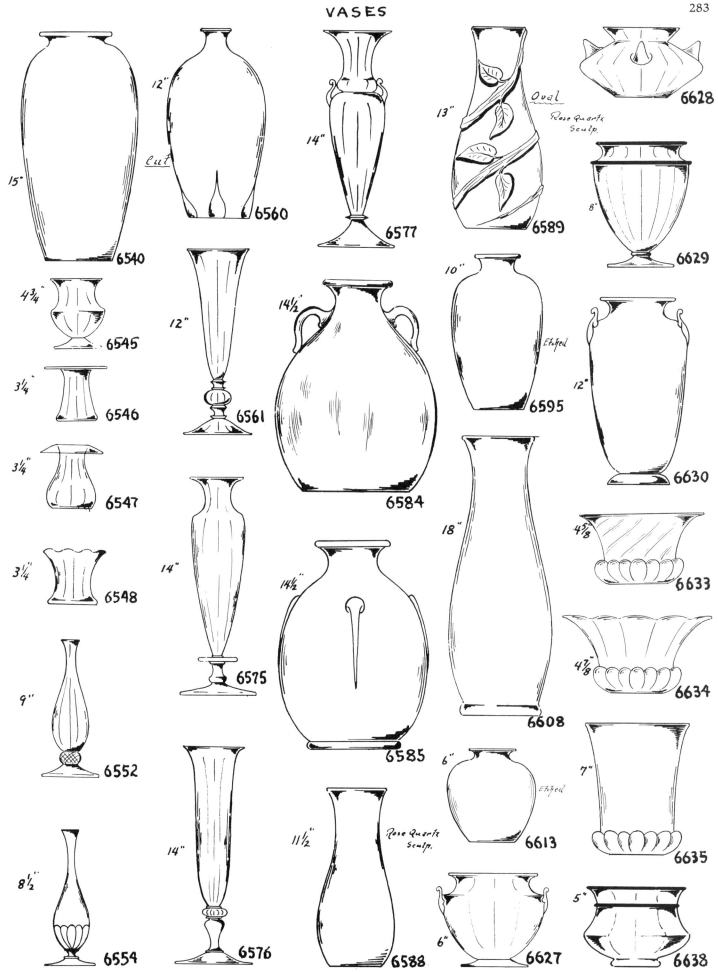

15" 6540

12" Cut 6560

14" 6577

13" Oval Rose Quartz Sculp. 6589

6628

8" 6629

4¾" 6545

3¼" 6546

3¼" 6547

3¼" 6548

9" 6552

8½" 6554

12" 6561

14" 6575

14" 6576

14½" 6584

14½" 6585

11½" Rose Quartz Sculp. 6588

10" Etched 6595

18" 6608

6" Etched 6613

6" 6627

12" 6630

4⅝" 6633

4⅞" 6634

7" 6635

5" 6638

VASES

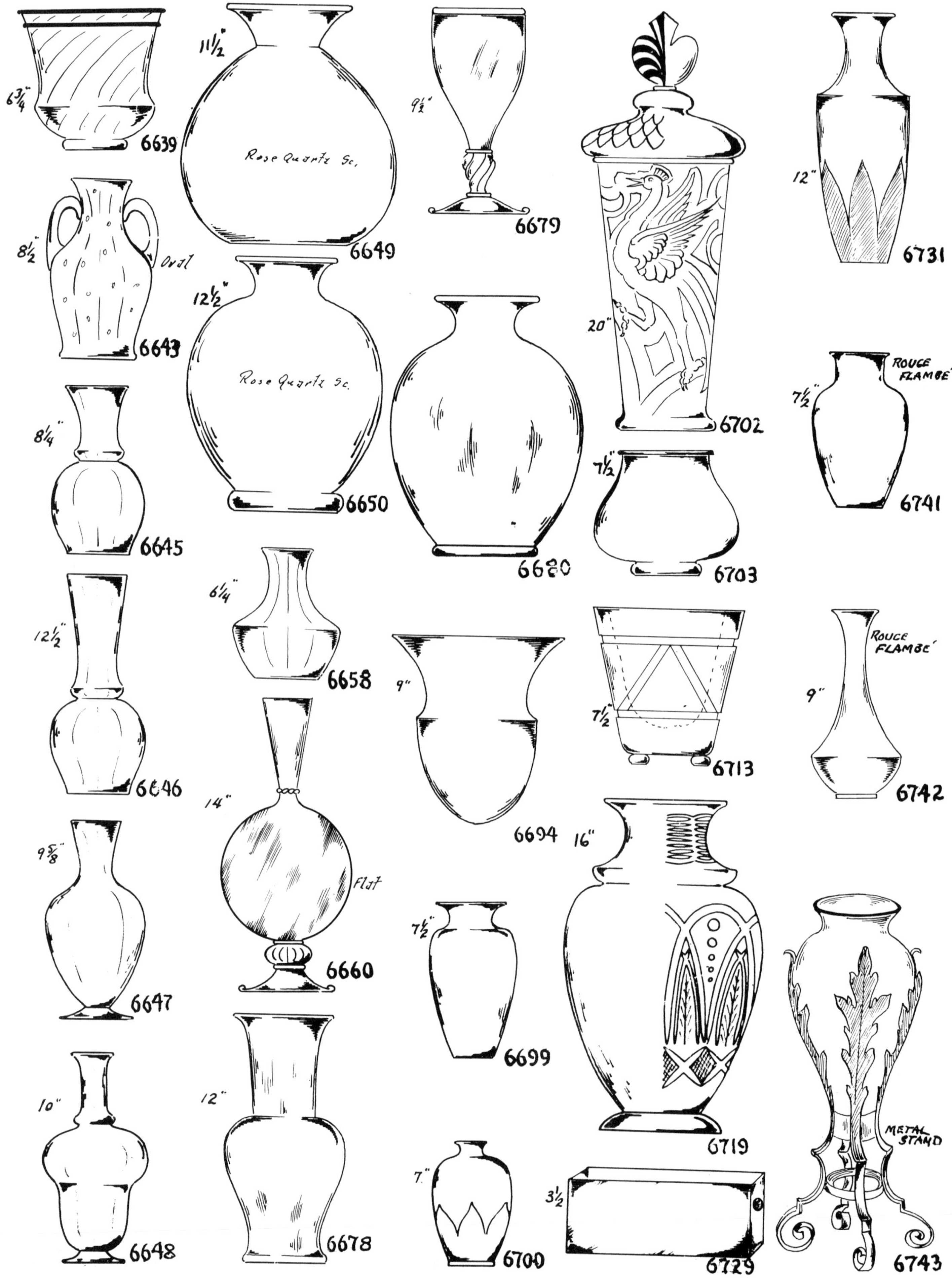

6639

6643

6645

6646

6647

6648

6649 — Rose Quartz Sc.

6650 — Rose Quartz Sc.

6658

6660 — Flat

6678

6679

6680

6694

6699

6700

6729

6702

6703

6713

6719

6731

6741 — ROUGE FLAMBE

6742 — ROUGE FLAMBE

6743 — METAL STAND

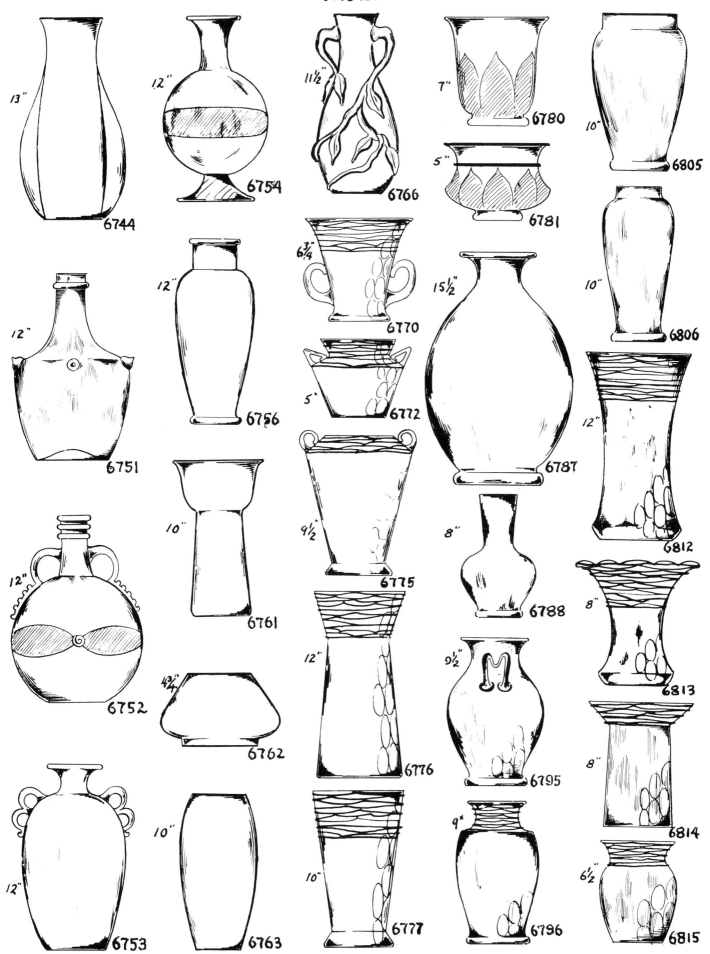

13" 6744

12" 6754

11½" 6766

7" 6780

5" 6781

10" 6805

12" 6751

12" 6756

6¾" 6770

5" 6772

15½" 6787

10" 6806

12" 6812

12" 6752

10" 6761

4¾" 6762

9½" 6775

12" 6776

10" 6777

8" 6788

9½" 6795

9" 6796

8" 6813

8" 6814

6½" 6815

12" 6753

10" 6763

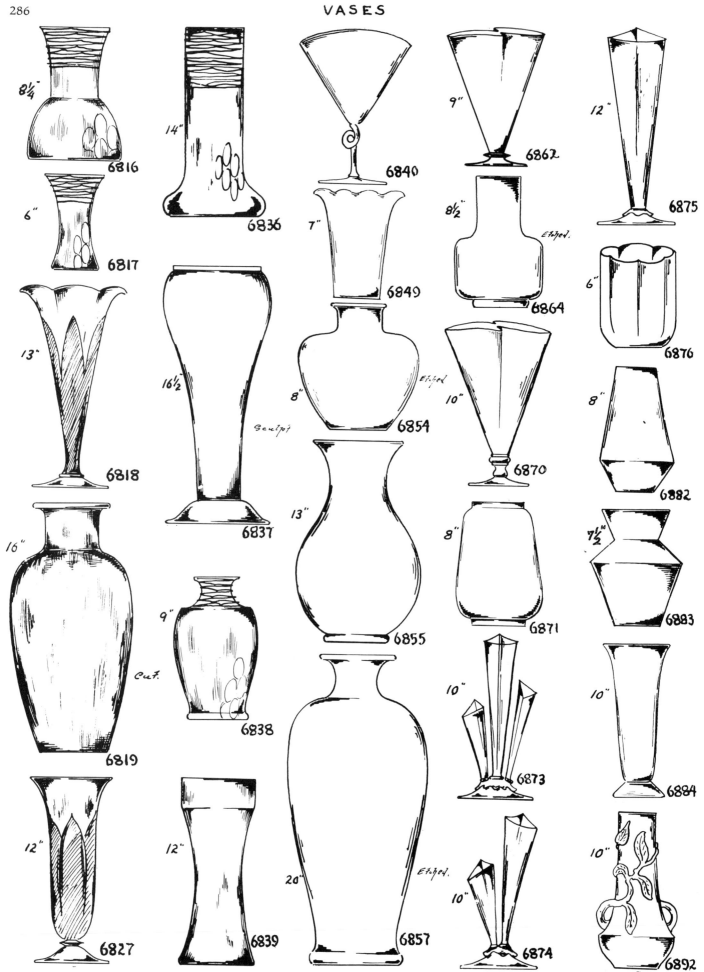

8¼" 6816

6" 6817

13" 6818

16" Cut. 6819

12" 6827

14" 6836

16½" Sculpt 6837

9" 6838

12" 6839

7" 6840

8" Etched 6854

13" 6855

20" Etched 6857

6849

9" 6862

8½" Etched 6864

10" 6870

8" 6871

10" 6873

10" 6874

12" 6875

6" 6876

8" 6882

7½" 6883

10" 6884

10" 6892

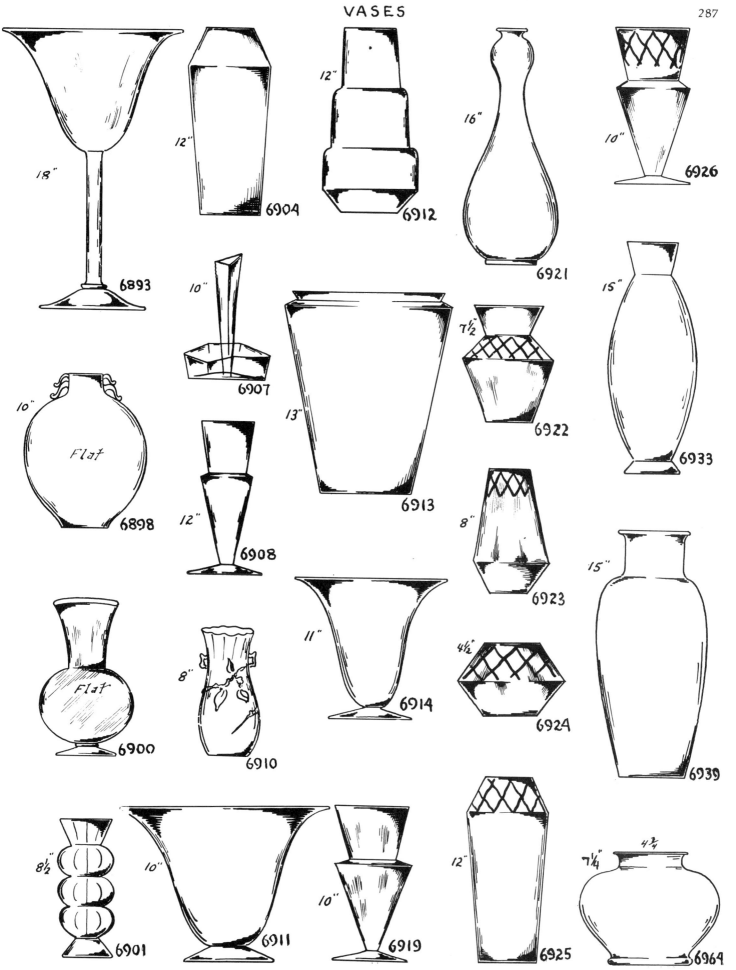

18" 6893

12" 6904

12" 6912

16" 6921

10" 6926

10" Flat 6898

10" 6907

13" 6913

7½" 6922

15" 6933

8" 6908

12" 6908

8" 6923

15"

11" 6914

4½" 6924

6900 Flat

8" 6910

6939

8½" 6901

10" 6911

10" 6919

12" 6925

7¼" 4¾" 6964

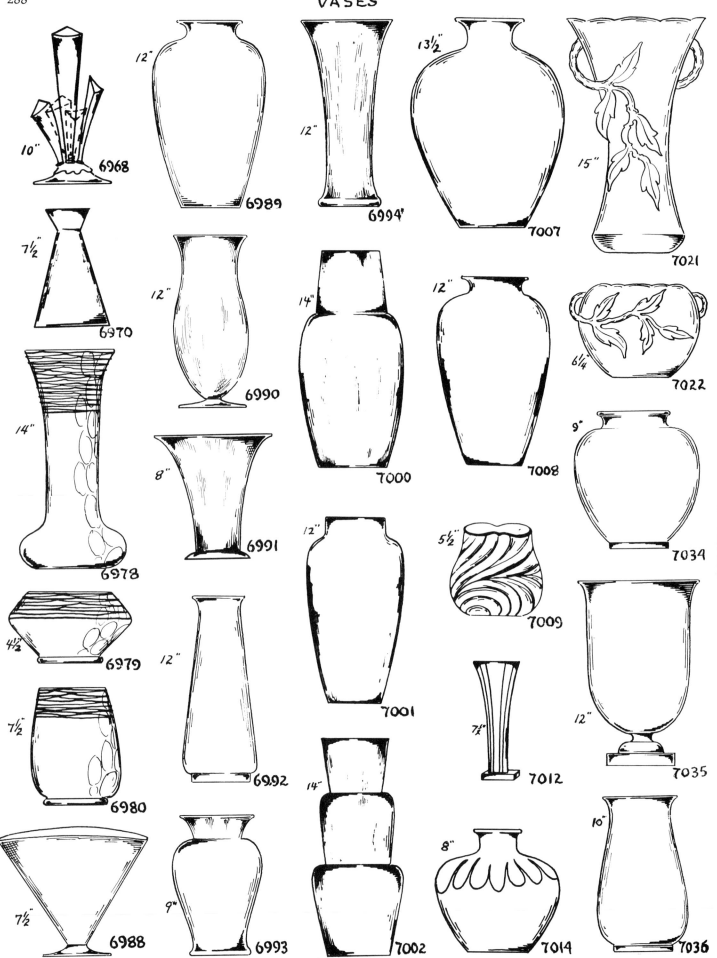

10"   6968

7½"   6970

14"   6978

4½"   6979

7½"   6980

7½"   6988

12"   6989

12"   6990

8"   6991

12"   6992

9"   6993

12"   6994

14"   7000

12"   7001

7002

14"   7002

13½"   7007

12"   7008

5½"   7009

7½"   7012

8"   7014

15"   7021

6¼   7022

9"   7034

12"   7035

10"   7036

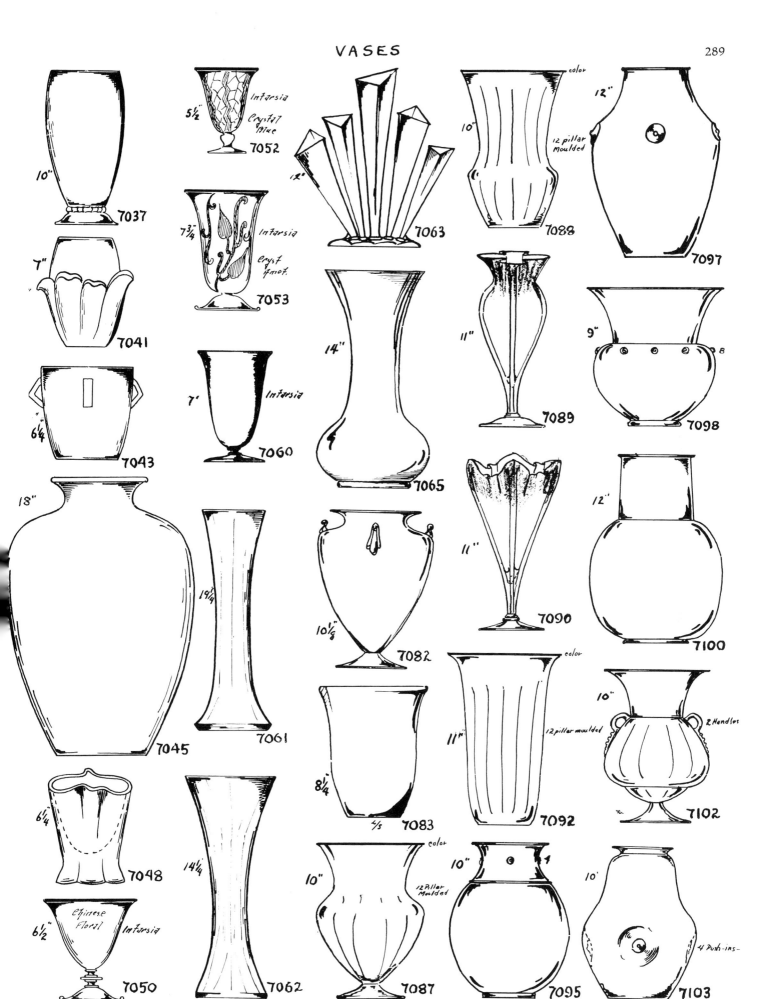

10" 7037

7" 7041

6¼" 7043

18" 7045

6¼" 7048

6½" Chinese Floral Intarsia 7050

5½" Intarsia Crystal Blue 7052

7¾" Intarsia Cryst Amot. 7053

7" Intarsia 7060

19¼" 7061

14¼" 7062

12" 7063

14" 7065

10⅞" 7082

8¼" 4/5 7083

10" color 12 Pillar Moulded 7087

10" color 12 pillar Moulded 7088

11" 7089

11" 7090

11" color 12 pillar moulded 7092

10" color 7095

12" 7097

9" 7098

12" 7100

10" 2 Handles 7102

10" 4 Push-ins- 7103

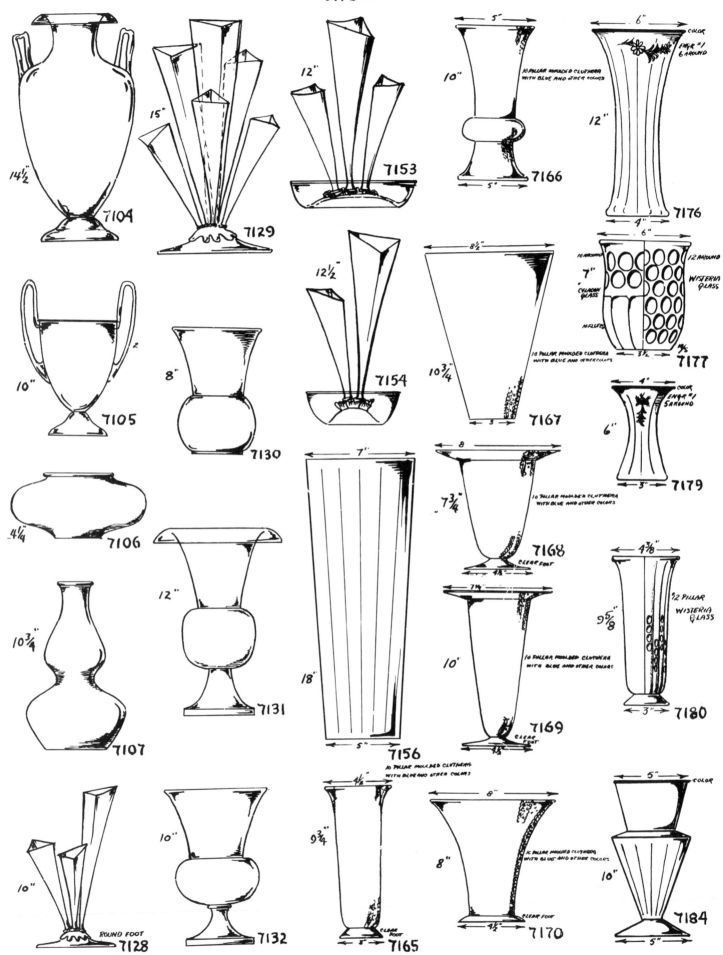

$14\frac{1}{2}$ 7104

15" 7129

$12\frac{1}{2}$ 7154

12" 7153

10" 7166

10 PILLAR MOULDED CLUTHERA WITH BLUE AND OTHER COLORS

6" 7176

12"

4"

COLOR
ENGR #1
6 AROUND

10" 7105

8" 7130

$10\frac{3}{4}$ 7167

$8\frac{1}{2}$ 7167

3"

10 PILLAR MOULDED CLUTHERA WITH BLUE AND OTHER COLORS

6" 7177

7" CELADON GLASS

10 AROUND   12 AROUND

WISTERIA GLASS

FLUTES

$3\frac{1}{2}$

$4\frac{1}{4}$ 7106

12" 7131

$10\frac{3}{4}$ 7107

7" 7156

18"

5"

8 7168

$7\frac{3}{4}$

10 PILLAR MOULDED CLUTHERA WITH BLUE AND OTHER COLORS

CLEAR FOOT

$4\frac{1}{2}$

$7\frac{1}{4}$

10" 7169

10 PILLAR MOULDED CLUTHERA WITH BLUE AND OTHER COLORS

CLEAR FOOT

$4\frac{1}{2}$

4" 7179

6"

COLOR
ENGR #1
SARGEANT

3"

$4\frac{3}{8}$ 7180

$9\frac{5}{8}$

12 PILLAR WISTERIA GLASS

3"

10" 7128

ROUND FOOT

10" 7132

$9\frac{3}{4}$ 7165

$4\frac{1}{2}$

10 PILLAR MOULDED CLUTHERA WITH BLUE AND OTHER COLORS

CLEAR FOOT

5"

8 7170

8"

10 PILLAR MOULDED CLUTHERA WITH BLUE AND OTHER COLORS

CLEAR FOOT

$4\frac{1}{2}$

5" 7184

10"

COLOR

5"

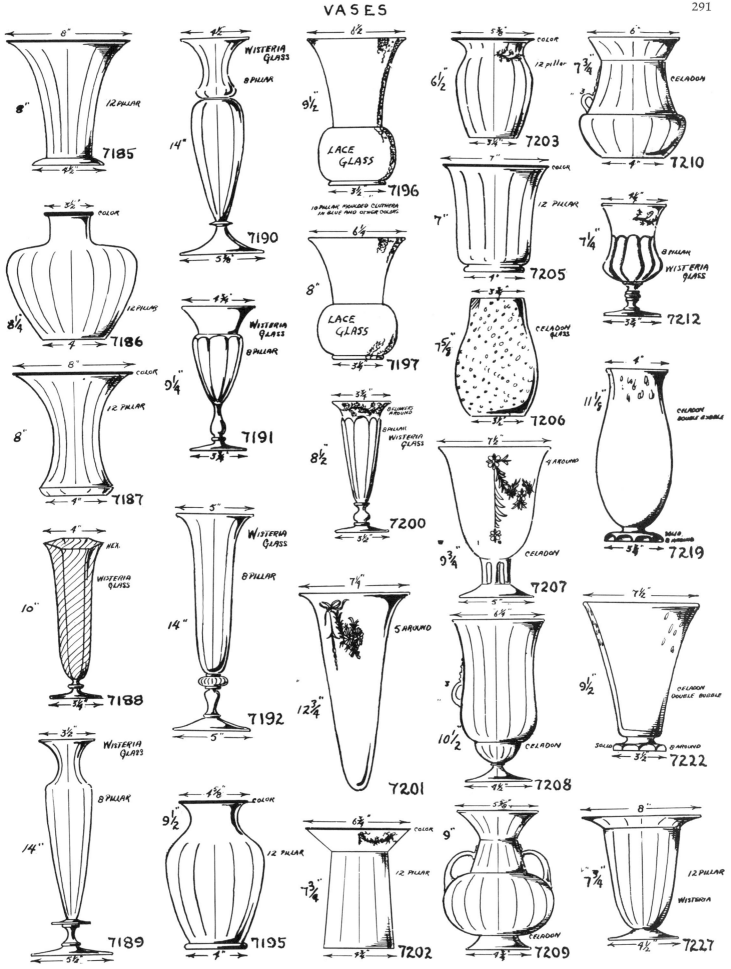

8"
8"
12 PILLAR
4½"
7185

4½"
WISTERIA GLASS
8 PILLAR
14"
7190
5⅞"

6½"
9½"
LACE GLASS
3½"
7196
10 PILLAR MOULDED CLUTHERA
IN BLUE AND OTHER COLORS

5⅝"
COLOR
12 PILLAR
6½"
3¼"
7203

6"
CELADON
7¾"
3"
4"
7210

3½"
COLOR
12 PILLARS
8¼"
4"
7186

1¾"
WISTERIA GLASS
8 PILLAR
9¼"
3¼"
7191

6¼"
8"
LACE GLASS
3½"
7197

7"
COLOR
12 PILLAR
7"
1"
7205

3¼"
CELADON GLASS
7⅝"
3½"
7206

4½"
WISTERIA GLASS
8 PILLAR
7¼"
3¼"
7212

8"
COLOR
12 PILLAR
8"
4"
7187

3¾"
8 FLOWERS AROUND
8 PILLAR
WISTERIA GLASS
8½"
3½"
7200

7½"
4 AROUND
CELADON
9¾"
7207

4"
CELADON DOUBLE BUBBLE
11⅛"
SOLID 8 AROUND
3¼"
7219

4"
HEX.
WISTERIA GLASS
10"
3¼"
7188

5"
WISTERIA GLASS
8 PILLAR
14"
5"
7192

7¼"
5 AROUND
12¾"
7201

6¼"
3
CELADON
10½"
4½"
7208

7½"
CELADON DOUBLE BUBBLE
9½"
SOLID
8 AROUND
3½"
7222

3½"
WISTERIA GLASS
8 PILLAR
14"
7189
5½"

4⅝"
COLOR
12 PILLAR
9½"
4"
7195

6¼"
COLOR
12 PILLAR
7¾"
5¼"
7202

5⅝"
9"
CELADON
4¼"
7209

8"
12 PILLAR
WISTERIA
7¾"
4½"
7227

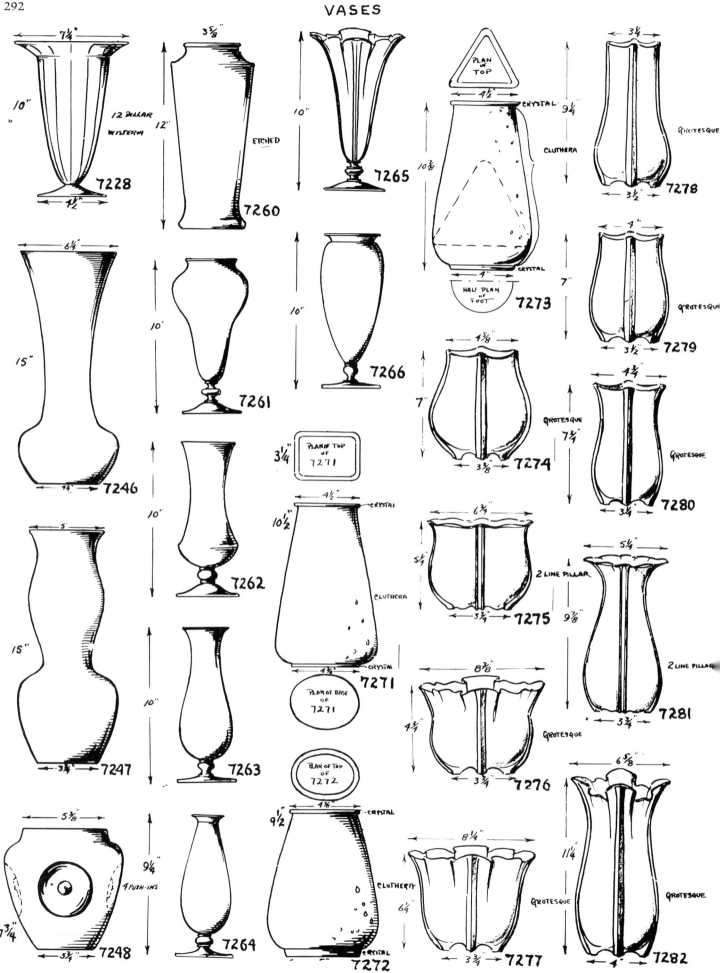

7228 12 PILLAR WISTERIA 10" 7¼" 12" 4½"

7260 3⅝" ETCHED

7265 10"

7273 PLAN OF TOP CRYSTAL CLUTHERA 4½" 10⅞" 4" CRYSTAL HALF PLAN OF FOOT 9¼"

7278 GROTESQUE 3¼" 3½"

7246 6¼" 15" 10" 1¾"

7261 7262 7263 7264

7271 PLAN OF TOP OF 7271 3¼" 4½" CRYSTAL CLUTHERA CRYSTAL 10½" 4½" PLAN OF BASE OF 7271

7272 PLAN OF TOP OF 7272 4⅜" CRYSTAL CLUTHERA CRYSTAL 9½" 6¼"

7266 10"

7274 4⅝" 7" GROTESQUE 3⅜"

7275 6¾" 5½" 2 LINE PILLAR 3¾"

7276 8⅜" 4¾" GROTESQUE 3¾"

7277 8¼" 6¼" GROTESQUE 3¾"

7279 4" 7" GROTESQUE 3½"

7280 4¾" 7¾" GROTESQUE 3¾"

7281 5¼" 9⅞" 2 LINE PILLAR 3¾"

7282 6⅝" 11¼" GROTESQUE 4"

7247 5" 15" 10" 3¾"

7248 5⅜" 9¼" 4 PUSH-INS 7¾" 3¾"

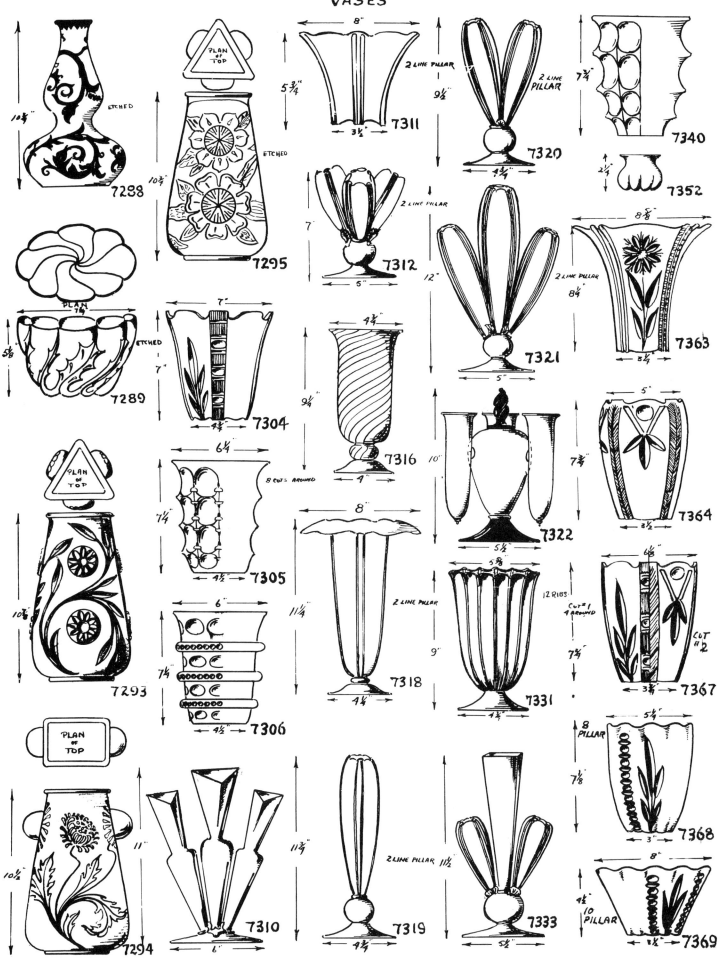

10⅞" ETCHED
7288

10⅜" ETCHED
7295

PLAN OF TOP
ETCHED

PLAN 7½"
5⅝" ETCHED
7289

5¾"
8"
3½"
7311
2 LINE PILLAR

7
7312
2 LINE PILLAR
5"

9½"
2 LINE PILLAR
7320
1¾"

12"
2 LINE PILLAR
7321
5"

7¾"
7340

2¼"
7352

8⅝"
2 LINE PILLAR
8¼"
7363
3½"

PLAN OF TOP
10⅝"
7293

PLAN OF TOP
11"
10½"
7294

7"
4½"
7304

6¼"
7¼"
8 CUTS AROUND
4½"
7305

6"
7½"
4½"
7306

9¼"
4¾"
7316
4"

8"
11¼"
2 LINE PILLAR
7318
4¼"

10"
5½"
7322

5⅝"
9"
12 RIBS
7331
4¾"

5"
7¾"
7364
3½"

4⅝"
CUT #1 4 AROUND
7¾"
CUT #2
7367
3½"

8 PILLAR
7⅛"
7368
3"

8"
4½"
10 PILLAR
7369
3½"

7310
6"

11¾"
2 LINE PILLAR 11½"
7319
4¾"

7333
5½"

5¼"

VASES

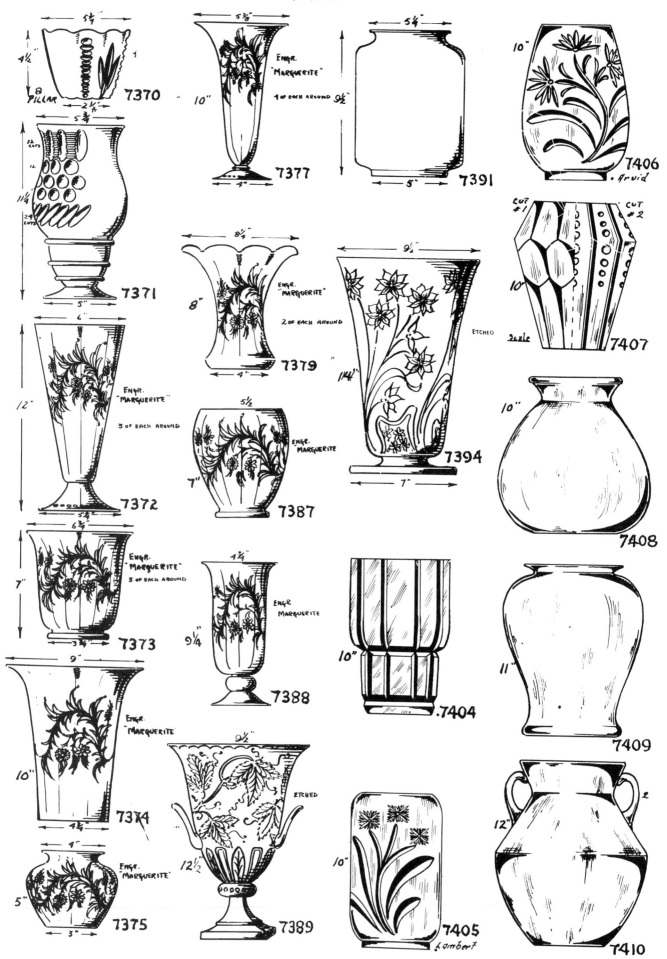

7370

1

8 PILLAR

5½"

4½"

2¼"

7371

12 CUTS

12

11¼"

24 CUTS

5¾"

5"

7372

ENGR. "MARGUERITE"

3 OF EACH AROUND

12"

6"

5½"

7373

ENGR. "MARGUERITE"

3 OF EACH AROUND

6½"

7"

3½"

7374

ENGR. "MARGUERITE"

9"

10"

4½"

7375

ENGR. "MARGUERITE"

5"

3"

7377

ENGR. "MARGUERITE"

1 OF EACH AROUND

5⅜"

10"

9½"

4"

7379

ENGR. "MARGUERITE"

2 OF EACH AROUND

8¼"

8"

4"

7387

ENGR. "MARGUERITE"

5½"

7"

7388

ENGR. MARGUERITE

4¾"

9¼"

7389

ETCHED

9½"

12½"

7391

5¼"

9½"

5"

7394

ETCHED

9¼"

11¼"

7"

7404

10"

7405

10"

L. Lambert

7406

10"

Arvid

7407

CUT #1

CUT #2

10"

Scale

7408

10"

7409

11"

7410

12"

2

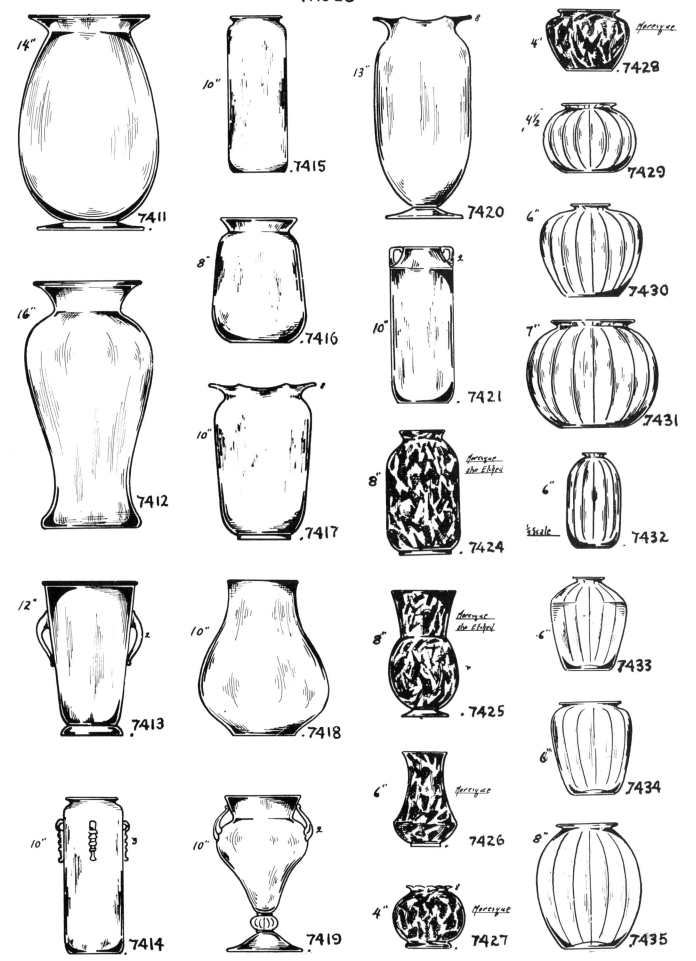

14" .7411

10" .7415

13" 8" .7420

4" Moresque .7428

4½" 7429

16" .7412

8" .7416

10" .7417

2 10" .7421

6" 7430

7" 7431

8" Moresque also Etched .7424

6" ½ scale 7432

12" 2 .7413

10" .7418

8" Moresque also Etched .7425

6" 7433

10" 3 .7414

10" 2 .7419

6" Moresque 7426

4" Moresque .7427

6" 7434

8" .7435

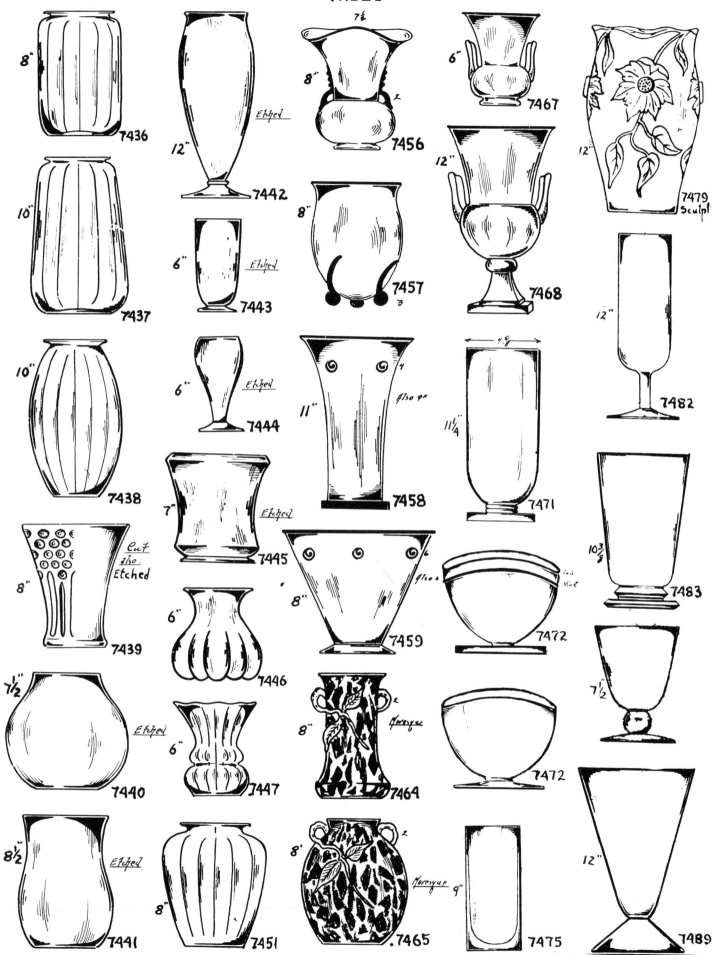

7436 8"

7437 10"

7438 10"

7439 8" Cut also Etched

7440 7½"

7441 8½" Etched

7442 12" Etched

7443 6" Etched

7444 6" Etched

7445 7" Etched

7446 6"

7447 6" Etched

7451 8"

7456 7½" 8"

7457 8" 3

7458 11" also 9"

7459 8" also 6"

7464 8" Moresque

7465 8" Moresque 9"

7467 6"

7468 12"

7471 11¼" A

7472

7472

7475 9"

7479 12" Sculpt

7482 12"

7483 10⅜"

7489 12"

7½"

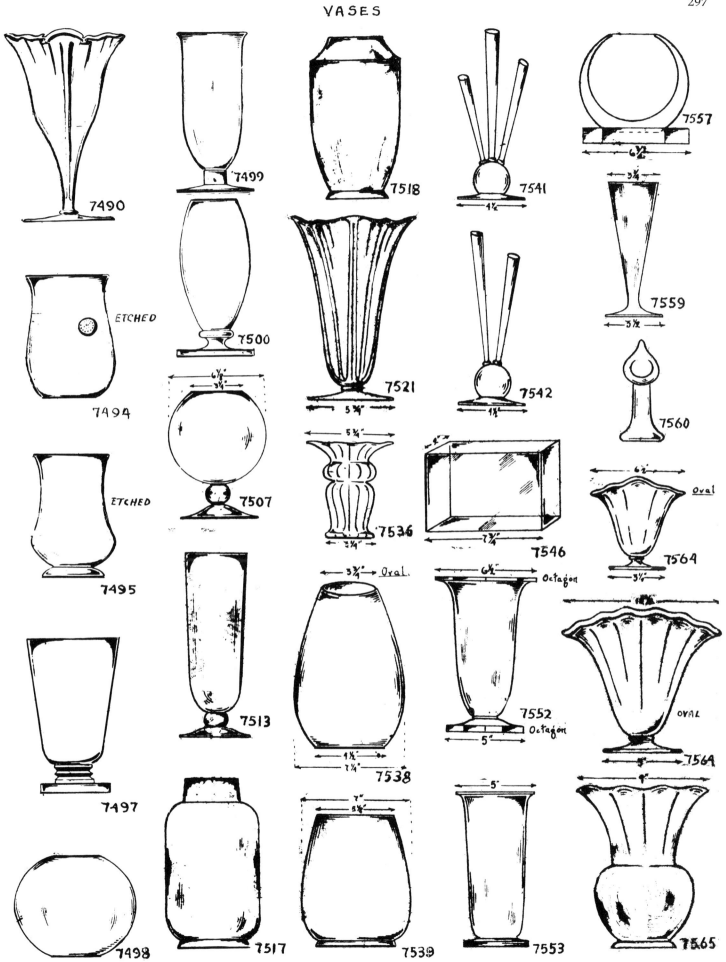

7490

7499

7518

7541

7557

6½"

ETCHED

7494

7500

6⅛"
3¾"

7507

7521

5 ¾"

7542

1⅛"

3¾"

7559

3½"

7560

7536

3¾"

7546

7¾"

Oval

7564

3½"

6½"

ETCHED

7495

7497

7513

3¾" Oval

7538

1½"
7¼"

6½" Octagon

7552
Octagon
5"

OVAL

7564

5"

7564A

7498

7517

7" 5⅜"

7539

5"

7553

7565

VASES

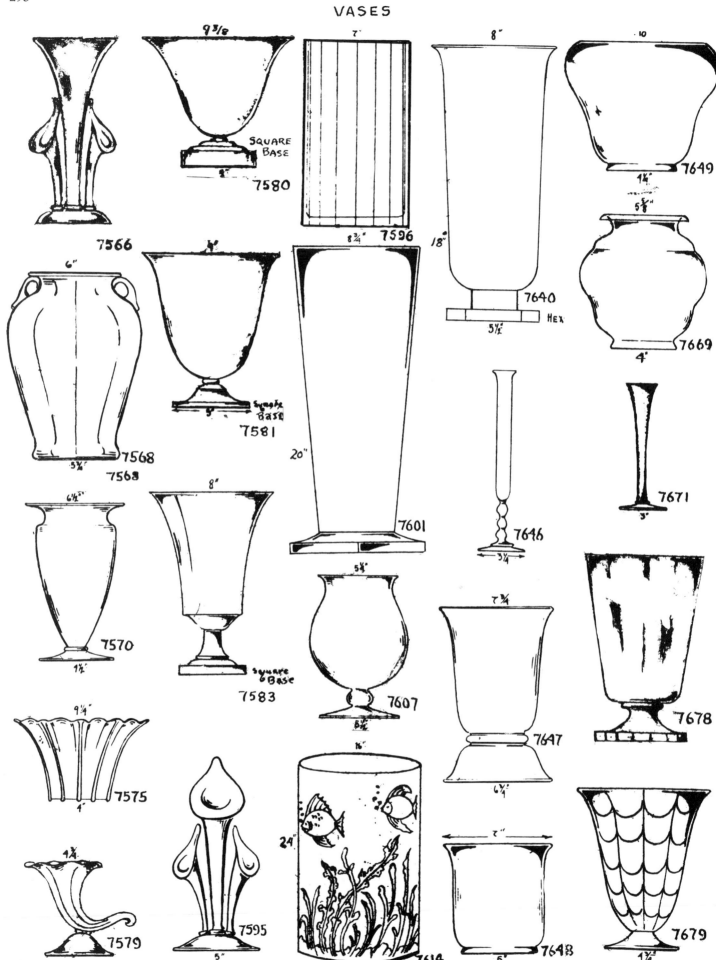

7566

9 ³⁄₈
SQUARE BASE
7580

7"
8 ³⁄₄"
7596

8"
18"
7640
5½"
HEX

10
1¼"
7649

5 ⁵⁄₈"
4"
7669

6"
7568
7569

5"
Square Base
5"
7581

20"
7601
5¾"
8½"
7607

7 ³⁄₄"
7647
6 ¼"

6½"
7570
1½"

8"
square Base
7583

9¼"
7575
4"

7646
3¼"

7671
3"

7678

4¾"
7579

5"
7595

18"
24"
7614

7"
5"
7648

1¾"
7679

VASES

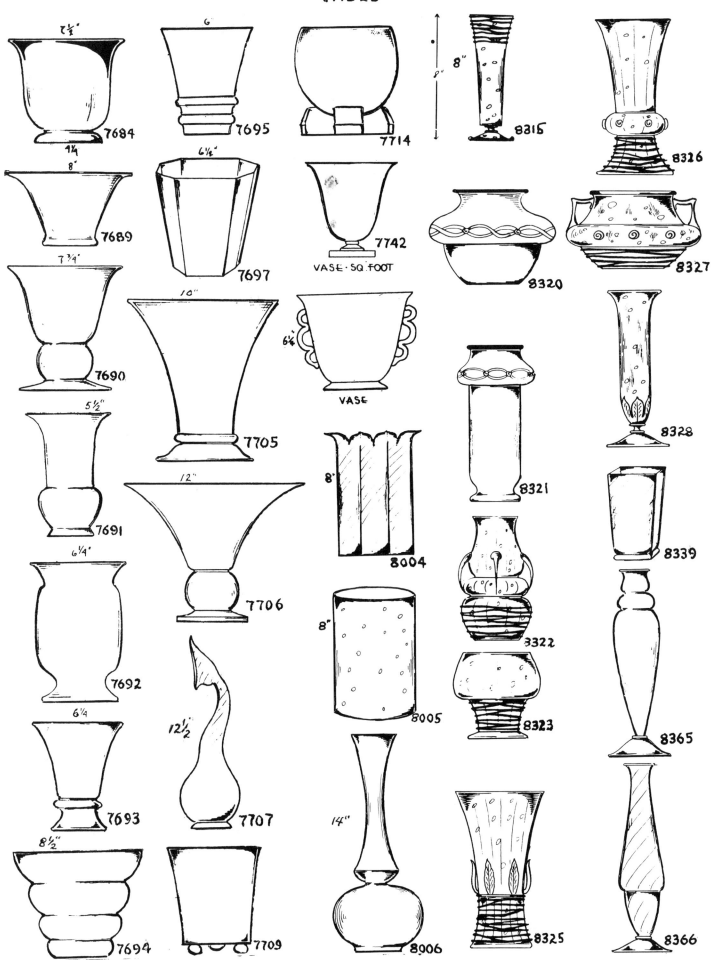

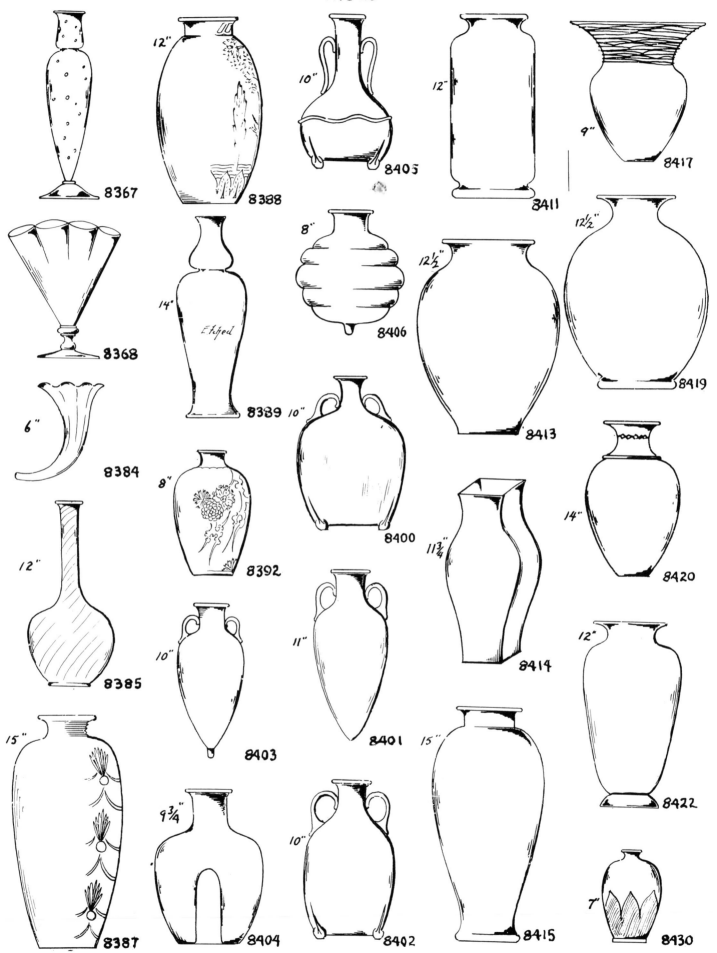

8367

12" 8388

10" 8405

12" 8411

9" 8417

8368

14" Etched 8389

8" 8406

12½" 8413

12½" 8419

6" 8384

8" 8392

10" 8400

11¾" 8414

14" 8420

12" 8385

10" 8403

11" 8401

15" 8415

12" 8422

15" 8387

9¾" 8404

10" 8402

7" 8430

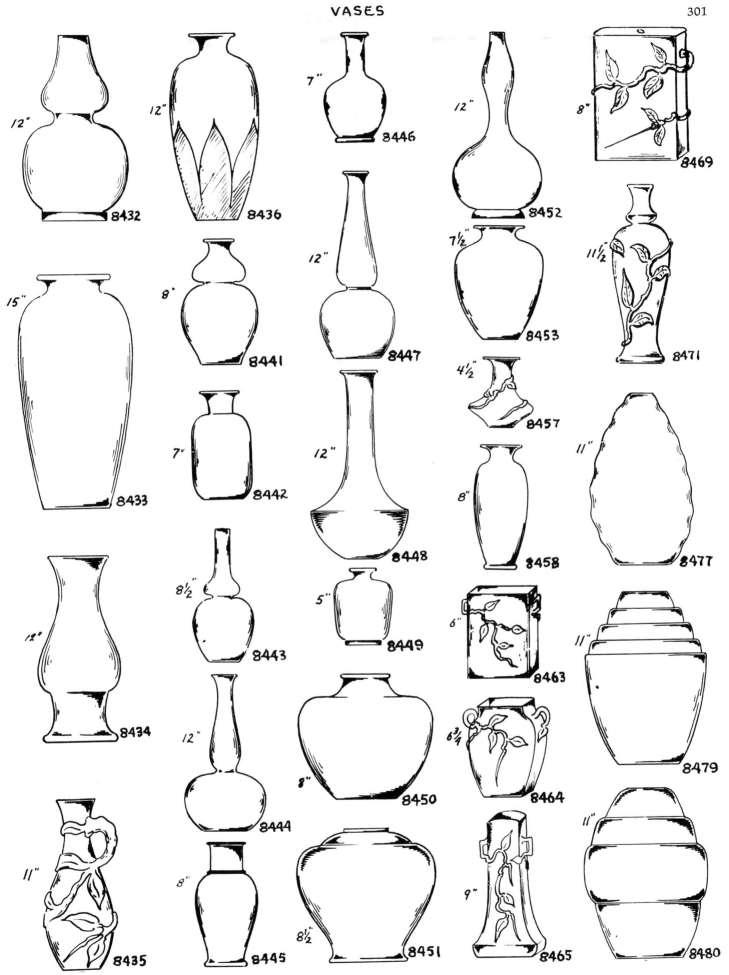

12" 8432

12" 8436

7" 8446

12" 8452

8" 8469

15" 8433

8" 8441

7" 8442

12" 8447

7½" 8453

4½" 8457

11½" 8471

12" 8448

8" 8458

11" 8477

12" 8434

8½" 8443

5" 8449

6" 8463

11" 8479

11" 8435

12" 8444

8" 8450

6¾" 8464

11" 8480

8" 8445

8½" 8451

9" 8465

VASES

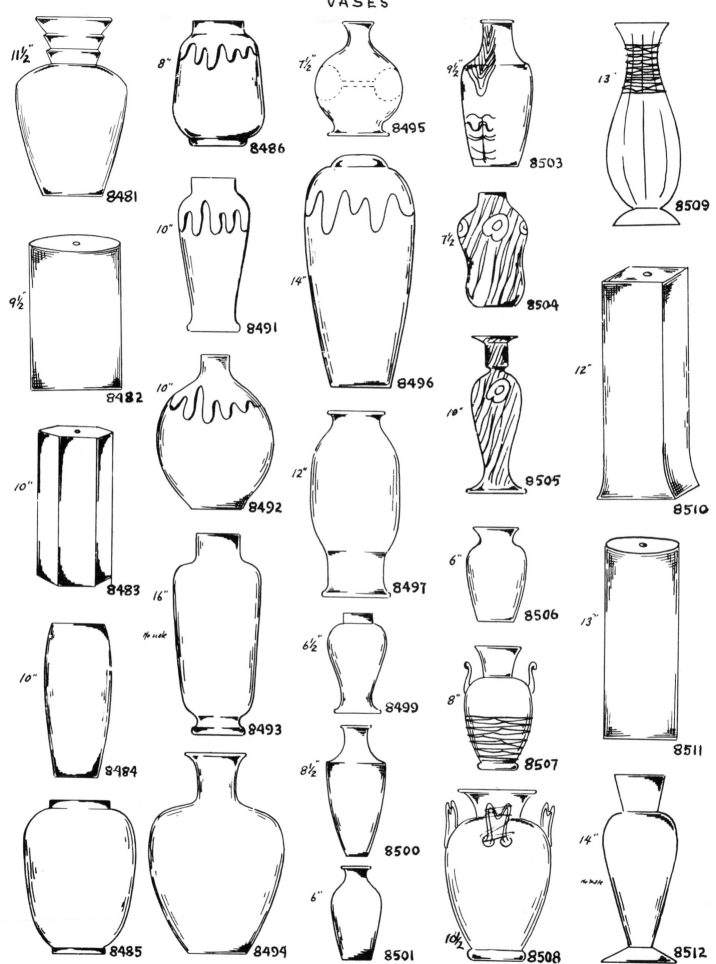

11½" 8481

8" 8486

7½" 8495

9½" 8503

13 8509

9½" 8482

10" 8491

14" 8496

7½" 8504

12" 8510

10" 8483

10" 8492

12" 8497

10" 8505

16" No scale 8493

6½" 8499

6" 8506

10" 8484

8½" 8500

8" 8507

13" 8511

8485

8494

6" 8501

10½" 8508

14" No scale 8512

VASES

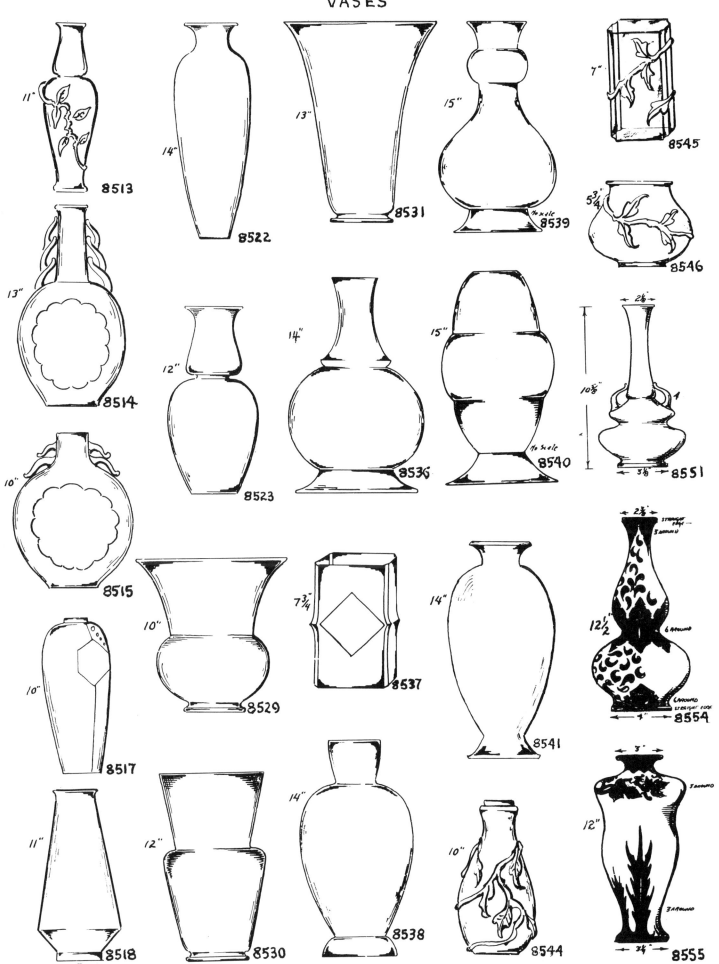

11" 8513

14" 8522

13" 8531

15" 8539

7" 8545

5¾" 8546

13" 8514

12" 8523

14" 8536

15" 8540

2⅛"
10⅞"
3⅜"
8551

10" 8515

10" 8529

7¾" 8537

14" 8541

2⅜"
12½"
1"
8554

10" 8517

11" 8518

12" 8530

14" 8538

10" 8544

3"
12"
2¼"
8555

VASES

AQUARIUMS

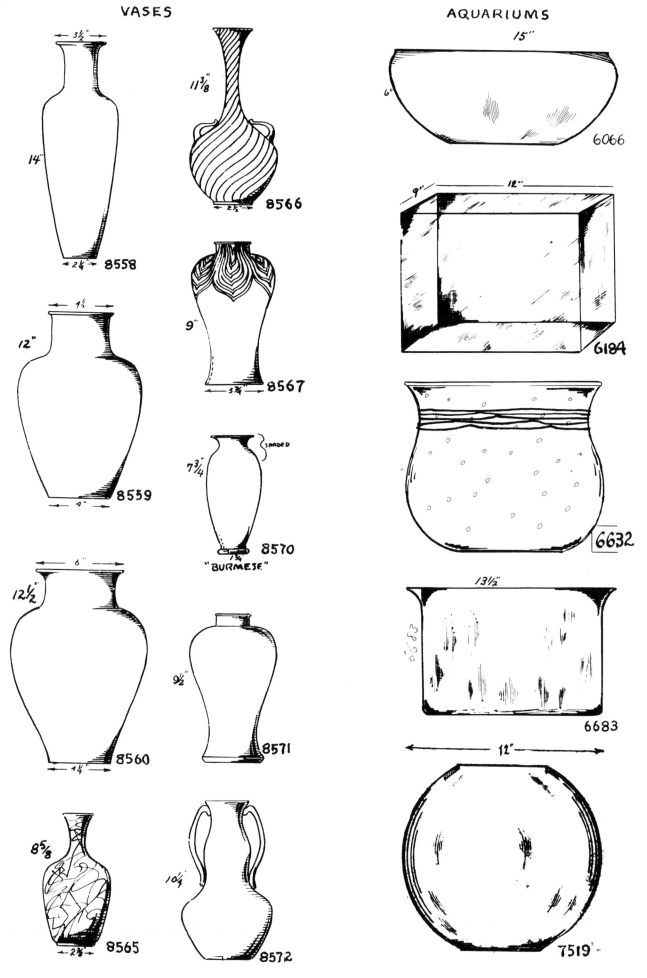

3½"
14"
2¼"
8558

11³⁄₈"
2½"
8566

9"
3¾"
8567

7³⁄₄"
SHADED
1¾"
8570
"BURMESE"

1½"
12"
4"
8559

6"
12½"
1¾"
8560

8⅝"
2⅜"
8565

9½"
8571

10¼"
8572

15"
6"
6066

9"
12"
6184

6632

13½"
6683
6683

12"
7519

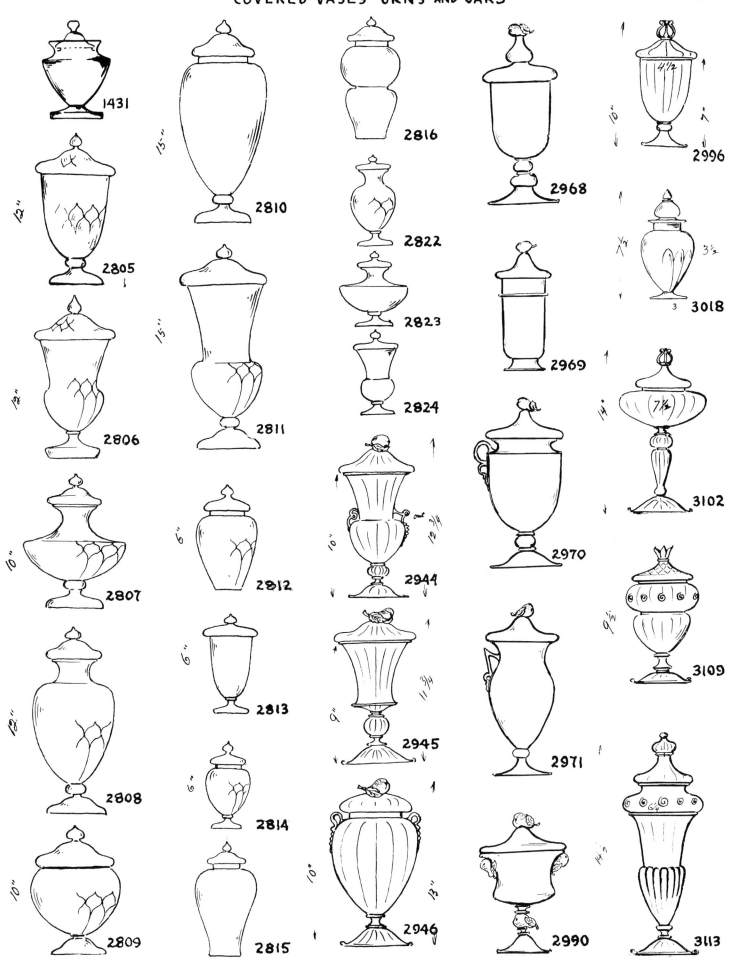

1431

2805

2806

2807

2808

2809

2810

2811

2812

2813

2814

2815

2816

2822

2823

2824

2944

2945

2946

2968

2969

2970

2971

2990

2996

3018

3102

3109

3113

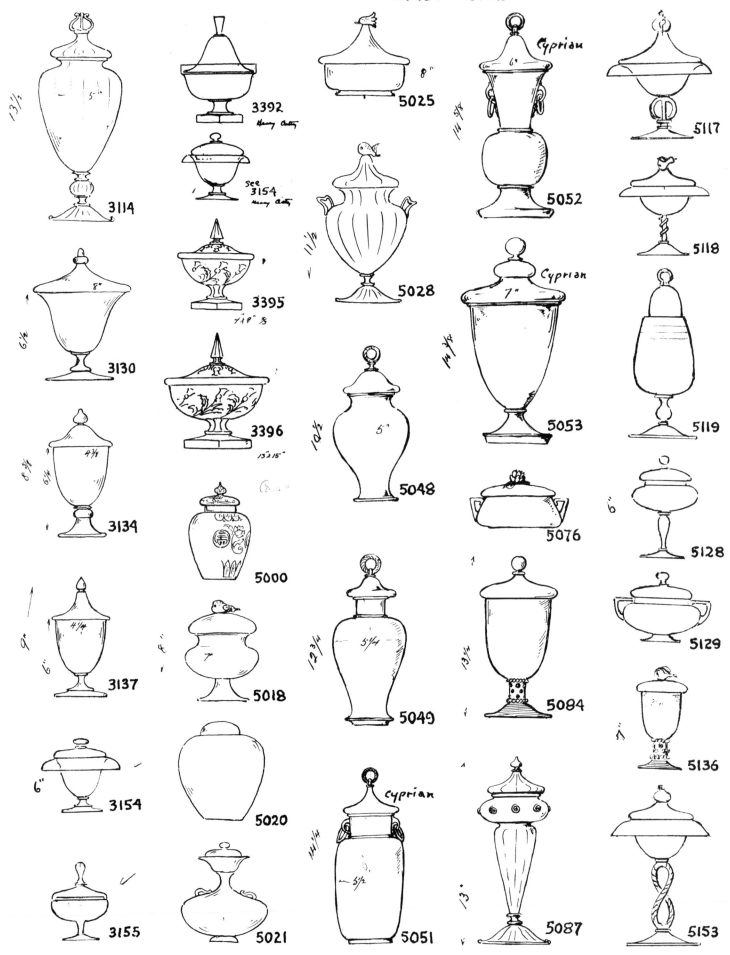

13½

3114

5-in

8"

3130

6½

4⅝
6¼
8⅜

3134

9"
6"
4¼

3137

6"

3154

3155

3392

Henry Cutting

See
3154
Henry Cutting

3395

7¼9" 8

3396

13x15"

5000

5018

7"

8"

5020

5021

8"

5025

11½

5028

10½

5"

5048

12¾

5¼

5049

Cyprian

14¼

5½

5051

14⅝

6"

5052

Cyprian

14¾

7"

5053

5076

Cyprian

5084

13¾

13"

5087

5117

5118

5119

6"

5128

5129

5136

5153

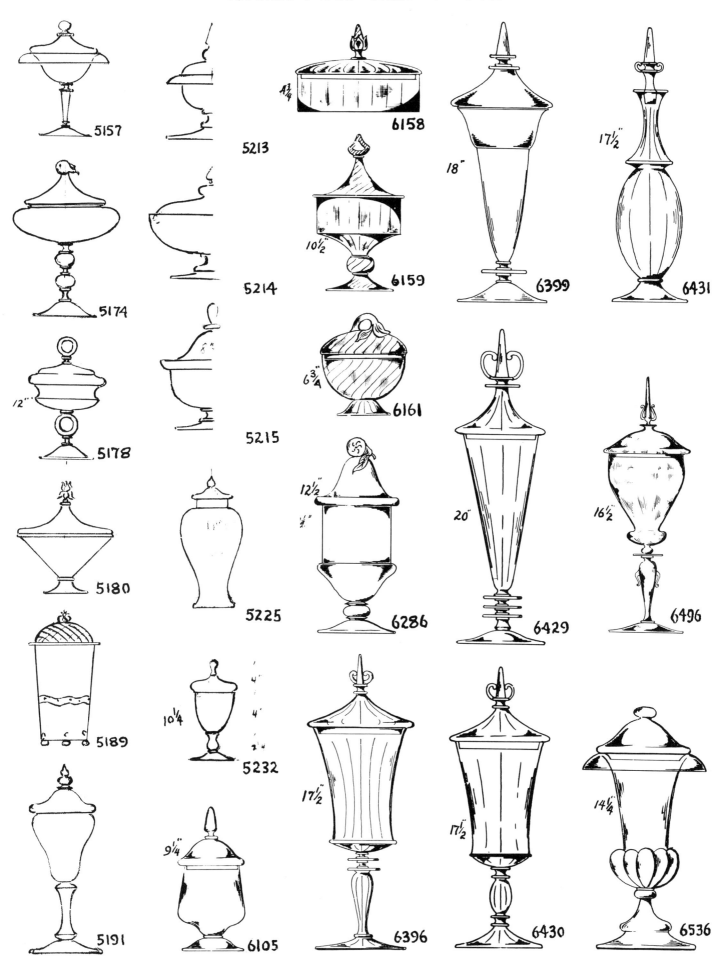

5157

5213

4¾"
6158

18"
6399

17½"
6431

5174

5214

10½"
6159

12"
5178

5215

6¾"
6161

16½"
6496

5180

5225

12½"
¼"
6286

20"
6429

5189

10¼"
5232

17½"
6396

17½"
6430

14¼"
6536

5191

9¼"
6105

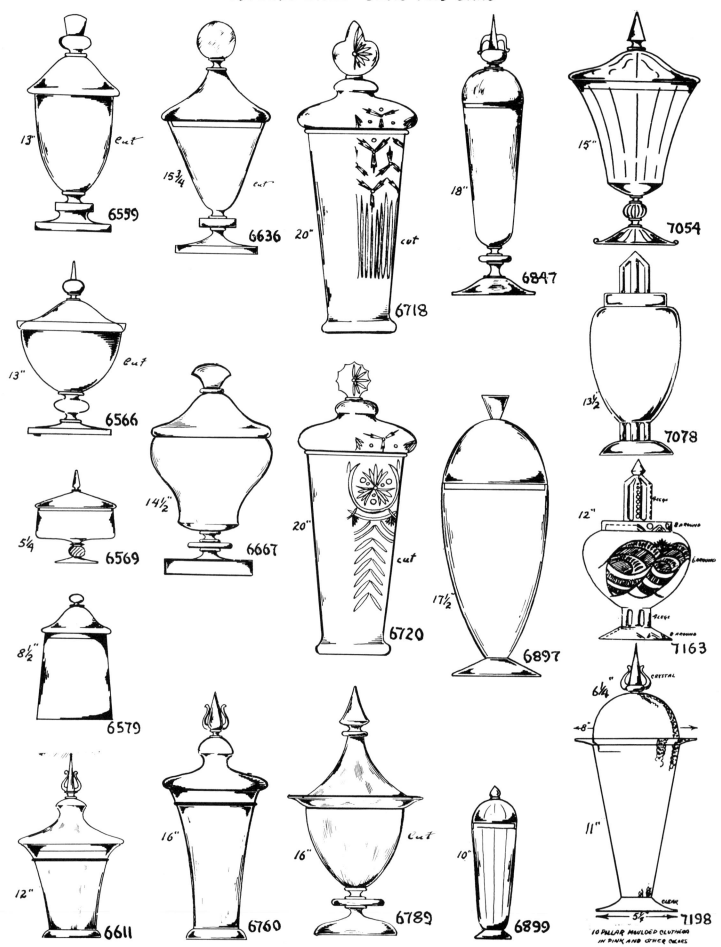

13"   cut
6559

15¾"   cut
6636

20"   cut
6718

18"
6847

15"   7054

13"   cut
6566

5¼"   6569

14½"   6667

20"   cut
6720

17½"   6897

13½"   7078

12"   6 rings
12"   7163

6¼"   CRYSTAL
8"
11"   CLEAR
5½"   7198

8½"   6579

12"   6611

16"   6760

16"   cut
6789

10"   6899

10 PILLAR MOULDED CLUTHRA
IN PINK AND OTHER COLORS

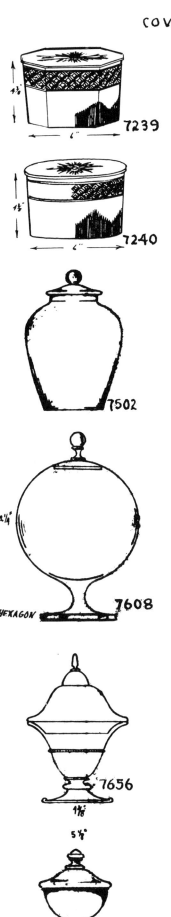

7239

7240

7502

7608

HEXAGON

7656

7670

10 3/8"

7703

14 3/4"

7721

6 1/4"

7745

COVERED · BOWL

16"

8007

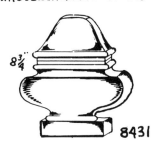

8 3/4"

8431

CRACKER JAR

353

LUMINOR

4 1/4"

3300

WATCH AND CLOCK HOLDERS

INK WELLS

1218

3 3/4

3056

1335

4 1/2

3057

1 1/4

7645

10 1/2

3051

10 1/2

3052

BOOK END

5032

8 1/2

3053

DESK SET

7 3/4

3054

BLANK	CUTTING	ENGRAVING	TOTAL	NAME

5073 Letter Rack
Stamp Box
Ink   Carved **30**ᵗʰ set
Corners
pen tray

7 3/4

3055

Appendix
of the
1932
Steuben Catalog

"In the following pages are sketched all of the designs referred to in the catalog proper.

"The numbers or names of the designs are shown, together with the numbers of the pieces to which they are applied. Any design, however, may be applied to pieces other than those shown, for which we would be glad to quote, upon your special request.

"Due to the limited space, objects are not drawn to scale; nor designs drawn to a fine accuracy. Consult the catalogue proper for size. To be appreciated, Steuben Glassware must be seen for its charm of color, grace of line, and beauty of design, all of which may not be apparent in sketches."

312

CATALOG No. 938
Decoration—MARLENE

CATALOG No. 938
Decoration—BIRD

CATALOG No. 938
Decoration—MATZU

CATALOG No. 938
Decoration—10018

CATALOG No. 2683
Decoration—TEAZLE

CATALOG No. 2683
Decoration—PUSSYWILLOW

CATALOG No. 2683
Decoration—STAMFORD

CATALOG No. 2683
Decoration—SHELTON

CATALOG No. 2683
Decoration—HUNTING

CATALOG No. 2687
Decoration—COMPTON

CATALOG No. 2687
Decoration—CANTON

CATALOG No. 2909
Decoration—T-9

CATALOG No. 2989
Decoration—DUCK

CATALOG No. 2989
Decoration—HUNTING DOG

CATALOG No. 2989
Decoration—PHEASANT

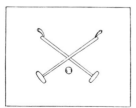

CATALOG No. 2989
Decoration—POLO

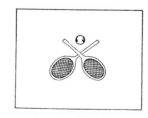

CATALOG No. 2989
Decoration—TENNIS

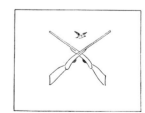

CATALOG No. 2989
Decoration—GUNS

STEUBEN DIVISION OF CORNING GLASS WORKS
CORNING, NEW YORK

CATALOG No. 5000
Decoration—MATZU

CATALOG No. 5000
Decoration—CHINESE

CATALOG No. 6030
Decoration—T-11

CATALOG No. 6034
Decoration—GRAPE

CATALOG No. 6034
Decoration—MATZU

CATALOG No. 6034
Decoration—MARLENE

CATALOG No. 6078
Decoration—FLORAL

CATALOG No. 6078
Decoration—FIRCONE

CATALOG No. 6078
Decoration—SEA HOLLY

CATALOG No. 6078
Decoration—NEDRA

CATALOG No. 6078
Decoration—MARLENE

CATALOG No. 6078
Decoration—MATZU

CATALOG No. 6112
Decoration—CHANG

CATALOG No. 6123
Decoration—T-10

CATALOG No. 6126
Decoration—NOYON

CATALOG No. 6183
Decoration—THISTLE

CATALOG No. 6199
Decoration—SCULPTURED

CATALOG No. 6268
Decoration—WARWICK

CATALOG No. 6268
Decoration—QUEEN ANNE

CATALOG No. 6272
Decoration—INDIAN

CATALOG No. 6389
Decoration—MARLENE

CATALOG No. 6391
Decoration—
SCULPTURED

CATALOG No. 6406
Decoration—ACANTHUS

CATALOG No. 6415
Decoration—THISTLE

CATALOG No. 6415
Decoration—ACANTHUS

CATALOG No. 6468
Decoration—FLORIDA

CATALOG No. 6501
Decoration—MANSARD

CATALOG No. 6505
Decoration—SHIRLEY

CATALOG No. 6505
Decoration—SHIRLEY

CATALOG No. 6505
Decoration—SHIRLEY

CATALOG No. 6505
Decoration—SHIRLEY

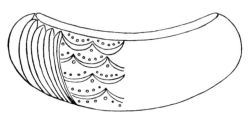

CATALOG No. 6515
Decoration—CUT No. 1

CATALOG No. 6559
Decoration—CUT No. 1

CATALOG No. 6596
Decoration—TORINO

CATALOG No. 6599
Decoration—
BURLINGTON

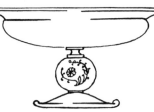

CATALOG No. 6626
Decoration—BURLINGTON

CATALOG No. 6626
Decoration—BURLINGTON

CATALOG No. 6626
Decoration—BURLINGTON

CATALOG No. 6636
Decoration—
HEAVY CUT

CATALOG No. 6680
Decoration—
LION

CATALOG No. 6687
Decoration—
HEAVY CUT

CATALOG No. 6688
Decoration—
HEAVY CUT

CATALOG No. 6727
Decoration—
VIRGINIA

CATALOG No. 6763
Decoration—
CUT No. 1

CATALOG No. 6768
Decoration—
TORINO

CATALOG No. 6768
Decoration—TORINO

CATALOG No. 6768
Decoration—TORINO

CATALOG No. 6828
Decoration—CUT

CATALOG No. 6828
Decoration—CUT

CATALOG No. 6844
Decoration—POUSSIN

CATALOG No. 6856
Decoration—SCULPTURED

CATALOG No. 6861
Decoration—WELLINGTON

CATALOG No. 6869
Decoration—MARINE

CATALOG No. 6869
Decoration—T-3

CATALOG No. 6869
Decoration—T-12

CATALOG No. 6869
Decoration—T-14

CATALOG No. 6880
Decoration—SAND BLASTED

CATALOG No. 6893
Decoration—GRAPE

CATALOG No. 6928
Decoration—BAYARD

CATALOG No. 6936
Decoration—LEAVES

CATALOG No. 6936
Decoration—WARWICK

CATALOG No. 7007
Decoration—BOOTHBAY

CATALOG No. 7035
Decoration—HEAVY CUT

CATALOG No. 7036
Decoration—HOLLYWOOD

CATALOG No. 7046
Decoration—REGAL

CATALOG No. 7050
Decoration—INTARSIA

CATALOG No. 7051
Decoration—INTARSIA

CATALOG No. 7053
Decoration—
INTARSIA

CATALOG No. 7078
Decoration—
LA FRANCE

CATALOG No. 7233
Decoration—ELDRED

CATALOG No. 7234
Decoration—
MOSELLA

CATALOG No. 7236
Decoration—
CHATHAM

CATALOG No. 7237
Decoration—
DANBURY

CATALOG No. 7238
Decoration—
STRAWBERRY
MANSION

CATALOG No. 7245
Decoration—STERLING

CATALOG No. 7245
Decoration—STERLING

CATALOG No. 7245
Decoration—STERLING

CATALOG No. 7250
Decoration—ELKAY

CATALOG No. 7250
Decoration—ELKAY

CATALOG No. 7250
Decoration—ELKAY

CATALOG No. 7289
Decoration—CUT PUNTY

CATALOG No. 7307
Decoration—ENGRAVED

CATALOG No. 7349
Decoration—
ENGRAVED No. 2

CATALOG No. 7372
Decoration—
RENWICK

CATALOG No. 7373
Decoration—
RENWICK

CATALOG No. 7374
Decoration—
RENWICK

CATALOG No. 7375
Decoration—RENWICK

CATALOG No. 7376
Decoration—RENWICK

CATALOG No. 7377
Decoration—RENWICK

CATALOG No. 7378
Decoration—RENWICK

CATALOG No. 7379
Decoration—RENWICK

CATALOG No. 7380
Decoration—RENWICK

CATALOG No. 7381
Decoration—RENWICK

CATALOG No. 7387
Decoration—
RENWICK

CATALOG No. 7388
Decoration—
RENWICK

CATALOG No. 7389
Decoration—
STRAWBERRY
MANSION

CATALOG No. 7391
Decoration—
HARTWICK

CATALOG No. 7391
Decoration—
VALERIA

CATALOG No. 7391
Decoration—PEONY

CATALOG No. 7401
Decoration—TRAYMORE

CATALOG No. 7401
Decoration—TRAYMORE

CATALOG No. 7401
Decoration—TRAYMORE

CATALOG No. 7401
Decoration—TRAYMORE

CATALOG No. 7402
Decoration—MARGUERITE

CATALOG No. 7402
Decoration—RENWICK

CATALOG
No. 7403
Decoration—
MARGUERITE

CATALOG
No. 7403
Decoration—
MARGUERITE

CATALOG No. 7403
Decoration—
MARGUERITE

CATALOG No. 7403
Decoration—MARGUERITE

CATALOG
No. 7403
Decoration—
RENWICK

CATALOG
No. 7403
Decoration—
RENWICK

CATALOG No. 7403
Decoration—
RENWICK

CATALOG No. 7403
Decoration—RENWICK

STEUBEN DIVISION OF CORNING GLASS WORKS
CORNING, NEW YORK

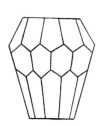

CATALOG No. 7407
Decoration—CUT No. 1

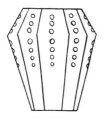

CATALOG No. 7407
Decoration—CUT No. 2

CATALOG No. 7424
Decoration—WINTON

CATALOG No. 7425
Decoration—SCULPTURED

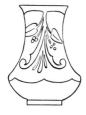

CATALOG No. 7426
Decoration—MARIGOLD

CATALOG No. 7439
Decoration—
SCULPTURED LEAVES

CATALOG No. 7440
Decoration—EVELYN

CATALOG No. 7441
Decoration—GORDON

CATALOG No. 7442
Decoration—MAPLEWOOD

CATALOG No. 7442
Decoration—MAYFAIR

CATALOG No. 7442
Decoration—DELWOOD

CATALOG No. 7443
Decoration—ALICIA

CATALOG No. 7444
Decoration—GRETA

CATALOG No. 7445
Decoration—ROSARIO

CATALOG No. 7471
Decoration—T-6

CATALOG No. 7471
Decoration—T-7

CATALOG No. 7471
Decoration—T-34

CATALOG No. 7471
Decoration—T-100

CATALOG No. 7471
Decoration—T-114

CATALOG No. 7472
Decoration—RENWICK

CATALOG No. 7472
Decoration—MARGUERITE

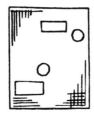

CATALOG No. 7473
Decoration—T-37

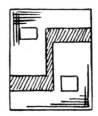

CATALOG No. 7473
Decoration—T-101

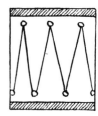

CATALOG No. 7473
Decoration—T-23

CATALOG No. 7475
Decoration—T-109

CATALOG No. 7475
Decoration—T-102

CATALOG No. 7475
Decoration—T-103

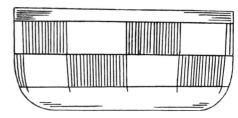

CATALOG No. 7476
Decoration—T-102

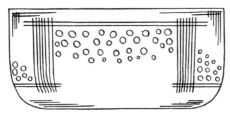

CATALOG No. 7476
Decoration—T-103

CATALOG No. 7481
Decoration—RIVIERA

CATALOG No. 7481
Decoration—RIVIERA

CATALOG No. 7481
Decoration—RIVIERA

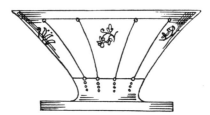

CATALOG No. 7481
Decoration—RIVIERA

CATALOG No. 7482
Decoration—T-35

CATALOG No. 7482
Decoration—T-36

CATALOG No. 7482
Decoration—T-25

CATALOG No. 7483
Decoration—T-27

CATALOG No. 7483
Decoration—T-29

STEUBEN DIVISION OF CORNING GLASS WORKS
CORNING, NEW YORK   XI

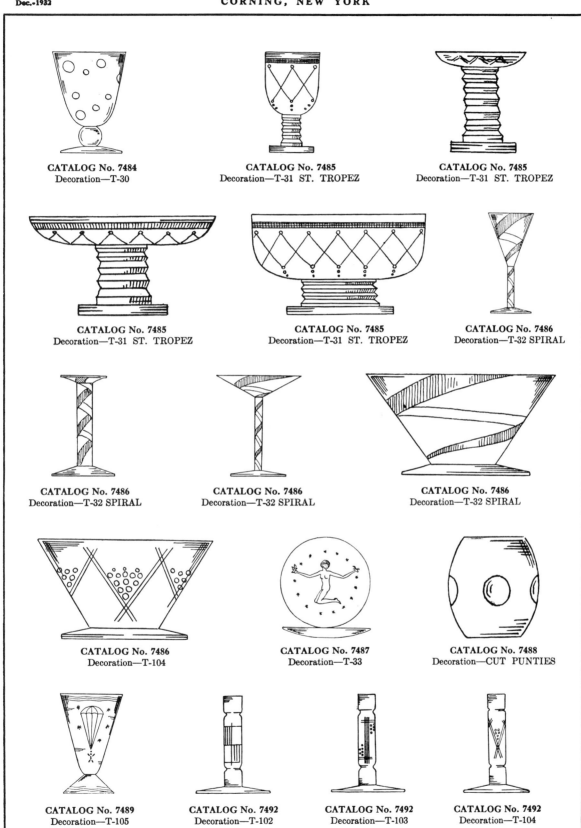

CATALOG No. 7484
Decoration—T-30

CATALOG No. 7485
Decoration—T-31 ST. TROPEZ

CATALOG No. 7485
Decoration—T-31 ST. TROPEZ

CATALOG No. 7485
Decoration—T-31 ST. TROPEZ

CATALOG No. 7485
Decoration—T-31 ST. TROPEZ

CATALOG No. 7486
Decoration—T-32 SPIRAL

CATALOG No. 7486
Decoration—T-32 SPIRAL

CATALOG No. 7486
Decoration—T-32 SPIRAL

CATALOG No. 7486
Decoration—T-32 SPIRAL

CATALOG No. 7486
Decoration—T-104

CATALOG No. 7487
Decoration—T-33

CATALOG No. 7488
Decoration—CUT PUNTIES

CATALOG No. 7489
Decoration—T-105

CATALOG No. 7492
Decoration—T-102

CATALOG No. 7492
Decoration—T-103

CATALOG No. 7492
Decoration—T-104

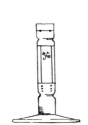

CATALOG No. 7492
Decoration—T-112
RIVIERA

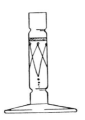

CATALOG No. 7492
Decoration—T-113
ST. TROPEZ

CATALOG No. 7492
Decoration—T-114

CATALOG No. 7494
Decoration—MILLEFIORI

CATALOG No. 7495
Decoration—SCULPTURED

CATALOG No. 7497
Decoration—T-106

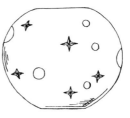

CATALOG No. 7498
Decoration—T-107

CATALOG No. 7499
Decoration—T-108

CATALOG No. 7500
Decoration—T-110

CATALOG No. 7500
Decoration—T-111

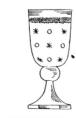

CATALOG No. 7501
Decoration—T-115 EMPIRE

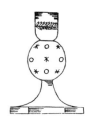

CATALOG No. 7501
Decoration—T-115 EMPIRE

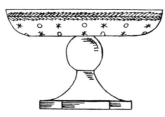

CATALOG No. 7501
Decoration—T-115 EMPIRE

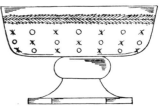

CATALOG No. 7501
Decoration—T-115 EMPIRE

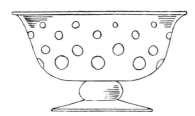

CATALOG No. 7503
Decoration—T-114

CATALOG No. 8413
Decoration—BRISTOL

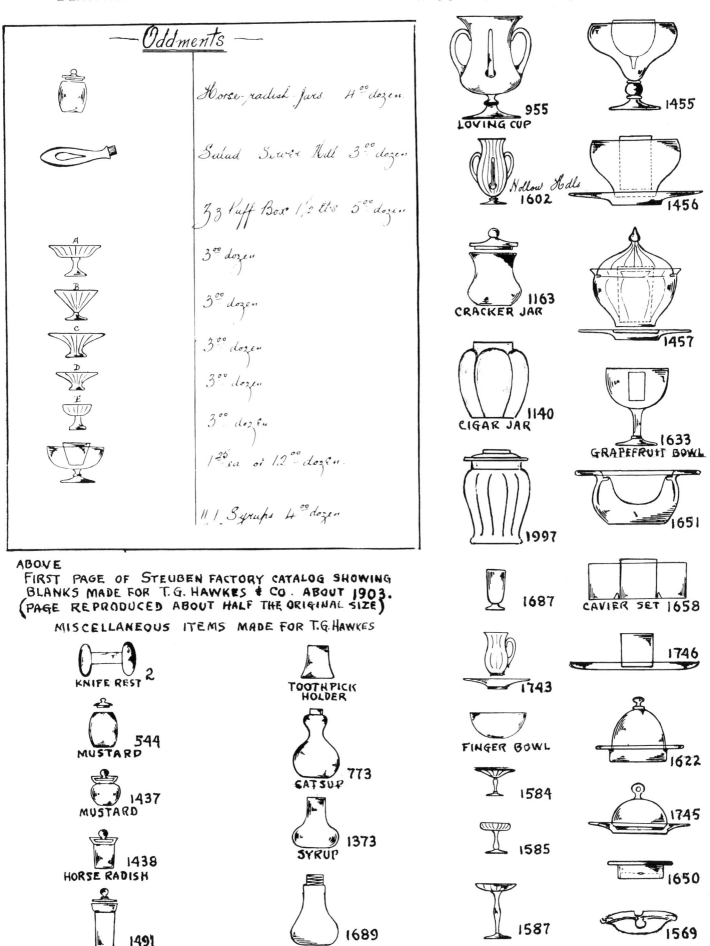

Oddments

Horse-radish Jars   4.00 dozen

Salad Server Hdl   3.00 dozen

3 3 Puff Box 1/2 lbs   5.00 dozen

3.00 dozen

3.00 dozen

3.00 dozen

3.00 dozen

3.00 dozen

1.25 ea or 12.00 dozen

1 Syrups   4.00 dozen

955 LOVING CUP

1455

1602 Hollow Hdls

1456

1163 CRACKER JAR

1457

1140 CIGAR JAR

1633 GRAPEFRUIT BOWL

1997

1651

1687

CAVIER SET 1658

1743

1746

FINGER BOWL

1622

1584

1745

1585

1650

1587

1569

ABOVE
FIRST PAGE OF STEUBEN FACTORY CATALOG SHOWING
BLANKS MADE FOR T.G. HAWKES & CO. ABOUT 1903.
(PAGE REPRODUCED ABOUT HALF THE ORIGINAL SIZE)
MISCELLANEOUS ITEMS MADE FOR T.G. HAWKES

KNIFE REST 2

TOOTHPICK HOLDER

544 MUSTARD

773 CATSUP

1437 MUSTARD

1373 SYRUP

1438 HORSE RADISH

1491

1689

BLANKS MADE FOR T.G. HAWKES & CO. BY STEUBEN GLASS WORKS

BON BONS, NAPPIES, TRAYS, ETC.

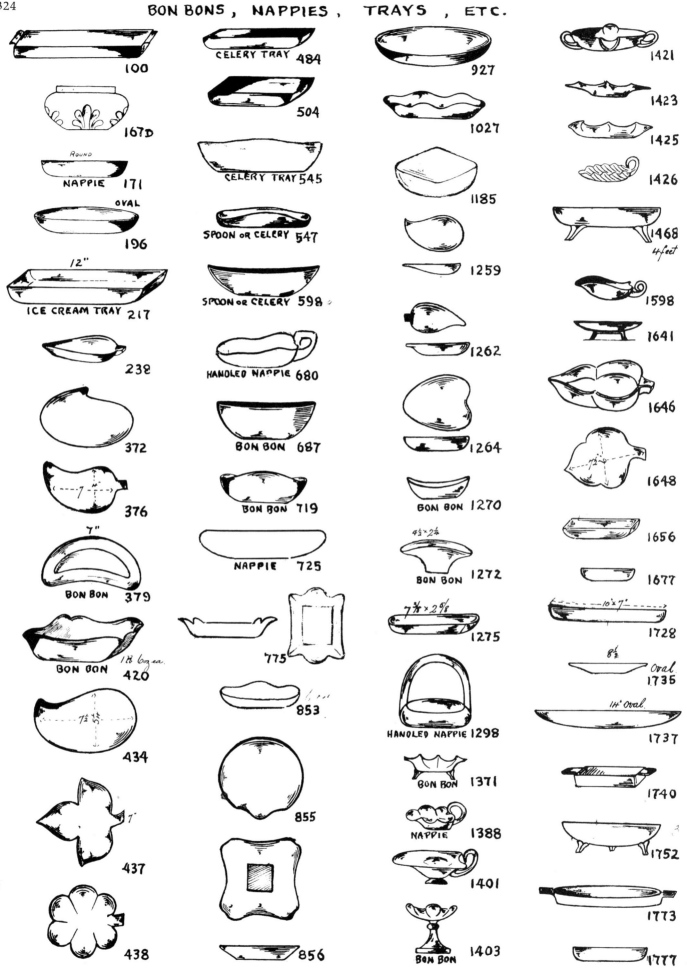

100

CELERY TRAY 484

504

167D

ROUND
NAPPIE 171

CELERY TRAY 545

OVAL
196

SPOON OR CELERY 547

12"
ICE CREAM TRAY 217

SPOON OR CELERY 598

238

HANDLED NAPPIE 680

372

BON BON 687

7"
376

BON BON 719

7"
BON BON 379

NAPPIE 725

BON BON 1lb 6oz ea. 420

775

853

7½ 5in
434

855

7"
437

438

856

927

1027

1185

1259

1262

1264

BON BON 1270

4½ × 2½
BON BON 1272

7⅜ × 2⅝
1275

HANDLED NAPPIE 1298

BON BON 1371

NAPPIE 1388

1401

BON BON 1403

1421

1423

1425

1426

1468
4 feet

1598

1641

1646

1648

1656

1677

10" × 7"
1728

8½
Oval
1735

14" Oval
1737

1740

1752

1773

1777

BLANKS MADE FOR T. G. HAWKES & CO. BY STEUBEN GLASS WORKS

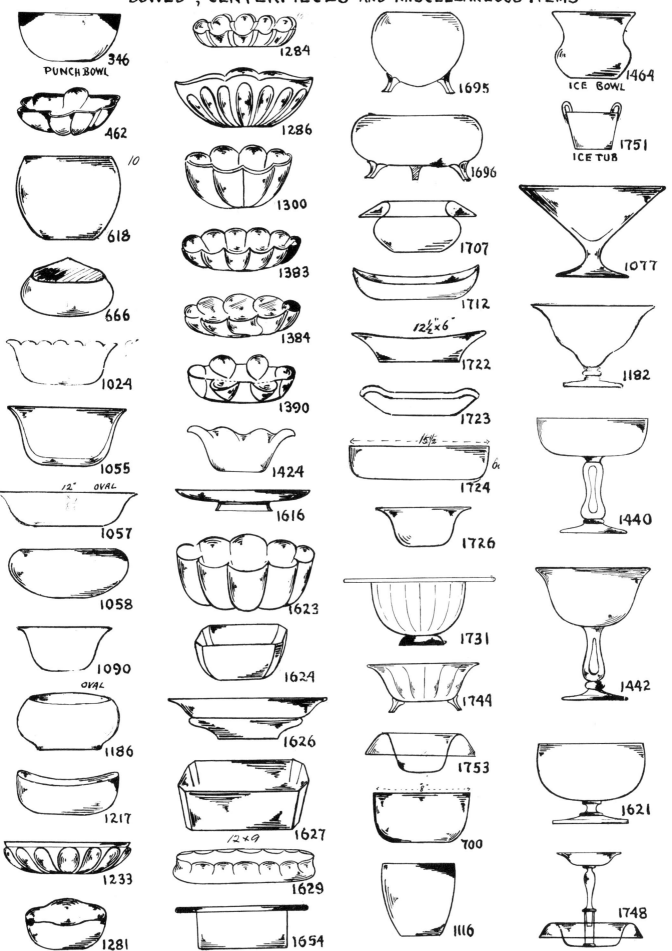

346
PUNCH BOWL

462

618
10

666

1024

1055

1057
12" OVAL

1058

1090

1186
OVAL

1217

1233

1281

1284

1286

1300

1383

1384

1390

1424

1616

1623

1624

1626

1627
12 x 9

1629

1654

1695

1696

1707

1712

1722
12½" x 6"

1723

1724
15½

1726

1731

1744

1753

700
8

1116

1464
ICE BOWL

1751
ICE TUB

1077

1182

1440

1442

1621

1748

BLANKS MADE FOR T. G. HAWKES & CO. BY STEUBEN GLASS WORKS

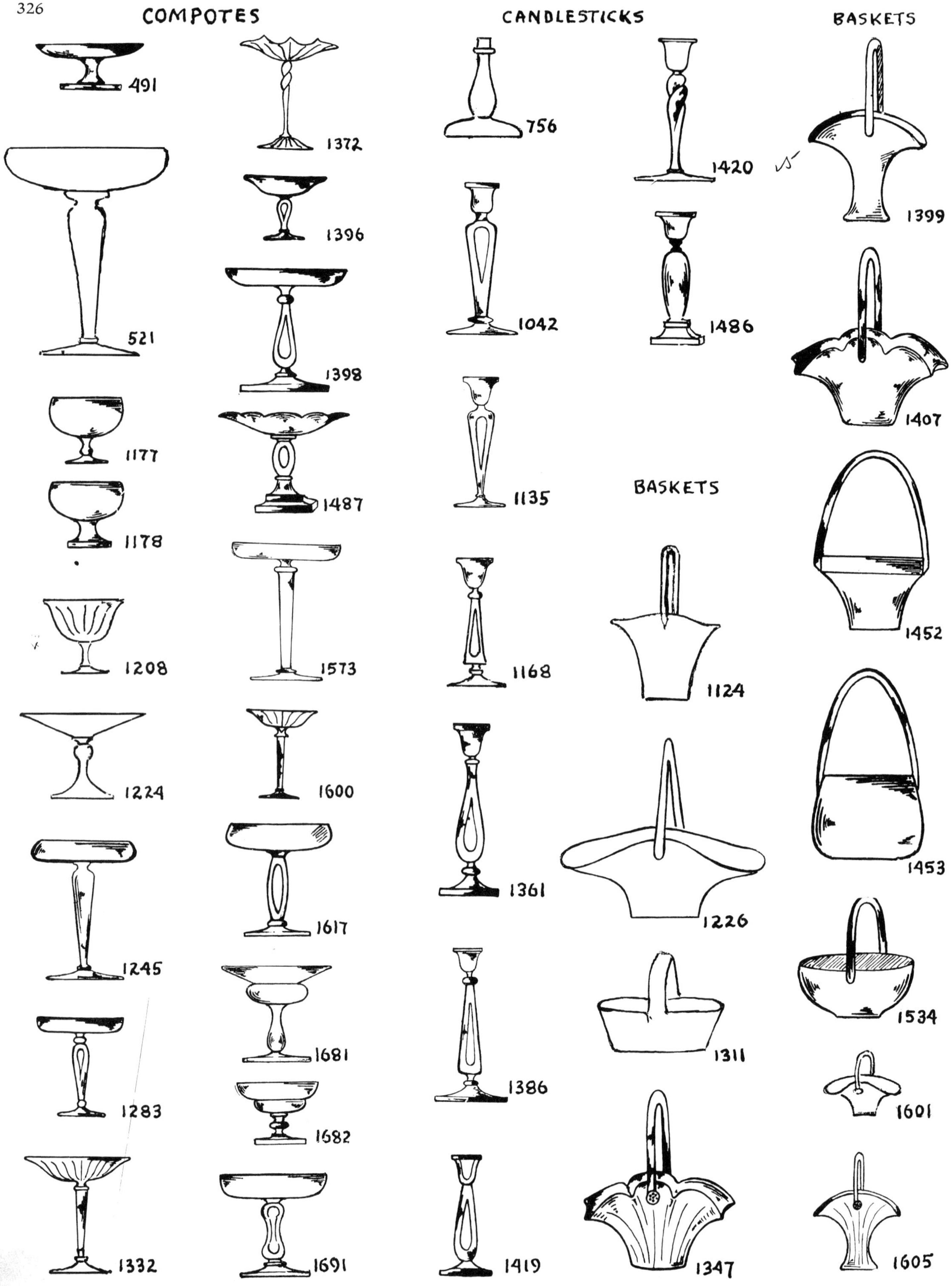

COMPOTES

491

1372

521

1396

1177

1398

1178

1487

1208

1573

1224

1600

1245

1617

1283

1681

1682

1332

1691

CANDLESTICKS

756

1420

1042

1486

1135

BASKETS

1168

1399

1361

1407

1124

1386

1226

1452

1419

1311

1453

1347

1534

1601

1605

BLANKS MADE FOR T. G. HAWKES & CO. BY STEUBEN GLASS WORKS

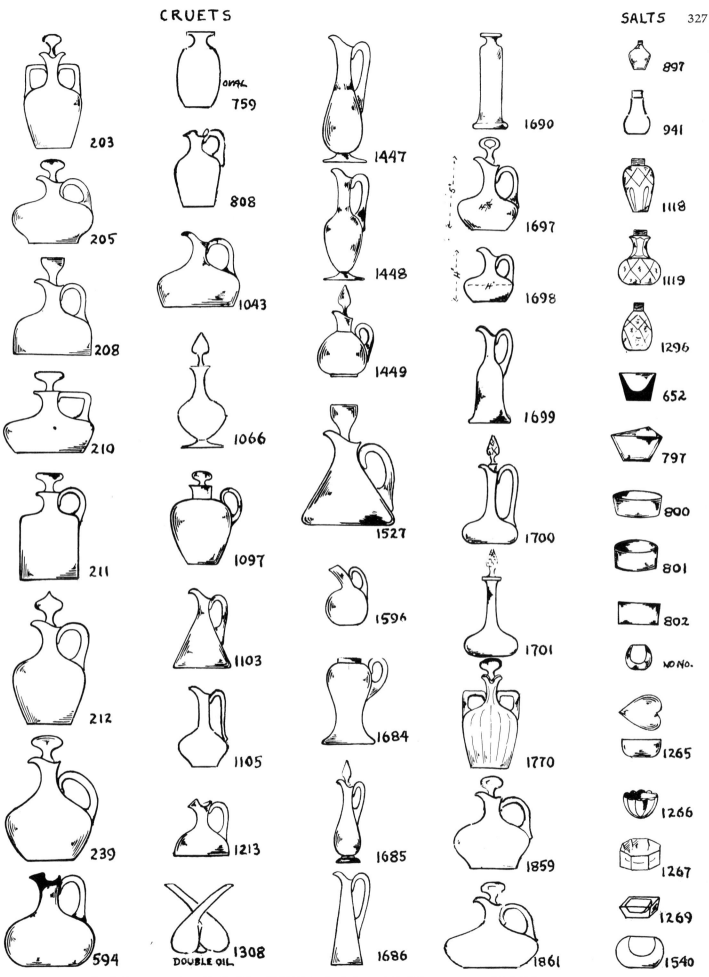

CRUETS

SALTS 327

203

759 OVAL

808

1043

205

208

210

1066

1527

1596

1447

1448

1449

1690

1697

1698

1699

1700

897

941

1118

1119

1296

652

211

1097

1701

1684

797

800

801

802

NO NO.

212

1103

1105

239

1213

594

1308 DOUBLE OIL

1685

1686

1770

1859

1861

1265

1266

1267

1269

1540

BLANKS MADE FOR T. G. HAWKES & CO. BY STEUBEN GLASS WORKS

328

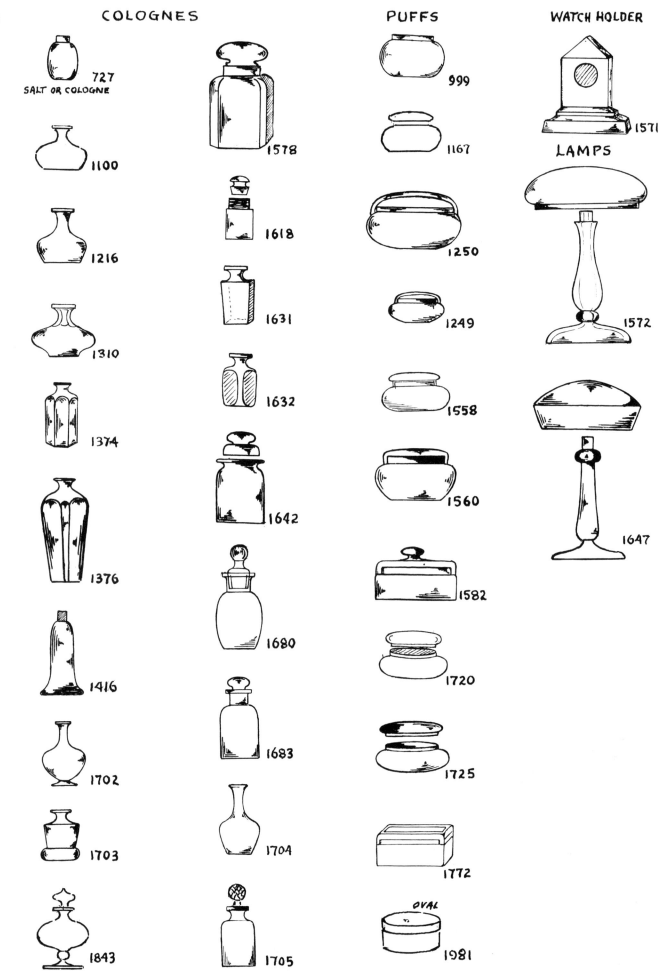

COLOGNES

727
SALT OR COLOGNE

1100

1216

1310

1374

1376

1416

1702

1703

1843

1578

1618

1631

1632

1642

1680

1683

1704

1705

PUFFS

999

1167

1250

1249

1558

1560

1582

1720

1725

1772

OVAL
1981

WATCH HOLDER

1571

LAMPS

1572

1647

BLANKS MADE FOR T. G. HAWKES & CO. BY STEUBEN GLASS WORKS

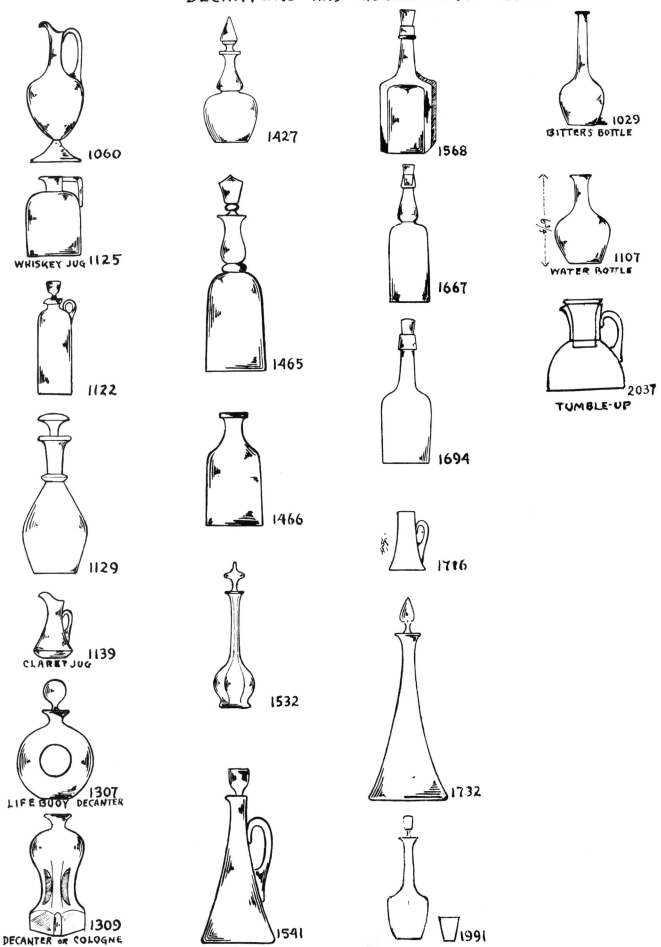

1060

WHISKEY JUG 1125

1122

1129

1139
CLARET JUG

1307
LIFE BUOY DECANTER

1309
DECANTER OR COLOGNE

1427

1465

1466

1532

1541

1568

1667

1694

1716

1732

1991

1029
BITTERS BOTTLE

1107
WATER BOTTLE

2037
TUMBLE-UP

BLANKS MADE FOR T.G. HAWKES & CO. BY STEUBEN GLASS WORKS

VASES

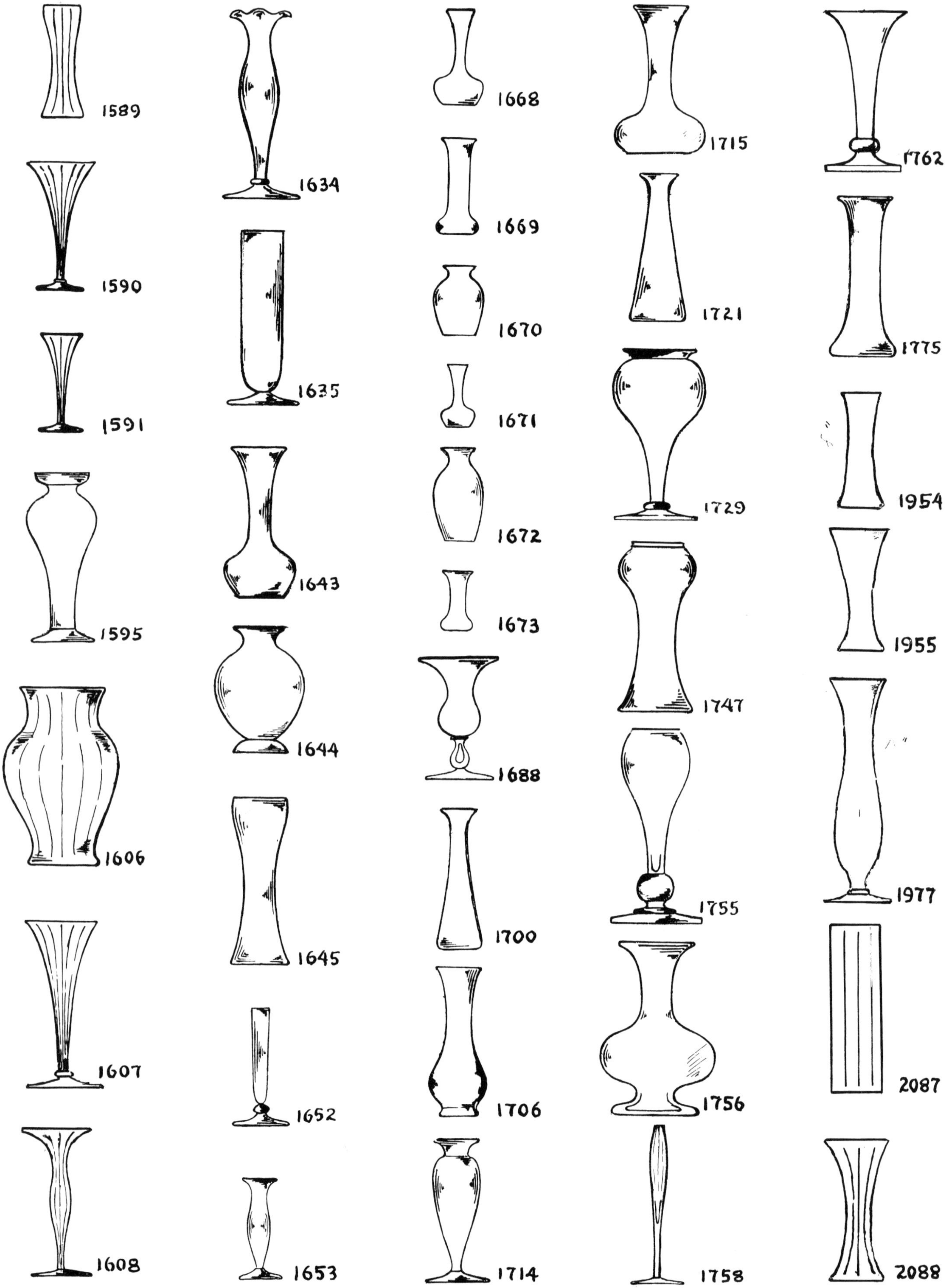

1589

1590

1591

1595

1606

1607

1608

1634

1635

1643

1644

1645

1652

1653

1668

1669

1670

1671

1672

1673

1688

1700

1706

1714

1715

1721

1729

1747

1755

1756

1758

1762

1775

1954

1955

1977

2087

2088

BLANKS MADE FOR T. G. HAWKES & CO. BY STEUBEN GLASS WORKS

VASES

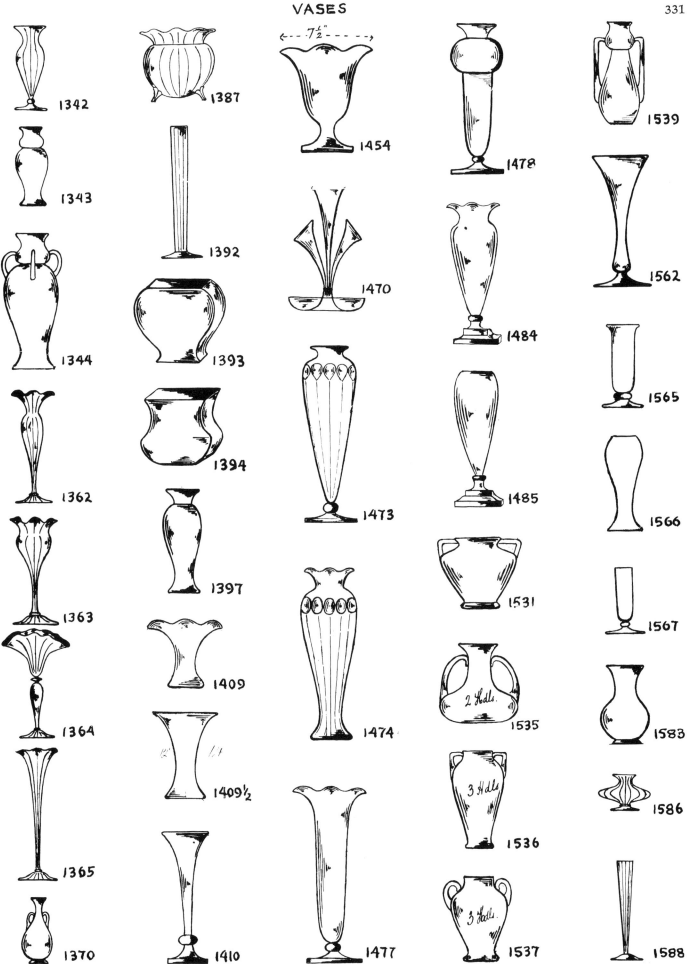

BLANKS MADE FOR T. G. HAWKES & CO. BY STEUBEN GLASS WORKS

VASES

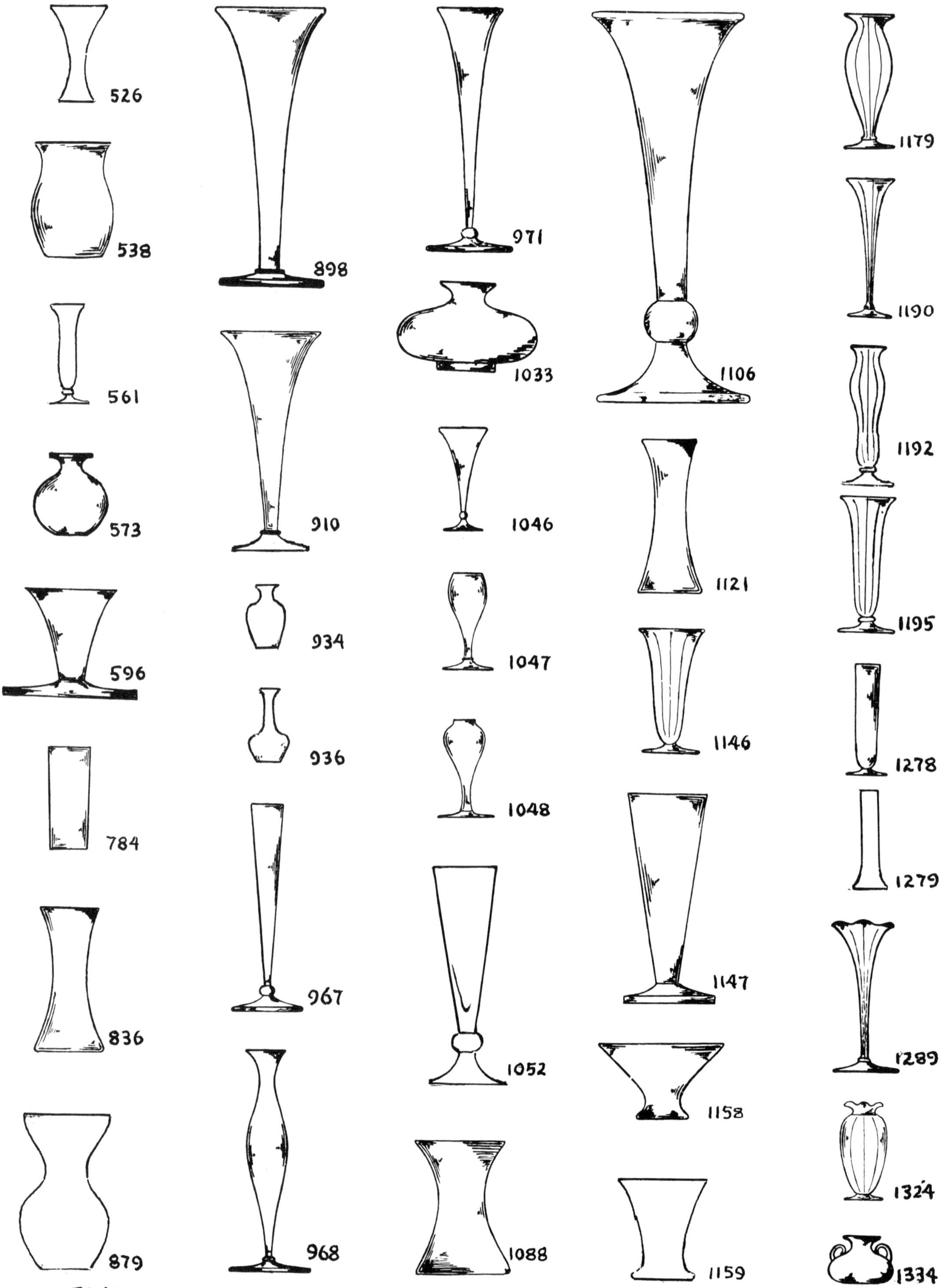

526

538

561

573

596

784

836

879

898

910

934

936

967

968

971

1033

1046

1047

1048

1052

1088

1106

1121

1146

1147

1158

1159

1179

1190

1192

1195

1278

1279

1289

1324

1334

BLANKS MADE FOR T. G. HAWKES & CO. BY STEUBEN GLASS WORKS

965

966

1089½

1089½

1133

1133

1234

1234

1400

1400

1404

1404

1406

1406

1451

1451

1458

1458

1460

1460

1469

1469

1636

1636

1637 *Hollow Hdls*

1637

1638

1638

1639 *Hollow Hdls*

1639

1640 *Hollow Handles*

1640

1665

1665

1710

1710

1718

1718

1741

1741

1958

1958

1086 *4 feet*

1243

1405

1435

1564 *oval*

1709

MISCELLANEOUS ITEMS

1462

1593 **PRESERVE DISH**

1657 **HONEY JAR**

MARMALADE JAR *NO NO.*

1211 **MARMALADE JAR**

1313

1461

1763

1028 *5½×4 Oval*

MAYONNAISE 1028 *8×6 Oval*

1574

1575 **MAYONNAISE**

1575 **MAYONNAISE**

1576 **MAYONNAISE**

1764

1765

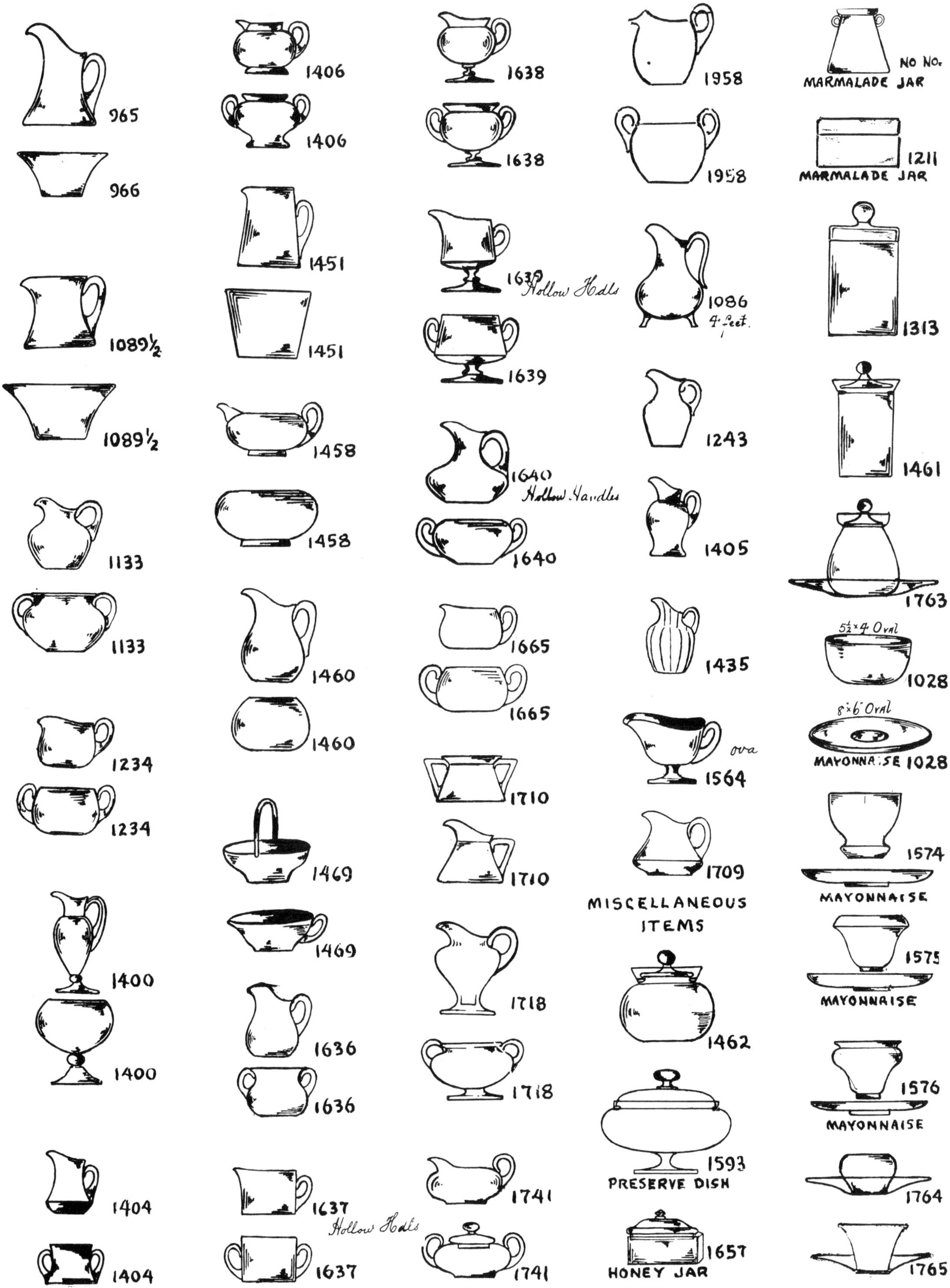

BLANKS MADE FOR T. G. HAWKES & CO. BY STEUBEN GLASS WORKS

PITCHERS

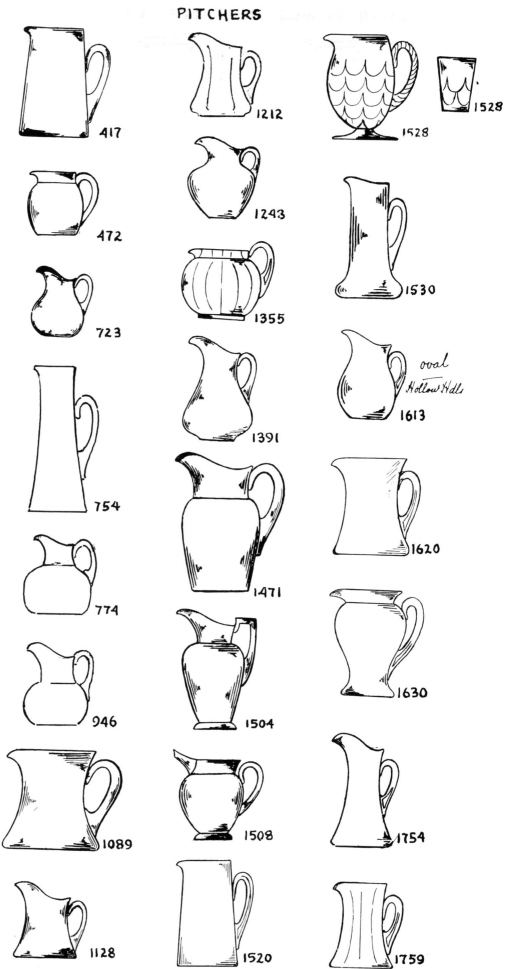

417

1212

1528 1528

472

1243

723

1355

1530

754

1391

1613 oval Hollow Hdle

774

1471

1620

946

1504

1630

1089

1508

1754

1128

1520

1759

BLANKS MADE FOR T. G. HAWKES & CO. BY STEUBEN GLASS WORKS

GOBLETS

CATALOG LISTING OF STEMWARE ITEMS MADE TO MATCH No.1044 GOBLET (ABOVE) AND No.1104 GOBLET (BELOW)

350

1044

1044

1060

1085

1085½

1104

1110

1255

1260

1413

1459

1463

1467

1619

Heavy Stem Ware

Large Goblets	5 50 per do
Small "	4 00
Saucer Champ	3 50
Tall "	3 50
Hollow Stem	6 00
Claret	3 00
Wines	3 00
Cocktail	3 00
Sherry	3 00
Cordial	2 50
½ Pt Tumbler	3 00
Whiskey "	2 50
Champ "	2 50
Soda "	6 00
Apollinaris "	3 50
Highball "	3 50
Finger Bowl	4 00
Lemonades	3 00
7" Plates	6 00
8"	7 50
13"	2 50 each
Decanters	9 00 dozen
" Sthrs	2 00
Qt Claret Decanters	12 00
" Sthrs	2 50
Pt	9 00
" Sthrs	2 00

ITEMS MATCHING No. 1044 GOBLET

Optical Stem Ware

+5%

Goblets	6 00 per doz
Sau Champ	6 00 " "
Claret	5 00
Cocktail	5 00
Wine	5 00
Sherry	5 00
½ Pt Tumbler	3 00
Whis	2 50
Champ	2 50
Finger Bowl	3 50
Twisted Plates	4 50
B & S Tumblers	5 00
Twisted Punch Plates	4 00
" " Cups	5 00

ITEMS MATCHING No. 1104 GOBLET

1413

1430 COCKTAIL

1541

1431 COCKTAIL

BLANKS MADE FOR T. G. HAWKES & CO. BY STEUBEN GLASS WORKS

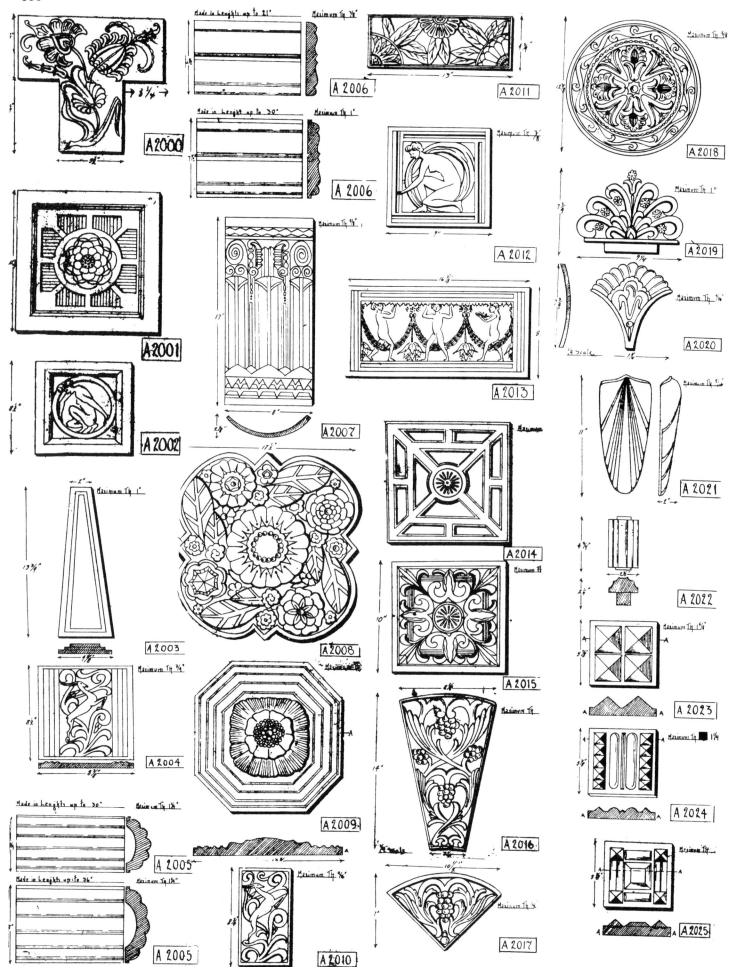

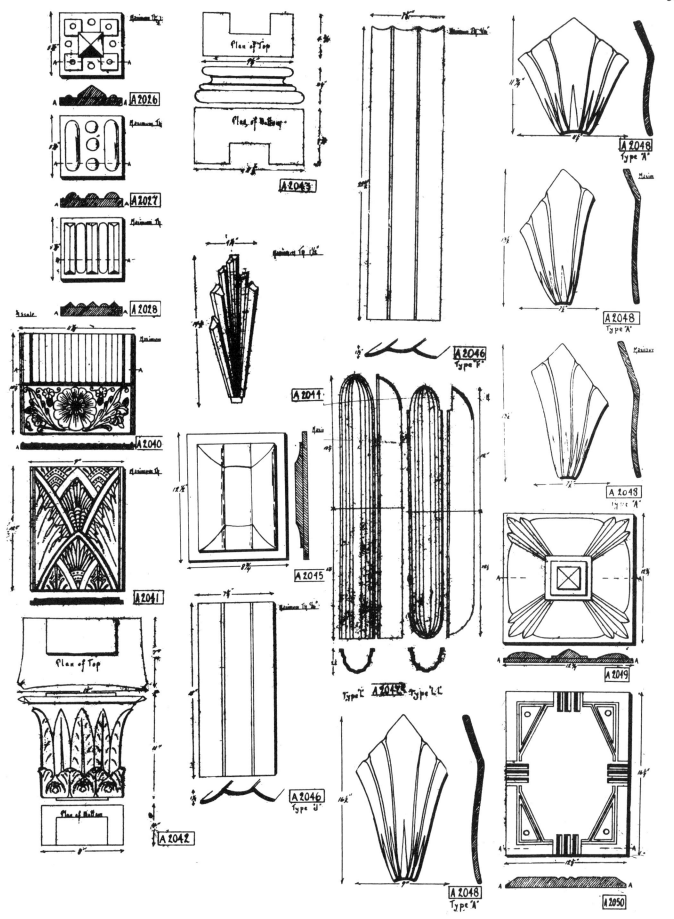

A 2026

A 2027

A 2028

A 2040

A 2041

A 2042

A 2043

A 2044

A 2045

A 2046 Type 'J'

A 2047 Type 'K' Type 'LL'

A 2046 Type 'K'

A 2048 Type 'A'

A 2048 Type 'A'

A 2048 Type 'A'

A 2048 Type 'A'

A 2049

A 2050

Plan of Top

Plan of Bottom

Plan of Top

Plan of Bottom

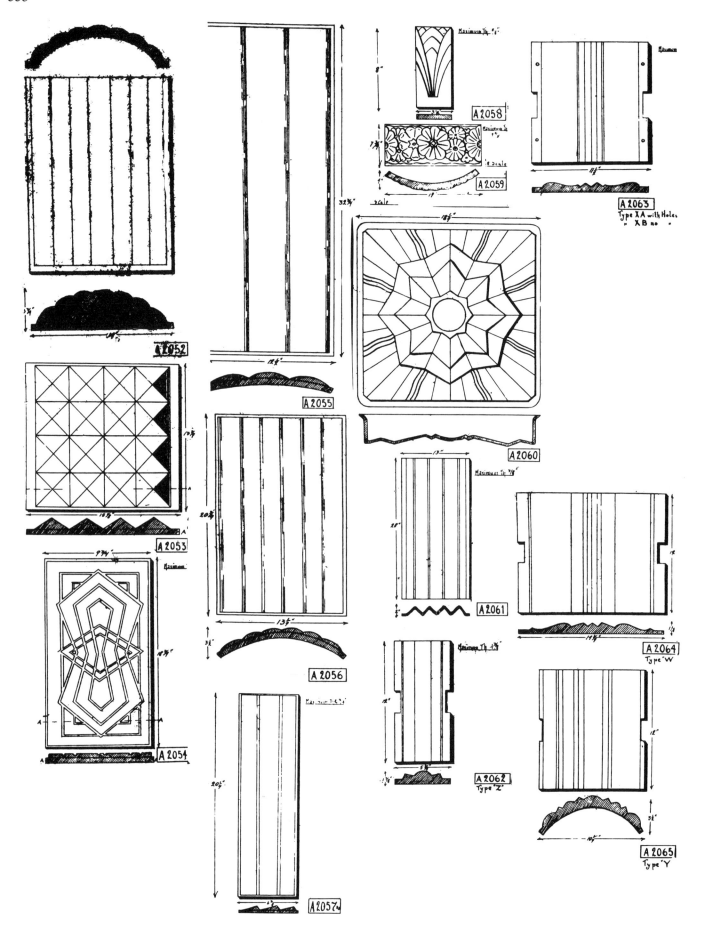

A 2052

A 2053

A 2054

A 2055

A 2056

A 2057

A 2058

A 2059

A 2060

A 2061

A 2062
Type "Z"

A 2063
Type XA with Holes
" XB no "

A 2064
Type "W"

A 2065
Type "Y"

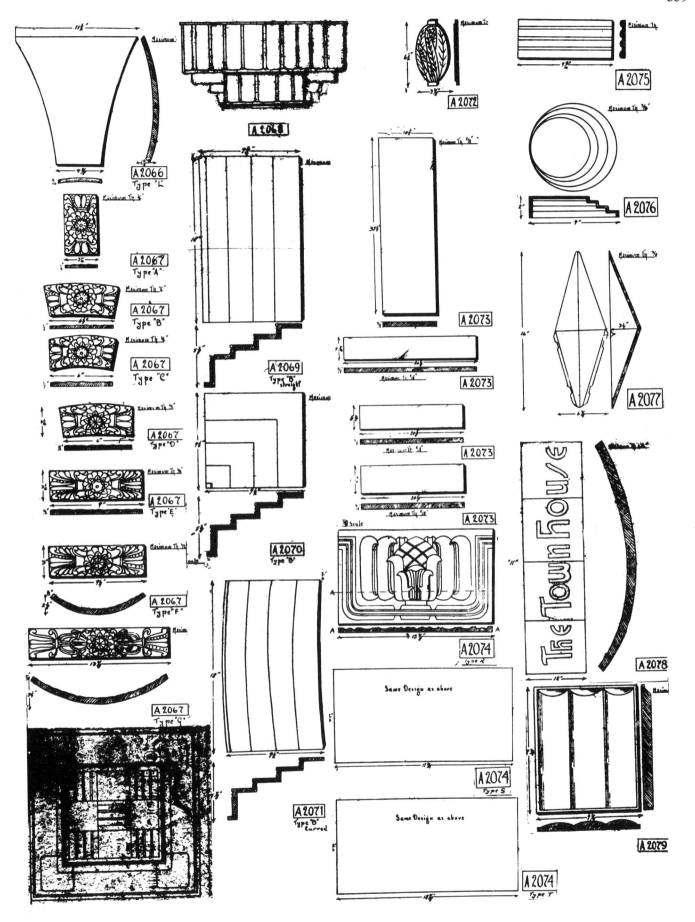

A 2066
Type "L"

A 2068

A 2072

A 2075

A 2067
Type "A"

A 2067
Type "B"

A 2067
Type "C"

A 2067
Type "D"

A 2067
Type "E"

A 2067
Type "F"

A 2067
Type "G"

A 2069
Type "B"
straight

A 2070
Type "B"

A 2071
Type "B"
Curved

A 2073

A 2073

A 2073

A 2073

A 2074
Type R

A 2074
Type S

A 2074
Type T

Same Design as above

Same Design as above

A 2076

A 2077

The Town House

A 2078

A 2079

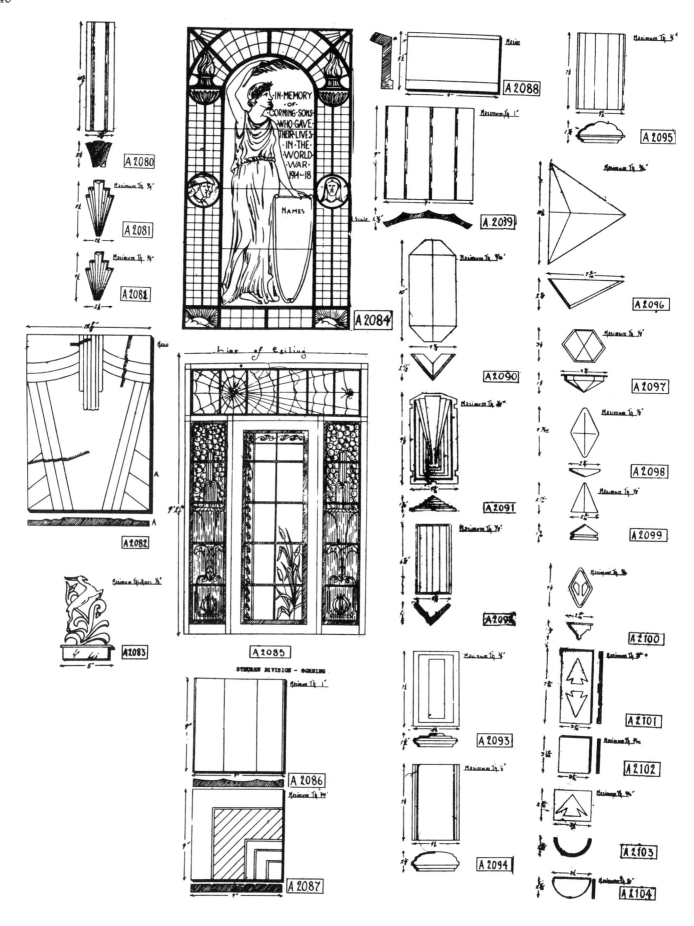

A 2080

A 2081

A 2082

A 2083

A 2084

A 2085

A 2086

A 2087

A 2088

A 2089

A 2090

A 2091

A 2092

A 2093

A 2094

A 2095

A 2096

A 2097

A 2098

A 2099

A 2100

A 2101

A 2102

A 2103

A 2104

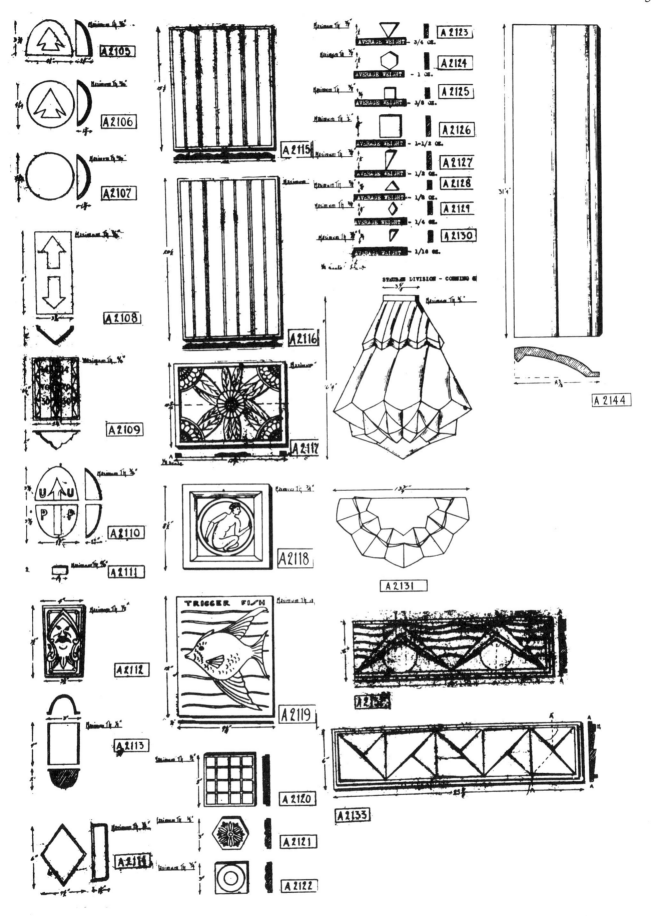

A 2105

A 2106

A 2107

A 2108

A 2109

A 2110

A 2111

A 2112

A 2113

A 2114

A 2115

A 2116

A 2117

A 2118

TRIGGER FISH

A 2119

A 2120

A 2121

A 2122

A 2123

AVERAGE WEIGHT - 3/4 OZ.

A 2124

AVERAGE WEIGHT - 1 OZ.

A 2125

AVERAGE WEIGHT - 3/8 OZ.

A 2126

AVERAGE WEIGHT - 1-1/2 OZ.

A 2127

AVERAGE WEIGHT - 1/2 OZ.

A 2128

AVERAGE WEIGHT - 1/8 OZ.

A 2129

AVERAGE WEIGHT - 1/4 OZ.

A 2130

AVERAGE WEIGHT - 1/16 OZ.

STEUBEN DIVISION - CORNING G

A 2131

A 2132

A 2133

A 2144

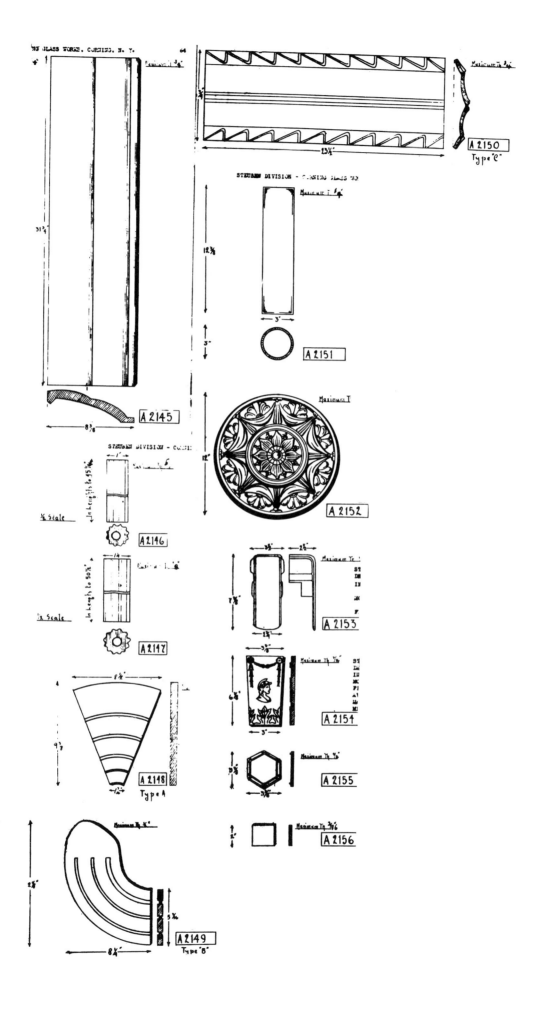

A 2150
Type "C"

A 2145

A 2151

A 2152

A 2146

A 2147

A 2148
Type A

A 2149
Type "B"

A 2153

A 2154

A 2155

A 2156

10

Additional Steuben Line and Lost Wax Items

THE FOLLOWING PAGES CONTAIN PHOTOGRAPHS TAKEN FROM EARLY STEUBEN CATALOGS showing cut glass, Aurene, and other items of the regular Steuben line. These catalogs were used by traveling salesmen and at the factory from about 1904 to 1912.

The lost wax items included were all made from about 1934, after Carder became art director of Corning Glass Works, until 1959.

Salesman's Catalog   STEUBEN CUT GLASS (1)   (See page 347.)

A. *Top:* Bonbons, cut Japan pattern. *Left,* No. 1404; *right,* No. 1405.
   Bottom: Nappies. *Left,* No. 1403, cut Japan pattern; *right,* No. 1403, cut Reese
      pattern.
B. *Top:* Bowl, No. 1402, cut Favorite pattern.
   Bottom: Bowls. *Left,* No. 1225, cut Empire pattern; *right,* No. 1225, cut Cornell
      pattern.
C. *Top:* Bowl, No. 1225, cut Concave pattern.
   Bottom: Bowls. *Left,* No. 1086, cut Yale pattern; *right,* No. 1381, cut Venus pattern.
D. *Top:* Bowl, No. 1381, cut Star pattern.
   Bottom: Bowls. *Left,* No. 1381, cut Reese pattern; *right,* No. 1381 cut Japan pattern.
E. Compotes. *Left,* No. 1092, cut Olympic pattern; *right,* No. 1331, cut Starlight pattern.
F. Compotes. *Left,* No. 1300, cut Wilbert pattern; *right,* No. 1072, cut Oregon pattern.
G. Candlesticks. *Left to right,* Nos. 1116 and 1246, cut Holland pattern; No. 1265 cut
      Rome pattern; No. 1245, cut Stepped pattern; No. 1116, cut Colonial pattern.
H. Candlesticks. *Left to right,* Nos. 1382, 1384, and 1385.

Salesman's Catalog   STEUBEN CUT GLASS (2)   (See page 348.)

I. *Left to right,* No. 1001, Whiskey Jug; No. 1339, Whiskey Decanter; No. 1430 Water
      Jug. All cut Tartan pattern.
J. *Left to right,* No. 1001, Whiskey Jug, cut Buzzsaw pattern; No. 1337, Decanter, cut
      Pembroke pattern; No. 1040, Whiskey Jug, cut Warsaw pattern.
K. *Left to right,* Decanters. No. 1341, cut Violet pattern; No. 1339 cut Bolton pattern;
      No. 1307, cut Electric pattern; No. 1301, cut Concord pattern.
L. Whiskey Bottles and Tumblers. *Left,* No. 1433, cut Baltic pattern; *right,* No. 1433,
      cut Sylvia pattern.
M. *Top;* Oil cruets. *Left to right,* No. 1281, cut Hilda pattern; No. 1052, cut Elite pattern;
      No. 1005 cut Whirlwind pattern; No. 1094, cut Atlantic pattern.
   Bottom: Left to right, Colognes. No. 1173, cut Cairo pattern; No. 1173 cut Brilliant
      pattern; No. 1006, cut Union pattern. String Box No. 1187, cut Maxim pattern.
N. *Left to right,* Water Bottle and Tumbler, No. 1268 cut Model pattern; Water Bottle and
      Tumbler, No. 1099 cut Crescent pattern.
O. Pitchers. *Left to right,* No. 1087, cut Daisy pattern; No. 1119, cut Domestic pattern;
      No. 1266, cut Bordon pattern.
P. Sugar Bowls and Creamers. *Left to right,* No. 1276, cut Teutonic pattern; No. 1199,
      cut Elk pattern; No. 1024, cut Norman pattern.

Salesman's Catalog   STEUBEN CUT GLASS (3)   (See page 349.)

Q. Lamp, No. 1306, cut Majestic pattern.
R. Vases. *Left,* No. 1253, cut Eureka pattern; *right,* No. 1294, cut Pekin pattern.
S. Shower Vase, No. 1386.
T. Vases. *Left to right,* No. 1124 cut Maple pattern; No. 1295, cut Ethel pattern;
      No. 1107, cut Hanover pattern.
U. Vases. *Left to right,* No. 1293 cut Pembroke pattern; No. 1289, cut Felton pattern;
      No. 1168 cut Majestic pattern.
V. Vases. *Left to right,* No. 1400 cut Empire pattern; No. 1399, cut Plymouth pattern;
      No. 1401, cut Manhattan pattern.
W. Baskets. *Left,* No. 1089, cut Nevada pattern; *right,* No. 1123, cut Daisy pattern.

Salesman's Catalog   STEUBEN ENGRAVED GLASS   (See page 350.)

A. *Left to right,* Pitcher, No. 1284; Vases, Nos. 1285 and 1286, all skeleton molded and engraved.
B. *Left to right,* Vases Nos. 1319, 1343, and 1283, all skeleton molded and engraved.
C. *Left to right,* Decanters, Nos. 1347, 1349, and 1348, all skeleton molded and engraved.
D. *Left to right,* Engraved Vases, Nos. 1393, 1385, and 1394.
E. Sugar Bowl and Creamer, No. 1492, Spoon Holder No. 1493, all engraved Adams pattern.
F. Vase, No. 1494, and Jug, No. 1495, engraved Adams pattern.
G. Compote, No. 1499, Candlestick, No. 1495, engraved Adams pattern.
H. Engraved Stemware, No. 1350.

Salesman's Catalog   AURENE (1)   (See page 351.)

A. *Left to right,* Vases, Nos. 130, 167, and 203.
B. *Left to right,* Vases, Nos. 165, 152, and 143.
C. *Left to right,* Vases, Nos. 200, 141, and 158.
D. *Left to right,* Candlestick, No. 196; Vases, Nos. 195 and 179.
E. *Left to right,* Vases, Nos. 162, 131, and 159.
F. *Left to right,* Vases, Nos. 183, 175, and 184.
G. *Left to right,* Vases, Nos. 154, 134, and 193.
H. *Left to right,* Vase, No. 140; Comport, No. 186; Cologne, No. 189.
I. *Left to right,* Vases, Nos. 155, 144, and 132.
J. *Left to right,* Vases, Nos. 161, 153, and 201.
K. *Left to right,* Vases, Nos. 135, 137, and 207.
L. *Left to right,* Vases, Nos. 194 and 174; Candlestick, No. 169.

Salesman's Catalog   AURENE (2)   (See page 352.)

M. *Left to right,* Vases, Nos. 182, 181, and 180.
N. *Left to right,* Vases, Nos. 178, 177, and 176.
O. *Left to right,* Vase, No. 170; Comport, No. 172; Vase, No. 164.
P. *Left to right,* Vases, Nos. 225, 246, and 226.
Q. *Left to right,* Vases, Nos. 217, 238, and 216b.
R. *Left to right,* Vases, Nos. 220, 185, and 227.
S. *Left to right,* Vases, Nos. 208, 211b, and 209b.
T. *Left to right,* Vases, Nos. 258, 259, and 260.
U. *Left to right,* Vases, Nos. 253, 254, and 255.
V. *Left to right,* Vases, Nos. 130a, 219b, and 218b.
W. *Left to right,* Colognes, Nos. 190, 188, and 187.
X. *Left to right,* Vases, Nos. 163, 224, and 245.

Salesman's Catalog   AURENE AND OTHER COLORS   (See page 353.)

Y. *Left to right,* Bowls, Nos. 198, 199, and 197.
Z. Decanter and Wineglass, No. 206.
AA. *Left to right,* Vases, Nos. 221, 223, and 222.

BB. *Left to right,* Vases, Nos. 235, 261, and 236.
CC. *Left to right, Top:* Finger Bowl Plate, No. 204.
                Bottom: Finger Bowl, No. 204; Vase, No. 210; Bonbon, No. 192.
DD. *Left to right,* Vases, Nos. 242, 239, and 240.
EE. *Left to right, Top:* Finger Bowl and Plate, No. 171; Bonbon, No. 191.
                Bottom: Bonbons, Nos. 138, 205, and 139.
FF. *Left to right, Top:* Vases, Nos. 151, 150, and 158.
                Bottom: Vases, Nos. 210, 212, and 213.
GG. *Left to right, Top:* Vases, Nos. 312, 363, and 365.
                Bottom: Vases, Nos. 314, 364, and 313.
HH. *Left to right, Top:* Vases, Nos. 345, 360, and 355A.
                Bottom: Vases, Nos. 361, 362, and 354.
II. *Left to right,* Vases, Nos. 346, 366, and 309.
JJ. *Left to right, Top:* Vases, Nos. 357, 359, and 358.
                Bottom: Vases, Nos. 356, 367, and 355.

Salesman's Catalog   ENGRAVED PATTERNS   (See page 354.)

A. Stemware and Plates, engraved Antique pattern.
B. Compote, Bowl, and Candlestick, engraved Camillo pattern.
C. Plate, engraved Antique pattern.
D. Candlesticks, Bowl, and Plate, engraved Indian pattern.
E. Plate, engraved Indian pattern.
F. Candlesticks, Vase, Plate, and Bowl, engraved Quintin pattern.
G. Console set, engraved Sheraton pattern.
H. Plate, engraved Etruscan pattern.
I. Candlesticks, Compotes, and Bowl, engraved Etruscan pattern.
J. Plate, engraved York pattern.

Salesman's Catalog   STEUBEN TABLEWARE   (See page 355.)

A. Candlesticks, Compotes, and Master Salts or Peppers, No. 5223, cut decoration.
B. Candlesticks, Compotes, and Bowl, No. 3376.
C. Bowl, No. 3341; Covered Compote, No. 3343; Vase, No. 3351.
D. Candlesticks and Bowl, No. 3375.
E. Iced Tea Set, No. 3329, mat-su-no-ke decoration.
F. Compotes, Candlesticks, No. 3178, and Bowl, engraved Waverly pattern.
G. Compote, No. 3305; Candlestick, No. 3304; applied mat-su-no-ke decoration.
H. Candlesticks and Compotes, No. 6453; Stemware, No. 6404 variant.
I. Candlesticks, Compotes, and Bowl, No. 6405; Stemware, No. 6404.

VASES AND BOWLS MADE BY THE LOST WAX PROCESS IN THE 1930s.   (See page 356.)

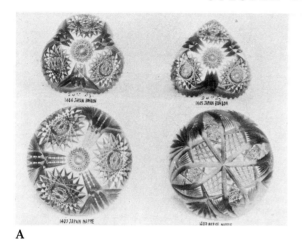

A

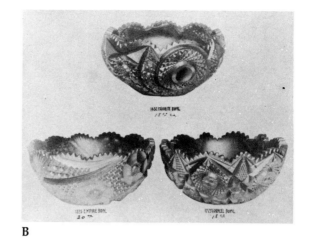

B

C

D

E

F

G

H

I

J

K

L

M

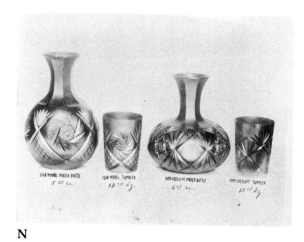

N

O

P

Q

1253 EUREKA

1294 PEKIN

R

1386 SHOWER VASE

28 ea.

S

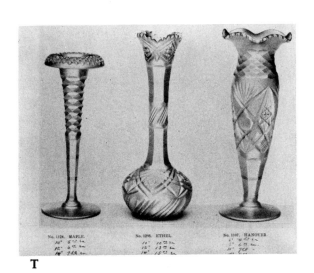

No. 1124. MAPLE.

No. 1248. ETHEL.

No. 1107. HANOVER.

T

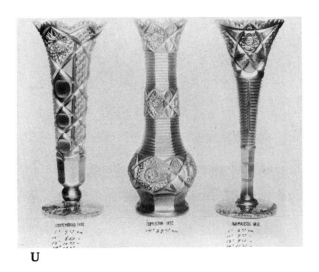

U

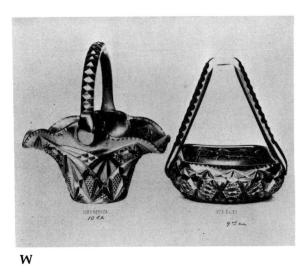

V

W

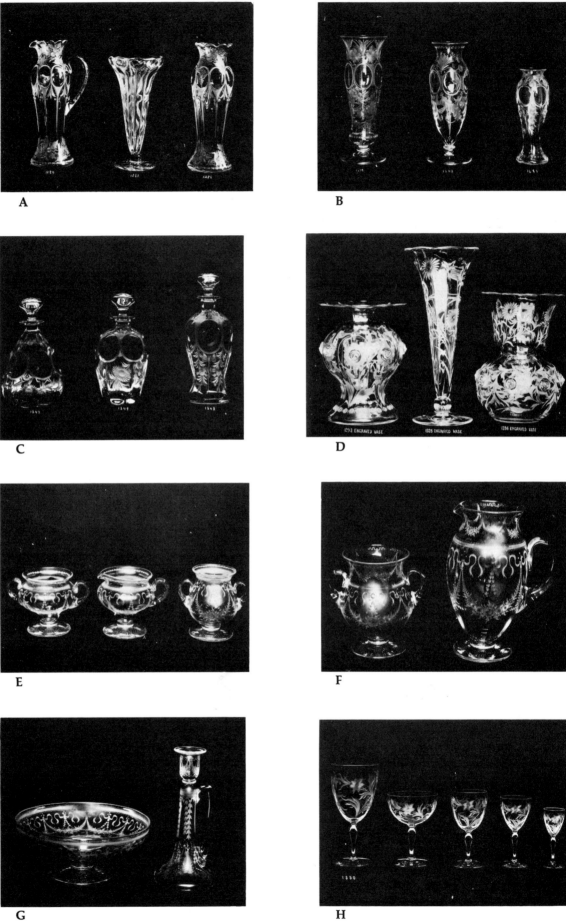

A

B

C

D

E

F

G

H

A

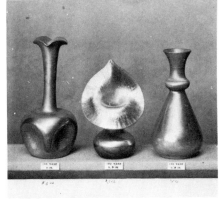

B

C

D

E

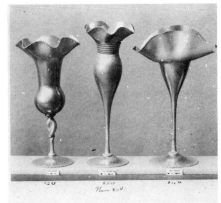

F

G

H

I

J

K

L

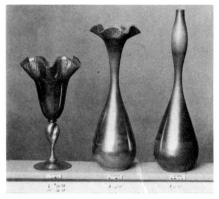

M

N

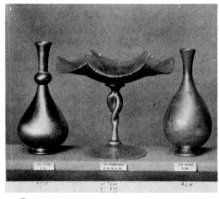

O

P

Q

R

S

T

U

V

W

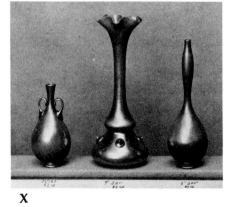

X

Y

Z

AA

BB

CC

DD

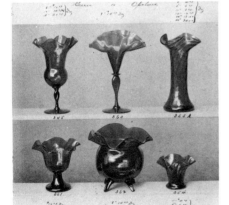

EE

FF

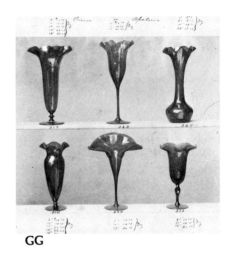

GG

HH

II

JJ

A

B

C

D

E

F

G

H

I

J

A

B

C

D

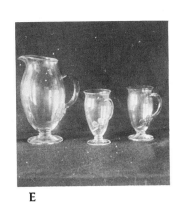

E

F

G

H

I

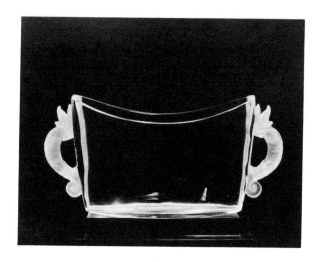

Notes

1. D. R. Guttery, *From Broad-Glass to Cut Crystal* (London: L. Hill, 1956, pp. 1–11), gives a historical description of the region and its early glass industry.

2. This and further quotations are from Carder's unpublished autobiographical notes and from his conversations with the author.

3. John Northwood II, *John Northwood* (Stourbridge: Mark and Moody, Ltd., 1958), pp. 32–43.

D. B. Harden; K. S. Painter; R. H. Pinder-Wilson; and H. Tait; *Masterpieces of Glass* (London: Trustees of the British Museum, 1968), pp. 49–51. The original Portland Vase of Roman cameo glass (late first century B.C. to early first century A.D.) is in the British Museum.

4. Northwood, op. cit., p. 36. John Northwood and his studio did "cutting up," "smoothing," and "polishing" on Wedgwood's jasperware copies of the Portland Vase in the 1870s.

5. Hugh Wakefield, *Nineteenth Century British Glass* (London: Faber & Faber, 1961), p. 29.

6. Wakefield, op. cit., p. 47. "It will be noticed that these decorative adjuncts of the 'sixties and early 'seventies were being used mainly on objects of clear uncoloured glass. As yet there was little sign of a serious revival in the use of coloured glass..."

7. Wakefield, op. cit., p. 49, states: "The revival of color became noticeable about the middle of the 'seventies..."

8. Northwood, op. cit., pp. 74–79.

9. Wakefield, op. cit., p. 40. "The words 'rock crystal' were used in Thomas Webb's pattern books in 1879 of a table set engraved with animal scenes by F. E. Kny; and almost immediately afterwards the name of William Fritsche... in the same technique...."

10. Polished engraving had also been done in Germany as early as the eighteenth century.

11. Northwood, op. cit., pp. 109, 114; Wakefield, op. cit., p. 41.

12. Northwood, op. cit., p. 127.

13. *Catalog, National Competition of Schools of Science and Art and Art Classes*, 1889. Department of Science and Art of the Committee of the Council on Education, South Kensington (London: Eyre and Spottiswoode, 1889) p. A.

14. Children of Annie and Frederick Carder: Caleb Stanley Carder, born September 6, 1891, died of diabetes in 1899. Buried in Holy Trinity Cemetery, Wordsley, Staffordshire. A terra-cotta memorial designed and modeled by F. Carder marks his grave. (John Northwood's grave is also in this churchyard.) Cyril Frederick Carder, born June 6, 1893, killed in action in France, July 18, 1918. Gladys Mabel Carder (Mrs. Gillett Welles), born November 10, 1889, died October 12, 1969, in Hudson, Ohio.

15. Catalog, *The Exhibition of the Royal Academy of Arts, MDCCCXCIII* (London: William Clowes and Sons, Ltd., 1893), No. 1768.

16. Frederick Carder, *Report of a Visit to the Principal Glass-making Districts of Germany and Austria* (Staffordshire County Council, 1902).

17. The Baron Steuben Motor Hotel now occupies this site.

18. Carder named the Steuben Glass Works after the New York State County of Steuben, in which Corning is located. The name is pronounced Stoo-ben' locally.

19. Carder's notes, written in 1937, state (p. 21): "How well I remember making up my mind to come to America. One night just before I left the Works I went to see Mr. J. in his office and told him that I wished to give him two weeks notice to leave his employ. This being the custom in England at that time. His face went red and after a long pause (he) asked me why I wanted to leave him. I told him that no doubt he knew the reason and if he did not I was sorry that I could not enlighten him. He offered to double my wages—after refusing some months ago. I told him 'no.' He then offered to triple them and again I said 'no.' I told him that I had worked for him harder than if the place belonged to myself and that I could see there was only one thing for me to do and that was to get away, as my interest had gone."

20. *Corning Leader*, March 11, 1903.

21. *Corning Leader*, October 13, 1903.

22. Addison, New York, is fifteen miles northwest of Corning.

23. Carder received the Michael Friedsam medal in 1927 from the Architectural League "For Service in the Cause of Industrial Art."

24. No records have been located that give information on the number of shares of Steuben Glass owned by Carder, but it seems probable that most of the financial backing was done by the Hawkes family.

25. No manager was appointed for Steuben from August, 1919, to September, 1922.

26. In September, 1922, Glen W. Cole was appointed superintendent of the Steuben Division and Carder continued as art director. In May, 1923, Carder was again put "In charge" of the Steuben Division as manager, a position he held until February, 1932, when John Mackay was appointed manager of Steuben and Carder was made art director of Corning Glass Works, a position he held until he retired in 1959 at ninety-six.

Arthur A. Houghton, Jr., became vice-president of Steuben Glass, Inc., October 12, 1933.

27. Robert J. Leavy was office manager of the Steuben Division from 1917 to 1934; vice-president in charge of production and sales 1934 to 1962; executive vice-president of staff 1962 to 1964; retired 1964.

28. John J. Graham was in charge of the Steuben Division laboratory and mixing room from 1925 to 1932; assistant manager (Steuben blowing room B Factory Main Plant) 1932 to 1940; manager Optical Glass CGW Parkersburg, West Virginia, 1940 to 1945; production superintendent, Steuben Division, 1945 to 1964; manager of manufacturing, Steuben Division, 1964 to present.

29. Dr. Eugene Cornelius Sullivan, glass scientist, born Elgin, Illinois, January 23, 1872; B.S. University of Michigan, 1894; studied at University of Göttingen and University of Leipzig, Ph.D. 1899. Came to Corning Glass Works in 1908 as chief chemist. Co-inventor of Pyrex glass, 1915. Vice-president (manufacturing) Corning Glass Works from 1920 to 1927; president, 1928–1929; vice-chairman, 1930–1936; vice-chairman, director of research, 1936–1945; honorary vice-chairman, 1946–1949; honorary chairman, 1950–1962. Died Corning, New York, May 12, 1962 ("Eugene Cornelius Sullivan—Glass Scientist," Corning Glass Works Publication 1966).

30. From a transcript of taped conversation with Robert J. Leavy, Otto Hilbert, Paul N. Perrot, Robert Rockwell, Kenneth Wilson, Robert Brill, and Paul Gardner at Corning, October 9, 1965.

31. Present whereabouts unknown.

32. Carder kept the casting in his office in the main plant until 1944 and took it with him when he moved to the old Steuben office building that year (at that time the Vycor plant of Corning Glass Works). It remained on the stair landing in the Vycor plant until a few months after Carder retired in 1959, when the Corning Glass Works decided to dispose of it. It would have been smashed and the cullet remelted but for an interested employee, who felt it should be preserved and was told he could have it if he would remove it. He took it to his home in Lindley, New York. A few months later, an antique dealer from Owego named Cooper purchased it for $100 and took it to his shop, filled the crack in the nose, and covered the entire casting with gold paint. When Robert Rockwell learned it was in Owego, he immediately went to see Cooper and in 1960 bought it for $300. Rockwell brought it back to Corning, removed the gold paint, and installed it in his collection at the Rockwell Department Store.

33. The Frederick Carder Elementary School, Corning, New York.

34. LP record, *The Fieldstone Porch Presents Conversations with Carder on Steuben,* c. 1963. Produced by Cecily and Gerry Philpot, The Fieldstone Porch, Glenbrook, Connecticut.

35. Just when or why a mistake was made in Carder's age remains a mystery. In the summer of 1963, Carder's housekeeper discovered a watch, tucked away for years, inscribed to him on the occasion of his twenty-first birthday, September 18, 1884. This led interested friends to send to England for verification. Carder had announced he would celebrate his ninety-ninth birthday on September 18, 1963. A few days before then, the verification of September 18, 1863, as Carder's birth date was received. He was almost antagonistic at the news and refused to discuss it, so Rockwell, who felt the facts should be known, decided to force the issue and publicly announce the new date at the birthday party.

From time to time, newspapers and other publications have used the name Frederick C. Carder. While Carder was alive, he always denied he had a middle initial with the same profane emphasis that he used when his surname was spelled Carter ("My name is Carder—with a 'd' for 'damn' "). A copy of his birth certificate in the author's possession gives no middle name or initial.

36. Robert Koch, *Louis C. Tiffany, Rebel in Glass* (New York: Crown Publishers, Inc., 1964), p. 126.

37. Tests on Aurene and Favrile conducted at Corning Glass Works Sullivan Research Center, 1966 and 1967, by Harrison P. Hood.

38. Gladys Carder Welles stated that her father also said the name was suggested by the aurora borealis.

39. Frederick Carder, "Glass and Glass Making As I know it." Handwritten, 1920, Unpublished. p. 16.

40. Trademark No. 43,287, registered September 6, 1904, United States Patent Office, Carder, op. cit., p. 16.

41. Carder, op. cit., p. 16.

42. Trademark issued June 1, 1915.

43. Northwood, op. cit., pp. 71, 105. Stevens & Williams were making Verre de Soie in 1885–1886.

44. Not to be confused with Tiffany's Cypriote glass, which it in no way resembles. See Koch, op. cit., p. 127.

45. Carder stated this "chemical" was either potassium or sodium nitrate. Tests by Dr. Harvey Littleton at the University of Wisconsin, December, 1967, showed potassium nitrate would produce bubbles when mixed with the powdered glass on the marver and picked up on a molten glass gather.

46. A type of bubble and streaked glass called Clutha was made in the 1880s and later by James Couper & Sons, Glasgow, Scotland. Thomas Webb & Sons made a similar type called Old Roman. (Wakefield, op. cit., p. 53.)

47. The several types of decorations that Carder called Intarsia during the period from about 1906 onward have led to misunderstandings. In addition to the three types described in the text, a fourth technique is on record.

In May, 1960, Carder discussed this Intarsia with Paul Perrot, who had received inquiries regarding it from Guy Robert, manager of export, Kosta Glasbruk, Sweden. At that time Carder stated that his first attempts at Intarsia occurred in 1916 and 1917, but commercial production was not launched before 1920 or 1921, and he gave the following description of the process to Perrot, who forwarded it to Robert in a letter dated May 9, 1960: "Laying out fragments of colored glass, cut out to a pattern, on the flat of a marver and then picking them up with a cylindrical gather of clear glass which was rolled over it. The gather was then returned to the pot of clear glass to receive a covering layer, after which the object was formed." Obviously this is not the same technique used to produce the

Intarsia made about 1930. Up to the present no pieces made at Steuben by this technique have been identified.

Another notation in the Corning Museum files indicates this type of Intarsia may have been attempted as early as 1914.

48. Harden; Painter; Pinder-Wilson; and Tait; op. cit., p. 25.

49. William B. Honey, *Glass* (London: Victoria and Albert Museum, 1946), p. 22.

50. Honey, op. cit., p. 23.

51. A catalog notation is as follows:

"Millefiori Glass

January 1, 1926

#1 12" Plate—$85.00 each	#6 7½" Plate—$30.00 each
#2 12½" Plate—$35.00 each	#7 8" Bowl—$85.00 each
#3 10" Plate—$50.00 each	#8 5½" Bowl—$50.00 each
#4 8" Plate—$30.00 each	#9 10" Plate—$75.00 each
#5 8" Plate—$30.00 each	#10 12" Plate—$100.00 each"

These designs are not identified, but they are probably similar to those illustrated.

52. These applied decorations were a variation of the mat-su-no-ke type made at Stevens & Williams in the 1880s and later. Carder also made this type at Steuben.

53. E. M. Elville, *English Tableglass* (London and New York: Country Life, Ltd. and Charles Scribner's Sons, 1951), p. 176, et seq.

54. Not to be confused with the English technique called Intaglio done in the late nineteenth century and since, using stone wheels with the engraver holding the glass object under the wheel. (Northwood, op. cit., p. 114, et seq.; Wakefield, op. cit., pp. 41, 42.) Steuben intaglio engravings were cut with copper wheels also with the engraver holding the glass under the wheel.

55. Elville, op. cit., pp. 152, 153.

56. Wakefield, op. cit., pp. 39, 40.

57. A page in Carder's handwritten notes dated August 9, 1912, gives the following formula for "Printing Ink":

170 Burgundy pitch	200 Wax
40 Asphalt	160 Fe_2O_3
8 Mastic	+ 1 tumblerful of terps.

Added notation: "think it would be better to drop some of the Fe_2O_3, say 140 instead of 160."

58. Hydrofluoric acid.

59. Carder's "gelatin" was composed mainly of glue and glycerine melted together to form a mass about the consistency of molasses when heated in a double-boiler type of container. This was poured over the plaster-of-Paris model while hot; after cooling, it formed a pliable mold that could be peeled from the undercuts in the plaster model and later from the wax casting.

60. Carder used a basic mixture of beeswax and paraffin, which could be melted and poured into the gelatin mold. After cooling, this wax would set to about the hardness of a wax candle.

61. Honey, op. cit., p. 7.

62. Honey, op. cit., p. 142.

63. A catalog notation dated March, 1926, lists the following:

PÂTE DE VERRE FIGURES

#1—Figure	50.00 each
#2—Medallion Head	25.00 each
#3—Small Figure	25.00 each
#4—Large Figure	50.00 each
#5—Small Head	25.00 each
#6—Figure	25.00 each

6272 vase Black over Jade Indian 18.00 ea.

Plaque Figure Pâte de verre 50.00 ea.

Plaque Mille Fleur eng. Fish des. 100.00 ea.

These objects have not been identified, with the exception of vase No. 6272, which is in the catalog line drawings.

Glossary

ANNEALING OVEN OF LEHR: A heated chamber with a continuous moving conveyor belt into which newly made glass objects are put to cool. The temperature at the opening of the oven where the glass is placed is just below the softening point of the glass. It diminishes gradually during the movement of the object through the lehr, to about room temperature at the end, where the object emerges. Glass objects cooled in this manner are relatively strain-free and will not shatter with ordinary temperature changes.

AT THE FIRE: Used in referring to an operation or technique executed by the glassworker in the blowing room while the glass is in a molten state or still workable, before being sent to the lehr.

BATCH: The mixture of raw materials melted to produce glass.

BATCH CARTS: Carts (usually made of iron at Steuben) used to wheel the batch from the mixing room to the glass furnace, where it is placed in the glass pot for melting.

BIT GATHERER: See SHOP.

BLANK: Undecorated glassware, usually made to have a cut, engraved, or acid-etched decoration added later.

BLISTER: A bubble so near the surface of the glass that it may break when touched and leave a pit.

BLOWPIPE OR BLOWING IRON: A hollow iron tube varying in outside diameter from ½″ to 1½″ and usually from 3′6″ to 4′8″ in length (some special irons are 5′6″ in length). A ring about ⅛″ thick called a "nose" is welded at one end to hold the gather of glass more firmly. The other end is rounded slightly to fit the lips of the worker.

CASING: Covering one color of glass with one or more layers of another color.

CHAIR: The glassblower's seat—a bench having low iron arms extending forward on each side to allow him to roll the blowing iron back and forth in forming the ware. Also the term used to describe the shop or team of glassworkers.

CORD: See STRIAE.

CRACKLE OF CRACKLING: An intentional effect obtained by dipping the expanded gather into water while hot. This causes the glass to crack. After it is reheated, the cracks fuse but the scars of the cracks remain, giving a decorative effect. (Not to be confused with ice glass.)

CRIMP: To form a crimped edge by use of a crimp mold.

CRIMP MOLD: A mold made of radiating iron or wood ribs mounted on a base plate. These ribs vary in number, thickness, and height depending on the form of crimp desired. The top rim of the hot glass object is pushed against the ribs to form the crimped edge.

CROWN GLASS: Window glass made by spinning out a large flat disk of glass from the blowing iron, leaving a bull's eye in the center where the iron was attached.

CULLET: Broken glass.

CUT GLASS: Glass ornamented by cutting designs into its surface.

DECOLORIZER: A substance used to counteract the coloring effects of impurities. When iron impurities in the sand cause a greenish tint, manganese dioxide (sometimes called glassmakers' soap) can be added to make the glass appear colorless. If glass to which manganese dioxide has been added is exposed to the sun under certain conditions, it will gradually acquire an amethyst tint, which generally deepens on continued exposure to the sun's rays.

DRAGLADING: Ladling the hot glass from a pot into a container (usually an iron kettle) filled with water. This is done when it is desirable to save the glass. The term is said to have been derived from the words "drag ladle."

FETTLING: A term used in nineteenth-century English potteries to describe the process of putting handles and spouts on the ware.

FLASHING: In general, Carder used this term synonymously with casing. He sometimes indicated it meant a very thin layer of glass over a heavier matrix. See CASING.

FLINT: In general, this term is used to designate lead glass. It originally derived from the use of ground flint pebbles in the glass batch.

FOOT: The base of a goblet or other object.

FOLDED FOOT: A foot with the outer rim folded back and fused to the glass, making a double thickness at the edge, like a hem on a cloth garment.

FORK: A wooden pole about 4 to 5 feet long, having on one end two iron or wood prongs covered with asbestos. The fork is used to carry stemware and other relatively small pieces to the lehr after they have been completed by the gaffer.

FRACTURE OR FLY: The spontaneous shattering or cracking of a glass piece. This usually results from changes in temperature and occurs when an object has not been properly annealed. See ANNEALING OVEN.

FREE-BLOWN: Fashioned offhand on the blowing iron with the aid of glassmakers' tools, as opposed to glassware formed by blowing or pressing in a mold.

FRIGGER: Usually a trial piece made by apprentices learning how to blow glass offhand. Sometimes poorly made pieces or those that are not regular factory production items are called friggers. So-called end-of-day pieces are often in this category.

FRIT: Partially fused or calcined ingredients of the glass batch, before they have become vitrified.

FROST: Powdered glass made by crushing thinly blown glass bubbles. Used by Steuben in making Cintra, Cluthra, and Moss Agate glasses.

FURNACE: A circular structure in the blowing room built of bricks and fired clay blocks, reinforced with iron rods; it housed the clay pots in which the glass was melted. The furnace was usually fueled by coal or gas. Steuben's first furnace held ten pots; its second, sixteen.

GADGET or SNAP: A spring clip or snap to hold the foot of a wineglass, vase, or other footed object, while the body or bowl is being finished by the glassworker. It is used instead of the pontil when a pontil mark is to be avoided or when the shape of the foot makes this type of tool advisable.

GAFFER: Chairman. See SHOP.

GATHER: The mass of glass picked up or "gathered" by dipping the blowing iron into the molten glass batch in the glass pot or tank. A small gather was also picked up on the pontil rod to "stick up" the object and transfer it from the blowing iron to the pontil, to allow finishing the top.

GATHERER: A workman who gathers the molten glass from the glass pot.

GLASS POT: The clay pot or container in which the glass batch is melted. Pots are placed in the arched openings of the furnace.

GLORY HOLE: A small furnace usually fired by gas in which the glass gather or partly formed object can be reheated during production. The opening of the furnace is used by some factories to reheat pieces instead of a glory hole.

HOOKED DECORATIONS: Applied threadings pulled up and down with a hook-shaped tool to form chevrons, feathers, and other line decorations.

JACKS: See WOOD JACKS.

KETTLE: An iron receptacle mounted on wheels and partly filled with water. It is capable of holding the contents of a pot of glass, which are ladled into it from the glass pot while the glass is molten. See DRAGLADING.

KILN: A furnace or oven used to anneal large glass pieces that could not be cooled in the lehr. Prior to the invention of the lehr, glass pieces had to be annealed in ovens or from the heat of the glass furnace.

LEHR: See ANNEALING OVEN.

MARVER: A plate of cast or wrought iron polished smooth on which the gatherer or glassblower rolls or "marvers" the glass gather when it is first brought from the pot on the blowing iron, to make it smooth and true. Also used in other glass production processes, for example, Cintra, Cluthra, etc. Marble slabs were also used as marvers.

MERESE: A wafer or button of glass used singly or in twos or threes to connect parts of hand-blown objects, such as segments of stems. Shapes of mereses vary as necessity demands. The most common are disks, flattened pellets, and pulley-shapes.

METAL: Glassworkers often refer to the glass as the "metal." "Best metal" usually meant fine lead glass.

MOVE: Fred Schroeder, foreman of the Steuben blowing room from about 1904 until the 1930s, stated that in the Steuben factory a "move" was a half-day's work. They might say, for example, "We made fifty-two five-pound jugs in a move."

PALLET: A flat piece of iron or wood that is held against the bottom of an object while the workman continues the forming process.

PARISON: The gather of hot glass after it has been partly or wholly inflated by the glassblower.

PIG or TOWER: A block of iron about 8" square at the base and tapering to about 1" at the top. There are semicircular notches of various depths in the top, which are used to support the blowing or pontil iron as the glassworker is rotating the object, when reheating it, at the glory hole or furnace.

PINCHERS or PINCERS: A spring tool made of iron with two blunt points; it operates like tongs, and is used to pick up bits of glass, such as flowers, fruit, and other applied decorations. Pincers are also made with points of varied sizes and designs for use in making "pinched" decorations and finishing handles.

PONTIL or PUNTY: A solid rod of iron about the same length as the blowpipe, but a trifle smaller in diameter. The end of this rod is dipped into the molten glass, and the small portion of hot glass that adheres is pushed against the base of the partly formed glass object. The gaffer then separates the top of the glass object from the blowing iron, thus transferring it from the blowing iron to the pontil rod. After the top is finished, the object is broken away from the pontil, leaving the pontil mark. This mark is often left as it comes from the rod; or it can be ground out and polished.

PRUNTS: Dabs or blobs of hot glass applied to objects as decorations. These dabs (prunts) are left plain as they are applied, or shaped with seallike iron stamps in many designs ranging from raspberries to animal and human heads.

PUCELLAS: A steel spring tool that is tong-shaped and has blades with smooth, polished edges. These blades have many uses in forming the free-blown pieces.

REEDING: Hand-applied threading. In Steuben pieces, this is irregularly applied as contrasted to machine threading, which is evenly spaced and of uniform thickness.

RESIST: The wax preparation used to protect the glass from the acid during etching. The surfaces of the glass not covered with resist are etched by the acid; they form the sunken parts of the design.

RIGAREE: Applied glass bands or ribs tooled with indented horizontal lines. These were used in a variety of designs.

SERVITOR: See SHOP.

SHEARS: A short-bladed, steel, cutting tool, similar to tin shears, used by the gaffer or other workman to cut off any excess while shaping the hot glass.

SHOP: The group of glassworkers who function together as a team in fashioning free-formed glass pieces. The size of the group varied with the type of ware being made. Carder described a typical shop as consisting of three men and three boys, as listed below:

Gaffer—the master glassblower, head of the shop or "chair"

Servitor—the chief assistant

Blower—second assistant

Bit Gatherer—boy who gathers bits of glass, such as "legs" and "feet," to be applied by the Servitor to the glass object

Sticker Up—boy who looks after the pontils, and when the article is stuck to the pontil by the Servitor, helps the Gaffer by warming it at the glory hole. He also cleans the excess glass from the blowing and pontil irons after they are removed from the finished piece

Taker In—boy who carries finished articles to the lehr

STICK UP: To affix the pontil iron to the partly finished object.

STRIAE: Cords or veins visible in the glass. Usually considered flaws, these result from improper melting of the glass batch.

STRIKING: The change in the color of glass effected by sudden cooling or heating during the production process. This effect is produced intentionally in opalescent glasses by spraying the hot glass with cool air. It is also the technique used in developing the purple color in Carder's Tyrian glass and in other art glass such as Amberina.

THREADING: Evenly applied threads of glass, usually done with a threading machine, in contrast to reeding, which was applied freehand. See REEDING.

WOOD BLOCK: A heavy block of wood having a quarter-sphere depression that was used to give the hot glass gather a symmetrical form in the early stages of shaping an object.

WOOD JACK: Steel spring tool of pincer type with wooden prongs used in shaping the hot glass. The wood in this tool is always charred before use and is kept from burning by dipping in water during use. Charred wood will not leave marks or scratches on hot glass, and so can be used to rub or push the glass into any desired shape.

Bibliography

BOOKS AND PAMPHLETS

Angus-Butterworth, L. M. *British Table and Ornamental Glass*. London: L. Hill, 1956.

Barret, Richard Carter. *Identification of American Art Glass*. Manchester, Vermont: Forward's Color Productions, 1964.

Beard, Geoffrey W. *Nineteenth Century Cameo Glass*. Newport, England: Ceramic Book Company, 1956.

Corning, New York, Museum of Glass. *Frederick Carder—His Life and Work*. Corning, 1952. Catalog of a special exhibition. Text by Thomas S. Buechner.

Corning, New York, Museum of Glass. *Glass from the Ancient World: The Ray Winfield Smith Collection*. Corning, 1957. Catalog of a Special Exhibition.

Elville, E. M. *The Collector's Dictionary of Glass*. London and New York: Country Life, Ltd., and Charles Scribner's Sons, 1951.

————. *English Tableglass*. rev. ed. London: Country Life, Ltd., 1960.

Ericson, Eric E. *A Guide to Colored Steuben Glass 1903–1933*, 1st ed. Loveland, Colorado: The Lithographic Press, 1963.

————. *A Guide to Colored Steuben Glass 1903–1933*, Book Two. Loveland, Colorado: The Lithographic Press, 1965.

Freeman, Graydon La Vern. *Iridescent Glass*. Watkins Glen, New York: Century House, 1956.

Grover, Ray and Lee. *Art Glass Nouveau*. Rutland, Vermont: Charles E. Tuttle Co., 1967.

Guttery, D. R. *From Broad-Glass to Cut Crystal, A History of the Stourbridge Glass Industry*. London: L. Hill, 1956.

Harden, D. B.; Painter, K. S.; Pinder-Wilson, R. H.; and Tait, H. *Masterpieces of Glass*. London: Trustees of the British Museum, 1968.

Honey, William B. *Glass; A Handbook for the Study of Glass Vessels of all Periods and Countries and a Guide to the Museum Collection*. London: Victoria and Albert Museum, 1946.

Janneau, Guillaume. *Modern Glass*. London: The Studio Ltd., 1931.

Koch, Robert. *Louis C. Tiffany, Rebel in Glass*. New York: Crown Publishers, Inc., 1964.

Mariacher, Giovanni. *Italian Blown Glass from Ancient Rome to Venice*. New York: McGraw-Hill, 1961.

McKearin, George S., and Helen. *American Glass*. New York: Crown Publishers, Inc., 1948.

————. *Two Hundred Years of American Blown Glass*. New York: Crown Publishers, Inc., 1949.

Northwood, John II. *John Northwood*. Stourbridge: Mark and Moody, Ltd., 1958.

Revi, Albert Christian. *American Cut and Engraved Glass*. New York: T. Nelson, 1965.

————. *Nineteenth Century Glass, Its Genesis and Development*. New York: T. Nelson, 1959.

Rockwell, Robert F. *Frederick Carder and His Steuben Glass 1903–1933*. West Nyack, New York: Dexter Press, Inc., 1966.

Thorpe, W. A. *Collections of Glass at the Brierley Hill Public Library*. Brierley Hill, England, 1949.

Van Tassel, Valentine. *American Glass*. New York: M. Barrows, 1950.

Wakefield, Hugh. *Nineteenth Century British Glass*. London: Faber & Faber, 1961.

Watkins, Lura W. *American Glass and Glassmaking*. London: M. Parrish, 1950.

ARTICLES

Bardrof, Frank E. "Frederick Carder: Artist in Glass." *The Glass Industry*, April, 1939, pp. 136–41.

Buechner, Thomas S. "The Glass of Frederick Carder." *The Connoisseur Year Book*, 1961, pp. 39–43. The Connoisseur, 28 and 30 Grosvenor Gardens, S.W. 1.

————. "The Life and Work of Frederick Carder." *The Rotarian*, September, 1957.

Carder, Frederick. "Artistic Glass from 1910 to the Present Day." *The Glass Industry*, March, 1934, pp. 28–29.

Ericson, Eric E. "The Rockwell Collection of Carder's Steuben." *Hobbies*, May, 1963.

Kamm, Minnie Watson. "Aurene Glass." *The Spinning Wheel*, October, 1949, pp. 18–20.

————. "Frederick Carder, Artist in Glass." *The Spinning Wheel*, October, 1950, pp. 36–41.

"The Life and Work of Frederick Carder." *Gaffer*, March, 1952, pp. 3–7, 14. Editorial.

Perrot, Paul. "Frederick Carder's Legacy to Glass." *Craft Horizons*, May/June, 1961, pp. 32–35.

————. "A Tribute to Frederick Carder." Abstract from a talk given in 1959.

"A Pictorial Demonstration of Glassmaking." *Antiques*, August, 1930, pp. 141–43. Editorial.

"Rhythm in Glass Ornaments." *Arts and Decoration*, June, 1938. Editorial.

Tolman, Ruel P. "Cameo Glass." *Antiques*, November, 1937, pp. 236–39.

Turner, W. E. S. "The Art of Frederick Carder." *Journal of the Society of Glass Technology*, XXIII, 1939, pp. 41–43.

OTHER SOURCES

The Borough of Stourbridge, Official Guide, 3rd ed. London, England: Pyramid Press Ltd., 1959–1960.

Brierley Hill Official Handbook, 2d ed., 1956–1957. Cheltenham and London: Ed. J. Burrow & Co., Ltd., 1956.

Brierley Hill Staffordshire Official Handbook, 3rd ed. Cheltenham and London: Ed. J. Burrow & Co., Ltd.

Carder, Frederick. "Autobiographical Notes." Handwritten, 1937. Unpublished.

———. "Autobiography of an Englishman." Handwritten, 1955. Unpublished.

———. "Glass and Glass Making As I Know It." Handwritten and typed copy, 1920. Unpublished.

———. "Notes for a talk on European Trip." Handwritten, dated December 1, 1902.

———. "Report of a Visit to the Principal Glass-making Districts of Germany and Austria," Staffordshire County Council, 1902.

Data from association with Mr. Carder as his assistant, 1929 to 1943.

Interviews with Carder's family, friends, associates in the Steuben and Corning Glass Works, Corning residents, and collectors of Carder Steuben glass.

Museum and private collections of Carder and Stevens & Williams glass in the United States and England.

Philpot, Cecily and Gerry. *The Fieldstone Porch Presents Conversations with Carder on Steuben*, c. 1963. LP record. The Fieldstone Porch, Glenbrook, Connecticut.

Steuben and Corning factory records.

Tape recordings.

Visits to Stourbridge, Wordsley, Brierley Hill, Dudley, and Birmingham, England.

Index

(*Italic* figures refer to illustrations)

(Roman numerals preceded by the word Plate refer to the color section)